New Directions in Sociology
(Vol. 1)

ADOLESCENTS AND THEIR MUSIC

Garland Reference Library
of Social Science
(Vol. 804)

New Directions in Sociology

General Editor, Peter W. Cookson, Jr.

ADOLESCENTS AND THEIR MUSIC
If It's Too Loud, You're Too Old
edited by Jonathon S. Epstein

ADOLESCENTS AND THEIR MUSIC

If It's Too Loud, You're Too Old

Edited by
Jonathon S. Epstein

GARLAND PUBLISHING, INC.
New York & London / 1994

Library of Congress Cataloging-in-Publication Data

Adolescents and their music : if it's too loud, you're too old / edited by Jonathon S. Epstein.
p. cm. — (New directions in sociology; v. 1) (Garland reference library of social science; v. 804)
Includes bibliographical references and index.
ISBN 0-8153-0614-8 (alk. paper) (hardcover)
ISBN 0-8153-2138-4 (paperback)
1. Rock music—Social aspects. 2. Rock music—History and criticism. 3. Music and youth. I. Epstein, Jonathon S. II. Series.
III. Series: Garland reference library of social science; v. 804.
ML3534.A3 1994
306.4'84—dc20 93-33839

Paperback cover design by Karin Badger.

Printed on acid-free, 250-year-life paper
Manufactured in the United States of America

For my wife Margarete and my children Helena and Jacob;
Boogie Chillun!

Contents

Series Preface

It is entirely appropriate that the first volume to appear in the New Directions in Sociology series should be Jonathon S. Epstein's edited volume *Adolescents and Their Music.* By analyzing the relationship between popular music, postmodernism, and youth culture, the contributors to this volume break new intellectual ground that is theoretically significant and empirically compelling. Perhaps because I am a sociologist, I have a deep faith in the power of social analysis to transform our thinking and, in the end, change society for the better. Sociologists have always been questioners, able to face the world, as it were, without the aid of received truth, sacred or secular. Part of the historical mission of the discipline is to break the chains of illusion created by ideology, magical thinking, and idle speculation.

So why is it that so much of sociological research lacks a sense of excitement? Is it the dead hand of outworn theory? Methodologies that obscure rather than illuminate? Professional training that devalues imagination and values the routines of "normal science"? Whatever the answers to these questions, the fact remains that sociology is in need of new inspiration. It is cliche to point out that we live in a rapidly changing transnational society that is being reshaped by a technological revolution and by a social revolution, the dimensions of which we have yet to comprehend. Sociology is the ideal discipline to record and interpret these changes because it is sensitive to social structures and social processes. In a world where the individual is seen as the natural unit of analysis, sociology is iconoclastic because in social inquiry, the group is the unit of analysis. It is absolutely critical, therefore, that sociologists engage fully in contemporary society and embrace the intellectual challenges presented to us by a world that is increasingly uprooting itself from the past.

The purpose of New Directions in Sociology is to publish sociological research that is daring, contemporary, and forward-looking. Jonathon Epstein is a young sociologist with imagination and the kind of intellectual hunger that is needed if the discipline is to break new theoretical and empirical ground. In this volume he has brought together a team of social analysts who focus on popular culture by unpacking the relationship between rock music and the larger society. Normally, we do not think of rock music as a matter of serious sociological interest, but Epstein makes it clear that rock music is, in fact, a social narrative that is ripe in research potential. The varieties of rock music are social scripts that challenge conventional thought and provide young people with a form of discourse that makes sense of a world that, oftentimes, appears to be senseless, or at least deeply confusing. Young people are living in a world they never made but are required to understand. Rock music is protest, passion, and, sometimes, just plain fun. As the contributors to this volume make clear, however, it would be a mistake to overlook the rich sociological resource that popular music provides.

In reading *Adolescents and Their Music,* I was struck with how differently the contributors approached the themes of popular music, youth culture, and postmodern society. I hope that this book will be used extensively in sociology classes and be read by the public. The issues that these chapters address are critical if we are to understand the culture that exists and the culture that is emerging.

Peter W. Cookson, Jr.

Acknowledgments

Over the past two years, while editing this volume, I have learned a number of important lessons. Foremost among these lessons was the realization that editing a book is hard work and cannot be done alone. A number of people have contributed their time, intellect, and energies to making this book a reality. While I can't thank them all in the space allocated, I would like to mention a few who have gone "above and beyond."

To my colleagues at Kent State I would like to extend my hand in appreciation. Their support has been overwhelmingly positive. Denzel Benson, Jerry M. Lewis, Lee Spray, Scott A. Reid, and Gayle Ormiston have all been strong supporters of this project.

Among the sociological community I would like to express my gratitude to Rebecca Adams and David Pratto at the University of North Carolina at Greensboro. Deena and Michael A. Weinstein, from DePaul and Perdue, respectively, have avidly encouraged this project since its inception. Without their enthusiasm the book would not have been written. Among the community of rock musicians, a number of individuals have been most gracious in their willingness to discuss this project with me from their point of view: Tom Araya of Slayer, Geoff Tate of Queensrÿche, Kory Clarke of Warrior Soul, Geddy Lee of Rush, Michael Persh, Davey Holmbo, Greg Arpo, Rich Lovsin and Michael Rand of Rhythm Corps and Fish have all gone beyond what could be reasonably expected. Further thanks are in order for Jim Filiault at Metal Blade Records and Lisa Grey at Atlantic Records.

Finally I would like to dedicate this volume to my friend and mentor, the late James K. Skipper, Jr. He was the first of my many teachers who saw the importance of this work. His input and storytelling will be sorely missed.

And thus begins the web. . . .

May 1, 1993
Kent, Ohio

INTRODUCTION

Misplaced Childhood: An Introduction to the Sociology of Youth and Their Music

Jonathon S. Epstein

This text primarily concerns itself with the concept of "youth subcultures." Generally speaking, when the term "youth subculture" is used in everyday discourse, it is at best a vague indicator that signifies that the unique lifeworld of what can broadly be defined as "youth" is being set apart and considered as an entity separate and distinct from the world of "adults." While this conception, youth is that which is not adult, is clearly not a very good one, it is apparently enough to justify broad and heated discussions about the status of youth across most of America's major institutions: education, the judicial system, churches, and, most importantly, the media.

The term "youth subculture" has been used in American sociology since it was introduced by Talcott Parsons in his classic text *The Social System* (1951). Broadly defined, "youth subculture" refers to the expressive form of young people's shared social and material experience. A youth subculture is distinguished by the distinct values, beliefs, symbols, and actions which certain youth employ to attend to, and cope with, their shared cultural experience. From the Parsonian, qua functionalist, perspective, this subcultural expression is generally in opposition to, and often in direct contradiction with, societal (read "white middle-class adult male") values, norms, and expectations. Not surprisingly, then, most early work in the sociology of youth subcultures concerned itself with urban underclass youth, who by any measure differed significantly from what the functionalist would consider the "mainstream" (cf. Cohen 1955; Suttles 1969; Yablonsky 1970).

The bias towards underclass "social pathology" was deeply imbedded in the sociology of this time period. It can be rightly pointed out that "social pathology" is a structural, not psychological, phenomenon. However, it is not difficult to see how this concept spilled over into social-psychological theorizing, particularly in reference to juvenile delinquency. For example, Edwin Sutherland's (Sutherland and Cressey, 1978) cultural transmission theory (often referred to as the theory of differential association), which concerns itself with the acquisition of values and norms favorable to the commission of delinquent acts. It is primarily organized around the social psychology of learning. Yet the actor's relation to space and social structure is also critical to the current understanding of Sutherland's conceptualization. That is, lower-class youth are more likely to become involved in deviant subcultures because of the excess of definitions that favor deviance in these youths' social world, a remarkable example of circular reasoning.

Other theorists of this era were much more direct in equating delinquency with lower-class subculture. Walter Miller (1958) clearly identifies the culture of the lower class as the ideal milieu for the creation of delinquent youth subcultures. According to Miller, the six "focal concerns" of the lower class (toughness, trouble, smartness, fate, excitement, and autonomy) have a direct impact on the creation of gangs, what Miller referred to as "single-sex peer groups." Miller apparently did not believe that other teens from other social classes shared these focal concerns, this worldview, which made it less likely for them to become involved in negative behaviors.

Albert Cohen (1955) shared Miller's concern with lower-class culture. Unlike Miller, however, Cohen saw the family as the primary location for the learning (or in Cohen's scheme of things, the *not* learning) of cultural values. For the current generation of social scientists/theorists, who have become accustomed to the definitions of delinquency offered by the field of social work, Cohen should appear to be pretty much correct.

However, it must be kept in mind that for Cohen, and indeed for many in the helping professions, the primary problem in lower-class families is that they teach lower-class values, which is just another way of saying that they do not teach middle-class values. This alone makes it very difficult for lower-class youth to "measure up" in the middle-class world of school and work.

By the mid-1960s it was clear that the earlier conception of youth subculture, best described by movies such as *Blackboard Jungle* or *The Wild One* and by musical heroes like Elvis Presley, i.e., cigarette-smoking, leather-clad white trash hoodlums, had been rendered all but irrelevant by the "youth movements" of that era. It was difficult to deny, for example, that the "hippies" were a "real" subculture, despite the fact that your daughter might be one. Suddenly youth subcultures were not just for dead-end kids with no future aside from the one they subculturally constructed for themselves; youth subcultures were for everyone. Functionalist studies of subcultures tapered off at this historical juncture and were replaced by a wave of British scholarly works which attempted to correct the obvious biases of functionalist theorizing.

It seems ironic that this social class bias was carried over into the proliferation of subcultural studies of the 1970s, most of which were at least informed by critical/Marxist theorizing (Hebdige 1979; Frith 1981). British subcultural studies celebrated working-class youth culture with an abandon that equaled the functionalists' quasi-scientific moralizing on the subject. While the functionalists argued, from Merton (1968), that working-class youths formed subcultures in order to achieve higher social status through the alternatives provided by those subcultures, the British argued that lower-class youth created subcultures in order to both *reaffirm* their social class status and to resist the attempts of "mainstream" society to strip them of their class-based identities. For both positions, youth subcultures remained a predominantly working-class phenomenon.

The fact that many middle-class, and even upper-middle-class, youth subcultures had not only formed but also become quite viable and long lived (cf. Epstein and Sardiello 1990), remained problematic from both perspectives. Why, for example, would it be necessary for upper-middle-class youth to create an alternative to the achievement ideology from which they were the most likely to benefit? For the functionalist, these youths needed no alternative value structure since they already had access to the culturally accepted means to achieve the goals that American society held like a carrot before them. For the British theorists, it was clear that middle-class youth needed no subcultural reinforcement since their lifestyle was already strongly affirmed by both societies' value structure and the expression of that normative structure in British culture.

This disjuncture in sociologists' thinking about subcultures was, in fact, quite problematic. American sociologist Robert Merton (1968) attempted to account for this apparent inconsistency with the addition of a fifth alternative to his already overworked "modes of cultural adaption." He called this additional adaptive mode "rebellion." For a group to fit this category, they must both accept and reject the goals of a culture and at the same time accept and reject the means to attain those goals. Clearly there is an inherent flaw in the logic of this scheme. How is it possible for a group to both accept *and* reject a means/goals scheme? Merton's assertion that what these groups are actually doing is offering alternatives to existing structures remains accepted within the discipline of sociology despite the obvious post hoc logic imbedded in its rhetoric and its lack of explanatory utility.

Into the seventies and eighties American sociology continued to conceptualize youth subculture as a primarily working-class phenomenon. Most work during this era focused on the undeniably critical problem of inner-city gangs and the cycle of poverty that was an inherent part of this phenomenon. Unlike the previous work, however, these studies attempted to place the experiences of these youths into a larger cultural framework. As a result, some twenty-five years after its inception, rock music began to be considered by academics a vital, and perhaps the primary, expression of youth culture.

Rock music has played a central role in youth culture for over thirty-five years. American teen culture was permanently changed, in 1956, when Elvis Presley appeared on the Ed Sullivan show from the waist up only. For the first time, American youth had a hero who was just like them, a young

(Presley turned 21 in 1956), defiant, leather-clad dynamo, who oozed sexuality and angst. Presley was the perfect hero for the new age, the kind of teen idol that every parent was almost required to hate. The days of the Tin Pan Alley, moon-in-June, carefully-crafted-by-adults, to-be-crooned-by-adults, pop song had ended (Epstein et al. 1990). To many adults it was clear that youth culture had turned ugly, into something menacing and fearful, made all the more problematic by the fact that it was now white middle-class youth who made up this subculture (Epstein et al. 1990). As Willis (1978) points out:

> Early rock 'n' roll was seized upon by the young in the mid-1950s in America and in England as their very own music. It was mainly theirs because it so clearly was not their parents'. . . . [T]he live performance of the stars (particularly Elvis Presley) was openly sexual in a way that only American Negroes had been held to be capable of before. Parents and established society could not condone such open subversion of traditional values. *The dissociation of one group is the association of another* [emphasis added]. A large scale musical genre became, perhaps for the first time, truly available to the young. This was the beginning, the first distinctive awakening, of what we refer to generically as youth culture. (46)

What is important about Willis's contention is the importance placed on association being derived from dissociation. Rock music continues to play a central role in youth culture in part due to its confrontational and antagonistic stance toward adult values. As generations of rock fans grow up, and have families of their own, they bring their music with them into adulthood. This makes it necessary for rock music to change, to mutate, in order for it to remain a viable center of youth culture. Once a music is co-opted into the mass culture, it can no longer be considered confrontational, as is demonstrated by the Beatles song "Revolution." "Revolution" was once considered a controversial song about radical political change; now it is used in television commercials to sell shoes. This kind of occurrence suggests that the boundary between popular music, which is heard on top forty radio and is used in advertising, and rock music is not impermeable.

Grossberg (1990) argues that the distinguishing factor between popular music and rock music is the degree of investment the fan has in a musical genre. He states:

> The power of rock and roll depends upon that part of the population which makes an investment in it, which empowers it within their lives, which differentiates both the music and themselves. Rock and roll fans enact an elitism in their relation to music. Rock and roll does not belong to everyone, and not everything is rock and roll. . . . While a rock and roll fan may enjoy other forms of popular music, the boundary is always drawn. (115)

There are several crucial points imbedded in Grossberg's argument concerning the creation of music subcultures. First, musical preference contributes to the creation of subcultural identity. What you listen to, or do not listen to, partially defines who you are within youth culture. Grossberg refers to the groups created by this phenomenon as "nomination groups" (115). Secondly, the importance of rock and roll for its fans depends primarily on the extent to which it functions within their lives as a method of granting definition to experience. That is, commitment to a particular genre of rock music depends primarily on the effectiveness of that music to structure the meaning of life experience. Thirdly, rock music functions within the wider context of social experience; it is created in response to larger social, cultural, political, sexual, or economic events. It is the ability of a genre of music to define these events for its fans that leads to the creation of different subcultures.

Grossberg's introduction of the concept of nomination groups into the study of youth culture implies a youth culture that is graduated. A nomination group can be considered a precondition to the formation of a subculture. While not all nomination groups become subcultures, all subcultures begin as nomination groups. Grossberg emphasizes, "nomination groups . . . function, by naming rock and roll, to create not subcultures but what are only nominal groups" (115). The ability for a genre of rock music to add definition to experience is the crucial element in the creation of a music subculture. The extent to which music becomes the focal point of a nomination group, by which the group both defines itself and is defined as such by outsiders, distinguishes a nomination group from a subculture. It is important to note that, for Grossberg, youths' use of rock as a symbol is separate and distinct from the conception of popular music as a commodity. It is not so for Simon Frith.

According to Frith (1981), rock music can best be understood sociologically in terms of its production and consumption as a commodity. Rock music is produced commercially to sell within a free market system. As such, the producers of this music, the multinational record companies, trade associations, and even the musicians themselves, are primarily concerned with selling music for profit. The difficulty, for the industry, is attempting to determine what will sell.

Most record companies approach the problem of determining what is marketable by what can be termed "saturation marketing" (Epstein 1991). Huge numbers of what the industry refers to as "product," the individual recordings of specific musical groups, are released into the marketplace. The vast majority of this "product" is never heard by anyone outside of the music industry network, which is comprised of record company employees, music journalists, radio programmers, club owners, and buyers for retail record stores.[1] Out of the dozens, and in some cases hundreds, of recordings released by a specific company, only a handful will actually be profitable. When a recording generates a "buzz," or begins to attract significant attention by either the music press or the consumers themselves, the company mounts a full-scale promotional campaign in order to maximize the potential market for that product. In the process, the company will generally neglect the majority of other bands whom they hold under contract.

Frequently, other companies are also aware of the success of a particular "product" and go on a contract-signing spree in an attempt to sign acts which are close enough in style to the current big seller in an attempt to cash in on that band's success. This method is generally quite successful, causing the market to become glutted with sound-alike bands. This brings the process full circle as the companies now have to identify new trends.

Both the existence and the quality of popular music can be understood within this mass-culture-for-profit framework. Mass art is produced for profit and both its content and form is determined by that pursuit (Frith 1981).

Interestingly, Frith does not reject the notion that rock music is central to the experience of youth. Despite its capitalistic orientation, popular music is the defining element of youth subcultures. According to Frith, "all adolescents have the same problems, all adolescents pass through peer groups, all adolescents use music as a badge and a background, a means of identifying and articulating emotion" (1981; 217).

Frith maintains that adolescent music subcultures are related to social class; what he terms the suburbs vs. the streets. Regardless of the social class of the listener, however, music functions within youth subculture as a way of defining the self (Kotarba 1990), creating collective excitement (Weinstein 1991a), and bringing about a sense of solidarity and subcultural consciousness (Sardiello 1990; Martin 1979). It is important to note that what the music does for adolescents is, for the most part, removed from the machinations of the music industry. They are in fact different issues, however intertwined.

In recent years there has been an increasing amount of scholarly interest in the role that popular music and music subcultures play in the values, attitudes, and behaviors of adolescents (Epstein and Pratto 1990; Verden et al. 1989; Schlattman 1989; Lemming 1987). While most of these studies attempt to establish a cause-and-effect relationship between involvement and commitment to popular music and behavior, little effort has been made to examine these relationships within a theoretical framework (Lewis, 1980a; Lewis 1980b). Conversely, those scholars who examine popular music subcultures from a theoretical perspective generally lack empirical grounding for their assertions (Grossberg 1990; Weinstein 1985; Straw 1990; Frith 1981; Hebdige 1979; Willis 1978). Frith (1985) has called for a combining of the two approaches into what he calls "low theory."

The research that has been empirically focused has generally used taste in popular music as an indicator for specific behaviors. For example Lewis (1980a) compared musical preference and self-reported drug use among sixteen-year-old Californians. His results indicated that the preferred music for his sample was heavy metal, and that heavy metal listeners were more likely to use drugs: "heavy metal people, in all drug categories, tended to have at least tried the drug [drug not specified] once or twice in greater proportion than the others" (179). Lewis argues that the frequency of drug use among heavy metal fans is a result of the "newness" of this particular style of music as opposed to its being a result of the content of the music. If Lewis is correct, however, it would imply that once heavy metal became an established rock form it would cease to be the music of choice for rebellious youth and would be replaced by a new musical form. This does not appear to be the case.

Heavy metal remains among the most popular music genres for white adolescents ten years after Lewis's article. Heavy metal is an electric guitar-based music which relies on high volume, distortion, and relatively simple song structure for its unique sound. Historically, heavy metal can be considered a continuation of a genre of rock music originally created by the power trios of the 1960s, most notably the Jimi Hendrix Experience and Cream (Epstein and Pratto 1990). These groups worked within a musical framework that was highly derivative of Chicago-style blues. In fact, a number of songs recorded by these early power trios were originally written and recorded by notable blues artists such as Robert Johnson, Muddy Waters, Albert King, and Bo Diddley. As successive generations of heavy metal bands emerge, the genre moves further away from its blues roots.

The 1970s group Led Zeppelin is most often cited as the first heavy metal group (Curtis 1987). It can be argued, however, that the British band Black Sabbath, who were contemporaries of Led Zeppelin, are more likely candidates for this distinction (Epstein and Pratto 1990). There are several reasons for this break with traditional thinking. Today's heavy metal is more akin to the music of Black Sabbath stylistically. This is evidenced in overall sound, song structure, and lyrical content. The themes of alienation and apocalypse present in today's heavy metal can be traced back to Black Sabbath's early works such as "War Pigs," "Paranoid," "Wheels of Confusion," and "Lord of This World." Black Sabbath was also the first rock band to make extensive use of satanic symbolism, which has become a frequent issue among heavy metal detractors in recent years. The band's early concerts prominently featured an upside-down crucifix as a prop (Pareles and Romanowski 1983), and a number of their songs were sung in the first person narrative form, using Satan as the narrator. Finally, Ozzy Osbourne, Black Sabbath's original vocalist, is still considered a top heavy metal performer.

All of this discussion, of course, is quite irrelevant to the experience of adolescents but quite important for the understanding of youth as a cultural category. Youth, according to Weinstein (chapter two of this volume), was once considered a transitional category located between adult responsibilities and childhood dependencies. However, this is no longer the case. Youth has now become a floating signifier that marks out a specific way of being that is neither age-specific nor relevant for the adolescence it parodies. In this manner adolescents have become detached from "youth."

This detachment is the primary reason for rock music remaining a music of adolescents despite the co-optation of the music by the nonadolescent adult consumer. As more and more rock music becomes an identifier for youth as a floating signifier, the boundary of what is acceptable adolescent subcultural music moves further away from the mainstream. Heavy metal has resided on this boundary since it was introduced into the popular music scene in the late 1960s. The fact that it continues to define the boundary between adolescent and mainstream music can be considered the reason it has remained the music of choice for marginal youth. The tremendous commercial success of heavy metal obviously brings the concept of "marginality" into question.

Heavy metal has generally been considered a working-class, white, male phenomenon (Frith, 1981). As Weinstein (1985) points out:

> The music evokes themes of exuberant aggression through its ear shattering amplification, its strutting leatherclad stars who have been applauded by their imitative fans for trashing their instruments onstage and their hotel rooms offstage, and its lyrics which express aggression in every possible dimension. The extreme rock genre that exemplifies the male youth is heavy metal. Ominously named

> groups such as Judas Priest, Black Sabbath, AC/DC, Iron Maiden and Scorpions attract almost all-male audiences with attire that make the Hell's Angels appear effeminate.... (12)

In recent years, however, heavy metal has begun to attract larger numbers of female fans. The success of "lite metal" bands such as Bon Jovi and Winger, as well as the success of several talented female heavy metal artists, may contribute to this change in audience characteristics. Lita Ford, Doro Pesch, and Fiona are three better-known examples of recently successful female heavy metal artists.

Black artists have also begun to cross over into the heavy metal market. There has been a small black presence in heavy metal for some time, primarily in interracial bands. Among the more popular are Jimi Hendrix, the late Philip Lynott, leader of the Irish band Thin Lizzy, Doug Pinnick of Kings' X, and Jon Butcher. The success of the New York quartet Living Colour, who toured with the Rolling Stones in 1989, has paved the way for other black bands to participate in the otherwise white heavy metal community. Other black bands, such as Bad Brains and Fishbone, who do not fit the stereotypical style that is expected of them by a segregated music industry (Perry 1988), have begun to receive favorable notices in the rock press. Audiences for these bands remain largely white (Epstein and Pratto 1990). The integration of the white rock music scene would appear to be a positive step towards a more tolerant society. There has, however, been considerable criticism directed towards what is perceived as the "selling out" of black music. According to Perry (1988), this criticism takes two related positions. The first is concerned, outwardly, with the style of the music itself. It is argued that by attempting to reach a larger (implying white) audience, black artists have lost sight of the cultural roots of their music. This position is essentially about what should or should not be considered "authentic" African-American music. Nelson George, perhaps the most well-known, and vocal, black music critic, describes this phenomenon as being the result of the "black American artists [who] want to be Barry Manilow" (Perry 1988; 57). This line of criticism, while not without merit, is difficult to define due to the impossible task of attempting to determine what is, and what is not, "authentic" black music. Who decides, for example, that the music of Bobby Brown is not an authentic expression of black music, while the music created by Public Enemy or Ice T is "authentic"?

The second criticism directed towards the crossover phenomenon is rooted in the rhetoric of black nationalism. This argument points to the racism imbedded in the music industry that is primarily economic in nature. It is pointed out that blacks are underrepresented in the music industry, particularly in upper-managerial positions, that blacks are paid less than their white counterparts, and that black promoters, radio stations, and retail outlets are frequently overlooked in the promotion of more well-known black artists. The end result, then, of crossover is the threat it poses to black American capitalism by denying the importance of the smaller black-owned and -operated music industry concerns which cannot compete with the industry.

The struggle over the purpose of African-American music has found its strongest articulation in a genre of popular music alternately dubbed hip hop or rap (Rose 1989). Rap is a style of music which originated among poor black youth in the South Bronx of New York City in the mid-1970s (Rose 1989). Rap spread through the dance clubs in New York's black neighborhoods and quickly became a serious force in popular music (Pareles and Romanowski 1983).

The primary focus of rap is lyrical content which continues the oral tradition of black America (Rose 1989). Rap relies on relatively simple syncopated rhyme patterns and rhythmically repetitive song structure. Most instrumentation on rap recordings is created by what is referred to as sampling, or the computer-generated playback of prerecorded musical sounds. A great deal of this prerecorded music is borrowed from the work of other artists. For example, on the 1989 album *Loced After Dark,* rap artist Tone Loc made use of guitar and drum samples from the Van Halen song "Jamie's Crying," keyboard samples from Gary Wright's "Love Is Alive," and guitar samples from Foreigner's "Hot Blooded." Other rappers have used samples of speeches by Martin Luther King, Jr., Malcolm X, and other well-known personalities, both black and white.

During its early years, rap's lyrics focused on the classic themes of all rock music: sex, partying, and the remarkable talents of the musicians themselves. Recently, however, rap has arguably become the most politically conscious style of popular music. A number of rap artists have become strongly committed to a militant and aggressive stance on issues of social justice and black nationalism. Artists like NWA (Niggas with Attitude) and Public Enemy have taken an openly hostile position toward a society which they consider blatantly racist, a society which holds no promise for the young blacks who make up the bulk of their audiences. According to Simpson (1990):

> The basic sound, propelled by a slamming polyrhythmic beat, is loud and raw. The lyrics, a raucous stew of street corner bravado and racial boosterism, are often salted with profanity and sometimes with demeaning remarks about whites, women and gays. The fact that they are delivered by young, self-consciously arrogant black men in a society where black youths make many whites uneasy doesn't help either. (60)

Like heavy metal, rap is a music dominated by males, both artists and fans. The few women who have been successful in rap have been less aggressive than their male counterparts. More often than not, these women create music that is a crossover between rap and pop. Several woman rappers, however, have taken a more assertive stand on social, particularly feminist, issues. Among the more well known of these women are Queen Latifah and Salt 'N' Pepa. It remains to be seen how rap is used by young African-American women.

This discussion points out that what is broadly conceived as youth subculture in American culture is a highly problematic issue. Does youth subculture reflect the cultural experiences of youth or does it merely exist as a separate entity? How is it that youth use their music to grant definition to experience? Do popular cultural forms support, reflect, and reinforce dominant ideologies or do these forms offer alternatives? In the following chapters these issues will be explored from a variety of complimentary perspectives. The organization of the text falls loosely into three categories; youth culture and its relationship to popular music, specific music subcultures, and empirical studies.

Deena Weinstein, Larry Grossberg, and Donna Gaines are perhaps the early 1990s' best-known rock 'n' roll intellectuals. Weinstein's definitive treatment of heavy metal, aptly titled *Heavy Metal: A Cultural Sociology* (1991a), has been the topic of intense debate in the mass media; has dragged Dr. Weinstein, rather reluctantly, into the pages of such influential periodicals as *Rolling Stone;* and at this writing, is the only sociology text ever to serve as a prop in a Broadway play. Her chapters in this volume continue her excellent scholarship. Her discourse on the disappearance, or perhaps the total absorption, of youth subcultures into the postmodern fabric stands in stark contrast to the celebration of youth in the work of her predecessors Simon Frith and Dick Hebdige. She has provided the first clearly postmodern treatment of American youth subcultures by severing the ties that have long bound American cultural sociology to its European roots. Hers is a sustained attempt to consider rock music in light of its relation to the general practical problematic of the social group that uses it; that is, youth. To that end she provides an inquiry into the sense and meaning that rock has for the specific group—youth—that uses it in the constitution of its daily life, and what this music means for youth as a social group faced with specific problems in contemporary social structure.

Lawrence Grossberg provides a similar treatment of American youth. Unlike Weinstein, however, Grossberg is unwilling to embrace totally the extreme postmodernist position. He considers the category of youth within the postmodern to be potentially liberating and empowering. Yet, in some very concrete ways, youth is the most silenced population, in intellectual, social, and political terms. With this in mind, Grossberg attempts to answer a number of specific questions: What is the status of the category of youth? What is the political significance of the category? What is its place in the field of political possibilities? In doing so, he opens up a discussion that attempts to rethink the articulation of ethnicity as a structure of investment and identity.

Donna Gaines returns the discussion of youth culture to its natural habitat: the suburbs and streets. Among suburban youth, the quintessential members of rock culture, the problem of "nothing to do, nowhere to go" is an ancient tradition. What concerns Gaines is the possible alternatives which emerge for kids who are left cold and alienated from the mainstream. Her chapter follows a "narrative" form that merges the sociological imagination with a journalistic attention to "the story." In this manner, she is working in the tradition of the first "suburban sociologists": Herbert Gans, David Reisman, and C. Wright Mills.

In the next chapter, Weinstein once again returns to a discussion of youth. Youth, she contends, can be best understood in terms of its cultural history as a modern idea. If it is nothing else, "youth" is a term that discriminates certain phenomena and marks them off from others. Youth is not a fixed or natural definition, however convenient it might be if it were. As people continuously interpret their world, even their most crucial terms keep changing their meanings. "Youth" is no exception. As a term in the discourse on the young it has a cultural history which Weinstein attempts to explicate.

Working from similar concerns, Daniel Dotter outlines, within a sociohistorical framework, the relationship between rock music and social deviance in the early years of the genre. He examines the role of mass media and other groups in the presentation and interpretation of this link and then goes on to sketch the early sociocultural changes in rock and roll based on this initial and continued association with socially deviant behavior and the specifically youth-oriented values which ultimately emerged, in the late sixties, as youth culture.

Robert Sardiello focuses his discussion on what is almost unquestionably the most visible, cohesive, and apparently permanent rock subculture: the Dead Heads. It is his contention that the Grateful Dead and its audience resemble an extended family drawn together by a concert ritual that closely resembles a religious festival. In his chapter he uses ethnographic data based on interviews and observations to analyze Grateful Dead concerts as secular rituals and describes the mythic nature of Dead Head unity in terms of the shared meanings the members of this group use to interpret their subcultural reality and define their identity.

Joseph Kotarba offers a postmodern reading on the fans of the heavy metal band Metallica. Over the past several years Metallica has become perhaps the most successful heavy metal band since Led Zeppelin's heyday in the 1970s. It is Kotarba's contention that Metallica has come to represent a specific world view that is epitomized by the current postmodern turn in American culture. Metallica, for Kotarba, is the emblematic rock band for youth culture of the nineties.

Venise Berry explores three controversial issues in rap music: sex, violence, and racism, and their relation to the social, cultural, and historical reality of urban black American youth. Her analysis draws on a variety of sources. It incorporates the discourse on rap from previous literature with worksheet responses collected from black high school participants in an Upward Bound program in a southwestern state and also with personal comments from a discussion group with twenty-four Upward Bound juniors and seniors. Her contribution to a sparse literature on rap is included with the hope that it will engender further sociological investigation of this vital urban musical form.

While popular music has consistently been attacked by groups who consider it a threat to sacred moral or social traditions, Thaddeus Coreno confronts the possibility that there is in actuality a lack of a genuinely threatening popular music. He does not share the opinion of rock music detractors, who view a good deal of popular music as a threat to the cultural and moral fabric. Instead, he considers the music that they condemn as an offense to a middle-class sensibility and moral code to offer, in reality, very little oppositional substance. In this way he is concerned with the absence of politically threatening music in a youth subculture that is widely seen as being the site of rapid social change. Coreno outlines the many reasons that rock music does not offer a viable oppositional discourse for youth. He then portrays avant-garde music as a more or less authentic source of cultural power for its listeners.

Emily Edwards examines the possible relationship between the content of popular music and adolescents' world view. She considers the possibility that just as high amounts of violence on television are expected to generate a "mean world" perception among heavy viewers, expectations about love, sex, and relationships may be as easily cultivated if a consistent enough message is presented in popular songs. The shaping of expectations should also be greater for adolescents who listen a lot than for those who spend little or no time listening. If messages presented in popular music are consistent with messages presented in other media on the same topic, the cultivation effect of that message is strengthened. Her chapter is an attempt to determine if there is an aggregate message or a consistent portrait of relationships presented in popular music of the 1980s.

Jerry M. Lewis, well known within the field of sport-crowd violence, turns his attention in this volume to the related phenomenon of rock concert violence. His analysis focuses on the social structural response to rock-crowd violence and provides suggestions for a clearer understanding of how these events occur and, conversely, how they might be prevented.

The purpose of Amy Mohan and Jean Malone's chapter is to describe an emerging musical category, alternative, in terms of the value system it communicates to its audience within a framework they derive from Adorno. Alternative music has its origins in the underground music of the 1960s and in British punk of the 1970s, the lyrics of which stressed pessimism, alienation, and intellectual criticism of commonly held social values. Because of these origins, alternative music genres, while stylistically diverse, adhere to a common value system which revolves around social criticism and alienation.

Their study used the method of content analysis to determine the extent of social criticism in alternative music and examined a variety of other values to measure the extent of alienation. For comparison, the extent of social criticism and alienation was also measured in a sample of songs from the pop mainstream. The expectation is that alternative music will contain more social criticism than mainstream pop, as well as more negative themes in general. This chapter also attempts to develop a relatively new method of content analysis for use in the study of popular songs by focusing on the manifest content of song titles.

No studies to date have examined the constructs of identity salience, psychological centrality, and authenticity of professional or semi-professional rock and roll musicians. Research that has dealt with identity and role-related issues tacitly assumes that the musicians identify highly with the role. The analysis presented in Scott A. Reid, Jonathon Epstein, and D.E. Benson's chapter demonstrates that semi-professional rock and roll musicians have a high level of salience for the role identity of musician and find it to be psychologically central. The rock musician role is clearly important to semi-professional musicians in that it is a major role identity in comparison to the other role identities they may possess. This research provides the first empirical support for this assumption.

This chapter is an important contribution to the literature on the sociology of rock and roll in that it is the first such study to facilitate the larger task of investigating how semi-professional and professional rock and roll musicians differ in terms of their identity structures and corresponding behavioral outcomes.

The final chapter of this volume is an annotated bibliography put together by Stephen Groce and Jonathon Epstein. Included in this annotated bibliography are what we believe to be the best and most sociologically relevant of the recent scholarly works on popular music. This annotated bibliography suffers, as does any attempt such as this, from our own sociological biases as well as from our inability to be exhaustive and inclusive. However, it is our hope that sociologists and others working in the area of popular music research, as well as those of us who teach courses on the sociology of popular music, will benefit from the compilation.

The sociology of youth and their music is a rich, broad area of study. The works included in this volume offer only a small portion of the other excellent works currently available. It is my hope that this volume will increase the discourse on the sociology of rock music and its audience in the discipline of sociology and contribute to the sociological understanding of America's postmodern youth.

NOTES

1. This activity creates an "insider" subculture which has yet to be fully explored within the literature, although Weinstein (1991) does discuss some of its characteristics.

REFERENCES

Carducci, Joe. (1990). *Rock and the Pop Narcotic*. Chicago: Redoubt.

Clarke, John, Stuart Hall, Tony Jefferson, and Brian Roberts. (1976). "Subcultures, Cultures and Class." In Stuart Hall and Tony Jefferson, (Eds.), *Resistance Through Rituals*. London: Hutchinson. 9–74.

Cohen, Albert K. (1955). *Delinquent Boys*. Glencoe, IL: Free Press.

Curtis, James. (1987). *Rock Eras: Interpretations of Music and Society 1954–1984*. Bowling Green, OH: Bowling Green University Popular Press.

Dotter, Daniel. (1987). "Growing Up is Hard To Do: Rock and Roll Performers as Cultural Heroes." *Sociological Spectrum* 7(1): 25–44.

Epstein, Jonathon S. (1991, October). "Understanding Youth Subcultures: A Working Paper in Theory Construction." Paper presented at the annual meeting of the Mid-South Sociological Association, Jackson, Mississippi.

Epstein, Jonathon S., and David J. Pratto. (1990). "Heavy Metal Rock Music, Juvenile Delinquency and Satanic Identification." *Popular Music and Society* 14(4): 67–76.

Epstein, Jonathon S., and Robert Sardiello. (1990). "The Wharf Rats: A Preliminary Examination of Alcoholics Anonymous and the Grateful Dead Head Phenomena [sic]." *Deviant Behavior* 11:245–257.

Epstein, Jonathon S., David J. Pratto, and James K. Skipper, Jr. (1990). "Teenagers, Behavioral Problems and Preferences for Heavy Metal and Rap Music: A Case Study of a Southern Middle School." *Deviant Behavior* 11:381–394.

Frith, Simon. (1981). *Sound Effects*. New York: Pantheon.

———. (1985, April)." Is Pop Music Culture?" Paper presented at the Conference on Music and Society.

———. (1987). *Art into Pop*. New York: Methuen.

——— (Ed.). (1988a). *Facing the Music*. New York: Pantheon.

———. (1988b). *Music for Pleasure*. New York: Routledge, Chapman and Hall.

Frith, Simon, and Andrew Goodwin (Eds.). (1990). *On Record*. New York: Pantheon.

Gaines, Donna. (1991). *Teenage Wasteland: Suburbia's Dead End Kids*. New York: Pantheon.

Giroux, Henry A. (1983). "Theories of Reproduction and Resistance in the New Sociology of Education: A Critical Analysis." *Harvard Education Review* 53(3): 257–293.

Giroux, Henry A., and Roger I. Simon, (Eds.). (1989). *Popular Culture, Schooling and Everyday Life*. New York: Bergin and Garvey.

Grossberg, Lawrence. (1990). "Is There Rock After Punk?" In Simon Frith and Andrew Goodwin (Eds.), *On Record*. New York: Pantheon. 111–123.

Hebdige, Dick. (1979). "Style as Homology Signifying Practice." In Simon Frith and Andrew Goodwin (Eds.), *On Record*. New York: Pantheon. 56–65.

———. (1981). *Subcultures: The Meaning of Style*. London: Methuen.

Kotarba, Joseph A. (1990, August). "Adolescent Use of Heavy Metal Rock as a Resource for Meaning." Paper presented at The American Sociological Association Meetings.

Lemming, James S. (1987). "Rock Music and the Socialization of Moral Values in Early Adolescence." *Youth and Society* 18(4): 363–383.

Lewis, George H. (1980a). "Toward a Uses and Gratifications Approach: An Examination of Commitment and Involvement in Popular Music." *Popular Music and Society*. 7(1): 10–18.

———. (1980b). "Popular Music, Musical Preference and Drug Use Among Youth." *Popular Music and Society* 7(2): 176–181.

———. (1987). "Patterns of Meaning and Choice: Taste Cultures in Popular Music." In James Lull (Ed), *Popular Music and Communication*. Beverly Hills: Sage. 198–211.

McDonald, James R. (1987). "Suicidal Rage: An Analysis of Hardcore Punk Lyrics." *Popular Music and Society*. 11(3): 91–102.

Markson, Stephen L. (1990). "Claims Making, Quasi-Theories, and the Social Construction of the Rock 'n' Roll Menace." In Clinton Sanders (Ed.), *Marginal Conventions: Popular Culture, Mass Media and Social Deviance*. Bowling Green, OH: Bowling Green State University Popular Press.

Martin, Bernice. (1979). "The Sacrilization of Disorder: Symbolism in Rock Music." *Sociological Analysis*. 40(2): 87–124.

Merton, Robert K. (1968). *Social Theory and Social Structure*. New York: Macmillan.

Miller, Walter. (1958). "Lower Class Culture as a Generating Milieu of Gang Delinquency." *The Journal of Social Issues*. 14: 5–19.

Pareles, John, and Patricia Romanowski. (198[illegible]). *The Rolling Stone Encyclopedia of Rock and Roll*. New York: Summit Books.

Parsons, Talcott. (1951). *The Social System*. Glencoe, IL: Free Press.

Perry, Steve. (1988). "Ain't No Mountain High Enough: The Politics of Crossover." In Simon Frith (Ed.), *Facing the Music*. New York: Pantheon. 51–87.

Polk, Kenneth. (1984). "The New Marginal Youth." *Crime and Delinquency*. 30(3): 462–480.

Rose, Tricia. (1989). "Orality and Technology: Rap Music and Afro-American Resistance." *Popular Music and Society*. 13(4): 35–44.

Rosenbaum, Jill L., and Lorraine Prinsky. (1991). "The Presumption of Influence: Responses to Popular Music Subcultures." *Crime and Delinquency*. 37(4): 528–535.

Sardiello, Robert. (1990). "The Ritual Dimensions of Grateful Dead Concerts." Unpublished master's thesis. University of North Carolina at Greensboro.

Schlattmann, Tim. (1989). "Traditional, Nontraditional and Emotionally/Behaviorally Disturbed Students and Popular Music Lyrics." *Popular Music and Society*. 13(1): 23–35.

Schutz, Alfred. (1977). "Making Music Together: A Study in Social Relationship." In Polgin et al. (Eds.), *Symbolic Anthropology*. New York: Columbia University Press. 106–119.

Simpson, Janice. (1990, February 5). "Yo! Rap Gets on the Map." *Time*. 60–62.

Snow, Robert P. (1987). "Youth, Rock 'n' Roll and Electronic Media." *Youth and Society*. 18(4): 326–343.

Straw, Will. (1990). "Characterizing Rock Music: The Case of Heavy Metal." In Simon Frith and Andrew Goodwin (Eds.), *On Record*. New York: Pantheon.

Sutherland, Edwin, and Donald Cressey. (1978). *Criminology*. Philadelphia: Lippincott.

Suttles, Gerald. (1968). *The Social Order of the Slum*. Chicago: University of Chicago Press.

Verden, Paul, Kathleen Dunleavy, and Charles H. Powers. (1989). "Heavy Metal Mania and Adolescent Delinquency." *Popular Music and Society*. 13(1): 73–82.

Vincent, Richard. (1989). "Clio's Consciousness Raised? Portrayal of Women in Rock Videos." *Journalism Quarterly*. 66(1): 155–160.

Vincent, Richard, et al. (1987). "Sexism on MTV: The Portrayal of Women in Rock Videos." *Journalism Quarterly*. 64(4): 750–755.

Weinstein, Deena. (1985). "Rock: Youth and Its Music." *Popular Music and Society*. 9(3): 2–15.

———. (1991a). *Heavy Metal: A Cultural Sociology*. New York: Lexington.

———. (1991b). "The Sociology of Rock: An Undisciplined Discipline." *Theory, Culture and Society*. 8(1): 97–109.

Wicke, Peter. (1990). *Rock Music: Culture, Aesthetics and Sociology*. New York: Cambridge University Press.

Willis, Paul. (1978). *Profane Culture*. London: Routledge and Kegan Paul.

Yablonsky, Lewis. (1970). *The Violent Gang*. New York: Penguin.

Adolescents and Their Music

Rock: Youth and Its Music*

Deena Weinstein

Since it burst upon the American cultural scene in the mid-1950s rock music has been a center of controversy, a phenomenon that, it seems, cannot be treated neutrally. In public discourse rock has been reviled as an agent of moral and civil corruption, and hailed as a stimulant to social reconstruction. The more general public polemics about rock have been reproduced in academic discourse, where scholars and critics debate about whether rock music is an authentic artistic endeavor or a mere fabricated commodity, whether it represents genuine social forces seeking to contest established institutions or is but a cunning sort of mystification serving to lull its listeners into acquiescence or worse while appearing to stimulate them. Missing from both the everyday and academic discourse has been any sustained attempt to consider rock music in light of its relation to the general practical problematic of the social group that uses it, that is, youth.

To understand rock's global import requires an inquiry into the sense and meaning that it has for the specific group that uses it in the constitution of its daily life. To that end, this chapter explores what rock music means for youth as a social group faced with specific problems in contemporary social structure.

The approach to be taken in analyzing rock music as a function of the problems of youth in contemporary post-industrial societies is based on the theoretical views defined by Jean-Paul Sartre, Karl Mannheim and José Ortega y Gasset. Each of these thinkers coordinated cultural phenomena and social dynamics in terms of the specific situations of social actors within the total social structure. Sartre's "being-in-situation," Mannheim's sociology of knowledge and Ortega's idea of the reciprocity between self and concrete circumstances frame an inquiry in which significations are anchored in the practical problems faced by the members of a social group relative to the larger social structure in which they must act. That is, the isolated cultural object (here rock music) and the global social dynamic (for example, Weberian "rationalization") are mediated by the specific groups' aspirations, dilemmas and life-chances. As Mannheim puts it:

> Only when we know what are the interests and imperatives involved are we in a position to inquire into the possibilities of the present situation, and thus to gain our first insight into history. Here, finally, we see why no interpretation of history can exist except in so far as it is guided by interest and purposeful striving.[1]

The "interests and imperatives" are called here aspirations, dilemmas and life-chances. Rock music will be used as an index of youth's aspirations. Such circularity is not vicious, but is, rather, a consequence of the general condition that social facts refer to one another in dialectical patterns of reciprocity and opposition. The starting point here, which in another study would be the conclusion of an analysis of data on record sales and radio listenership, is that rock music is youth music and should be understood as such for sociological investigation.

Prevailing Approaches

Rock music has been traditionally understood within either a cultural or a societal framework. The cultural debate focuses on the *intent* of rock as a cultural object: is it produced as art or as commodity? The societal argument involves the *effect* of rock music: does it create social progress, does it function to maintain the status, or does it harm youth. These perspectives form the context within which rock is discussed by most of the rock press, scholarly analysts of popular music, parental groups, rock fans and rock artists.

Neither the cultural nor the societal debate about rock music remains static, in part because the music itself changes thematically and stylistically. The section below on the historical diversification of rock will address this issue. For example, when rock music becomes tied to movements for "progressive change," critics on the left tend to praise it both as culturally authentic and as an agent of change, whereas when rock seems to abandon a narrowly political dimension such critics tend to brand it as a commodity that bolsters the status quo.

The cultural debate centers on whether or not rock music is intended as art, that is, as the authentic expression of creative individuals. As art, rock might be viewed as "high culture" (seemingly aspired to by early '70s groups such as Pink Floyd, Genesis, and Emerson, Lake and Palmer) or as an urban derivative of a more rural "folk culture" (as the early works of Little Richard and Chuck Berry, or Bob Dylan's sixties' output, were understood). As appreciators of art, audiences are active, informed and critical. Record reviewers who lament the lack of greater achievement in the later album of an artist than in an earlier release, or who denounce the record because it is hook-laden, commercial-sounding or formulaic, hold the standard of rock as artistic expression. So do fans who complain that a group has sold out.

If, in contrast, rock is not intended as art for self-conscious appreciators it is culturally interpreted as a commodity produced for the purpose of profit. Thus, the other side of the cultural debate over rock holds that the music is a tool of capitalism. In works unambiguously entitled "Rock for Sale" (Michael Lyndon) and *Rock 'n' Roll is Here to Pay* (Chapple and Garofolo) the creation of rock is interpreted as being shaped not by authentic expression but according to commercial standards to enable it to appeal in the marketplace to the mass audience. The standards for a successful commodity sharply contrast with those of art: a commodity is packaged with an audience in mind that is passive and unreflective, and that wants no challenges or surprises. Since rock as commodity is aimed at the largest possible number of consumers it must be geared to the lowest common denominator. Celebrity and image (hence the crucial importance of public-relations-marketing-advertising specialists) rather than artistic profundity and proficiency are the requirements of successful audience appeal. According to Simon Frith, rock critics work within this cultural debate: ". . . records and songs are valued for their artistic intensity, for their truth to experience; yet they are condemned for commercialism, the belief in a continuing struggle between music and commerce is the core of rock ideology."[2]

In contrast to the terms of the cultural debate, rock has also been debated in a social context which focuses not on the intentions of its producers but on the effects of the music/lyrics on the general society. The antipodal positions in this societal controversy are that rock is a force for change and that it is a force to maintain the *status quo* or that its influence is negative. Yet both positions share the assumption that some of the possibilities for social change are dependent upon the youth of the society—adults function at best to train or restrain the young, but youth is the locomotive factor in altering patterns of human relations.

Those who believe that rock is a factor that promotes social change come from both ends of the ideological spectrum. From the inception of rock those on the right have been hostile to it. Reacting against either the beat of the music ("jungle music" arousing the young to frenzy) or the lyrics (especially those advocating sexual promiscuity and drug use, and those involving satanic themes) rural and small-town fundamentalist preachers, former Vice President Spiro Agnew, and members of the John Birch society, among others, have warned against the music. Periodically a minister will organize a mass rally to burn or, if environmental protection laws proscribe burning, smash rock records. An article in the John Birch Society's *American Opinion*, for example, claims: "Rock music, universally in high regard among a whole generation of adolescents, has somehow evolved as one of the major influences on our children—and, through them, on our nation's future."[3] The author, embedded in the post-World War II cold-war mentality, claims that rock music is a Communist plot:

> Music is now the primary weapon used to make the perverse seem glamorous, exciting, and appealing. Music is used to ridicule religion, morality, patriotism, and productivity—while glorifying drugs, destruction, revolution, and sexual promiscuity.[4]

With the demise of the Evil Empire and the attendant collapse of the Soviet threat, a more universal symbol of evil has been invoked: Satan. Rock has been seen as part of a campaign to recruit adolescents for the forces of satanism. Christian fundamentalists have argued: "Satan has gotten a real foothold in rock. . . . Satan will use this dark side of rock to lead Christians into sin."[5]

Those in favor of change, whether it is called progressive or revolutionary, also interpret rock music as capable of effecting or at least initiating movement toward securing their desired ends. The author of *The Age of Rock*, for example, claims: "Rock music was born of a revolt against the sham of Western culture; it was direct and gutsy and spoke to the senses. As such, it was profoundly subversive. It still is."[6] Leftists of various stripes, rock musicians, fans, and mere onlookers believed that the music of the late sixties and early seventies contained radical criticism of the existing society and calls to arms for change. Songs such as Barry McGuire's "Eve of Destruction," much of Bob Dylan's work such as "Highway 61" and "Maggie's Farm," and John Lennon's "Imagine" are among the host of widely cited examples of criticism of the dehumanizing, unjust and militaristic aspects of contemporary society. Irwin Kantor cites those on the "progressive" side of the debate over the social consequences of rock:

> . . . several writers, such as Ralph Gleason, Paul Wolfe, and Susan Huck, agree that rock music has been central to the emergence of what Theodore Roszak calls a youth-oriented counter culture which radically diverges from the values and assumptions that have been in the mainstream of our society since the Scientific Revolution of the Seventeenth Century.[7]

As the optimism of the sixties' leftists faded in the wake of the world-wide repression of 1968; the horrors of Altamont, which indicated that love wasn't all you need or that youth did not have enough love to make a difference; and the shootings at Kent State a year later, which were seen as an explicit attack on progressive youth the tide of opinion about the social function or possibilities of rock changed.

Political progressives began to see rock more and more as a force that maintained the *status quo* rather than as something that would help to combat it. The ambivalence in this shift is recognized by Levine and Harig's review of the rock literature: "On the one hand it (rock) is seen as stimulating change, while on the other it is portrayed as serving to reinforce the structure and ideology of the capitalist system."[8] The argument that rock reinforces established institutions is based on the premise that the cathartic function of the music channels energies, including the anger and frustration caused by an oppressive and unjust society, into harmless release. Herbert Marcuse's analysis of mass culture's repressive desublimation, which was argued most clearly in his 1964 *One-Dimensional Man,* is often cited. Others carry the argument further, using the understanding that rock is produced by the capitalist system to claim that it therefore must serve its ends. Capitalism's products are assumed to function for capitalist ends, creating profits as well as maintaining the *status quo* within which that economic system thrives. Michael Lyndon, for example, argues:

> In fact rock, rather than being an example of how freedom can be achieved within the capitalist structure, is an example of how capitalism can, almost without a conscious effort, deceive those whom it oppresses. Rather than being liberated heroes, rock and roll stars are captive on a leash, and their plight is but a metaphor for that of all young people and black people in America.[9]

The debate on the social impact of rock shifted in the eighties. No longer was its axis progressivism versus the *status quo*. The ascendancy of conservativism and religious fundamentalism, validated by the election and re-election of Ronald Reagan, changed the poles of the polemic. Now the controversy was between those on the left who were reduced to arguing that rock had no social impact versus those on the right who claimed that it had negative effects such as suicide, sexual perversion and satanism. The most forceful proponent of the conservative camp was the Parents' Music Resource Center (PMRC).[10]

The Youth Group and Its Music

The debates in the rock literature over whether rock music is an authentic expression of creative impulse or a commercial commodity, and whether the music has progressive, reactionary or harmful social consequences, can be enlightened by considering the group that uses it in the constitution of its life. As the music of youth in the period following World War II, rock has been a response to the general and historically and socio-culturally specific problems that youth has encountered in the contemporary societies of the West. A sociological under-standing of rock, then is premised on a description of the structural situation of the contemporary youth groups, structural here not being understood in a static sense as a fixed position relative to others, but dynamically, as a set, in Mannheim's sense, of interests and imperatives, an array, as Max Weber had it, of "life-chances."

Youth, in the sense that is meant here, is not primarily a biological or even a psychological category, but a sociological one. Forming a distinctive social group, adolescents are the products of an industrial society. Extended training (education) is necessary to fit individuals to be competent contributors to ongoing institutional projects. Further, young people, in the chronological sense, are not generally needed in and might even be disruptive of the labor market. The adolescent as a social type is betwixt and between childhood dependency and adult responsibility, in the sense of Mary Douglas, an anomaly who does not fit into any fixed category and is, therefore, impure from the society's standpoint, that is, a "danger."[11] The special tension between dependency and responsibility that structures adolescent life is, from the viewpoint of youth, both a blessing and a curse. To be beyond dependency, but still dependent, and moving towards responsibility, but not responsible yet, releases the adolescent into a suspended state of social freedom that tends to become an end-in-itself. This is especially so in light of the possibilities of the young body to enjoy intense pleasures and to recover relatively quickly from physical stress. This freedom, however, is circumscribed and, indeed, checked by the double pressure to acknowledge continued dependency and to undertake responsibilities and to prepare for future self-responsibility. Youth experiences its freedom and spontaneity as both intensely and intimately real, and as precarious and fleeting. The freedom and vitality that shoot forth in the social space of adolescence tend to become, indeed, fetishes, icons of an evanescent distinction.

The freedom opened up by the transition from dependency to responsibility places the youth group in a particularly privileged position to problematize society as a whole. That is, adolescents are able to make of participation in society a problem to be faced prior to any dilemma about how to participate. Children are taught to have ideas of what they would like to "be" when they grow up. Adolescents have the privilege and torment of raising the question of whether they want to be anything that the society holds out as a possibility for them. In the sense of Georg Simmel, the very "form" of the youth group is to question the category of "form" itself and, in strictly Simmelian terms, to oppose to it the solipsism of unlimited or at least overflowing "life."[12] Not all adolescents, of course, carry their freedom to a questioning of form itself, but all of them in some way decide what they do in terms of that utmost possibility. Some adolescents seek to remain as children, whereas others seek to short-circuit freedom and become responsible immediately; but either of these strategies is undertaken against a prevailing possibility of escaping, albeit momentarily, from either pole. In circumstances of intense social conflict youth may even hypostatize its freedom into an image of an ideal society in which freedom is perpetual and social relations need not be formally mediated. The adolescent who is suspended in freedom yet is pulled backwards into dependency and pushed forward into responsibility is a marginal being in the Simmelian sense, someone who is similar to the stranger or the wanderer, but not the same.[13] The model for the stranger is the trader who is here today and stays tomorrow, but who is never one with the group to which s/he refers, despite performing an often necessary function in its social life. The stranger, then, problematizes the absoluteness of particular forms, but not of social form itself. The wanderer does problematize form in itself but does so as a confirmed outsider, so in a sense, form is no longer a problem, but is merely an environing condition like an inert object that provides either advantages or disadvantages, or a mixture of both. Like the stranger the adolescent is relevant to a larger social group, but like the wanderer the adolescent escapes any fixed definition within that group. Thus, form itself is a problem that structures the adolescent's being-in-the-world: it is neither accepted in a demystified way, as in the case of the stranger, nor is it treated as a thing, as for the wanderer. Form, for the adolescent, can be opposed, played with, shunned or desperately grasped, but it cannot be fully subjectified or objectified.

The general structural predicament of the adolescent typically appears in the conscious form of a dualism between freedom and constraint. The latter is interpreted alternately as being treated as a child when one is capable of exerting one's own will, and as being forced into a system of obligations and responsibilities that must alienate one from one's new-found will. Freedom, in contrast, is interpreted as doing what one wants. The content of such vacant freedom is found primarily in direct bodily pleasures or in thinly veiled sublimations of those pleasures, though a counterpoint of existential loneliness and of resentment against the constraint of form may arise and sometimes becomes the dominant theme. The dualistic consciousness of the adolescent may be described in Freudian terms as a dichotomous choice, without any mediating terms, between release of the id and subjection to the super-ego. There is a failure to acknowledge the executive function and powers of the ego at the very moment that the ego is being most strongly affirmed in the form of a will to power and pleasure, and as a repository of treasured feelings. Rock music is, at its heart, a response to and an enhancement of this dualistic consciousness of youth, catering to the desires for freedom and the immediate goods that the independent and irresponsible life offers, or holding out a utopia in which the suspension of coercive routine is the normal state of affairs.

Caught between the moment of suspended freedom and the transition from dependency to responsibility, the typical dualistic consciousness of youth is modified by the counter-tendencies to sink back into childhood and to advance towards adulthood. The complex dialectic of adolescent mentality is the ground of the many ambivalences of youth, to which rock music appeals. Most of rock music is what Freud called a "compromise formation,"[14] in this case between the wish to remain in the stage of youth and the counter-wish to become a self-sustaining member of the wider society, or less frequently between the wishes to be free and to sink back into childishness. There is a kind of music that can be here called "pure rock," which expresses clearly the typical dualistic consciousness that counterposes spontaneity to regimentation, vitality to sociality, and the irreplaceably pleasurable event to the routine performance of social roles that are alien to the self. Songs such as the Rolling Stones' "Satisfaction," and "You Can't Always Get What You Want" would be examples of such "pure rock." And there is also the conventional pop music that romanticizes and mystifies the everyday life of everyman, particularly in its sexual dimension. The bulk of rock music falls between the poles of pure rock and pop, reflecting and representing the fundamental ambivalence between the thirst for freedom, pleasure and momentary execution of will, and the imperative of transiting from dependency to responsibility. The general compromise formation is diversified historically according to the vicissitudes of youth's life chances in the economy and the demands made upon it by the polity, and socially, according to the different sub-groups that make up youth.

Historical Diversification

As a compromise formation appealing to the ambivalent aspirations of youth, the style and content of rock music changes in relation to the specific life chances (interests and imperatives) that the youth group encounters in successive historical periods. The periodization of rock music, which has become integral both to the merchandising of rock as nostalgia and to the critical and academic literature concerned with the music, may be grounded on broader historical transformations. Rock began in the mid-1950s and expressed the search of the first generation of suburban youth for a position from which to declare itself independent of parental standards and to rationalize and satisfy, simultaneously, its desires for the free play of immediate pleasure. In the first era of rock, white middle- and working-class youth used the music of poor Southern whites and urban blacks to distance themselves from the norms of bureaucratic careerism and programmed suburban consumption. By the late 1950s, however, the raw origins of rock had been smoothed out by the process of commercialization. The youth group had become solidified as a separate category in society with substantial purchasing power in a generally expanding economy. Rock merged with pop and "youth culture" tended to spill over into the wider social life.

Economic conditions, reflected in the baby boom and suburbanization, were the environing determinants of the first era of rock. The next phase of the music's historical development was politically conditioned by the draft and more generally by the blacks' quest for social justice and the movements opposed to the Vietnam War. In this period the youth group no longer sought support in other sub-cultures but generated its own musical expressions and went in some cases so far as to create utopian visions of a society that would incorporate the spontaneous exercise of will and the venting of primal emotions. The hedonism and protest of mid-to-late 1960s rock reflected the life chances of youth under the "guns and butter" policies of Lyndon Johnson's administration: employment opportunities were expanding but one might be called to arms. The combination of affluence and vulnerability led to the formation of a counter-culture in which intense sensualism, enhanced by drugs, was mixed with political utopianism in an uneasy blend that was ideologically reflected in the debate between "cultural" and "political" revolution. Rock music was an integral component of the counter-culture, expressing its hedonism and its moralism, its dependence upon the "affluent society" and its rejection of the "warfare state" and of organizational discipline and consumership.

The next era of rock music was conditioned by the economic decline that began with the inflation of the early 1970s and ran through the recession of the early 1980s. In the wake of the baby boom the relative proportion of youth in the society declined at the same time as employment opportunities contracted. The competition engendered by the struggle for places in the society was reflected in the separation of the youth groups into fragmented sub-cultures, each of which was expressed by a particular style of music. In the mid-1980s a momentarily expanding economy and an awakening fear of militarism seemed to be supporting a "new wave" of rock music expressing multiple syntheses of the styles that were diversified in the 1970s.

Most generally the historical sequence of rock music follows a dialectical pattern in which periods of consolidation of the youth group alternate with periods of dispersion. An era of consolidation is most marked when adolescents have expanding economic opportunities ahead of them and experience political threats to the realization of their hopes, as was the case in the 1960s. In contrast, dispersion is most pronounced when economic opportunities are contracting and the youth group is not jeopardized politically. Political quiescence and economic expansion, as occurred in the 1950s and 1980s generate an individualistic cohesiveness, a shared style without a distinctive and militant "consciousness of kind." There has yet to be a period of both economic decline and political threat. Such an era might be adverse to rock music because of the limitations it would place on freedom and enjoyment. The wavelike rhythm of consolidation and dispersion is not an imminent historical dynamic but is derivative of economic cycles and political conflicts which themselves do not have a fixed periodicity: it is an empirical generalization that has the use of being a diagnostic measure of the situation of youth.

Sub-Group Diversification

In addition to the dialectical changes in rock described above, there are synchronic variations that are manifest in different rock genres and life styles that make specific appeals to subsets of youth. As a category youth is not an undifferentiated mass. Adolescents behave more or less homogeneously: their significant differentiations come to the fore or are submerged on different occasions and in different contexts. Among the more important distinctions dividing the broader youth group are those of gender, race, age (best understood as junior high school, high school and college age groups), geographical location (for example, urban versus small town, coast versus heartland), and social class affiliation (roughly working class versus middle class).

Each of these synchronic distinctions is, of course, relative to diachronic variations. In periods of consolidation the more static structural differences tend to become blurred, whereas in times of dispersion they tend to become sharpened. For example, in the 1960s specialized taste groups were often submerged in a thematic consensus on protest and pleasure, and a musical fusion of diverse styles (for instance, Dylan, Hendrix and Joplin), whereas in the 1970s diverse themes and styles arose that were based on structurally and demographically grounded sub-groups. The following brief exploration of the division of youth on the basis of gender will draw primarily upon the music of the 1970s, which brings out the correspondence between variations in musical genre and differences of gender more clearly than does the music of other periods. Synchronic distinctions, however, are present in every period and are merely highlighted by the type-case.

The ambivalence felt about entering the society, its intensity and its particular expressions are in part a function of the socialization patterns to which individuals have been exposed. In American society and with little variation in all modern societies boys are allowed greater freedom than are girls. Boys are permitted from an earlier age to be less supervised by adults, to go further from home, to be away from home for longer periods of time, including at night, than are girls. Boys are encouraged to be active in their bodily movements and are dressed to permit such activity. Girls, in contrast, are urged to be quiet and still, and are clothed in ways that hinder movement (clothes that are binding, that expose underwear easily if one is active, and that are easily dirtied and torn by activity). Boys are allowed to be aggressive vocally (cursing) and physically (fighting); such opportunities are not extended to girls. Boys are expected to be "naughty" ("He's all boy!") and to have little ability to defer gratification, whereas girls are supposed to be patient and "good," conforming to stipulated rules and constantly planning for a future and deferring present happiness for some ideal storybook ending of happily-ever-after. As a result of these socialization patterns the male has more problems with the transition from youth to adulthood, since the adult role is closer to the female pattern of low aggression, strict conformity to the "rules" and supervision by adults (bosses and spouses). The music that male youths (especially those in high school who are beginning clearly to see their adult options) enjoy reflects their ambivalence. They tend to admire the proficiency of artists who are committed to their careers. One often hears them complaining about how long it takes a certain artist or group to come out with a new album, implying that it is wrong for the artists not to be hard at work at their music. On the other hand, the music evokes themes of exuberant aggression through its ear-shattering amplification; its strutting, muscular and often black-leather-clad stars who have been applauded by their imitative fans for trashing their instruments on stage and their hotel rooms offstage; and its lyrics which express aggression in every possible dimension.

The strong rhythm section and the high amplification characteristic of hard rock appeal to males more than to females. Hard rock is redolent with themes of getting one's pleasure now and of misogyny. Pleasure is not of the world of the adult; at best society metes out small dollops of it in return for what Freud terms "unpleasure" (*unlust*). The anti-female bias of hard rock can be traced to the cultural representation of woman as a check on vitality and a guardian of social responsibility, sharply contrasting with the active hedonism of male youthfulness. A "macho" stance, not necessarily one that is cultivated within a life-style to which music is integral, is a compromise formation for men in general, who are in society but do not want be of it.

The extreme rock genre that exemplifies the male youth is Heavy Metal.[15] Ominously named groups such as Judas Priest, Black Sabbath, AC/DC, Iron Maiden, Anthrax, and Manowar attract a mainly male audience. Fans of the more radical subgenre, death metal, are almost exclusively young men. The music admires the very qualities that the male youths must sacrifice in order to become members of society. For many of them Heavy Metal sublimates these qualities and therefore allows them both to have their cake (behave as an adult) and eat it too (feel naughty and aggressive through participation in the music).

Rock music serves as a compromise formation for females, too, although in a sharply contrasting way to that in which it caters to males. In accordance with the passive and obedient female socialization pattern, the music directed to female youth is soft, both in terms of its beat and its amplification. The lyrical themes are almost exclusively concerned with romance and the rock stars are soft-spoken, often blond, non-threatening, and somewhat androgynous in appearance. Several studies conclude that girls "favour 'safe' pop idols rather than the rebel imagery of Elvis Presley."[16] Rock music that appeals to female youth serves to ease tensions about sexual activity, which whether or not young women are actively engaging in it, is threatening to female selfhood. For women, who are socialized to fit into society, it is this relatively wild act, in which one is a raw and pleasure-seeking being for a moment, that is in some sense their destiny and their major vulnerability. The fears of rape, of being used (of being seen not as a person but only as a sexual object), and of becoming pregnant are never far from a teenage girl's concerns. Romance is a way of taming these fears as well as preparing one to partake in sexual relations, engage in courtship and ultimately secure a husband.

The extreme rock genre that exemplifies the female youth is Soft Rock, which like Heavy Metal came to prominence after the period of consolidation of the 1960s ended. Whereas Heavy Metal heightened and disciplined the hard aspects of acid rock, customizing it for a male taste group, soft rock muted and tamed folk rock, adapting it to a predominantly female audience. Such performers as Cat Stevens, James Taylor, Jackson Browne and Carole King transformed the protest themes of the 1960s into sentimental commentaries on manners and mores, often keying in on the vicissitudes of romance and the illusions of youth. The soft rock performers cultivated a normal, if "laid back," appearance and often strove for acoustical effects and an intimate atmosphere even in their large-scale performances, evincing the comfort and security ultimately sought by females. More recently there has been an upsurge of harder female rock by female performers such as Joan Jett, Chrissie Hynde and Pat Benatar stressing the themes of independence, sexual expression and love of pleasure.

This development responds to the aspirations of a generation of women who seek a compromise between the two tendencies of the 1970s and to a return to traditional femininity coincident with institutional openings towards equal opportunity, and indicates the beginnings of consolidation.

Madonna has capitalized on this ambivalence of young women.

Although the preceding discussions of the gender differences among youth and the types of music that respond to the particular problems highlighted by them oversimplify gender roles, the arguments hold for each male and female to greater and lesser degrees, and in addition the relevant cultural object, in this case music, tends to emphasize the differences and, indeed, to reinforce them.

Conclusion

The foregoing analysis of rock music in terms of its relations to the opportunities and imperatives encountered by youth in the contemporary post-industrial societies of the West can be used to inform the debates over the global, cultural and societal import of rock that dominate the current and recent literature on this form of music. The cultural debate over whether rock is an authentic creative expression or merely a commodity for sale can be enlightened by referring to the distinction made in the discussion of rock as a compromise formation between pure rock and pop. Pure rock, which expresses directly the dualistic consciousness of freedom in opposition to societal constraint tends to be authentic, whereas pop music, which romanticizes the adult world, tends to be merely a commodity. In between the two poles, where most of rock music falls, there is often a mix of genuine creative intent and programmed and formulaic commodity production. Indeed, some of the most sensitive and authentic rock is a commentary on the tensions within the mixed mode from the creator's viewpoint, and on the ambivalence of youth itself (Rush "Subdivisions," Bruce Springsteen "Backstreets") One should not make the mistake of confusing high sales figures with the intent to produce a commodity. Those listeners who follow a particular group or artist are aware of when the performer has "sold out" and when the music is "real," and they are, perhaps, the best judges in the cultural debate, at least as it pertains to specific cases.

Similarly, the social debates over whether rock music supports the *status quo* or favors progressive change, or whether it is merely neutral or harmful to youth, can be illuminated by reference to the remarks above on the historical process of rock. In periods of expanding economic horizons for and political threats to youth, rock music will tend to become politically confrontational, whereas in periods of contracting economic horizons and political quiescence, rock will tend, if only by neglect, to support prevailing institutions. Of course, the deeper social debate is not merely over the content of rock music but over the question of whether rock's appeal to the adolescent idea of freedom constitutes liberation, repressive desublimation, or evil. If one views liberation as the creation of a solidary community that is now only potential, rock music will appear, for the most part, to be reactionary. On the other hand if one sees liberation as a release of vitality that is dammed by repressive social roles, then at least pure rock will be interpreted as a genuine social expression of revolt, the quintessence, one might argue, of modernism, created for and often by the social group whose members have the temporary privilege of problematizing society as a whole, of affirming, if only momentarily, life against form.

Whether or not "rock 'n' roll is here to stay" has been a concern of both friends and foes of the music. The latter believed that it was a fad that, like the hula hoop and goldfish swallowing, would soon fade into oblivion or be relegated to the warehouse of nostalgia. Adherents of rock, in contrast, were treated every so often to thematic songs proclaiming the immortality of the music ("Rock and Roll Ain't Noise Pollution—Rock and Roll Will Never Die," AC/DC) or rallying the faithful with chants of "Long Live Rock and Roll" (Rainbow). From the perspective taken in the foregoing discussion the continued existence of rock music is understood as a function of the continued existence of youth as a social category, as a social group with distinctive structural problems in contemporary society. And despite a demographic shrinkage in the number of people and the proportion of the population in the age group from thirteen to nineteen, the social category of youth is expanding. On one end the category of childhood is shrinking. For various reasons, people as young as eight or nine years old are sharing in the youth life-style in terms of consumption of products such as clothing, leisure activities from video games and television programs to record purchases, and knowledge of the "real world"—sexual, political, ecological, etc.[17] On the other side of the demographic distribution the expansion of youth may be witnessed in people in their twenties and many in their thirties and forties who have not become adults.[18] As a result of prolonged involvement in school, high unemployment rates and psychological factors there are a host of people in their twenties and thirties who are "still" living at "home" with their parents. Also, there has been a great increase in the number of adults who remain single and who marry but choose to remain childless. These situations encourage the prolongation of youthful life-styles. And rock stars are not switching to adult music; in deep middle age members of the Rolling Stones and The Who still rocked with much of the fervor and passion that they had decades earlier. Grey-haired rockers, fans and musicians, have increased the size of the youth category. And as long as youth as a social category survives, so will the musical expression of youth, rock, endure.

NOTES

*Originally published in *Popular Music and Society* 9 (1983):2–15. Reprinted with permission of the author.

1. Karl Mannheim, *Ideology and Utopia* (New York: Harcourt, Brace and World, 1936), pp. 260–261.

2. Simon Frith, *Sound Effects: Youth, Leisure and the Politics of Rock 'n' Roll* (New York: Pantheon, 1981), pp. 10–41.

3. Gary Allen, "More Subversion Than Meets the Eye," in *The Sounds of Social Change,* eds. R. Serge Denisoff and Richard A. Peterson (Chicago: Rand McNally, 1972), p.151.

4. Ibid., p. 165.

5. Richard Peck, *Rock Rock Rock: Making Musical Choices* Greenville, S.C.: Bob Jones University Press, 1985), p. 34.

6. Jonathan Eisen, *The Age of Rock* (New York: Vintage, 1969), p. xv.

7. Irwin Kantor, "This Thing Called Rock: An Interpretation," *Popular Music and Society,* 3 (1974), pp. 204–205.

8. Mark H. Levine and Thomas J. Harig, "The Role of Rock: A Review and Critique of Alternative Perspectives on the Impact of Rock Music," *Popular Music and Society,* 4 (1975), p. 200.

9. Michael Lyndon, "Rock for Sale," in *Side-Saddle on the Golden Calf,* ed. G.H. Lewis (Pacific Palisades: Goodyear, 1972), p. 316.

10. Deena Weinstein, *Heavy Metal: A Cultural Sociology* (New York: Lexington/Macmillan, 1991), Chapter 7.

11. Mary Douglas, *Purity and Danger* (Baltimore: Penguin, 1966).

12. Georg Simmel, "The Conflict in Modern Culture," in Georg Simmel: *On Individuality and Social Forms,* ed. Donald N. Levine (Chicago: University of Chicago Press, 1971), pp. 373–393.

13. Georg Simmel, "The Stranger" and "The Adventurer," in Levine, op. cit., pp. 143–149, 187–198.

14. Sigmund Freud, *The Interpretation of Dreams* (New York: Basic Books, 1955).

15. Deena Weinstein, op. cit., Chapter 4.

16. Michael Brake, *Comparative Youth Culture* (London: Routledge and Kegan Paul), p.154.

17. Neil Postman, *Amusing Ourselves to Death* (New York: Penguin, 1986).

18. See Chapter 4.

REFERENCES

Allen, Gary, 1972. "More Subversion than Meets the Ear." Pp. 151–166 in R. Serge Denisoff and Richard A. Peterson (eds.), *The Sounds of Social Change*. Chicago: Rand McNally.

Brake, Michael, 1985. *Comparative Youth Culture: The Sociology of Youth Cultures and Youth Subcultures in America, Britain and Canada*. London: Routledge & Kegan Paul.

Chapple, Steven and Reebee Garofolo, 1978. *Rock 'N' Roll is Here to Pay: The History and Politics of the Music Industry*. Chicago: Nelson-Hall.

Douglas, Mary, 1966. *Purity and Danger*. Baltimore: Penguin.

Eisen, Jonathan, 1969. *The Age of Rock*. New York: Vintage.

Freud, Sigmund, 1955. *The Interpretation of Dreams*. New York: Basic Books.

Frith, Simon, 1981. *Sound Effects: Youth, Leisure, and the Politics of Rock 'n' Roll*. New York: Pantheon.

Kantor, Irwin, 1974. "This Thing Called Rock: An Interpretation." *Popular Music and Society* 3:203–214.

Keniston, Kenneth, 1972. *Youth and Dissent*. New York: Harcourt, Brace & Jovanovich.

Levine, Mark H. and Thomas J. Harig, 1975. "The Role of Rock: A Review and Critique of Alternative Perspectives on the Impact of Rock Music." *Popular Music and Society* 4:195–207.

Lyndon, Michael, 1972. "Rock for Sale." Pp. 313–321 in G.H. Lewis (ed.), *Side-Saddle on the Golden Calf*. Pacific Palisades: Goodyear.

Mannheim, Karl, 1936. *Ideology and Utopia*. New York: Harcourt, Brace and World.

Marcuse, Herbert, 1964. *One-Dimensional Man*. Boston: Beacon.

Peck, Richard, 1985. *Rock Rock Rock: Making Musical Choices*. Greenville, SC: Bob Jones University Press.

Postman, Neil, 1986. *Amusing Ourselves to Death*. New York: Penguin.

Simmel, Georg, 1971a. "The Adventurer." Pp. 187–198 in Donald N. Levine (ed.), *Georg Simmel: On Individuality and Social Forms*. Chicago: University of Chicago Press.

Simmel, Georg, 1971b. "The Conflict in Modern Culture." Pp. 375–393 in Donald N. Levine (ed.), *Georg Simmel: On Individuality and Social Forms*. Chicago: University of Chicago Press.

Simmel, Georg, 1971c. "The Stranger." Pp. 143–149 in Donald N. Levine (ed.), Georg Simmel: *On Individuality and Social Forms*. Chicago: University of Chicago Press.

Weinstein, Deena, 1991. *Heavy Metal: A Cultural Sociology*. New York: Lexington/Macmillan.

The Political Status of Youth and Youth Culture*

Lawrence Grossberg

I

I want to start with four observations: first, as Ellen Wartella and Byron Reeves (1985) have demonstrated, there is a long and replete history of research on the relationship between youth and media, often constructed in a context of concern and fear about the deleterious nature of the relationship. Second, if youth is part of the last category in the list of subordinated populations—servants (i.e., racial and subordinated populations), women, and the young—it is surprisingly treated as an unproblematic category in almost all of the research that surrounds and constructs it. It is, at the very least, surprising how under-theorized it has remained. One could not get away with a similar acceptance of commonsense notions for any other "subordinated" group. Perhaps this is because, in some very concrete ways, youth is the most silenced population in society, not only in intellectual but in social and political terms as well (despite being the noisiest). This brings up the first of the two questions I want to raise here: What is the status of the category of youth? What is the political significance of the category? What is its place in the field of political possibilities? Here I can do no more than open up discussion, comparable perhaps to Stuart Hall's and others' attempts to rethink the articulation of ethnicity as a structure of investment and the articulation of identity as a structure of social positions and differences (see Rutherford, 1990). This involves rethinking identity as a space of identification and belonging rather than as as an effect of interpolation.

The third observation is that youth is always overdetermined, inflected not only by race, gender, ethnicity, sexuality, and class, but also by spatial location (in terms of both nations and regions and the different forms of social space—e.g., urban, suburban, rural, and small town), and by generational identity (where one plugs into the history of specific social formations). This is crucial, for it prevents us both from overgeneralizing any particular notion of youth, and also from reducing the category to a historical epiphenomenon (as many cultural constructionists would have it). The final observation, which will bring me back to the question of youth and media, is that youth is not merely an audience fraction of the media. The very existence of youth, at least in the twentieth century, is intimately tied to the media and vice versa: we might say that, perhaps more than any other social identity, youth always exists, as a style, with and within the media. This is the second question I want to raise here: how to position youth, not only within history, but as itself a historical space always and already implicated with the media.

This is to go beyond the assertion that the meaning of youth is, and must remain, uncertain. It is not merely a question of the historical construction of the category, or the rearticulation of its meaning, or even of its occasional existence as a site of social struggle. Nor is it merely that the reference of youth is contestable: somehow located between, yet overlapping with, both childhood and adulthood, it is simultaneously identified with and differentiated from adolescence and young adulthood. It is true, of course, that the social identity of "youth" is undefinable. Youth is a term without its own center. It is a signifier of change and transition, caught between the ignorance and innocence of the child, and the perceived dogmatism and inflexibility (perhaps even the corruption) of the adult. Youth cannot be represented, for it is an identity largely defined by and for the adults who, in a variety of ways, invest in it and use it to locate themselves. But there is more to it, for the very register of its reference is constantly at stake; both the signifier and the body of youth—its existence as an articulated unity of practices—are always mobile. Youth moves within and across the multiple planes of historical existence: biological (chronology, development), economic, social, ideological, phenomenological, libidinal, affective, stylistic and attitudinal (not in the social-psychological sense but in the sense in which we say, "She has an attitude."). Youth *is* a historical construct, for its existence depends upon the deterritorialization of rites of initiation which give social temporality—moments of transition—their own place and space. Youth exists in and as a complex field of vectors which are constantly deterritorializing and reterritorializing the body of youth, spatializing the temporality of transition. Youth exists only as a mobile and flexible alliance or distribution of practices; yet its mobility and flexibility must constantly be disciplined, stabilized or even homogenized. This is at least in part the function of the various institutions and apparatuses which operate on youth, including, I might add, the various academic apparatuses which, in their research formulations, organize youth into various formations, into various conceptions of "the proper" forms of youth.

Most of us, whether knowingly or not, start with a commonsensical demographic conception of youth in which age is linked to economics: youth as either market or audience. In either case, whether youth resists or accedes to the position, youth is defined in its relation to processes and practices of commodification. And this commodity status is simply reproduced in its status as a chronological independent variable, for as Pierre Bordieu (1984) has argued, such variables are themselves always the articulated unity of diverse fragments. Their stability has to be actively maintained, reconstructed in the face of both real and potential challenges. For they are never without meaning, never without reference to material bodies in social space, never independent of their place within the space of power relations.

II

My own commitment to cultural studies leads me to examine those formations which try to construct the agency, the political possibilities of youth. Since the 1960s, there is a clear tendency to see youth as a new political agent, if not the new revolutionary agent.

One of the most influential models has been subcultural theory, derived from deviancy theory and symbolic interactionism and politicized in the work of the Centre for Contemporary Cultural Studies (Hall and Jefferson, 1976; Hebdige, 1979). While acknowledging the diversity of positions, I think it is still possible to describe the general thrust of this work. It began with the assumption that the experience of the members of a subculture is determined by their social position, i.e., by their place within an objective set of social relations, and in particular, by the articulation of their class and generational positions. "Generation" was not simply equivalent to age, but described a particular historical moment and the social psychological experience of that moment. In terms of the latter, subcultural theory focused on the centrality of the construction of identities. In terms of the former, generation was largely a matter of cultural relations and practices: the fact and ideology of affluence, the omnipresence of mass communication, the different dimensions of the postwar social experience, the rapid expansion of education, and the growing visibility of youth style (manifested most apparently in rock culture).

Yet, as various participants in this project have admitted, they often "got the balance wrong": while their descriptions defined the subculture generationally, their explanatory model often assumed that the relevant experience that held the subculture together (both as a population and a style), what was often described as "the fit," was rooted almost entirely in its members' class position (a position which was generally working class; researchers' occasional efforts to describe middle-class subcultures never quite fit the model) and in the normativity of the masculine gender. In fact, their accounts of subcultures rarely actually needed generational identifications: the trajectory of upward mobility which, in conjunction with the working class condition of many of the subcultures, defined the dominant contradictions, was part of the broader cultural milieu.

The subordination of the subcultural population, a subordination defined both positionally and experientially, was constituted by the dominant culture and ideology. But the subculture, by constructing its own style, by rearticulating the fragments of various formations of the dominant culture (into the space of their own youth culture), was able to express its experiences and respond to its lived contradictions in creative ways. On the one hand, that style homologously represented the experience (the relationship of representation was understood differently depending upon different assumptions about the mediating term—e.g., as an image, a structure of feeling, a signifying practice). On the other hand, the style enabled its members to live with the contradictions in their experience by creating an identity—often but not always a forbidden identity—which "resisted" both the dominant culture and the parent (class) culture. But this resistance is "imaginary" since it takes place within the specular realm of culture, on the terrain of the dominant ideology. It offers only a magical solution to the lived contradiction, and the subordination, of the subculture's members. While the contradictions are the result of real social conditions, positions, and subordinations, the style/identity can only respond at the level of culture/ideology/identity, and thus, the contradictions remain firmly in place.

This work has been widely influential, even while it has been seriously criticized (Clarke, even within the tradition of cultural studies; see, e.g., Clarke, 1990). At the same time, cultural studies have reinflected the model by generalizing the notion of appropriation as a form of articulation. This enables the critic to reject the assumption that audiences are passive cultural dopes, without giving up the recognition that they are often duped by cultural practices. After all, if people are cultural dopes, what is the point of criticism or education? But, on the other hand, if they are never duped, then there is similarly no point to such activities. Some cultural analysts have expanded the notion of subculture beyond the parameters of the original model, thus holding on to the notion that such appropriation is a form of resistance which differentiates and privileges some (marginal) consumers (or cultural practices) from the mainstream mass cultural audiences (or practices), usually by virtue of their subordinate position. But other critics, while rejecting this dualism, recognize that youth itself, regardless of class (although not independently of it) already constitutes a space of subordination and discipline. At its best, these works, building upon subcultural theory's linkage of youth and generation (e.g., McRobbie, 1991; Hebdige, 1988), have begun to talk about the importance of style as a place of identification and belonging for youth. These critics question the different forms and significances of the generational identification of various youth fractions, and of their different relations to style. This route opens the possibility of accounting for the differences between subcultural styles, and for the "fit" that holds any style together, questions that the original subcultural investigations were unable to answer because, within their model, experience was largely determined elsewhere (in class relations). The result was that any subcultural style remained incapable of rearticulating the positions and identifications of the subcultural population.

At this point, I want to consider a different and, in some ways, more interesting model of the political status of youth: John and Margaret Rowntree's (1968) attempt to see (1) youth as a class formation and (2) the rise of youth culture in the context of shifts in the mode of production and class relations. Based on the postwar Fordist compromise, the Rowntrees argued that the amelioration of the lot of the working class in the United States was resulting in "class-shifting." That is, while following the common argument at the time that focused on the "embourgeoisment of the working classes," the Rowntrees argued not for the disappearance of class differences (the typical liberal view), but for the appearance of a new proletariat, a potentially revolutionary class which, like the working class before it, was exploited by the new relations of postwar capitalism. In fact, in a somewhat prescient move, they identified two such classes: the masses of the "backward countries" and the young of the United States. What is crucial about their argument is that both were exploited and alienated, albeit in different ways, by virtue of their position in the changing mode of production.

The Rowntrees focused their analysis of the changing mode of production on the role of the state in advanced or monopoly capitalism: on the one hand, the state guaranteed the continued imperialistic and neocolonialist structures within which central capital could export its necessary labor to the periphery. And on the other hand, presaging arguments about post-Fordism, the state was seen to support two industries which had an increasingly important role, both quantitatively and qualitatively, and which crucially depended upon and shaped the youth population: defense and education. "These two industries embody the most acute and potentially explosive contradictions of this variant of the capitalist mode of production (as, for instance, heavy industry embodied the most explosive contradictions in the 1930s)." These industries were necessary to absorb the surplus labor of youth (even as youth absorbed vast quantities of social and economic resources). This goes beyond the more common recognition that the temporal expansion of youth (partly through the spatial expansion of education) was necessary to keep the baby boomers from destabilizing the Fordist labor market.

Moreover, the Rowntrees argued, these two industries were basically unproductive. And it is this unproductivity which defined the nature of the economic exploitation and social "immiseration" of youth. To put it simply, youth was as alienated by its economic position as the working classes had been by theirs: "Not only is the young worker's product taken from him, but the dilemmas of monopoly capitalism make his work increasingly unproductive and therefore subjectively repugnant. In addition, the young are alienated . . . from their own potential" (as adults). As youth became conscious of their exploitation ("student as nigger"), of their complicity in the suppression of other peoples (the university as knowledge factory for the war machine) and of themselves as a unity, they became self-conscious of themselves as a class (the traditional Marxist term and the condition for revolutionary agency).

While I do not want to take the time to criticize this vision—history has already made most of its weaknesses apparent—I do want to make two points. First, despite their conflation of education and knowledge production (which are not necessarily equivalent, as their increasing disarticulation in the 1990s demonstrates), the Rowntrees were correct to point to the conjuncture of education and defense as what Deleuze and Guattari (1977) describe as machines of antiproduction and to the special relation which exists between youth (at least, the baby boom that followed the Second World War) and these economic apparatuses. This has serious implications for any attempt to locate youth within the space of economic relations. Second, despite the obvious historical errors in their account—apparently, youth lost its class self-consciousness somewhere along the way, perhaps as it moved from its necessary role in antiproduction to its role in both Fordist and post-Fordist modes of production—at least a part of their case is strengthened by contemporary developments: the increasing impoverishment of youth in American society and their increasing use in temporary and part-time minimum wage jobs that offer few benefits, little chance of advancement and no security—in short, no future.

Both of these visions of the political agency of youth share three assumptions which I wish to challenge. First, they assume that economic power is always expressed in and constructs class formations. This makes it more difficult to adequately describe the economic articulations of youth—the ways youth both deconstructs and reinforces class identifications. Moreover, the changing places and fortunes of youth in the economy seem to escape a simple class analysis, for they depend less on the relations of labor and capital, the basic contradiction underlying class relations, than upon the changing articulations of the relations between the forces and the relations of production.

Second, both views see youth as a transitional period during which individuals search for a viable adult identity, a moment of initiation. Against this commonsense view, Erik Erikson (1968) argued that youth searches for "fidelity," for something worth believing in and trusting. Erikson emphasized youth as a time of passion and intensity, of identification and belonging. Youth is "impelled to find a faith, a point of rest and defense, a touchstone by which they can accept or reject, love or hate, act or not act" (Baker, 1989). Youth does not so much involve an ideological search for identity as an affective search for appropriate maps of daily life, for appropriate sites of involvement, investment and absorption. This involves youth in a constant shuttling between extremes. Searching for something worthy of their passion, they "have no choice but to talk in extremes; they're being wrenched and buffeted" (Baker, 1989) by all of the competing (and in the contemporary world, unworthy) demands of the historical formation. Perhaps this is because, even more than children, they are "always episodes in someone else's narrative, not their own people but rather brought into being for someone else's purposes" (Steedman, 1986).

The final assumption, closely tied to the first two, is that the identity of youth depends on its place in a system of difference, as the other to some dominant term. That is, it is assumed that age as a dimension of power must operate in the same way as we assume gender and race to operate. As Stuart Hall (1991) puts it, identity is "a structured representation which only achieves its positive through the narrow eye of the negative. It has to go through the eye of the needle of the other before it can construct itself." Regardless of whether this is an adequate model of racial and gendered systems of identification and belonging, I believe it is entirely inadequate for an understanding of youth. And it is not merely a matter of the continuous rather than discrete nature of age as a variable. Rather it depends upon what I have just described as the affective extremism of youth. Locating youth on an affective plane emphasizes its positivity and brings us closer to Hall's (1991) recent notion of ethnicity as "the moment when people reach for those groundings [in imaginary, knowable places, in the identities of specific places] and the reach for those groundings." Or, in other words (Hall, 1989), "by ethnicity we mean the astonishing return to the political agenda of all those points of attachment which give the individual some sense of place and position in the world, whether in relation to particular communities, localities, territorialities, languages, religions or cultures."

III

Youth is not merely an ideological construction and what is at stake is not merely a question of what it means to different groups. There are real material stakes in the struggle to construct youth in particular ways. Youth has not, in the first instance, to be located within a meaningful system of social differences; it has to be organized, disciplined, controlled, distributed, and subjugated to the spatial and temporal maps of the dominant socal formations. For youth is always more than childhood, more than a time of growing up, more than the innocent passing of time. Youth involves an excessiveness, an impulsiveness, a maniacal irresponsibility which escapes time and potentially goes on forever. Youth is a material problem; it is a body—the individual body and the social body of generations—that has to be properly inserted into the dominant organization of spaces and places, into the dominant systems of economic and social relationships. As a body, it has to be located in its own proper places and its movements have to be surveyed and constrained. And as a body, its gendered and racial identities have to be neatly defined, its behavior regulated and its sexuality policed.

The affective extremism of youth suggests, then, a different model—not youth as a stage of difference, or as a potential outsider, but youth as a territory which is becoming minor. This has nothing to do with numbers or even with resistance per se; it has everything to do with an alternative way of living in the dominant, with a deterritorialization of the dominant maps from within. Youth is not an identity but a distribution of practices and affects, the product of a territorializing machine which organizes the places and spaces of a minor mattering map. Youth is constantly producing lines of flight that attempt to escape the dominant organization of everyday life. Or rather, its lines of flight are always located within the dominant field but they respeak it, stuttering the dominant language, as Deleuze and Guattari (1987) might say. Youth's mobility of investments, its sense of itself as a transition which celebrates the transitory, is also an investment in mobilities. Such a minor articulation is not without its own mattering maps, its own lines of articulation which anchor youth into the real world, but according to a minor system of investment. This is the significance of style (and ultimately of the media) in youth culture, for its minoritarian politics are more a matter of style than of age or social position or experience. But style is itself determined by and within the dominant cultural and institutional contexts, as well as the structures of capital investment.

Let me try to specify this more historically by considering how youth was reconstructed in the postwar years. For the baby boomers were shaped, and their bodies and lives positioned within, a complex, interactive, and often contradictory set of social formations and apparatuses. My argument is that a particular generation was identified with "youth" and invested with a certain power within and by a broad range of social discourses. This was the first generation of children isolated by business (and especially by advertising and marketing agencies) as an identifiable market; and despite its social differences and its cultural diversity, the economic strategies were surprisingly successful in constructing a rather coherent generational identity and a singular marketing cluster (an "identity in difference"). But while it was a generation constructed for economic (and nationalistic) reasons, economics was not the only basis for its privileged position in society. If the war had been fought, rhetorically at least, to protect the American dream, it was the conjunction of the family and consumerism that defined the postwar images of that dream. This was a crucial moment in the history of American identity. As postwar America struggled to understand its new position in the world—the kid among nations who had suddenly grown up and become the leader—it had to relocate its own sense of difference. If America had always defined itself by its open-ended future, by its ongoing effort to realize the American dream as a still undefined and certainly unrealized possibility, by the fact that it had not and could not grow up, it needed now to understand how that was still possible. Its response was to continue investing its identity in the future by finding a more definitive, already existing embodiment of that future. The baby boomers became the living promise of the possibility of actually achieving the American dream. They were to be the best-fed, best-dressed, best-educated generation in the history of the world. They were to be the living proof of the success of the American experiment.

The fragility of this process meant that youth would be ambivalently valued: on the one hand, nurtured as a time directed beyond the present (the American dream), a time for constructing new mattering maps projected into an unknown future. On the other hand, youth was envied and feared as a heightened experience of the present, as a challenge to the viability and necessity of existing social norms and regulations. This ambiguity was reconciled by making youth into an identity, marking its difference—as a demographic category, a commodity, and an audience—and developing appropriate structures of disciplinization. Youth had to be both spatialized (confined within privileged discourses and institutions) and identified (led into the appropriate adult identities). Society had to develop strategies to "program" the mobility, the positive "otherness" and the uncertainty of youth into the normalcy of adulthood (through the specific historical alliance of family, school, psychology, medicine, and criminal justice systems, as well as economic discourses and cultural discourses).

As society attempted to shape the body of youth—to organize its material, ideological, and affective life by monitoring its needs, aspirations and behavior, the baby boomers gained an independent existence as youth apart from these social institutions. After all, such practices can never fully control their effects. This left a space, within which the privileged place of youth enabled it to rearticulate its own territorialization by foregrounding the sense of its own difference, a difference which had already been constructed for it. If youth represented the promise and identity of "America," its most valued commodity, then why should it not celebrate itself as an end in itself, as a distinct and independent formation standing apart from, if not in radical opposition to, the adult world that had created it and endowed it (unintentionally, no doubt) with such powers. It is not that youth was somehow inherently rebellious, but that its identity was given, at a particular moment, by its very self-incarnation of a radically alternative space, a minor modulation of the dominant maps of everyday life.

This unique position was formed at the intersection of youth's alienation from the adult world, and the sense of its difference which had been constructed by that world. This position was articulated into a series of minor rearticulations of the adult realities of everyday life. If society demanded that youth be under constant surveillance, then youth would constantly expose itself in order to hide in the very surfaces, not only of its different styles (Hebdige describes this politics of youth as "spectacle") but of its moral and sociological indeterminacy. If society demanded that youth be consumers, they could consume themselves as fetish-objects. If society located the body of youth in the spaces of domesticity, consumption, and education (with any transgressions resulting in specific sites of incarceration for the youthful offender), then youth could construct its own places in the space of transition between these institutions: in the street, around the jukebox, at the hop (and later, at the mall). These are all spaces located between the domestic, public, and social spaces of the adult world. What the dominant society assumed to be no place at all—merely a transition—became the privileged site of youth's investment and eventually, the spatial coordinates of youth culture. The anonymity of these places offered the possibility of avoiding social surveillance, a social version of the desperate effort to construct a space of privacy in one's room, surrounded by the music. Of course, these new deterritorializations and reterritorializations, these articulations in a minor key, these spaces of transition, could be carried back into the dominant places. Thus, young girls often had to transform the private into the public and the public into the private, the bedroom into the site of collective style, and the space of domesticity into the place of social practices of dancing, makeup, etc.

Here we can begin to understand the natural union of youth and media culture, for it here that we must locate the emergence of rock and youth culture. The articulation of rock and youth transformed a transitional culture into a culture of transitions (and the transitional body of youth into a body of transitions). For it was this popular culture, with rock at its center, that territorialized the space of youth, constituting youth by the distribution of its own practices. This distribution defined youth by the places and spaces of its own mattering maps. And yet, simultaneously, rock located youth within a binary machine that marked its difference rather than its positivity. Rock mapped the specific structures of youth's affective alienation on the geographies of everyday life. Just as rock functioned by continually generating its own difference, both internally and externally, from mere entertainment (read boredom), so the specific territorialization of youth's positivity was stratified, mapped onto the grid of socially defined differences. Rock was a response to a certain kind of loneliness and uncertainty: it was about the ways in which youth itself offers new possibilities of identification and belonging through the construction of temporary mattering maps. For youth inhabited a place in the social order which demanded that it live daily life according to someone else's maps, someone else's dreams, someone else's trajectories. Youth was subordinated to its already defined place within a social narrative that was told before it arrived. Youth, in the rock formation, became its very difference from the adult world, a world that, above all else, was regulated, disciplined, and boring. It was the radical rejection of boredom as the very negation of youth that came, in the 1950s, to define both youth and rock. Rock's territorializing machine was deployed in the service of a differentiating project, linked to the project of mapping boundaries, of marking the differences between youth (fans) and adults (boredom).

For rock was always about the transitions between investments and differences. It was not only a territorializing, but a differentiating machine as well. It displaced the question of identity and self-identity into the narcissistic production of a binary distribution within rock itself. Instead of being different because one had a socially guaranteed identity, rock constructed temporary differences through people's places within different mattering maps and cultural alliances. Investment became the source of a transitory difference. Anonymity and difference replaced identity itself as transition became the key value. Rock was about the control one gained by taking the risk of losing control, the identity one had by refusing identities. Its only stability was in the investment one made into the formation itself. It reified its own transitional status, locating itself as a permanent "between" or "becoming." It constituted itself as a space of "magical transformations" in the face of youth's own necessary transformation into its own imagined other: adulthood. Youth celebrated its own impossibility in rock.

Ultimately, the register of that difference was the body and its politics was fun. The body was not merely the site of a static system of pleasures; rather pleasure was always located within an economy of movement: dance, sexuality, style, and taste are all inseparable pieces of a common body. The music itself, in its volumes and rhythms, in the particular tones, colors, and grains of voice to which it is always returning, not only foregrounded the body in motion, but continuously undermined the ability of any identity to control or even claim the body as its own. The body of youth in rock was always a body on display, to others and itself, as the mark of a celebration of energy and fun. They mattered because they were at the heart of rock, and rock mattered. Rock touched, fragmented, multiplied, and propelled the bodies of its fans. It created a flexible and transitory body which was put into place against the various emotional narratives and alienating experiences of youth's everyday life. Of course, fun is not the same as pleasure. Rock was not about pleasure—it was just as often about displeasure and pain, and it did not always seek to transform the latter into pleasure. Rather, it celebrated its ability to avoid, or rather, to rearticulate the dominant structures of everyday life (noise, repetition, etc.) into a new economy, an economy of the affective deployment of energy against the debilitating economies of boredom, a minor use of boredom in the service of fun.

IV

Once again, since the 1980s, youth itself has become a battlefield on which the current generations of adolescents and preadolescents, baby-boomers and baby-busters, parents, corporate and corporate media interests (and, we might add, politicians and academics) are fighting over territories, investments, and powers, fighting to articulate and thereby construct youth's experiences, identities, practices, discourses, and social differences. This struggle encompasses a fractious and often contradictory set of social formations, defined not only by the proliferation of postwar generations but also by the attenuation of the relationship between age and "youth" in favor of youth as an affective identity stitched onto a generational history. This is a struggle located in the space of the contradiction between those who experience the powerlessness of their age (adolescents and college students) and the generations of baby boomers who have attached the category of youth to their life trajectory, in part by redefining it as an attitude ("You're only as old as you feel"). For the baby boomers, youth is something to be held on to by cultural and physical effort. But the whole point about being young is that one doesn't have to work for it.

The specific configuration of youth which was articulated in the postwar rock formation is being displaced and reshaped. (Consider that hip hop is perhaps the only available model for an alternative youth culture today; hence youth-oriented media and even rock culture itself find that they must increasingly use its styles and rhythms, although this has not always forced them to question their racism.) The structure of normalcy which had disciplined and controlled the "extremism" of youth depended on the construction—differently from each direction—of a stable boundary between youth and adults. As this collapses, or more accurately, as it is being actively eroded, the "Right" (e.g., in the discourses of Tipper Gore, Allan Bloom, and William Bennett) is attempting to reconstruct it, albeit differently, within the image of a corrupt adult world threatening and simultaneously insulating a perfectly innocent youth. At the same time, one finds images which, while echoing the 1950s, actually suggest that neither adulthood nor youth defines normal and predictable categories. This is not nostalgia, or if it is, it is a nostalgia for an imaginary past, a past we know we did not live through even as we desire to relive it: a nostalgia for nostalgia. All of the generations of postwar youth are caught in this inability to choose or even differentiate between youth and adult. If the baby-boomers seem to refuse to give up their youth, contemporary youth (the baby busters) increasingly demands its adulthood. And preadolescents desire nothing so much as to skip entirely the process of growing up (which for them often means skipping the teenage years) in order to be just what they must inevitably become: adults. "The goal seems to be to get to thirty as fast as possible, and stay there. Starting out, we are eager, above all else, to be finished" (Leavitt, 1985; see also Coupland, 1991).

The struggle is physical and economic as well. The material, social and mental state of youth in America is—let us not say in crisis, but rather simply dismal. Yet this fact is erased from the maps constituting the terrain of struggle. Even the *New York Times* (Brazelton, 1990) has acknowledged that America is "failing its children" and compares the status of children in America unfavorably with some Third World nations: "Children endure more deprivation than any other segment of society. Yet . . . the U.S. could reduce this tragedy with remedies that are available right now." The fact that it isn't—that we aren't—suggests that the worsening condition of youth is not innocent, that it itself must be placed within the territory of the struggle.

> The emergency we are facing is an unprecedented adolescent health crisis—one that has serious repercussions for our economy and our social well-being. For the first time in the history of this country, young people are *less* healthy and *less* prepared to take their places in society than were their parents. . . .
>
> Unhealthy teenagers—those who are alienated or depressed, who feel that nobody cares, who are distracted by family or emotional problems, who are drinking or using drugs, who are sick or hungry or abused or feel they have no chance to succeed in this world—are unlikely to attain the high levels of education achievement required for success in the 21st century. And thousands of these young people will experience school failure, which for many will be a precursor to an adult life of crime, unemployment, or welfare dependency. (National Commission on the Role of the School and the Community in Improving Adolescent Health)

The struggles over youth are being enacted in the media as well, in a broad range of texts that are clearly punctuated by images and relations of youth. The television screen is filled with baby boomers' nostalgic look back on their own youth, on the images from their own youth, and on their own youthfulness. Images of the transgressions of age have exploded: young people becoming old, old people becoming young, old and young people switching places. Not coincidentally, it is only quite recently that television has bothered to, or been able to, represent youth peer culture ("Beverly Hills 90210"). But this success is simultaneously framed and balanced by programs extending the representation to cover the entire expanse of the postwar youth generations (the twenty-somethings, thirty-somethings, and even forty-somethings). But even more clearly, we can see the struggle over youth in the different, and in some cases, new ways in which youth—its experiences, practices and discourses—is represented: youth as embodying all of the (negative) characteristics of adulthood; youth as radically different from adulthood, often in threatening and alien ways; youth as the repository of adult fantasies of innocence and/or irresponsibility; youth as the salvation of the world or at least of parents; youth as the site of victory and luck; youth as the last champion of justice; youth as possibility; youth as utter failure; and youth as unavoidable closure. This diversity signals, at the very least, the contradictions in people's feelings about youth. Youth seems to have become the dominant topic and audience for popular culture. The media (even the vast majority of rock) speak as if from a position of youth, for youth; but they actually speak as adults, for adults. Thus it is increasingly common to find the baby-boomer heroes and heroines of prime-time television confronting their ambiguous relations to both youth and adulthood, appropriating the former category and dissolving it into their reluctance to enter into the latter. Perhaps all this encodes a new resentment of youth by a generation that was never taught to be adults or even to value that identity, and whose identity is still imbricated in their investment in youth.

The category and body of youth are being reshaped. I am neither proclaiming the end of youth nor interpreting a mere change in its meaning. I am pointing to its rearticulation, and reterritorialization, not only as a cultural category but as a social and material body as well. That body is torn apart by the contradictions between the different generations and territorializations of youth. The very sites and forms of its public existence are being restructured (from marches to malls); its rhythms and drugs are changing as well. The issue is not whether the various discourses about youth are referentially accurate but that they are themselves part of the context in which youth is organized. The discourses and practices that interpenetrate, surround, and shape youth have now become a major battleground. Those generations which have invested their identities in the category of youth are now attempting to produce new articulations in an attempt to control, resist, alter, or sustain the dominant conceptions of their own identities and futures. And those generations of "children" and "young people" who might assume the category for themselves not only confront new demands from the world but also new discourses which offer them little guidance or solace. But both groups are caught in their own dilemma: the minor discourse has become majoritarian. The deterritorializations which defined the territory of rock and youth have been largely confined, and the differentiating power of rock—the difference of youth—has become unnecessary. And this is inseparable from the changing effectivity of the media or at least of rock culture. For its very territorializing power has overwhelmed its differentiating effects. Within rock culture, differences matter less and less, and the territorializing machine of rock seems increasingly to rearticulate itself into mechanisms of the social distribution of leisure. Thus, once again, this new space of youth is marked and mapped by rock culture, now operating as a minor discourse become major. Its mobility has been constrained, its territorializing power weakened, and it itself dispersed into the social distribution of leisure. Even more, its differentiating power has itself dissolved into the tolerance of a space without, or with a different organization of, affective investment.

But this struggle is not merely sociological. It has to be located within a larger political and economic project: a struggle over the political possibilities of the nation. Thus the contemporary uncertainty surrounding youth, and the struggles over youth and youth culture, cannot be reduced to a mere token of a more universal struggle to discipline youth because it is such a powerful—if potential—site of antagonism and resistance. This is, at best, a romantic desire based on images of youth from specific times and places. There is nothing intrinsic about youth which makes it politically resistant. To say that youth is a time of transition when change and experimentation are encouraged, to say even that it is a moment of a certain kind of rebellion, is not the same as saying that it constitutes some sort of political undercurrent or threat. And there is little evidence, especially in the past decade, that contemporary generations of youth pose any such radical challenge to the status quo. Conservative attempts to reinflect and redeploy the place of youth in American society and culture must be determined elsewhere, by a trajectory which connects youth to the struggle over the politics of culture.

I believe that this "political struggle" with and over youth, more than anything else, defines the context of and mediates the relations between youth, popular culture, and the state. At such moments as the present, the sites, forms, and rhythms of youth's public existence are restructured. The discourses and practices that interpenetrate, surround and shape youth (largely leisure and popular culture practices, but also practices of family, education, drugs, etc.) have become a major battleground. In this context, neither youth nor its relations to the media can be described or interpreted apart from the specific context which constitutes not only the significance of the relation, but the relation itself and the very body of youth. Hence the "problem of youth and media" cannot be reduced to a mere question of constructing a specific set of texts "communicating" the "right" message to kids, as if such communication could be isolated from the whole context of communication and the world. (How, for example, are we to communicate to youths the importance of dissent or of avoiding drugs when it is clear to them that we live in a country which doesn't value or even tolerate real dissent but does allow itself to become saturated with drugs?) We need to go much further, not only by listening to youths but also by legitimating them, their experiences, their feelings, and their practices. Even more, as academics, we need to see the signifying, institutional, and material machinery by which youth is constructed, disciplined, and controlled. We need to see how youth is made into a subject, an identity, and an agent, and how each of these is now being taken away. And finally, we need to see how these practices are being taken up in broader efforts to redirect the trajectory of American society.

NOTE

*This paper was originally given at the conference, "Are the Kids Alright?—Early Adolescence and the Media," at the Pennsylvania State University in April, 1990. I would like to thank the conference organizers, Bea Mandel and Michael Ludwig, for inviting me. This paper draws in part on material from my book, *We Gotta Get Out of This Place: Popular Conservatism and Postmodern Culture* (Routledge, 1992).

REFERENCES

Baker, W. (1989). "The Global Teenager." *Whole Earth Review*, 65.

Bourdieu, Pierre (1984). *Distinction: A Social Critique of the Judgement of Taste*. Trans. R. Nice. Cambridge, MA: Harvard University Press.

Brazelton, T. B. (1990). "Why Is America Failing Its Children?" *New York Times Magazine*, September 9.

Clarke, Gary (1990). "Defending Ski-jumpers: A Critique of Theories of Youth Subcultures." In S. Frith and A. Goodwin (eds.), *On Record*. New York: Pantheon, 81–96.

Coupland, Douglas (1991). *Generation X: Tales for an Accelerated Culture*. New York: St. Martin's.

Deleuze, Gilles, and Felix Guattari (1977). *Anti-Oedipus: Capitalism and Schizophrenia*. Trans. R. Hurley, M. Seen and H.R. Lane. New York: Viking.

——— (1987). *A Thousand Plateaus: Capitalism and Schizophrenia*. Trans. B. Massumi. Minneapolis: University of Minnesota Press.

Erikson, Erik H. (1968). *Identity: Youth and Crisis*. New York: Norton.

Hall, Stuart (1989). "The Meaning of New Times." In S. Hall and M. Jacques (eds.). *New Times: The Changing Face of Politics in the 1990s*. London: Lawrence and Wishart, 116–134.

——— (1991). "Old and New Identities, Old and New Ethnicities." In A.D. King (ed.). *Culture Globalization and the World-System*. London: Macmillan, 41–68.

Hall, Stuart, and Tony Jefferson (eds.). (1976). *Resistance Through Rituals: Youth Subcultures in Post-War Britain*. London: Hutchinson.

Hebdige, Dick (1979). *Subculture: The Meaning of Style*. London: Methuen.

——— (1988). *Hiding in the Light*. London: Routledge.

Leavitt, David (1985). "The New Lost Generation." *Esquire*, May.

McRobbie, Angela (1991). *Feminism and Youth Culture*. London: Macmillan.

National Commission on the Role of the School and the Community in Improving Adolescent Health (n.d.). *Code Blue: United for Healthier Youth*.

Rowntree, John, and Margaret Rowntree (1968). "Youth as a Class." In *International Socialist Journal*, 25.

Rutherford, John (ed). (1990). *Identity: Community, Culture, Difference*. London: Lawrence and Wishart.

Steedman, Carolyn (1986). *Landscape for a Good Woman: A Story of Two Lives*. London: Virago.

Wartella, Ellen, and Byron Reeves (1985). "Historical Trends in Research on Children and the Media: 1900–1960." *Journal of Communication*, 35.

The Local Economy of Suburban Scenes

Donna Gaines

Introduction

Among suburban youth, the problem of "nothing to do, nowhere to go" is an ancient tradition. Lacking access to affordable or even available public transportation, many young people are left stranded, isolated, bored by their limited options. After-school activities organized for young people by adults do not always captivate the imagination. School, family life, and community may offer little in the way of edification, enjoyment, and spiritual growth.

Some kids wait out their sentence, mark time, planning to escape and never return. They get good grades, go to college or try their luck elsewhere. But with college moving out of reach and American frontiers dwindling, many more just linger on. They hang on, living at home after high school, stuck in dead-end service jobs, paying off cars, maybe trying to finish up at the community college. Dreams fade far into a future that seems ominous.

The statistical category for youth is the age group from fourteen to twenty-four. And during that period of a person's life it is parents, the school, and then the town, the police, and a bad economy that dictate where you can go and what you can do.

For some kids, this is brutal. What alternatives emerge for kids who are left cold, alienated from the mainstream? School is something they learn to tolerate in varying degrees; some survive and are graduated, others defect—they drop out. Adults have always felt that sports were an activity that would redirect youthful energy in a positive way. But sports are not an answer for everyone. Artistic pursuits may not be encouraged or nurtured in a school setting. Outside of school, sex, clothes, food, drugs, rock and roll, and, more recently, gangs may be among the activities people seek out to allay suburban boredom.

Without a car, young people really have to be creative. Otherwise, they are shipwrecked, at the mercy of parents, friends, and cabs they cannot afford. City kids can take a train or bus, jump a fare risking arrest, or they can walk. But in suburban and rural areas, without wheels, kids are in perpetual lock-down.

Some kids scrape enough money together to revive an old bomb and this provides transportation to and from more central cultural activities—band practice, parks, friends' houses, shopping malls, rifle range, the beach, or wherever else friends are hanging out. After the 1980s crackdown on drunk driving, hordes of young people became "D.W.I. outlaws." Caught driving while intoxicated, the driver can have his or her license suspended and become shipwrecked until age 21. Broke, bored, and locked down in their suburban homes, kids learn to be creative.

In suburbs, suicide and substance abuse have often been linked to boredom, isolation, and alienation. At the extreme, in an attempt to kill time, focus restless energy, and make something out of anomie, some young people do end up killing themselves, their parents, or each other.

The present effort is to explore what else is there for kids to do in the suburbs besides conform, self-destruct or waste away. Young people do create opportunities and seize possibilities for positive, creative action. Often, they labor with few economic resources and without adult intervention.

While they vary in scope, depth, and longevity, the *scenes* and *subcults* of suburbia that I will examine are retreats, refuges, and outlets organized by kids, for kids. It is here that young people are able to carve out space and place, to reinvent themselves in more rewarding ways.

Suburban Landscapes

It was late September on Long Island but it was still warm enough to do the things they'd been doing all summer. The five guys had been friends for years and they were now all just over twenty-one. Though cash-rich enough for the bars or the dance clubs, they were neighborhood guys who still enjoyed congregating in the Carle Place High School parking lot they had hung around in since junior high. On the night of September 21, 1991, they returned to familiar terrain, to the parking lot on Cherry Lane. Tonight, much like any other night, they had been cruising around in their cars, looking for something to do.

In this small, white ethnic, nonaffluent, turnpike town, adventure usually came in the form of pizza and beers, girls, fights, car races, and cruising. After the hunt, the guys often retired to enjoy the fine art of hanging out, street conversation in a parking lot. Maybe they'd hook up with other friends too.

By now they had jobs as carpenters, landscapers, maintenance men, and mechanics. One had dreams of entering the New York City Police Academy. They were accomplished at hobbies involving dirtbikes, weightlifting, and karate. They came from good families, in a nice small, close-knit community, less than an hour's drive from New York City. They had the hottest cars—Cadillacs, Camaros.

But the school yard was sometimes the site of rumbles. There were wars of class cultures; jocks against burnouts. There were race wars too; white ethnic guidos against blacks. Kids from neighboring high schools would come down as united forces, allied in support. These were the typical suburban turf wars in the 1990s that went on in a number of high schools across Long Island.

Although local nomadic teens tended to appropriate this space "after hours," even with the periodic rumbles there had been very little in the way of vandalism. The rumbles were few and far between. The adults rarely knew about them. They were more the stuff of myth and legend. But by now, as in a few other towns, local school district officials had hired a security guard to circumvent "minor mischief." There was security on weekends at the high school and also at the two elementary schools "just in case." To adults, unsupervised young people hanging out in unstructured settings was an activity that always spelled trouble. Security was primarily a preventive measure.

The guard on duty that night at Carle Place High School was a twenty-year-old Hispanic man with a wife and kid in Brentwood, in Suffolk County, a poorer, more socially stressed neighbor to the east. The security guard was also on probation for weapons and drug convictions in New York City. At around 2:30 A.M., a half-hour before the close of his shift, the guard pumped between nine and sixteen shots from an unregistered nine-millimeter handgun into the car in which the five young men were sitting. Two died and three others were left in critical condition. He was charged with attempted murder and murder. He claimed it was self-defense.

People sympathetic to the five guys, who knew them as "good kids," asked what a poorly trained "mental case" with a criminal record was doing with a gun anyway. Security guards are explicitly not supposed to carry weapons. This guard was known to take a hard line about hanging out. It may be a historic suburban tradition among youth, but to him, it was against the rules and he was determined to enforce them. In the local lingo, that made him a "dick."

Others in the town, also familiar with the five, knew them as "assholes" and were more inclined to feel sorry for the plight of a guard trying to do his job. The five guys had a reputation for starting this sort of trouble. They weren't such nice guys; in fact, some said they were bullies, and were sure they must have taunted the poor guard into a frenzy. Before the fatal encounter, there had apparently been threats with baseball bats and weeks of cruel racial slurs. The security guard had told his wife he would need a gun, and he had apparently called the cops about it. But nothing was done, and the harassment continued.

But the people who supported the five guys, however, denied that it was racial. After all, all five got along well with another guard, who happened to be black. In any case, the night of the shootings, everyone did agree it was all the fault of a "senseless argument."

After the shootings, newspaper headlines described the dead men as "Five Friends Who Loved Cars." In the neighborhood this was seen as a euphemism, a polite way of saying the five guys were guidos. Like jocks, rads, brains or burnouts, guidos have their place in the status hierarchy of the American high school. So when the news broke about the five guys getting shot, reactions in neighboring towns ranged from sadness to glee. When I asked my friends, people who went to school with or knew the five guys, about the shooting, some people lamented that they really were good guys, and it was a shame. Others sneered and snickered that the security guard had done us all a public service.

But one outsider wondered what five males aged twenty-one to twenty-three were doing hanging around in a high school parking lot at 2:30 A.M. on a Saturday night? Didn't young people around here have anything better to do on a weekend night than tease a skinny, high-strung security guard? Is that all there was to do in the suburbs?

In the year following the schoolyard shooting, I tried to understand what else young people could turn to besides the making of mischief.

Much suburban youth crime is of the mischievous, disorganized kind, signifying random resistance to empty time and space: loitering, criminal trespass, vandalism, petty larceny, assault, public intoxication, breaking and entering. These are over and above status offenses—crimes committed in defiance of adult rule, crimes only if you are young, such as running away from home, curfew violation, and truancy.

Car theft, burglary, and drug trafficking have an economic base. But acts of recklessness and death-defiance are better explained by the social and cultural conditions experienced by suburban youth. The local economics of youth scenes and subcults are constructed and maintained outside the gaze of adult authority and the scope of established media. Such activity occurs in pockets; it is esoteric, occult. The following is an account of how such social organizations emerge organically, against a barren architectural and social backdrop, beneath the surfaces of the teenage wasteland.

From Scenes to Subcults

While the status hierarchy of the American high school does depend on presentation of self as part of a clique or social group at the high school, scenes and subcults occur outside of the boundaries of the institution. Membership in status groups (such as the "jocks" or "guidos" or "burnouts") may be discernible by what one wears, where one hangs around, who one's friends are and what one does *at school* (play sports, blast Morbid Angel, publish a fanzine). In a different way, scenes and subcult membership may increase one's status by association with something in the larger world. Someone who is nothing in the classroom but is an active key player in a scene or subcult is less invested in dreary everyday life at school and more empowered in his or her personal everyday life.

It is worth taking a few moments to spell out what is meant here *analytically* by scenes and subcults. Historically, when we think of "scenes," we tend to think of the 1960s. In the early part of the decade, "swinging London's" Mods made the Carnaby Street *scene*. After that, the hippies made the *scene* panhandling, or at happenings in the Haight-Ashbury section of San Francisco. The notion of a "scene" emerged earlier in that decade, in descriptions of the Beat *scene* of poets and bohemians of New York City's Greenwich Village and the North Beach section of San Francisco. Before the 1960s, this form of social organization and interaction surfaced in discussions of pool hall hustling, and is associated with the idea of "hipness," or "hepness," a concept that is at the root of all postwar youth culture. Hipness can be traced as far back as the opium dens of the 1930s.

If we attempt to define the constituent elements of a "scene," with its prerequisite assumption of "hip" we note that it is urban, *sub*terranean, *sub*cultural, esoteric, insular, with highly specified meaning systems and linguistic, sartorial, and behavioral codes. Scenes, then, are exclusionary and impenetrable, unless you are "hip" (in the know). The scene is the place to be, where it happens, where people are involved; but only *certain* people, with shared understandings of what's up (or down).

Regardless of where it's at, and what it's based upon, any scene exists and is identifiable as such because it is bound to specifics of time, place, space, attitude, and cultural production. Music, dance, fashion, elixirs, poetry, and mood are shared in a community of spirit. To make the scene, you go there, check it out, and partake of it. That's it.

For examples of sociological investigations via case studies of scenes, see Sherri Cavan's *Hippies of The Haight* or Ned Polsky's *Hustlers, Beats and Others*. The legacy of American youth culture is full of people who have sought out alternatives, and who exhibit passion for their subcultural processes.

The notion of a "scene" reemerged with a stronger social self-awareness and a political sensibility in the early 1980s, with the development of post-punk hardcore music. The term was reformulated—as the "hardcore scene." Like that of the punks, the hardcore kids' scene was founded upon a "do-it-yourself-or-have-nothing" cultural practice ethic. The movement took root in bleak, decaying suburbs and urban sectors where disaffected kids resisted boredom by dissenting with purpose.

Where heavy metal music was hedonistic and celebratory, hardcore was critical of the social order, with a radical eye towards transformation. Unlike the hippie subculture, hardcore was not informed by leftist thought, any more than it was by populist, fascist, or anarchist doctrine.

Any hardcore scene that erupted invented itself from the start. Kids organized bands and appropriated space for practice and shows. Street sheets and fanzines were generated to spread the news, publicize shows, and articulate the nature of the scene. Fashions and modes of behavior were put forth as standards were set by participants. There was room for local variation in sights, sounds, and songs.

As an analytic device to illustrate the scene at its most insular, esoteric end of the continuum I offer the notion of *subcult*. Where the youth subcultures of 1960s hippies or 1950s gangs were visible to adults, the refuges of the 1980s were more underground and more heavily coded, benefiting from long-term isolation. On a continuum, as activity becomes more insular, less understandable to adult mainstream decoders (sociologists, journalists, psychologists, teachers, parents, critics) the closer to subcult status it moves.

Another crucial subcult to emerge in the 1980s was hip hop. As it was "discovered" by the mainstream rock press (*Rolling Stone, SPIN*) journalists found it necessary to include a "rap dictionary" sidebar so that meaning systems would be more standardized among the readership. While hip hop emerged in a very specific sociohistoric context, *rapping* is, a priori, a verbal articulation. Other scenes, the subcults of hardcore, thrash, and, say, death metal, rely less heavily on the verbally articulated message and may require a greater understanding of context on the part of the decoder. Given that, heavy intrusion and media "discovery" often do not degrade the integrity of a scene. Over time, there may be new innovations, or borrowed ones, but that's rock and roll.

In the postmodern world, where culture is plucked from a menu a la carte, the scene serves as an enclave wherein highly specified cultural practices and processes are organized. All the unique and discrete elements that separate one subcult from another, or from the more generalized "subculture" or "counterculture," will be identifiable as a scene.

Scenes & 'Zines

A robust hardcore scene generated from San Francisco, and involved a fanzine with a substantial international circulation, a college radio show, and eventually, a warehouse venue for bands to perform. *MaximumRocknroll*, the fanzine, the radio show, and The Warehouse Gillman St. scene, served as a model for kids across America. It may not have been the first, but it was one of the most well known, and it survived the longest.[1]

The role of the fanzine as an organizational vehicle in setting up, developing, and sustaining a scene is crucial. In the beginning, a fanzine may actually be nothing more than a street sheet, an elaborated flyer notifying potential participants of a show, or the birth of a new fanzine itself. A street sheet or occasional fanzine is typically irregular, amateur in the extreme—and proud of it. It will circulate as needed, in a narrow range of arenas. It travels a circumscribed route, wherever the publishing author happens to go. Arenas for distribution are created ad hoc; at a show, a deli, record or clothing store. If the publishing author has access to free postage at, say, a university or office job, the fanzine might be sent through the mail.

Initially, a mailing list of fans who should get the 'zine is developed around a core of friends, band members, fellow students, or work buddies. Another way is to obtain a band's mailing list. This will be comprised of fans who happen to be at the show and like the band enough to place their names and addresses in a notebook.

In addition, many local bands will send out newsletters announcing a show or news of the band's products available for consumption. These are fan club 'zines, dedicated to one band and its obsessive fans, rather than a particular scene. In the 1980s, thrash and hardcore scenes flourished. By the 1990s, post-thrash death metal and brutality bands depended upon their labels and created a very unified subcult. (Briefly, death metal is post-thrash, which is itself a hybrid of hardcore and heavy metal music.)

Alternatively, many post-hardcore bands of the 1990s are annoyed by the tag and may separate themselves out by having their own band 'zines. Such bands are arguably rock and roll bands, and may have only marginal ties to any scene. If they are popular, with a big local following, and if they play often, they might get interviewed in a scene 'zine anyway.

Either way, the occasional 'zine functions to organize people with common interests into a network that can be called upon for any number of cultural activities that constitute that scene—shows, protest mailings and vigils, advertisements for equipment, rides, housing—the whole range of the emergent community's needs.

If the occasional 'zine begins to routinize, published with some regularity, mailing begins to extend beyond a small circle of friends. In addition to a widening audience, the fanzine may begin to cover more "general interest" activities. After a while the fanzine functions to sustain the community which supports it. This places the community and the fanzine in a cozy symbiosis. The 'zine in question becomes the acknowledged scripture of the scene. Fans feed it and feed off it.

At a certain point, the routine 'zine will either expand its boundaries to include new musical forms or will become so regular that it begins to resemble a commercial enterprise. For example, *MaximumRocknroll* (*MRR*) began in 1982. By 1987, it was reaching about 13,000 hardcore fans in the USA, Europe, and Asia. It was running some forty to fifty pages of fine print, published monthly, and was known to rock critics and scholars, as well as kids outside the hardcore scene. *MRR* has become a recognizable cultural artifact.

As ever, *MRR* carries scene reports written by readers from towns and cities in almost every American state and many foreign countries. It has a logo, regular contributors, star columns, and a lively letters-to-the-editor section. *MRR* has opened itself up to discussions of social issues and some musical variations on hardcore. It has maintained a distinctive point of view, while retaining its scruffed-down form. By 1992, it is the archetype of the established 'zine.

MRR is widely available in comic book stores and now even in large chains such as Tower Records. The occasional 'zine and the more routine 'zine are not so recognized, and they soon become collectors' items. The difference between the sporadic, one-shot-deal occasional fanzine and the more routinized form is a matter of economic organization.

The routinized 'zine has developed a community of readers outside the locale and networking extends to the scene at large. It circulates more widely and often. Sometimes the type of scene it supports influences the 'zine's range of possibility.

Where the established fanzine like *MRR* extends to the universe of the scene—to all hardcore kids in scenes everywhere—the occasional fanzine is merely informed by this universe. The routinizing process takes the occasional 'zine out of the neighborhood and begins to move it into the universe of the scene.

Some 'zines start up with an already existing network. *Cadaveric Mutilation* is published in Suffolk County, Long Island in the remote town of Shirley. It is focused towards a highly developed death metal scene that is newer and rather distinct from the hardcore scene. Less accessible, more underground and subcult than hardcore, the death metal scene is highly organized and 'zines play a critical role in keeping it that way. There are death metal bands across the USA, Scandinavia, and Latin America.

The death-dedicated 'zine sustains and expands the community of Diecide and Morbid Angel fans, and the spirit of the Tampa scene, to fans of local Long Island death bands like Pyrexia and Suffocation. Conversely, the local unsigned or newly signed band will become known to fans of more established bands.

As such, *Cadaveric Mutilation* comes to the fan with loads of band flyers, product lists, and a network sheet of twenty-four bands and twenty-four other 'zines a fan might want to know about. There are "ads" for demo tapes and seven-inch EP's for death and brutality bands such as Incantation, on Relapse Records in Millersville, Pennsylvania; taped interviews of beloved bands put out by *Viruside 'Zine* in New Carlisle, Ohio; calls for submissions to a new *Embroyatomy 'Zine,* and more. In addition, this 'zine covers nondeath bands such as the Chiselers, widening its scope and making a crossover into the local hardcore/garage punk scene.

The ideological and aesthetic boundaries of scenes are less rigid on the local level because of neighborhood or workplace friendships, and lack of both anything better to do and places in which to do anything. People are willing to give some lip service to the ideals of hardcore—"support your local bands." More often, though, when incompatible bands are booked together as a matter of convenience, the club will be filled with loyal fans who leave after their band is done. The best shows are bookings of bands who have overlapping followers. A cluster of four or five such bands guarantees a full house, a decent take at the door, and a profit at the bar. The good 'zine helps organize this by keeping the spirit of community going in between shows, when people might drift away.

Beyond function, the quality of the 'zine will generally reflect whatever access the author has to the world of mechanical arts reproduction. If the author is lucky, he or she is in high school and takes an art class, or has a parent or a job with access to a lot of office supplies, computers, machines, or free postage, and friends to help. The 'zine takes time and interest and effort. Setting it up and distributing it may be a mission of sorts. The rewards are greater access to better scenes, endless artifacts, networking, and the production of a cultural room of one's own.

Regardless of their stage of development, scope, or depth, local scenes are always the result of a labor process involving an elaborate system of interactions, economic organization of resources, and accidents. Some scenes that are organized at the local level will need to invent themselves from scratch. But they always reflect back (or outwards) to scenes that are now part of a collective consciousness. People understand organically but also historically what they need to do to get things going.

The Black Pages

The process of organizing a scene is intrinsically tied to everyday life. In a given day while going about your business, it is very possible to see key players at the stores and on the streets of your town. For example, I met Mad Bill at a local convenience store about a year ago. He recognized me from somewhere and we started talking about local bands, the hardcore scene at home, and the crust-core scene around Tompkins Square Park on the Lower East Side of Manhattan. Mad Bill takes an active interest in bands he likes, whether they are hardcore, noize, death metal, garage, or skin. He calls this interest "MadHouse Productions." That might include a wide range of his activities. Most of this is not for profit. But organizing any scene does cost money and expenses have to be covered.

As such, Mad Bill is a scene entrepreneur. This means he puts out a fanzine, organizes shows, and keeps a clearinghouse of assorted "product" on hand—demo tapes, stickers, flyers, T-shirts, and souvenirs. He hooks bands up with studios, college radio, the underground (and mainstream) press; gives members pep talks and haircuts; and disseminates whatever information must be known.

Scene entrepreneurs are at the center of the scene, either as organizers, as collectors of scarce (or limited) resources, and as information and referral services. The scene entrepreneur uses the fanzine to pull people, bands, and places together.

Mad Bill published the first issue of *The Black Pages* at the end of 1990, and the second a few months after that. It is typical of fanzines to be published on an as-needed basis, either because the scene is active and there is lots of enthusiasm, or it is dying out and there is frustration. More often resources—writing time, paper, photocopying, a desired show or demo—are in limited quantity and this delays or prevents any regular publication.

Some 'zines are more "professional" looking than others. Whether they are sold in comic book or record stores, distributed at schools and shows, or affiliated with a radio station or club, slicked-down graphics are frowned upon. The typical fanzine looks like something the person slapped together. The more local the distribution, the more raw the design.

The Black Pages ran between ten and twenty pages, typed in uppercase letters. It was photocopied and then stapled into a 5 1/2 by 8-inch booklet. There were hand-drawn cartoons and band photos. Issue #1 opened up with a statement of intent:

> A new fanzine, devoted entirely to the local hardcore scene and its participants. We are not doing this for fame or fortune, but rather to keep people informed as to local happenings. Along with show related articles we will also do interviews with bands, clubs, sound studios, etc. We also welcome comments and articles written by our readers. Send all letters, ideas, articles, love letters, tapes, photos, hate mail, valuables, money etc. to: [address].

The center of the hardcore scene is, of course, its bands. The local bands that constitute the hardcore scene, according to Mad Bill, include hard rock, Gothic, and garage punk as well as hardcore bands. By the 1990s the hardcore sound had evolved, and it rarely exists anymore in pure form. Thrash, noize, metal, and funk influxes have long since transformed it. Post-hardcore, what these bands have in common is geography, proximity, shared venues, clubs, rehearsal studios, friends, and above all, the ethical conviction that they are in it for real. The scene is not a ticket for rock stardom, although bands may dream of some commercial support and recognition. All bands in Mad Bill's pantheon are "unsigned" to any major (or large independent) label. Most have been playing together for less than five years, and usually less than two years. The members are in their very early twenties, and are working, in school, or both. Many have played with members of each other's bands in various incarnations since high school. For example, some members of Creedmoor went on to become Ghouls. Suburban Trash was retired and the bass player joined NutJob. A member of the Nihilistics is now also a Chiseler.

Sometimes the members of several bands set up a side project that becomes a new band—Ghouls and Chiselers got together as Corporate Waste, to everyone's delight. This gives members a chance to digress from limited material, to switch instruments, and to experiment.

On the periphery of this scene are other bands that have been going at it for several years, or who aren't even remotely connected to hardcore music (or the scene). They will be included in the fanzine and people will go to their shows if they are "friends of the scene," viewed as supporting it. Rosary Violet, for example, is a self-identified "gronk" band (a mixture of Gothic, rock, and funk). Sea Monster and the CorpseGrinders have a hard rock Nazi-heroin mystique (although neither band embraces either the ideology or the substance). These older bands are known to the newer ones, and inspirational for their dedication and craft.

The boundaries of one scene will overlap with another and new people are always floating in and out. The bands organized into *The Black Pages* shuttle between clubs on Long Island and New York City. Because of the limited number of available venues at any given time, one locale will be hot, the other will not. Bands play together at local clubs, in shows organized by their members or managers or entrepreneurs like Mad Bill. Some bands are included into the scene because they are needed to fill a specific booking—or because they have been invited by one of the bands to perform with them.

These matchmaking ventures of bands and shows and players often work out like blind dates. A band often gets a show by offering to book three other bands (promising a large local following and a decent door take for the bar). But sometimes the "date" doesn't show. One night, for example, I.C.B. (In Cold

Blood), was hung when Rosary Violet had to back out of a show due to a scheduling snafu. Mad Bill was able to call in one of the bands that practices at Meat Market Melodies studio. They in turn brought in two other bands and saved the night.

Such scene ruptures often work out for the best—even band breakups will open up the door to bigger, better alternatives in the form of new bands. The Ghouls broke up and reunited with old members of Creedmoor and started Voodoo Eggplant, which lasted two weeks. A liaison between Ghouls and Chiselers generated Corporate Waste. Often these regenerated bands do not last, but they continue to form new bands with members of defunct groups. The scene is kept fresh and vital, if unstable, in this way.

Some local bands in this scene play at clubs in New York City, and have ties to the hardcore squatter community of the Lower East Side. They will play at downtown clubs as part of larger shows, at CBGB's, or locally to the same friends they see every day.

The night of the show all the friends, band members, and fans are summoned to show their support. Weeks of preparation will culminate in flyers and last-minute transportation emergencies. *The Black Pages* has chronicled many of the shows, local and in "the city."

Mad Bill's Madhouse Productions Ltd. also provides amateur video services for bands. No profit is made on this and the videotaped shows usually end up as everyone's treasured memory, to be watched over and over again. Advertised by Mad Bill as

> The Ultimate Alternative Music Video Compilation. . . . You won't find in any of the local disco-shithouse-guido-dickheads & bimbo moron infested mainstream dipshit kind of Z-100 [dance music radio station] vomit spewing so-called record stores.

The fanzine articulates a cultural and social vision, and *The Black Pages* offers one where community is the answer to the perils of living in the 'burbs. An editorial page thanks the bands and people in them, friends, and favorite "great places." Among them are Mama Gina's Pizza, Flipside, L.I. Rock and Meat Market Melodies rehearsal studios, The Right Track Inn, ABC

NO RIO, Black Cat, Spiral and Continental Divide clubs, Mike's Tattoo parlor, Revolution Rock clothing boutique, and "of course our good friends at Anheuser Busch . . . thanks for making the scene a great place to be."

Birthdays, good times, people, and places get their moment of appreciation. Taking a position on local cultural politics—the life and death of the scene—is implicit. Throughout the narrative, Mad Bill implores his readers to "do something!" Lines of cultural difference are drawn in cartoons and the "opinion page."

"What's Your Beef" draws clear lines in the local *kulturkampf*. This is a guest rant written by a friend of the 'zine and the scene, "Beef," in Mad Bill's larger second issue of *The Black Pages.* He bitches about people who complain, rock critics who cannot review shows properly, and poseurs who "heard the Ramones for the first time on WDRE!! (a Long Island commercial radio station claiming to play "alternative music"). These, the YUPPIE white-collar criminals of our modern times that should be burned on a very high mountain, are making us look bad!! So kill a yuppie for me!!" Beef goes on to say that if people want to "support a cause, listen to college radio." In fact, a number of the bands featured in the fanzine have been guests on college radio shows where their music is broadcast and they are interviewed.

Elsewhere, Mad Bill offers a critique of "Rad-Tards" featuring a peace-punk college "rad" kid interested in world beat, worthy causes, and everything politically correct and socially meaningful. In jams with a new-wave hair cut, anticorporate T-shirt, and skateboard, the P.C. vegetarian is implored by Mad Bill to "finish all your meat and you'll grow up."

There are also homespun comics, one by Beef and another by Ajax, of the Chiselers/Nihilistics. Beef chronicles the adventures of "Biff Bong Hitt," documenting "waste analysis" with acid, acid rain, bong fog, beer, butts, etc. Ajax Lepinski's "Bed Time Stories and Other Tales of Desperation and Woe" specifically the woeful tale of the blubbering Rat Bastard, are also included.

Girls are offered the chance to go out on a date with Phil De Graves, singer with the Chiselers. Elsewhere are rock star stage shots of NutJob guitarist Mike, Mug Shotz of a Chiseler show at Scandals in Bellmore, and Glenn, singer from Sycotic Sons. The text is sprinkled with doodles, cartoons, and occult and corporate symbol appropriations, the point being that this is for the scene, something anyone can do.

Central to every scene are its artifacts: record and tape demos, band photos, videos, flyers, fanzines, stickers, T-shirts with band logos. These are universal; they exist across America for any "unsigned" band. The processes—forming a band, setting up practice, booking shows, showcasing house parties, getting equipment, organizing fans, distributing music products—do not vary much from town to town.

The process of organizing a local death metal scene is essentially the same. Pyrexia started with two friends who were bored with thrash music. They got friendly with some guys from Suffocation. They got a demo tape with a singer and a guitarist and a drum machine. They auditioned a full band, got a logo, sent the demo out to death metal fanzines such as *Placental Drippings, Imminent Demise,* and *Cadaveric Mutilation.* They set up a basement rehearsal studio under the laundromat, started booking shows, got band shots, a post-office box, T-shirts, and stickers, and before long were in the death metal circuit, playing shows in the tri-state area.

On a given day in my neighborhood, where the five guys got shot for having nothing better to do than taunt some guy with racial slurs, band activity gives people something to do, someplace to be and something to belong to. Regardless of the nature of the scene, the roles and rules remain the same. There will be an entrepreneur like Mad Bill, musicians like Ajax, obsessive fans, managers, photographers, scribes, lovers, friends, family members, and producers.

The processes, products, and social relations that constitute the local scene are organic. They begin spontaneously, and even if they die out or transform, they are always ready to be reconstituted in the name of a reunion or memorial show. The scene can be taken out, set up, experienced, and tucked away. This is what Mad Bill calls "the retro-scene." It happens "instantly" because people have the shared memory of what it was and can recreate or simulate it for the night.

The local economy develops as people recognize innate talents that can be contributed. In the spirit of "do-it-yourself," the self-taught recording engineer, photographer, scribe, musician, fashion archivist, and entrepreneur create beauty and meaning where there was once only boredom and alienation.

Conclusion

Some sociology of music examines phenomena of established bands, known to the public, under contract to record companies, with media coverage and public relations apparatuses in place. Other methods of rock analysis look at social movements—the punks or hip hop nation. Subversive and socially progressive statements in art are considered. This is an exploration into how music shields young people from a world they perceive as dull and hostile, circumscribed by adults and an equally controlled music industry.

Isolated and alienated, stranded in decaying suburban turnpike towns with diminishing options and inflated great expectations, these are some of the things young people do to survive. This is what there is available in the way of local culture, beyond what is socially constructed for young people by adults.

Beyond the dull compulsions of adult-organized activities and the terrors of everyday life—gangs, drugs, race wars, rapes, unemployment, family violence, sexual abuse and exploitation, high school, suicide, and teenage pregnancy, young people are carving out autonomous spaces and investing life with meaning. Innovating their own music scenes and secluding themselves in "subcults," kids manage to survive, thrive, and revive their spirit in the teenage wastelands of suburban America. People act, they react, they create and recreate, and sometimes they reach higher ground.

NOTE

1. For a more detailed and empirically grounded discussion of the hardcore scenes of the 1980s, the history of *MaximumRocknroll,* and my notion of the "subcult," see my religion chapters in *Teenage Wasteland: Suburbia's Dead End Kids* (1992, Pantheon).

Expendable Youth: The Rise and Fall of Youth Culture*

Deena Weinstein

Youth, adolescence, can be understood in terms of its cultural history as a modern idea. If it is nothing else, "youth" is a term in discourses that discriminates certain phenomena and marks them off from others. It would be a mistake to think that there is some fixed or natural definition of "youth," however convenient it might be to have one. As people continuously interpret their world, even their most crucial terms keep changing their meanings. "Youth" is no exception. As a term in our discourses it has a history.

If you stop and think about it for a moment, you will probably find out that you are not clear about what you mean by the word "youth." Ordinarily it has at least three forms of distinct and sometimes divergent meanings: youth can mean a biological category defined by age, a distinctive social group, and a cultural construct.

"Youth" in the biological sense refers to an age group of human organisms who are going through a specific process of physical maturation. Cultures may find some ways of marking off this physiological group from others by codes and disciplines, particularly those pertaining to sexuality, aggression, and work or preparation for work. But the biological stratum doesn't get us very far. We know there is more to youth than hormonal changes and the like.

The social definition of youth is the center of the modern idea of youth. There are many technologically unsophisticated cultures in which there is no separate youth age-grade. One is either a child or an adult. The Jewish rite of passage of the bar mitzvah, part of which involves the statement to the thirteen-year-old boy who is the center of the ceremony, "Today you are a man," reflects the ancient Hebrews' lack of a youth age-grade.

The vast changes that gave rise to a modern life characterized by specialization, continuous innovation, an increasingly knowledge-based economy, high rates of mobility, economic surplus, and leisure created a socially defined period in the life cycle between the dependency of childhood and the responsibility of adulthood. The social definition of youth and its consequent marginalization as a group betwixt and between (not fully integrated into society) coincided with the industrial era. A socially defined period of transiting from being cared for to becoming a provider originated in the upper middle class in the period following the French Revolution and increased in length and spread throughout the population as surplus wealth, specialization requiring lengthy schooling, and the power of labor groups to restrict employment opportunities increased. Youth as a social group became universal in America after World War II. Since that time the number of years defining this age-grade has increased.

Youth Culture: "Talkin' 'Bout My Generation" (The Who)

When society isolates a group of individuals into a category, that group will begin to be defined for itself, both by its members and by others. The group develops its own distinctive values, ideals, sentiments, and activities. As the modern period proceeded, "youth" became, by the mid-1950s, a distinctive subculture, with symbols, practices, and folkways peculiarly its own; that is, "youth" became a cultural construct as well as a biological and social category.

The flowering of this subculture in the middle of the twentieth century was related to suburbanization, an extended and universal secondary school system (Coleman, 1961) and a nationwide electronic mass media. "Youth" gained a sharp cultural configuration through its music ("rock 'n' roll"), certain forms of attire, and a set of rituals and activities centered on leisure and entertainment.

The youth subculture was partly created by adolescents themselves and partly contrived by the consumer-goods industry. During "... the fifties, youth became an isolatable consumer market, with its own capital, its own desires and its own commodities" (Grossberg, 1984:107). There is controversy over the basis of this subculture:

> Certainly the agencies of pop culture (record companies and teenage magazines and clothes shops and so on) EXPLOIT young people ... the question is to what extent they MANIPULATE them. The picture the left offers is of teenagers as entirely passive consumers, buying, playing, acting just as commerce dictates, accepting the values that the media embody, stripped of any autonomous source of joy or creation or rebellion. ... (Corrigan and Frith, 1975:237)

Talcott Parsons coined the term "youth subculture," which for him developed "inverse values to [those of] the adult world of productive work and conformity to routine and responsibility" (Brake, 1985:40). Other investigators indicated that the youth culture, as "dress, adornment, music, dancing, and slang has the function of asserting independence from adult authority" (Roe, 1987:222–223).

Before youth had its own culture, its transitional status was obvious in its imitation of adult style. Holly Brubach describes the almost-grown woman prior to the full onset of the youth subculture, the ingenue. Played in movies by Audrey Hepburn, the ingenue "... sought to give the impression of being experienced beyond [her] years. ... Fashion was something girls learned by emulating their mothers ..." (Brubach, 1990:124). By the end of the 1950s, clothing distinctively different from, not imitative of, adults was being worn by young women.

The central feature of the youth culture, and its metonym, is its music. Rock 'n' roll has always symbolized youth.

> The whole adolescent milieu is penetrated at many levels by an active interest in music; . . . adolescent discourse centers around the language and terminology of rock and that music provides the core values. . . . (Roe, 1987:215)

Another scholar argues that the core of adolescents' personal identities is their musical taste. Such preferences, as well as the salience of music as such, serve ". . . to differentiate late-adolescents from adults" (Moffatt, 1989:151). A similar assessment of the function of music is given by Prinsky and Rosenbaum. They contend that rock music helps teenagers to identify with their peers rather than their families: "It is created by and for young people and may function for teenagers in delineating a rebellious subculture that stands apart from the adult world" (Prinsky and Rosenbaum, 1987:394).

The youth subculture, from its beginnings, was in opposition to, and not merely different from, the general (adult) culture. Markson elaborates on this point, claiming that attempts by family and school to direct and restrain adolescents were contested by them: "Rock emerged as part of the resistance to such disciplinization as a music of opposition to the enforcement of mainstream values" (Markson, 1989:4). Grossberg provides a similar interpretation. He contends that rock's denunciation of the family is not due to an antifemale bias, as some have contended: "A more accurate reading would see it as an attack on the institution itself, as a resistance to the very disciplinization which constructs its youth" (Grossberg, 1984:107).

The rebelliousness of 1950s rock 'n' roll is shown by many of its features, from Elvis Presley's sneer to lyrical complaints about the teenage role found in a host of songs such as Chuck Berry's "School Days" and the Coasters' "Yakety-Yak." Beyond symbolic content, the appeal of black and working class rock 'n' roll performers for middle-class white youth challenged mainstream norms. Rock 'n' roll reacted against sexual and racial disciplinizations. Its sexual side was held in check during the decade by the communications industry, which coded sex as "dance" and banned (now innocuous) numbers such as Mickey and Sylvia's "Love is Strange."

The disciplinary forces had less success with the incursion of the black sensibility. Initially, songs were whitened from their R&B originals in cover versions by such performers as conventionality's pinup boy, Pat Boone. But personalities like Little Richard and Chuck Berry could not be resisted. The "percentage of best-selling records by black artists increased from three in 1954 to twenty-nine in 1957" (Lipsitz, 1990:126). George Lipsitz concludes:

> At the very moment that residential suburbs increased class and racial segregation, young people found "prestige from below" by celebrating the ethnic and class interactions of the urban street. (1990:120)

The first decade of a distinctive youth culture is bounded by the years 1955–64, from the rise of Chuck Berry to the ascent of his most successful pupils, the Beatles. In its second decade youth culture remained music-centered, but transformed opposition to adult culture into self-conscious confrontation. During the first era youth was a group in itself, but in this second era it also became a group for itself.

> Somewhere in the nineteen-sixties, millions of people began to regard themselves as a class separate from mainstream society *by virtue of their youth and the sensibility that youth produced.* (Greenfield, 1987:48, emphasis added)

This second era was marked by an alternative source of rebellious authority to the prestige from below provided by black rock 'n' rollers. Blacks had become acceptable to the middle class: the popularity of Martin Luther King and the civil rights movement itself reflected/caused that change. Other evidence of the change in the cultural image of blacks was in the mass popularity of Motown and Stax musics, created by blacks, and whitened a bit by them. The new affront to bourgeois values was drugs, especially marijuana, which had been used by the fifties rebels, the beats. The beats were marginals who disdained the mainstream culture.

Beyond their symbolic value, the mood- and mind-altering properties of marijuana and LSD had a rebellious effect. Each privileged the interior monologue over the social conversation and each privileged the id over the superego directives of conventional society. In the experience of both drugs, clock time was absent; the Bergsonian *durée* was the only time that could matter. Accentuating

> . . . the "now," and the feeling of freedom to "walk around and feel the moment," led to a total breakdown of conventional notions of time. Industrial and job-oriented time is crucially concerned with order. . . . (Willis, 1975:108)

By the late 1960s the youth subculture was transformed into a counterculture. Still attached to biological and social youth, its way of life was explicitly, self-consciously understood as standing in opposition to mainstream/adult culture. Moreover, it was promoted by the young as a universally good culture, one that should be adopted by adults. "Turn on, tune in, drop out" was the official invitation, the raising of the gap between childhood dependency and adult responsibility into the human ideal. Youth culture as hegemon, in the late 1960s, expressed a loathing for aging. "I hope I die before I get old" was its rallying cry (now ashes in the mouth for more people than merely the originator of the phrase, the rather ancient and partly deaf Pete Townshend of The Who).

The Detachment of Youth Culture from Youth: "Rock 'n' Roll Nursing Home" (Iron Prostrate)

The fabled "sixties" ended sometime in the first half of the 1970s, decimated by a multiplicity of events, including the killings at Kent State, the end of the military draft, and the OPEC-induced economic recession. The end of the sixties was also the end of the youth culture as centered on the demographic grouping of young people. Youth culture persisted and youth, in its biological and social dimensions, certainly did not disappear; but the cultural formation of "youth" floated free from the social group of young people. No longer restricted to adolescents, "youth" became available to all. The youth culture got co-opted into the general leisure culture, and lost its moorings in a particular group. It became what postmodernists call a "floating signifier," a designation or identification that could be taken up by anyone as the emblem of a life-style. It was chic for adults to take up aspects of the youth culture in the late 1960s, but afterwards a youthful image, as defined by the leisure culture, became a normalized component of anything else that might be "chic," "trendy," "hip," or "in."

This process is not unique to "youth." Other floating signifiers are constantly being created as symbols are detached from socially relevant groups. One example is "family." Family can be used by baseball fans ("We are family," shouted the Pittsburgh fans the year their team triumphed), by gay couples who demand to be listed as dependents in health insurance plans, and unrelated members of communes.

The free-float of youth culture, the detachment of a social group from its set of significant symbols, creates two newly isolated entities, one cultural and the other social. The process bears some resemblance to the splitting apart of a compound such as water (H_2O) into its constituent elements, hydrogen and oxygen. Apart from one another the elements have different properties than the compound. Having been set loose from its biological and social moorings, the "youth" culture drifts around adolescents, drawing upon their significance, but only so much as to be fit for appropriation by anyone of any biological age or social position. "Youth" as a cultural category has been eviscerated and sublimated into a commercialized spirit of "youthfulness," haunting contemporary life at every turn. On the other hand, "youth" no longer belongs to young people as a cultural designation, as their own style of life, but belongs potentially to everyone in some way or other. Youth, in the sense of young people in a special biological and social predicament, has become marginal to "youth" as a cultural code of beliefs, values, sentiments, and practices. Youth does not have its own "youth," but instead has the "youth" that is given to it and to everyone else through the media. Young people do not have a culture that is theirs; they have become marginal to the idea of youth itself.

Youth culture became a free-floating signifier in the 1970s. Practices associated with the 1960s youth culture such as smoking pot, listening to rock music, and wearing long hair by males began to characterize adults. Many of these people had adopted these practices when they were young, and did not abandon them when they became adults. "When I became a man, I put away childish things" (1 Corinthians 13:11) was no longer the applicable rule. Youth culture was appropriated by the middle-aged as well as by those biologically classified as children. No longer did one hear about the much ballyhooed generation gap.

The music, too, was disconnected from adolescents; anyone was free to appreciate it. Simon Frith maps the rise and fall of youth culture:

> . . . the music business is no longer organized around rock, around the selling of records of a particular sort of musical event to young people. The rock era—born around 1956 with Elvis Presley, peaking around 1967 with *Sgt. Pepper*, dying around 1976 with the Sex Pistols . . . (Frith, 1988:1)

The reasons for this severance of the biological/social grouping from the cultural are complex. Partly the process is related to the meaning of youth in the contemporary world and partly it is due to the particular content of that cultural formation.

While the old are generally venerated in so-called traditional societies, contemporary society gives the place of honor to youth. In part this is a reflection of the distinction between cultures that are oriented to the past and those that are oriented to the future. The elderly are the embodiment of the past, youth are representatives of the future. The modern era, in whose ashes we now play, was future-oriented, had a sense of history rather than myth, and placed stress on the hope of progress. "In the 1950s, 'youth' came to symbolise the most advanced point of social change: youth was employed as a *metaphor* for social change" (Clarke et al., 1975:71).

Youth also came to be valued because of secularization. Christianity's promise to individuals of eternal life was erased as the Nietzschean rumor of the death of God gained wider circulation. Science's view of mortality usurped religion's hope. The body became the alpha and omega of existence when transcendence was no longer imaginable. Youth began to be equated with the immortality of the body.

"Youth" thus became more than a transitional stage; it was an ideal to which all aspired. Athletic and nutritional regimens became popular as means to "staying young" or regaining a "youthful" shape. Medical technology, ever sensitive to consumer demand, made face-lifts, tummy-tucks, and silicon implants popular practices.

The negative valuation of the old, the horror of aging, was keenly felt by youth itself by the late sixties. "Don't trust anyone over thirty," they repeated until they reached their own thirtieth birthdays. "I hope I die before I get old" was sung lustily by those who could not imagine in their worst nightmares or acid trips their being no longer young.

Rock, like youthful looks, is no longer the province of the young. It "is the sound of perpetual adolescence, making of adolescence a model for the whole of life . . ." (Duncan, 1984:199). Indeed, it is the rock that was firmly attached to biological/social youth during the hegemony of "youth culture" ("classic rock") that is most popular with the no-longer-young crowd. A critic complains:

> Invented for teens, who demanded new styles, top 40 radio now stands pat along with its original baby-boomer listenership. By feeding the Big Chill generation the illusion of eternal youth, radio is retarding creativity and aggravating audience passivity. (Eddy, 1986:83)

Further, as the postmodern era shifted the focus away from a future, as the death, not of God but of history, was proclaimed, the most valued temporal dimension became the present. Past and future are devalued, inconsequential. Youth ". . . had become the symbol of (post-)modernity, of the present, of the NOW, presided over by the 'brats' of the fashion, music, video-clip, and cinema world" (Chambers, 1987:241).

The free-float of youth culture is also due to the content of that culture. In an abstract sense the two central features of youth culture are its leisure/consumption focus and its opposition to mainstream culture. Both of these factors helped make the culture of youth appealing to those of all ages.

The spread of the consumer ethic (as a response to late capitalism's need to replace the more producer-oriented

"Protestant ethic") coincides with the free-float of youth culture. The centrality of work, of one's occupation, to a sense of self has been replaced by one's use of leisure.

> The seeds of an American youth culture can be found in the 1920s "youthful approach to consumption." Gradually this middle class definition of youthful leisure consumption spread to other class and age groups as well. Style, fashion, and consumption based fads became commonplace concerns. Indeed, an entire segment of the mass media was devoted to supplying the physical artifacts, cultural values, and artistic expressions of the youth culture to wider society. (Dotter, 1987:37)

The oppositional feature of youth culture also coincided with a long-term social trend, interpreted from different perspectives as the "crisis of authority," the rise of mass democracy, and the power of crowds. All refer to the decline of traditional elites. In all sectors of society, political, economic, familial, religious, and academic, those on the bottom resisted the rule and definition of the situation of dominant groups. "Question Authority" was a 1960s-era motto. Karl Mannheim termed this trend "levelling" and expounded upon it in his "Democratization of Culture" (Mannheim, 1971). If youth culture thumbed its collective nose at parental, school, and, in the sixties, political authorities, its gesture resonated with all those who were demanding their rights against traditional elites. The civil rights and student movements in the 1960s, and subsequently the women's, gay-rights, and the disabled-persons movements all work in the direction of levelling. They are resistances to what Foucault calls "disciplinization."

Listen to the music of youth cultures. From the 1950s era of Jerry Lee Lewis' "Great Balls of Fire," through pre-disco Rolling Stones songs like "Satisfaction" and "Sympathy for the Devil," the symbolic rebellion is evident. Rock is a resistance to disciplinization, a resistance to enforcement of mainstream values. Compare this attitude to the adult form of popular music, pop, with its emphasis on romance.

Reaction to the Free-Float by Youth: "Desperate Cry" (Sepultura)

Young people have responded to the extortion of "youth" from them in a variety of ways. As the youth culture of the 1960s dissipated into the youthfulness or youthful mystique of the leisure culture in the 1970s, most young people simply followed along, losing any special distinctiveness and merging into the youthful leisure culture as its distinctive representatives. Others, however, could not or would not adjust to the lack of an identity that would set them apart from other groups in the population. They confronted a special problem. The "youth culture" of the 1960s had dissolved and could not be reclaimed and, even more to the point, neither could a relatively confrontational youth subculture, such as that of the 1950s, be created.

The responses of the young people who became marginal are familiar and define many of the so-called "problems of youth" today. Some became "burnouts" and "dropouts," retreating into depression, drugs, and sometimes suicide, none of which were of great significance in discourse about "youth" before our postmodern age. "Deracination," a term used by anthropologists to categorize the elimination of the native, autochthonous culture of a people, particularly tribal peoples, can be applied to youth. The deracinated, such as American Indians on reservations or in cities, who are bereft of ability to lead meaningful lives and are not able to assimilate into the dominant culture, exhibit similar symptoms worldwide: depression; the widespread use of depressant drugs, especially alcohol; and very high rates of suicide. It is in this context that the suicide statistics of youth, rising sharply since 1970, can be usefully interpreted. During the decade of the 1980s, "the suicide rate among 15- to 19-year-olds has increased about 21 percent" (Leland, 1991:53).

Some young people have entered cults and authoritarian sects, which set themselves sharply off from the general culture. Such responses have complex psychological and social determinants, but it is wise to think of them first as culturally specific, as responses of the young to the "youth" of which they have been dispossessed.

Another response by young people to the usurpation of their culture has been the formation of subcultures, such as "punk" or "metal," which raised the symbolic stakes too high for the general leisure culture to co-opt them. These attempts to reattach a youth culture to a biological and social group began shortly after youth culture floated free from its social anchor and has continued since then, centered in the realm of rock, the one sphere in which the myth of the youth culture was embedded. Rock also was one of the few cultural spheres in which youth could be a producer, not merely a consumer, of cultural forms.

Punk, which originated as a form of music in New York around 1975, spread as a youth subculture to Britain shortly thereafter. Generally interpreted within an economic framework as working-class dissent, the British punk movement should also be seen as an attempt to reinstate a genuine youth culture. Its enemy was not the rich, not even the bourgeoisie; it was adults.

> Punks decried anyone or anything connected with the established social order as boring old farts (BOFs). They regurgitated the impulse behind the mod slogan of the '60s, "I hope I die before I get old." . . . (Cashmore, 1987:247)

Much of the punk style (mohawks, neon hair colors, safety pins through cheeks) cannot be appropriated by adults, at least by those who prefer to keep their jobs. The U.S. punk scene, centered in L.A. around 1980, cannot be understood in economic terms either. There were no dole-queue kids there. If anything, the U.S. punk fan's parents tended to be middle class.

Heavy metal, which appeared as a form of music around 1970, achieved subcultural status in Britain by 1974. This subculture, too, spread to the U.S. and to much of the industrial world by the end of the decade. One of the most frequent terms in the lyrics of heavy-metal songs, whatever their themes, is night. Night is a time of danger, obscurity, and mystery when the forces of chaos are strongest. But it is also the time for Bacchanalian revelry. Heavy metal's rhetoric and imagery puts forward Dionysian themes and themes of chaos. These themes are related in that both conjure with powers that the adult world wishes to keep at bay and exclude even from symbolic representation. Under the cover of night everything that is repressed by the respectable world can come forth. What is that respectable world? For heavy metal's youthful audience that world is the adult world (Weinstein, 1991).

Heavy metal, like punk, raises the stakes higher than adults can reach; for example, the style of very long hair for males. The focus on power in the subculture is exemplified by an emphasis on extreme sonic volume. Both adults and young children seem to have difficulty withstanding (appreciating?) loudness. This feature is a self-acknowledged gatekeeper, reserving the music for youth only. "If it's too loud then you're too old" is the often-repeated rallying cry.

During the 1980s there were repeated attempts by demographic youth to recapture a youth culture for themselves. Many of these efforts built upon the heavy metal and punk subcultures of the prior decade. Examples include hardcore, thrash metal, skate punk and death metal. All of these are sonically, physically, and lyrically too rough for little kids or adults. They are not commercial and receive no radio or MTV exposure. They are only known to cognoscenti and are not easily co-opted by the forces of commerce.

During the latter half of the 1980s, still another recapturing project was underway, which looked to the mythic past of the sixties. Centering around the Grateful Dead, the music, clothing style (especially tie-dyed T-shirts), and drugs of choice (particularly LSD) of the counterculture found a new audience among young people in the upper-middle class. Here the reattachment efforts were not aimed at excluding other demographic groups, but rather at embracing the final supernova of an attached youth culture.

By the early 1990s a new musical style emerged that has tried to speak to and for youth. Exemplified by groups such as Jane's Addiction and Nirvana, the style has been labeled "alternative." Coming from music that was once exclusive to college radio stations, the last bastion of the 1960s' progressive, free-format FM, these ready-for-prime-time, MTV-friendly bands play music with neopsychedelic elements over a guitar grunge and strong bass guitar/drum rhythm section. During the summer of 1991, an explicit, self-conscious attempt was made to reinvoke the sixties counterculture. A touring festival, with a variety of alternative music bands, and political and artistic sideshow called the Lollapalooza Festival, drew an avid audience of middle-class, college-aged youth. The tour was dubbed by the *New York Times,* rather appropriately, "Woodstock for a Lost Generation" (Reynolds, 1991:28).

Alternative music has had much commercial success. The accessible hit song by Nirvana, "Smells Like Teen Spirit," has won heavy rotation on a wide variety of radio formats, in addition to MTV. The rapidity of the process of usurpation by commercial culture (witness rap music as used on advertisements and by Hammer) may make Nirvana's title more accurate than they might have intended—only smelling like, rather than being, teen spirit.

Adult Reaction to Reattachment Efforts: "Welcome Home (Sanitarium)" (Metallica)

The wide range of attempts by young people to recapture a culture of their own has been met by a variety of adult reactions. The mainstream commercial rock industry ignored or actively derided the new subcultural musical styles. The worldwide Live Aid concert in 1986 decisively excluded youth-specific musics, most notably, given its popularity at that time, heavy metal. It wasn't until the 1990s that *Rolling Stone* magazine took any interest in metal or rap.

Indeed, it seems that the rise of youth-based rock has inspired an equal and opposite reaction.

> For these acts—Natalie Cole, Mariah Carey, Michael Bolton, Harry Connick Jr.—love can still conquer all, and cozy traditionalism warms over all of life. . . . It isn't just an alternative to Guns n' Roses and N.W.A. For a largely adult audience, it is a fortress against them. (Leland, 1991:52)

The sense of impending doom, ecological, economic, political, educational, and social, has replaced a sense of progress and of hope for a future world that is better than the current state of affairs. Much of the distinctively youth-based music, especially thrash metal, cogently and emotionally articulates this view. Against commercial music's message of "Don't Worry, Be Happy," young people belonging to youth subcultures worry a lot.

The reaction against insurgent subcultures has gone as far as efforts to suppress them. Although adults have disapproved of rock music since its introduction in the mid-1950s (Martin and Segrave, 1988), during the 1980s there was a strong concerted effort to resist it politically. This movement has been aimed not against rock music as such but at the youth-specific musics, particularly metal and rap (Weinstein, 1991). It is no accident that those who testified against heavy metal at United States Senate hearings in 1985 were representatives of parental interest groups (Parents' Music Resource Center and the Parent-Teacher Association), fundamentalist ministers, and physician-owners of psychiatric hospitals specializing in the treatment of adolescents.

Even more ominous than lawsuits against bands, banning concerts, and efforts at censorship was the exceedingly large increase in the number of adolescents sent to mental hospitals. *Newsweek*, among others, concluded that part of this was a response to youth behaving rebelliously.

> The "illness" for which many teenagers are committed is usually not the kind of delusional psychosis or thought disorder commonly associated with institutionalization. Instead, the diagnoses are commonly behavioral problems: "conduct disorder," "oppositional defiant disorder," and the popular "adolescent adjustment reaction." (Darnton, 1989:68)

Rosenbaum and Prinsky examined California hospitals with adolescent care programs.

> When these hospitals were given a hypothetical situation in which the parents' main problem with their child was the music he or she listened to, the clothes he or she wore, and the posters on his or her bedroom wall, 83% of the

> facilities believed the youth needed hospitalization. (1992:528)

Therapy often includes requiring the elimination of the music and its associated sartorial styles. In contrast, actions such as banning heavy metal T-shirts by school officials seem innocuous.

The moves to suppress youth subcultures that symbolically revolt against adult authority have had only episodic success. Indeed, these subcultures thrive on efforts to oppose them, because such endeavors vindicate the subcultures' claims to be genuinely countercultural. Not to minimize the threat of censorship, it is still true that First Amendment protections of expression are widely backed by the media and the courts, and help to shelter oppositional subcultures. The cultural war will go on, probably without either side winning the field.

Where does that leave youth? The present situation results from two failures. Firstly, the youth culture of the 1960s, as an ideal and ideology of a specific age-grade, was unable to become culturally hegemonic. Youth did not become the leading social group. Instead, the signifier "youth" was detached from the age-grade and made available to everyone. But, secondly, the free-floating signifier "youth" was unable to displace the cultural expression of young people altogether. Genuine youth subcultures have arisen that exist by marginalizing themselves from the leisure culture's free-floating definition of "youth." Thus, young people are now free to choose among an array of radically confrontational youth subcultures and the commercialized "youth" image.

That is a choice with which many are uncomfortable. They would like to be part of a generation with its own voice, as they suppose that 1960s youth were. In the present situation they can become marginal to the majority of young people by entering an exclusive subculture or they can blend in with pop fashion. Those who choose to reclaim "youth" for youth in oppositional subcultures carry the torch of rebellion, ready to light a conflagration if the circumstances ever permit a younger generation to coalesce again. At the same time, they alienate themselves from the bulk of their age-mates. These young people, doubly marginalized, have to criticize their own generation as well as the adult world. Youth cultures have not disappeared; the price of participation has simply become socially and emotionally higher. Youth is now the province and achievement of select groups of marginalized young people, who must actively establish their claim to it through cultural struggle.

NOTE

*Originally presented at the Annual Meetings of the American Sociological Association, Pittsburgh, Pennsylvania, August 1992. Reprinted by permission of the author.

REFERENCES

Brake, Michael. 1985. *Comparative Youth Culture: The Sociology of Youth Cultures and Youth Subcultures in America, Britain and Canada.* London: Routledge & Kegan Paul.

Brubach, Holly. 1990. "In Fashion: A Certain Age," *New Yorker* (November 5):122–128.

Cashmore, E. Ellis. 1987."Shades of Black, Shades of White," pp.245–265 in James Lull (ed.), *Popular Music and Communication.* Newbury Park, CA: Sage.

Chambers, Iain. 1987. "British Pop: Some Tracks from the Other Side of the Record," pp. 231–244 in James Lull (ed.), *Popular Music and Communication*. Newbury Park, CA: Sage.

Clarke, John, Stuart Hall, Tony Jefferson, and Brian Roberts. 1975. "Subcultures, Cultures and Class: A Theoretical Overview," pp.9-74 in Stuart Hall and Tony Jefferson (eds.), *Resistance through Rituals: Youth Subcultures in Post-War Britain*. London: Hutchinson.

Coleman, James S. 1961. *The Adolescent Society*. New York: The Free Press.

Corrigan, Paul and Simon Frith. 1975. "The Politics of Youth Culture," pp. 231–241 in Stuart Hall and Tony Jefferson (eds.) *Resistance through Rituals: Youth Subcultures in Post-War Britain*. London: Hutchinson.

Darnton, Nina. 1989. "Committed Youth: Why Are So Many Teens Being Locked Up in Private Mental Hospitals?" *Newsweek* (July 31):66–72.

Dotter, Daniel. 1987. "Growing Up Is Hard to Do: Rock and Roll Performers as Cultural Heroes," *Sociological Spectrum*: 25–44.

Duncan, Robert. 1984. *The Noise: Notes from a Rock 'n' roll Era*. New York: Ticknor & Fields.

Eddy, Chuck. 1986. "Radio '86: Dead Air," *Village Voice* (December 30):83–84.

Frith, Simon. 1988. *Music for Pleasure: Essays in the Sociology of Pop*. New York: Routledge.

Greenfield, Jeff. 1987. "They Changed Rock, Which Changed the Culture, Which Changed Us," pp.42–48 in Janet Podell (ed.), *Rock Music in America*. New York: H.W.Wilson.

Grossberg, Lawrence. 1984. "I'd Rather Feel Bad Than Not Feel Anything at All: Rock and Roll, Pleasure and Power." *Enclitic* 3(1–2):94–111.

Leland, John. 1991. "Welcome to the Jungle," *Newsweek* (September 23):52–53.

Lipsitz, George. 1990. *Time Passages: Collective Memory and American Popular Culture*. Minneapolis: University of Minnesota Press.

Mannheim, Karl. 1971. "The Democratization of Culture," pp. 271–346 in Kurt H. Wolff (ed.), *From Karl Mannheim*. New York: Oxford University Press.

Markson, Stephen L. 1989. "Claims-Making, Quasi-Theories and the Social Construction of the Rock and Roll," Paper presented at the American Sociological Association.

Martin, Linda, and Kerry Segrave. 1988. *Anti-Rock: The Opposition to Rock 'n' Roll*. Hamden, CT: Archon Book.

May, Herbert G., and Bruce M. Metzger. 1977. *The New Oxford Annotated Bible*. New York: Oxford University Press.

Moffatt, Michael. 1989. *Coming of Age in New Jersey: College and American Culture*. New Brunswick, NJ: Rutgers University Press.

Prinsky, Lorraine E., and Jill Leslie Rosenbaum. 1987. "'Leer-ics' or Lyrics: Teenage Impressions of Rock 'n' Roll," *Youth and Society* 18(4):384-97.

Reynolds, Simon. 1991. "Woodstock for the Lost Generation," *New York Times* (August 4):Section H, pp. 22ff.

Roe, Keith. 1987. "The School and Music in Adolescent Socialization," pp.212–230 in J. Lull, (ed.) *Popular Music and Communication*. Newbury Park, CA: Sage.

Rosenbaum, Jill L., and Lorraine Prinsky. 1991. "The Presumption of Influence: Responses of Popular Music Subcultures," *Crime & Delinquency* 37(4):528–535.

Weinstein, Deena. 1991. *Heavy Metal: A Cultural Sociology*. New York: Macmillan/Lexington.

Willis, Paul E. 1975. "The Cultural Meaning of Drug Use," pp. 106–118 in Stuart Hall and Tony Jefferson (eds.), *Resistance through Rituals: Youth Subcultures in Post-War Britain*. London: Hutchinson.

Rock and Roll Is Here to Stray: Youth Subculture, Deviance, and Social Typing in Rock's Early Years

Daniel Dotter

Introduction[1]

As an emerging expressive art form, rock and roll has been in existence almost four decades. For at least twenty of those years it has constituted the prime component of popular music in American society as well.[2] At the same time, the music has undergone innumerable shifts in style, content, and delivery.

Beginning in the mid-1970s and peaking today, we find the appearance of many historical and scholarly works analyzing rock and roll as a cultural art form (Belz, 1972; Gillett, 1983; Ward et al., 1986), as contemporary cultural history (London, 1984; Makower, 1989; Pielke, 1986; Marcus, 1975; Frith, 1981), as an impetus for political protest (Orman, 1984; Gitlin, 1987; Kaiser, 1988), and as a commercial mass-produced phenomenon (Denisoff, 1975; 1986; Chapple and Garofalo, 1977).

This growing body of work has addressed several questions, including the following:

1. What are the historical/artistic roots of rock and roll?
2. What is the relationship of the music to the wider cultural context in which it is produced (i.e., the mass media and related influences)?

3. What is the role of the artist in the production, dissemination, and interpretation of the music?
4. What is the social/psychological impact of rock and roll on its youthful audience (generally presumed to be negative)?
5. How has the commercialization of the music changed its artistic/cultural content?

These questions further suggest that from its very beginning, rock and roll music has undergone a unique evolution within contemporary popular culture: its artists and content have continually been a source of deviant subcultural identification, *and* each has been an object of commercial exploitation as well. At its inception, rock and roll music was a vehicle for youth protest and stylistic expression. It also represented a ripe frontier for control as a cultural commodity to be bought and sold.

Working from these broad concerns, this chapter has three purposes: (1) to document historically the link between rock music and social deviance in the 1950s and 1960s; (2) to examine the role of mass media and other groups in the presentation and interpretation of this link; and (3) to outline the early sociocultural changes in rock and roll based on this initial and continued association with socially deviant behavior and values in the emerging youth subculture.

I have chosen to focus on the early decades of rock because for at least twenty-five years the music was interpreted as belonging to subcultures disvalued by the white middle class: blacks and also white middle-class youth. The relationship between rock music and social deviance, viewed in an interactionist context (Blumer, 1969; Dotter and Roebuck, 1988), is a continuous result of two simultaneous processes: the deviance-generating activities of "claims-making" interest groups (Spector and Kitsuse, 1977; Markson, 1990) and social typing by the mass media and other groups (Klapp, 1962; 1964; 1969) that highlights the sociocultural *and* commercial nature of the music and its performers. Deviance-generation was tied into the emergence and development of the deviant youth subculture (Hebdige, 1979; Hall and Jefferson, 1976; Clarke, et al., 1976), especially in the late 1960s. As rock music became more commercialized, social typing helped break down the deviant youth subculture into a number of "taste publics" (Sanders, 1990). My historical perspective suggests that even when rock, its performers, and audiences seemed most revolutionary (and therefore most deviant), the subculture associated with the music and its production had already begun to change—to "de-revolutionize," as it were.

Before examining the historical links between rock and roll and social deviance, it is necessary to define the latter term more precisely. The cultural context of rock and social deviance in the 1950s and 1960s emerged from the music's relationship to its listeners and their associated social responses.

A Perspective on Social Deviance

Deviance Defined

Sociologists have long and passionately argued for one or another definition of social deviance. In his seminal work on deviant behavior, *Outsiders,* Howard S. Becker (1973:4–8) succinctly summarizes the most common of these definitions. The simplest view is a statistical one. Deviance is seen only in numerical terms—how far a person, thing, or situation varies from the average. In a sociocultural context, this definition is virtually meaningless, for a social response to a person or behavior considered to be deviant must be forthcoming in order to meet the sociological criteria of "deviance."

The second view is what Becker calls the "medical analogy." Deviance is "pathological," evidence of the presence of disease, indicative perhaps of the wholesale breakdown in the functioning of groups and their culture. For example, widespread drug use among the young may be seen as symptomatic of deeper conditions of social disorganization. Thus, the medical analogy implies that there is some higher, desired, agreed-upon state of social/psychological health.

The third perspective is more relativistic in its interpretation. Deviance is simply the failure to obey group rules.

This definition is nonproblematic only if one assumes that all actors *know* what the rules are and the *circumstances* under which they are to be obeyed.

The fourth stance is the most sociological and relativistic. It represents the core of the interactionist approach to deviance. According to Becker (1973:9), "*social groups create deviance by making the rules whose infraction constitutes deviance,* and by applying those rules to particular people and labeling them as outsiders." This view locates deviance or "differentness" in the social responses of particular groups to particular situations. The implication is that deviance in one social context may be seen as conformity in another. As such, this approach is the most fruitful for use in this paper. In the 1950s and 1960s, the response of large segments of conventional middle-class society was to condemn rock music, its performers, and the associated behaviors in youth and other subcultures.

Another interactionist, Edwin Schur (1971:24), has offered a more complete definition:

> Human behavior is deviant *to the extent that* it comes to be viewed as involving a *personally discreditable* departure from a group's normative expectations *and* it *elicits* interpersonal or collective reactions that serve to "isolate," "treat," "correct," or "punish" *individuals* engaged in such behavior.

The interactionist approach situates social deviance in the exchanges of meaning between groups (i.e., audiences, in the context of this paper). In this sense, rock and roll could not have emerged without at least one primary audience willing to structure its subcultural norms around the music. Similarly, the connection between rock and social deviance is a cultural creation involving other audiences in addition to the group that initially adopted and identified with the music.

"Claims-Making Activities" and the Social Construction of Deviance

Chief among these were audiences which engaged in "claims-making activities" (Spector and Kitsuse, 1977). Early rock audiences, such as parents, media critics, school officials, and religious and other leaders socially constructed most of music and its performers as deviant and disvalued. This labeling process relied upon media agents for dissemination of negative publicity at the same time that corporate structures in the recording industry promoted the music to the emerging youth subculture.

As claims-making groups, these moral entrepreneurs were amorphously structured as de facto rule makers and enforcers of community standards regarding the music, its performers, and listeners (Dotter and Roebuck, 1988). In the 1950s this labeling process centered on lifestyle deviance. By the middle 1960s the focus had shifted to include political deviance as well. Kai T. Erikson (1962:308) summarizes the interplay among audiences to social deviance on several levels: Deviance is not a property *inherent* in certain forms of behavior; it is a property *conferred upon* these forms by the audiences which directly or indirectly witness them.

This chapter, then, focuses on several audiences of early rock and roll: the growing white middle-class youth subculture developed after World War II; the parents of this generation; critics, performers, and other producers of the "new" music; and black groups which were the original creators of the form as both performers and listeners. These groups were interconnected by the mass media; first via radio and later via television. The next section briefly describes the primary listening audience of rock and roll in the 1950s and early 1960s.

Their Own Kind of Music: White Middle-Class Youth and Early Rock and Roll

The emergence of rock and roll coincided with the demographic and sociocultural development of a white middle-class youth subculture. In the 1950s especially, the music introduced this subculture to black musical styles and, to a lesser extent, to black culture generally (Dotter, 1987:30). For the first time, adolescents had a music of their own, even if they did not completely comprehend its black origins in rhythm and blues and doo-wop styles.[3]

A historian of early rock and roll, Charlie Gillett (1983:15), describes the impact of the burgeoning youth subculture:

> The growth of rock 'n' roll cannot be separated from the emergence, since the Second World War, of a new phenomenon: the adolescent or youth culture. Since the war, adolescents have made a greater show of enjoying themselves than they ever did before. Their impact has been particularly sharp because there were so few facilities that easily accommodated their new attitudes, interests, and increased wealth. Neither individual communities nor the mass communications industries anticipated the growth of adolescent culture, or responded quickly to it.

In the beginning, then, rock and roll listeners tended to be white, middle-class, and, it can be argued, female. By the late 1960s, rock's original adolescent audience had telescoped to include a wider range of ages and a more equal distribution of sexes. If the youthful audience broadened in the first fifteen years of rock and roll's existence, so too did the links between the music and social deviance. The next section details these historical concerns.

Rock and Roll and Deviant Behavior

The 1950s: Hail! Hail! Rock and Roll

Rock and roll as a distinctive form of American popular culture burst on the scene in 1955 and 1956. If it was not born then, at least white middle-class youth became aware of its existence. At the beginning, the early artists were hardly likely rockers, much less prototypical Americans.

Although he was not yet crowned the "King of Rock and Roll," Elvis Presley had already made his initial recordings in Memphis, Tennessee, during 1954. Robert Pielke, a rock historian (1986:28), describes Elvis's emergence:

> . . . a part-time truck driver walked into Sam Phillips's Sun Studios in Memphis to record a few of his country favorites in a style he had picked up from listening to black music and gospel. His name was Elvis Aaron Presley when he walked in, but he walked out as the "King of Rock and Roll." His early recordings were only regional hits, but to perceptive executives at RCA they told the story of the future. Elvis wasn't about to remain a regional phenomenon much longer.

Presley's appearance in 1954 was part of a larger trend in the recording industry: the marketing of white cover versions of songs originally recorded by black rhythm and blues artists. For example, "Sh-Boom" by the Chords was covered by the Crew Cuts; "Tweedle Dee" by Lavern Baker was also released by Georgia Gibbs; and "Sincerely" by the Moonglows was covered by the McGuire Sisters.

The initial impact was popularization among white youth of the original recordings as well as the cover versions. However, by the time Elvis and other important early rockers emerged in 1955 and 1956, rock and roll was fast becoming the music of middle-class white youth and covering effectively ended (Pielke, 1986:22–28).

Colonel Tom Parker marketed Elvis as a "sanitized" pop star to make the King more acceptable to white adults (whose teenaged sons and daughters were listening to the music). This public relations move has been well-detailed in several sources (Pareles and Romanowski, 1983:437–439; Ward, et al., 1986:130–131; Vellenga, 1988). During this period of time (1955–1957) there were a number of other artists helping to legitimate rock and roll for the white audiences. These include, most importantly, Bill Haley, Buddy Holly, Jerry Lee Lewis, and Ricky Nelson.

In the cases of Haley and Nelson (Brooks and Marsh, 1985:17–18; Belz, 1972:37–38; 51), other media in addition to recording fueled their careers. For example, Nelson was a long-time regular on the television series titled for his parents, "The Adventures of Ozzie and Harriet." Even more significant was Haley's part in placing rock and roll in movies, including *Rock Around the Clock* and *Blackboard Jungle*. The latter occasionally spurred rioting by teen viewers while the former also included performances by two important black artists of early rock and roll, Chuck Berry and Little Richard.

Practically all of the performers mentioned in this section (with the possible exception of Ricky Nelson) contributed to the link between early rock and roll and images of deviance among the young. For all of his latter-day acceptability, Elvis provided the easy target as a "lifestyle deviant" among these artists. His rhythm and blues/gospel roots were overshadowed by his sexually suggestive, myth-generating performances on the "Ed Sullivan Show." Even his biography was disvalued by most parents and, initially, critics, who were surprised by his popularity. In the words of Greil Marcus (1975:148):

> They called Elvis the Hillbilly Cat in the beginning; he came out of a stepchild culture (in the South, white trash; to the rest of America, a caricature of Bilbo and moonshine) that for all it shared with the rest of America had its own shape and integrity. As a poor white Southern boy, Elvis created a personal culture out of the hillbilly world that was his as a given. Ultimately he made that personal culture public in such an explosive way that he transformed not only his own culture, but America's.

In transforming America's culture, then, Elvis exemplified lifestyle deviance in a general nonconforming (and relatively safe) manner. His image prompted negative attitudes among middle-class adults and adoration among their children (as his records sold millions). But his was not the only deviant part to play among early rock and roll performers.

In May 1958, Jerry Lee Lewis canceled his tour of Britain several days after he arrived at Heathrow Airport with his new wife. The following account describes the reaction after Lewis introduced his wife, Myra Gale, to the English press (Ward, et al., 1986:178):

> The British had always suspected that American rock and roll stars were degenerates, but they hardly expected to have the evidence served up to them on a silver platter, and that's what Jerry Lee and Myra had just done. The news hit the wire services and traveled as fast as the electrons could carry it, and when it ticked out in the newsroom of the Memphis *Press-Scimitar*, a reporter did a

> little more digging and found out that the marriage had occurred five months before Jerry Lee's divorce became final, and that Myra Gale Lewis was not fifteen at all, but thirteen (well, almost fourteen).

Although Lewis's career did not end after this blatant moral breach, it never was quite the same again.

Similarly, in 1959, with rock and roll hardly five years old, Chuck Berry was arrested and charged with violation of the Mann Act (transporting a minor across state lines for immoral purposes), Little Richard became the first "born again" rock and roll star, Buddy Holly was killed in a plane crash (with Richie Valens and J.P. Richardson, the "Big Bopper"), and congressional hearings on "payola" scandals began (Ward, et al., 1986:208; Pielke, 1986:32).[4]

As America and the world unwittingly waited for the 1960s, it seemed rock and roll, with its flaunting of authority, excessive and immoral behavior, even greed, would give way to more conventional performers and performances.

The 1960s: The Kids Are Alright

In the 1960s the connection between rock and deviant behavior deepened to include not only lifestyle deviance but political deviance as well. The broadening of this relationship included British bands such as the Beatles, the Rolling Stones, and The Who, and also uniquely American variations led by Bob Dylan among other folk protest performers. At the same time, black artists were mainstreamed into the white-dominated recording industry. All of these elements coalesced at the Woodstock Music and Art Fair in August 1969.

By the time the Beatles toured America and appeared on the "Ed Sullivan Show" in 1964, their performer-image had been considerably cleaned up by manager Brian Epstein (much as Colonel Parker had done with Elvis).[5] The accounts of "Beatlemania" are legion (Coleman, 1984; Brown and Gaines, 1983; Shotton and Schaffner, 1983), and the artistic/cultural significance of the Beatles has been amply chronicled (Schaffner, 1978; Lewisohn, 1988). The importance of the Beatles for this chapter is as a transition image, involving rock as an art form, the telescoping of the rock audience to include older adults, and the politicized nature of rock and roll deviance.

In the early 1960s the Beatles represented no more deviant a posture than Elvis or the other early rockers. The length of the band members' hair and their British speech patterns seemed more eccentric than deviant to many adults, as did the frenzied response of teenagers to their music. As has been argued (Dotter, 1987:32), the Beatles were responsible for lending a measure of respectability to rock among adults—especially through the saccharine love ballads of Paul McCartney.[6]

However, by the mid-1960s the Beatles had become trendsetters in lifestyle deviance, freely experimenting with drugs in and out of the recording studio. The album cover design and art work of *Sergeant Pepper's Lonely Hearts Club Band* continue to stir controversy as to their "real" or hidden meaning; Beatles songs from throughout this period have been overanalyzed for references to drugs (e.g., "Lucy in the Sky with Diamonds" and "I Am the Walrus") (Sheff, 1981). Additionally, the Beatles as a group became involved with transcendental meditation under the guidance of Maharishi Mahesh Yogi (Coleman, 1984:335–345). Finally, on the eve of their last American tour during the summer of 1966, John Lennon's ill-fated remarks about the Beatles being more popular than Jesus were published in the U.S. for the first time after having been published in Britain, unsensationally, four months earlier (Coleman, 1984:312–314). His subsequent public apology cooled the situation, but to many people, young and adult, the incident represented the depth of rock and roll deviance (no matter what the context of the remarks).

While the later Beatles pushed lifestyle deviance in several directions, two other British bands of this time deserve mention: the Rolling Stones and The Who. These groups rose to popularity at roughly the same time as the Beatles, but neither brought respectability to rock in the 1960s. The acknowledged leaders of each band—Mick Jagger and Pete Townshend—cultivated a much rougher musical and cultural image than that generally associated with the Beatles. Jagger's deviant label was a kind of threatening sexuality (epitomized in "Satisfaction"). As a guitarist, Townshend's live performance histrionics are legendary. In addition to trademark displays of "power chords" and incessant "windmilling," he frequently ended concerts by smashing his guitar and abandoning it to the audience (Marsh, 1983; Barnes, 1988). These violent displays were politicized in the context of two youth anthems by The Who: "My Generation" in the 1960s and "Won't Get Fooled Again" in the early 1970s.

The Rolling Stones and The Who, then, were from the beginning more threatening than the Beatles—and therefore more deviant in the eyes of adults and critics. Each band had prototypical lifestyle deviants, and each was touched by the death of an original member (Brian Jones and Keith Moon). Furthermore, the bands' open identification with violence (lyrically and onstage) came at a time that the audience for rock was expanding to include not only teenaged girls but college students and young adults.

Each band was at the center of controversy concerning audience death at a live performance as well. In 1969, at a free Rolling Stones concert at Altamont Speedway in California, four people perished. Included was a male stabbed by members of the motorcycle gang Hell's Angels. The Angels claimed to have been hired by the Rolling Stones and the Grateful Dead as security guards (London, 1984:120–121).

In December 1979, at Cincinnati's Riverfront Coliseum, eleven ticketholders to a Who concert with "festival" non-reserved seating were killed in the rush to enter the building before the show began. Coroner's cause of death for each victim was asphyxia by compression of the chest (Fuller, 1981).

While the deaths at neither of these events were overtly political, both represented the deviant underside of rock—violence uncontrolled. The Rolling Stones incident occurred at the height of the counterculture and the Vietnam War. The tragedy surrounding the Who concert came ten years later, suggesting to many critics that hard rock and roll was not a harmless pastime, even if its audience and performers were older now.

The Beatles, the Rolling Stones, and The Who were British imports fashioning varying degrees of lifestyle and political deviance. By the late 1960s there were a significant number of American rock performers identified with the antiwar movement. The most important of these artists throughout the decade was Bob Dylan (Gitlin, 1987:197–203). His cryptic, sometimes unintelligible lyrics were open to wide interpretation, and he greatly expanded the rock audience among the young adult college population (Dotter, 1987:33). He began as a folk-protest singer, writing antiwar songs before there was an antiwar movement. He even toured England in the spring of 1965 with Joan Baez, producing the documentary film *Don't Look Back* (Kaiser, 1988:199–202; Rodnitsky, 1976). He lost much of his political appeal among his audience by "electrifying" his music in 1965 and 1966.

Two other important protest performers were Joan Baez and Phil Ochs. Baez appealed to both the antiwar and civil rights movements through her music. Her own attraction to the latter may have grown out of her marginal status in early life. Her father was a middle-class professional, but she suffered rejection by both whites and Mexicans for her part-Mexican heritage and her inability to speak Spanish (Rodnitsky, 1976:85–86). Unlike many protest performers, Baez would frequently get physically involved in activities (e.g., in Birmingham, Alabama, and Berkeley, California).

Similarly, Phil Ochs came from a middle-class background. After Dylan moved squarely into the rock mainstream, Ochs's popularity as a protest singer grew. By the late 1960s, however, his appeal had waned, because the antiwar movement had become increasingly militant—largely ignoring protest songs as a vehicle for leadership (Rodnitsky, 1976:73).[7]

The final connection between rock and roll and deviant behavior in the 1960s concerns the fate of black music and artists in a developing white industry. The Beatles and especially the Rolling Stones and The Who were profoundly influenced by urban black American rhythm and blues. Protest singers such as Dylan, Baez, and Ochs sang of the life of the poor and disenfranchised. Yet throughout the decade, much black rhythm and blues or crossover rock was hardly deviant, political or otherwise. Nor did it often get perceived as such by the media. In fact, according to Nelson George (1988), the 1960s was the beginning of forced artistic assimilation by black artists within a white-dominated industry.[8]

The most visible black performers of the decade who did not assimilate into white cultural/artistic standards were James Brown ("Soul Brother Number One") and Aretha Franklin ("Queen of Soul"). Brown, long known as hardworking on tour, projected conflicting images throughout the 1960s (Pareles and Romanowski, 1983:68). For his patriotic stance on Vietnam, he was labeled an Uncle Tom by radical blacks. Yet he also testified to black pride and "Black Power" in many of his songs, hurting his standing with whites in the industry (George, 1988:103).

Franklin's 1960s Atlantic albums and her cultural image were largely apolitical. Her fusion of blues and gospel spoke of intimate personal struggle, long the hallmark of urban and rural rhythm and blues (George, 1988:105–106; Pareles and Romanowski, 1983:202–203).

Two black performers with wide appeal among whites in the decade were Jimi Hendrix and Sly Stone (Gillett, 1983:386). While their lifestyle deviance was well-known and documented, each was something of a marginal, if not deviant, symbol to black audiences. Nelson George (1988:109) writes of the two:

> Sly was, alas, just as drug-crazed as Hendrix and just as enamored of "rock culture." He had an integrated band, not just racially but sexually, that looked as if the members had just wandered off the corner of Haight and Ashbury. No slick choreography around the Family Stone. . . . Like Hendrix he played gigs with rock acts at rock revues almost from the beginning.

Stone and Hendrix, then, were very much like Chuck Berry in the 1950s—to black audiences, they forsook black musical and cultural roots for white rock and roll. Thus they were lifestyle deviants to black *and* white adults.

Through the 1960s the audience of rock and roll had expanded considerably and the nature of rock deviance had evolved on a number of levels, as I have demonstrated. I turn now to a brief description of the Woodstock Music and Art Fair, considered by many to be the height of rock culture in the decade.

The Woodstock Music and Art Fair: Come Together

The lifestyle and political deviance associated with rock music, its performers, and its expanded audience was strikingly symbolized by the Woodstock Music and Art Fair (Makower, 1989). Staged August 15–17, 1969, the festival was called "An Aquarian Explosion of Peace and Music." Although referred to simply as Woodstock, the event actually took place in the 600–acre pasture of Max B. Yasgur's farm, some fifty miles south of Woodstock, New York. Attendance estimates run to half a million people (Pepper, 1989). Several of the thirty-one performers have already been mentioned in this analysis, including The Who, Joan Baez, Jimi Hendrix, and Sly and the Family Stone. There were three deaths (one heroin overdose, one burst appendix, and one person mistakenly run over by a tractor).

The purpose of the concert suggests its nonconforming stance (Pepper, 1989:10): To create a society, even if only temporary, that succeeded in sustaining peace and love throughout its existence and that tried to make the world a better place. There were no robberies, rapes or other crimes during the festival.

The twentieth anniversary of the event was observed with much media coverage and analysis (*Life,* 1989; *Rolling Stone,* 1989). Then, as now, Woodstock is usually considered the zenith of countercultural youth movement. Viewed in other terms, it may be argued that Woodstock took place *after* the movement (and the associated deviance I have detailed) had already begun to decline. Symbolically, Woodstock may have served both purposes: as a celebration of and also as an obituary for the 1960s. Rock and roll was becoming more and more conventional, even though a great show was made of its deviance. By the late 1960s rock music was the focal point of a large youth subculture, viewed as socially deviant by claims-making interest groups and as a lucrative commercial market by the recording industry. Furthermore, through the process of social typing in the mass media, the relationships of the music and performers to the various audiences had begun to change.

Deviant Subculture, Claims-Making, and Social Typing: The Creation of Cultural Images

The Emergence of Rock and Roll

From its beginning, rock and roll has represented a creative form of popular art with associated deviant lifestyles. This connection suggests that a process of social typing was at work in the 1950s and 1960s, transforming the music, the performers' lifestyles, and audience perceptions as well. This process was fueled by the recording industry as well as mass media in an attempt to popularize the "new" art form and render it acceptable to wider numbers of listeners in the expanding youth subculture.

At the same time, "claims-making" interest groups (Spector and Kitsuse, 1977; Markson, 1990) continued to view the subculture and its music as socially disvalued. During these early years of the emergence and evolution of rock music, these groups included media critics and elected officials, as well as religious and other community leaders.

In its first decade and a half of existence, then, rock music and the youth subculture associated with it were part of two simultaneous processes of social construction: the deviance-generating efforts of claims-making interest groups and the positive social typing of mass media, both of which tended to make cultural heroes of performers even as they and the subculture were exploited.

Claims-Making, Subcultural Style, and Deviance-Generation

Through most of the 1950s and 1960s, rock music, its performers, and the youth subculture that had formed around it were constantly assailed as socially deviant by a collection of amorphous claims-making interest groups (London, 1984; Orman, 1984). As has been pointed out, these groups included media critics, elected officials, and religious and other community leaders. Engaging in a process of deviance-generation, these moral entrepreneurs consistently attacked the threats to conventional society posed by rock music, its performers, and the youth subculture (Frith, 1988:4–5; Pielke, 1986:64–65).

Claims-making interest groups generate deviance in the following steps (Markson, 1990:33; Spector and Kitsuse, 1977):

1. Assert the existence of a particular condition, situation, or state of affairs in which human action is causally implicated.
2. Define the asserted conditions as offensive, harmful, undesirable or otherwise problematic to the society and amenable to corrective human action.
3. Stimulate public scrutiny of the condition from the point of view of the claims-makers.

In the 1950s, as I have demonstrated, the question of rock and roll deviance related to the objectionable nature of its general life-style. The music was "different" in content, style, and presentation, and therefore bad. Not that bad, however; performers such as Elvis Presley, Jerry Lee Lewis, and Chuck Berry were labeled as relatively nonserious threats to authority.

But the claim of lifestyle deviance generated against performers of rock and roll and its listeners intensified through the mid-1960s as the music and the youth subculture were increasingly associated with widespread recreational drug use and other specific forms of deviance (e.g., premarital sex). During the late 1960s this social construction of deviance was amplified to include political deviance, even criminality, as well. The identification of much of the music by claims-makers with antiwar sentiment and protest placed rock and its youth subculture in direct opposition to much of the larger society. Charles Kaiser (1988:190–191) describes the impact of the music and its widening political character:

> There would remain a lasting legacy, a culture of sound as well as words. Of all the elements that made up the sixties, this one had the deepest impact on the whole generation, all around the world. It helped shape a common political agenda, but its influence went far beyond politics. It was

> by turns steel-edged, sentimental, raucous, melodious, sophisticated and infantile, sometimes tinged with nihilism, but most often blazingly upbeat.

The music and its increasingly visible performers were the most important media elements in the evolution of the youth subculture during the late 1960s. As has been demonstrated, the normative content of the subculture moved from what I have called lifestyle deviance to political deviance. This shift of focus may be interpreted as a change in subcultural style. In this sense, the subculture represented a break from the dominant culture in an attempt to give expression to the unique experience of the former (Hall and Jefferson, 1976). Style, then, became a vehicle for social change (i.e., from lifestyle to political deviance).

The historical moment of a subculture is linked to its ritualistic style. John Clarke and his coauthors (1976:14) make the following observation:

> . . . some subcultures appear only at particular historical moments: they become visible, are identified and labeled (either by themselves or by others); they command the stage of public attention for a time; then they fade, disappear or are so widely diffused that they lose their distinctiveness.

If subcultural style is historically bounded, it is also mediated through several social channels. Especially relevant are the efforts of claims-makers in the family, church, school, media, and so on. A subculture thus offers solutions to particular problems or contradictions in the experiences of its members (Hebdige, 1979:81).

Simon Frith (1981:181–182) traces in a general manner the evolution of subcultural style by contrasting the concept of "teenager" (from the 1950s) with those of "youth" and "youth culture" (from the 1960s). The term "teenager" described a style of consumption (lifestyle deviance), of which rock and roll music was the conspicuous element.

"Youth," on the other hand, was an ideological concept (political deviance), and "youth culture" suggested that its adherents were consciously negating parental values (Frith, 1981:190). Broadly speaking, then, youth subcultural style implied resistance to white middle-class values *and* lifestyle.[9]

By the late 1960s, the youth subculture was firmly entrenched on American university campuses. Furthermore, it had largely transcended problems dealing with personal expressiveness and confronted the political activity of the dominant culture in the form of antiwar protest. Frith (1981:194) demonstrates the centrality of the Vietnam War for the transformation of subcultural experience:

> . . . the Vietnam War was experienced as a youth event, both by those people who survived the endless tedium, pointlessness, and fear of active service with drugs and rock 'n' roll, and by those people who had come to terms with their personal desperation and political determination not to be drafted. In the 1960s there was a *generation* of male Americans who had to define and evaluate their lives in terms of Vietnam, whether they fought there or not.

As the subcultural experience became more political, the role of rock music and its performers in expressing subcultural style evolved in the same direction. Even before Woodstock, music, performers, and subculture had been successfully generated as deviant by claims-makers. However, this process and accompanying moral entrepreneurship would gradually lose momentum if subcultural behavior and norms became institutionalized on a wide scale (Dotter and Roebuck, 1988). As opposition to the war mounted, rock music had moved into the commercial mainstream and positive social typing by mass media continued.

Social Typing and the Public Drama of Rock and Roll

According to Orrin Klapp (1962:11), social typing creates collective images in modern mass-produced society. These representations may be lifestyles, musical forms, or even broader cultural images (e.g., values). Furthermore, social types aid audiences in searching for collective identity. This process occurs in three ways (Klapp, 1969:219–229; Dotter, 1987:39–40): (1) by reinforcing cultural values and thereby defining selfhood; (2) by serving as a role model for seductive, deviant experience, suggesting that such disvalued behavior is possible and perhaps even to be admired; and (3) by creatively offering a transcendence of ordinary experience, a new set of guidelines that transforms cultural values.

The emergence of rock and roll proliferated the seductive and, to a lesser extent, transcending identity searches. Klapp (1964:263) emphasizes the public nature of these searches and hints at their media connection:

> Man's second life is now in the public drama. His dreams are taped, filmed, and projected. It may not be too long in our audience-directed society before the public drama becomes our first life—before the balance tips and the vicarious becomes real, and what one does at the office seems only an intermission for the real show. At least one must not discount the public drama. It is growing and finding new modes and techniques of power.

The public drama of early rock and roll was fueled in various ways by the recording industry and mass media. This process produced nonconventional, deviant social types for the 1950s and 1960s, exploiting ever-expanding audiences as it created a commercial demand. I turn to these concerns.

When rock and roll was "born," the recording industry and mass media had a unique task: to make the music and its performers acceptable to middle-class youth (and to a lesser degree, their parents). Rock's artistic emergence from black rhythm and blues is well-documented (George, 1988; Young, 1988). As I have demonstrated, the performers of the 1950s were instrumental in presenting early rock and roll in a culturally relevant (but deviant) framework for young white audiences. Nelson George (1988:68) writes of Chuck Berry's importance as a black purveyor of white teenaged subcultural images:

> As rock and roll's first guitar hero, Berry, along with various rockabilly musicians, made that instrument the genre's dominant musical element, supplanting the sax of previous black stars. . . . The electric guitar captivated legions of white kids, sending them into air-guitar solos in front of mirrors across the nation.

Perhaps even more effectively than Elvis, Chuck Berry articulated a cultural image for postwar white youth and the concern with sexual frustration and adult repression.

From a marketing standpoint, several developments aided the growth of rock and roll in this period. These include the appearance of 45-r.p.m. records, white performers moving from cover versions to their own original compositions, and the production of movies dealing with the youth subculture and associated alienation, such as *Blackboard Jungle, East of Eden, Rebel Without a Cause,* and *The Wild One* (Pielke, 1986:27–38).

Thus rhythm and blues became rock and roll with a youth-oriented subtext. It remained for the 1960s to supply the political, transcendental reality of the Woodstock Nation.

As the size of the counterculture swelled, rock's commercial possibilities were continuously exploited (Dotter, 1987). The appearance of British bands suggested a merging of musical styles and cultural interpretations. Increasingly, critical acceptance became predicated on commercial success.

As Pete Townshend (1985) of The Who writes, "Without urban R&B there would have been no Rolling Stones, Beatles, Kinks, or Who. . . . Our band was in the business of taking the best of American culture and selling it on to the British." He further outlines the later commercial success of the rock opera *Tommy* and its impact on the band, "We went from the ridiculous to the sublime—being told we were musical geniuses when really we were just a bunch of scumbags" (Barnes, 1988). Clearly, the political significance of the music depended on commercial viability.

In this sense, then, Woodstock represents the degeneration of rock's political deviance rather than its summit. As many performers suggested, they participated for the musical experience itself and not for any political ramifications. Indeed, Abbie Hoffman was forced from the stage by Pete Townshend when Hoffman attempted to make a political announcement during The Who's set (Makower, 1989:235–236).

Similarly, the commercial possibilities of black crossover to white audiences began to erode the unique character and message of rhythm and blues. This process, continuing today, is what Nelson George (1988) has called "the death of rhythm and blues." The cultural context of black popular music thus becomes indistinguishable from its white counterpart in an attempt to attract audiences.

This discussion has illustrated the relationship between mass media, audiences, and rock and roll as deviant popular culture in the 1950s and 1960s. The deviant character of this culture (whether lifestyle or political) was a commercial commodity, subject to social typing by the industry and mass media.

The Institutionalization of Deviant Subculture

By the mid-1960s, the process of social typing as applied to rock music had helped to foster a deviant youth subculture at the same time that it led to an increasingly commercial presentation of the music as popular culture. Central to these two developments was the evolution of the performer as a cultural hero (Dotter, 1987; Chapple and Garofalo, 1977).

In the early decades the cultural heroes of rock and roll occupied a precarious sociocultural position. On the one hand, they served as role models for seductive deviant experience, offering new guidelines for the youth subculture to follow with respect to lifestyle or political deviance. In so doing, they were constantly at odds with claims-makers attacking their credibility. On the other hand, these symbolic leaders of the deviant youth subculture were themselves transformed by the commercialization of their message. By 1969 and the passing of Woodstock, the deviant youth subculture had begun to splinter into a number of "taste publics" (Sanders, 1990; Arnold, 1970). The original creators and audiences of the music were older and hardly considered revolutionary. For even the most deviant of performers, recording and concert touring had become a business venture. In this context, commercial promotion demanded that rock heroes and their music be marketed to wider, more conventional groups. In the words of Clinton R. Sanders (1990:6):

> This promotion of deviant/innovative cultural materials within the interaction system surrounding cultural

> production is analogous to the "educational" efforts which organized groups of social deviants (homosexuals, ex-mental patients, alcoholics, and so forth) direct at the public in order to attack widespread negative definitions and ease the weight of social reaction.

Being the primary expressive mode for the deviant youth subculture, rock performers were revolutionary (and therefore disvalued by claims-makers) only as long as they and their music appealed to a relatively exclusive category of listeners. As rock increasingly *became* popular music in the 1970s, its performers and their symbolic deviance were institutionalized into a larger mass cultural framework (Dotter, 1987:35–38). Additionally, the political experience of the subculture lost much of its appeal with the end of the Vietnam War.

The initial decades of rock and roll music, then, are an especially fruitful source for the study of deviant subcultural identification and its stylistic expression in popular culture. The processes of social typing and deviance-generation provide a complex outline for sociocultural change.

Summary and Conclusions: Deviance-Generation and Sociocultural Change

This chapter has demonstrated the link between rock and roll music and social deviance in the 1950s and 1960s. The labeling or deviance-generation process involved claims-makers as well as cultural heroes. By the end of the 1960s, social typing had led to an institutionalization of deviant subcultural styles (including lifestyle and political forms).

Several key lines of inquiry have emerged from the analysis. First, the symbolic importance of music and performers for the expression of deviant subcultural styles is clear. I have examined the historical nature of homology in the early years of the deviant youth subculture's existence: the symbolic relationship between a group's values, lifestyles, subjective experience, and musical expression (Hebdige, 1979:113; Willis, 1978). Future research should extend the analysis to contemporary situations, such as the emergence of rap and its expression of subcultural styles.

Second, the process of deviance-generation suggests a labeling model involving several groups and layers of analysis. While I have incorporated various concepts central to the Marxian analysis of subculture, I believe we are best served by a pluralistic approach to the labeling process. As has been pointed out (Clarke, 1990), focusing strictly on the importance of social class in the genesis of deviant subculture tends to dichotomize the world into members and nonmembers, deviants and straights. The nature of the labeling process and deviance-generation is much more complex and volatile on either a structural or experiential level.

Finally, the importance of deviance-generation within the wider arena of sociocultural change deserves further attention. The link between the two is most evident during times of "moral panic," as the late 1950s and 1960s surely were (Cohen, 1980), but the labeling process suggests a more subtle and fundamental connection.

In the 1950s we were not sure if rock and roll was here to stay. Indeed, it survived to evolve over 30 years. The "straying" I have outlined in this chapter did much to encourage that creative, social evolution, even as performers and audiences were eventually exploited.

NOTES

1. A piece on rock and roll deserves expressions of gratitude as substitute liner notes. Each of these people contributed to this paper, but none had any hand in its shortcomings. Thanks to Jim Skipper for asking me to do it; to Mike Cappel for the album and books; to Clyde DeBerry and Charles Minifield for turning me on to Muddy Waters, James Brown, et al.; to Della Wills for her Aretha Franklin selections; to Paulette Cappel for her interest in Pete Townshend and *Empty Glass* (the artistic origin of this paper); and to Jackie Durham for her enthusiasm about Tom Petty and the Rolling Stones.

Special thanks to Doyle Kidd and Randy Shultz for everything—particularly the infrequent but boisterous "Boys' Night Out"; and to The Who for the band's unwitting inspiration to "carry on."

Extra special thanks to Susan Roach for introducing me to the local rock scene; to my students for teaching me about music and life; to Allan and Patsy McBride for sharing their family; to Rollo Richey for tolerating my presence between classes and setting up my computer; to Billy Williams and Martha Smithey, valued colleagues and friends, who offered irrepressible humor and listened; to Mike and Lynda Moore for reappearing at the appropriate instant.

Extra, extra special thanks to Marianne for asking all the right questions about rock and roll deviance and for supplying quite a few of the answers too; to Michelle and the kids for a really great time; and to Tom for going to the concert with me against his better judgment.

Heartfelt thanks to my Mom, Chardelle, for her continued love, encouragement, and support, and for caring about rock and roll only because I do.

This paper is for Josh and his generation.

2. It is practically impossible to identify the exact year of rock and roll's birth. Alan Freed, pioneering disc jockey who was later disgraced by payola scandals, claimed to have invented the term in 1951 and is generally credited with doing so (Denisoff, 1986:86; Belz, 1972:50–51; Chapple and Garofalo, 1977:56–61).

After moving to radio station WJW in Cleveland, Ohio, he originated the late-night "Moondog Rock 'n' Roll Party" (consisting of rhythm and blues recordings from independent labels) (Pareles and Romanowski, 1983:205). Many, if not most, sources provide the arbitrary date between 1954 and 1956 (Pielke, 1986:27–30; Belz, 1972:16). Likewise, I think it impossible to define rock and roll in a few words, nor do I offer a classification of its many early styles. The reader is referred to Gillett's (1983:23–35) five styles which generally cover the music's evolution through the 1950s and early 1960s. For the sake of convenience, I employ rock and roll as a generic term for the period covered by this research; rock is used in reference to the broad genre of the late 1960s, distinguishing it from related styles such as pop or folk music. In the years following Woodstock, this amorphous form of rock began to split into a number of more specific categories (Weinstein, 1991:12–13).

3. Doo-wop is a form of rhythm and blues–based harmony using repeated nonsense syllables (Pareles and Romanowski, 1983:162).

It represents a distinctive style and was initiated by black youths too poor to buy musical instruments (Pielke, 1986:12). Its usage soon spread to white singers as well.

4. Also in 1959, the male members of the Platters were arrested in Cincinnati with four nineteen-year-old women. Not being identified as rock and roll deviants, they were relatively unaffected by the incident, and no one was jailed (Ward, et al., 1986:208).

5. The drug and sexual excesses of the Beatles during early pre-America tours of Britain and Germany went unknown and uncriticized for years (Brown and Gaines, 1983:38–44).

6. At the same time in the U.S., the Beach Boys and related performers, purveyors of "Surf Rock" or "California Rock," presented a similar clean-cut image for rock and roll, boiling it down to surf, sand, fast cars, pretty girls, and sunshine. The cultural evolution of the Beach Boys, while interesting, is not covered here because the group never was seriously identified as politically deviant. The Beach Boys produced innocuous, middle-class rock which celebrated the American Dream, Southern California-style. Artistically, Brian Wilson, the group's creative energy, continued to evolve as a songwriter/producer, releasing the critically acclaimed but commercially less-successful *Pet Sounds* in 1966 (Gillett, 1983: 327–329). The music of the Jim Morrison-led band, the Doors, represents an interesting contrast. The dark lyrical content of the band's material and Morrison's controversial stage behavior broadened the artistic content of rock in a somewhat apolitical fashion (Densmore, 1990).

7. In the late 1960s John Lennon and Yoko Ono even became involved in the Peace Movement with outrageously-staged bed-ins and press conferences. Lennon no longer considered himself a pop star and defended their actions: "We are willing to become the world's clowns if it helps spread the word for peace" (Coleman, 1984:397).

8. Motown Records, headed by Berry Gordy, Jr., and known as the "Sound of Young America," produced a seemingly endless succession of classic records for both black and white audiences during the 1960s. Artists of the label included Smokey Robinson and the Miracles, the Temptations, the Four Tops, Marvin Gaye, Stevie Wonder, and Diana Ross and the Supremes, among others (Pareles and Romanowski, 1983:222–223). Through the 1960s and much of the 1970s, Motown remained the country's major black-owned business and producer of crossover hits (Ward, et al., 1986:384).

9. Paul Willis (1978) provides an analysis of the contrasting styles and identifications within the hippie and motorbike boy subcultures.

References

Arnold, D. 1970. *The Sociology of Subculture.* Berkeley, CA: Glendessary.

Barnes, Richard. 1988. Liner notes for *The Who: Who's Better, Who's Best.* MCAD-8031. Universal City, CA: MCA Records.

Becker, Howard S. 1973. *Outsiders: Studies in the Sociology of Deviance.* (Enlarged ed.). New York: The Free Press.

Belz, Carl. 1972. *The Story of Rock* (2nd ed.). Oxford: Oxford University Press.

Blumer, Herbert. 1969. *Symbolic Interactionism: Perspective and Method.* Englewood Cliffs, NJ: Prentice-Hall.

Brooks, Tim, and Earle Marsh. 1985. *The Complete Directory to Prime Time Network TV Shows: 1946–Present* (3rd ed.). New York: Ballantine.

Brown, Peter, and Steven Gaines. 1983. *The Love You Make: An Insider's Story of the Beatles*. New York: Signet.

Chapple, Steve, and Reebee Garofalo. 1977. *Rock 'n' Roll Is Here to Pay: The History and Politics of the Music Industry*. Chicago: Nelson-Hall.

Clarke, Gary. 1990. "Defending Ski-Jumpers: A Critique of Theories of Youth Subcultures." Pp. 81–96 in Simon Frith and Andrew Goodwin (eds.), *On Record: Rock, Pop, and the Written Word.* New York: Pantheon.

Clarke, John, Stuart Hall, Tony Jefferson, and Brian Roberts. 1976. "Subcultures, Cultures, and Class." Pp. 9–74 in Stuart Hall and Tony Jefferson (eds.), *Resistance Through Rituals: Youth Subcultures in Post-War Britain.* London: Hutchinson.

Cohen, Stanley. 1980. *Folk Devils and Moral Panics.* New York: St. Martin's.

Coleman, Ray. 1984. *Lennon.* New York: McGraw-Hill.

Denisoff, R. Serge. 1975. *Solid Gold: The Popular Record Industry.* New Brunswick, NJ: Transaction.

———. 1986. *Tarnished Gold: The Record Industry Revisited.* New Brunswick, NJ: Transaction.

Densmore, John. 1990. *Riders on the Storm: My Life with Jim Morrison and the Doors.* New York: Delacorte.

Dotter, Daniel. 1987. "Growing Up Is Hard to Do: Rock and Roll Performers as Cultural Heroes." *Sociological Spectrum* 7:25–44.

Dotter, Daniel L., and Julian B. Roebuck. 1988. "The Labeling Approach Re-Examined: Interactionism and the Components of Deviance." *Deviant Behavior* 9:19–32.

Erikson, Kai T. 1962. "Notes on the Sociology of Deviance." *Social Problems* 9 (Spring):307–314.

Frith, Simon. 1981. *Sound Effects.* New York: Pantheon.

———. 1988. "Introduction." Pp. 3–7 in Simon Frith (ed.), *Facing the Music.* New York: Pantheon.

Fuller, John G. 1981. *Are the Kids All Right?: The Rock Generation and Its Hidden Death Wish*. New York: Times Books.

George, Nelson. 1988. *The Death of Rhythm and Blues*. New York: Pantheon.

Gillett, Charlie. 1983. *The Sound of the City: The Rise of Rock and Roll* (2nd ed.). New York: Pantheon.

Gitlin, Todd. 1987. *The Sixties: Years of Hope, Days of Rage.* New York: Bantam.

Hall, Stuart, and Tony Jefferson (eds.). 1976. *Resistance Through Rituals: Youth Subcultures in Post-War Britain*. London: Hutchinson.

Hebdige, Dick. 1979. *Subculture: The Meaning of Style*. London: Methuen.

Kaiser, Charles. 1988. *1968 in America*. New York: Weidenfield and Nicholson.

Klapp, Orrin E. 1962. *Heroes, Villains, and Fools: The Changing American Character*. Englewood Cliffs, NJ: Prentice-Hall.

———. 1964. *Symbolic Leaders: Public Dramas and Public Men*. Chicago: Aldine.

———. 1969. *Collective Search for Identity*. New York: Holt, Rinehart, and Winston.

Lewisohn, Mark. 1988. Liner notes for *The Beatles: Past Masters* (Vol. 1 and 2). DIDX 2888 and DIDX 2889. EMI Records.

Life. 1989. "Woodstock: Where Are They Now?" (August):20–45.

London, Herbert I. 1984. *Closing the Circle: A Cultural History of the Rock Revolution*. Chicago: Nelson-Hall.

Makower, Joel. 1989. *Woodstock: The Oral History*. New York: Doubleday.

Marcus, Greil. 1975. *Mystery Train: Images of America in Rock 'n' Roll Music*. New York: E.P. Dutton.

Markson, Stephen L. 1990. "Claims-Making, Quasi-Theories, and the Social Construction of the Rock and Roll Menace." Pp. 29–40 in Clinton R. Sanders (ed.), *Marginal Conventions: Popular Culture,*

Mass Media, and Social Deviance. Bowling Green, OH: Bowling Green State University Popular Press.

Marsh, Dave. 1983. *Before I Get Old: The Story of The Who*. New York: St. Martin's.

Orman, John. 1984. *The Politics of Rock Music*. Chicago: Nelson-Hall.

Pareles, Jon, and Patricia Romanowski (eds.). 1983. *The Rolling Stone Encyclopedia of Rock and Roll*. New York: Summit Books.

Pepper, Jon. 1989. "1960s Flower Children Now Grown Up." *Monroe* (LA) *News-Star* (August 13):1D.

Pielke, Robert G. 1986. *You Say You Want a Revolution: Rock Music in American Culture*. Chicago: Nelson-Hall.

Rodnitsky, Jerome L. 1976. *Minstrels of the Dawn: The Folk-Protest Singer as a Cultural Hero*. Chicago: Nelson-Hall.

Rolling Stone. 1989. "Woodstock Remembered." 559:61–91.

Sanders, Clinton R. 1990. "A Lot of People Like It: The Relationship Between Deviance and Popular Culture." Pp. 3–13 in Clinton R. Sanders (ed.), *Marginal Conventions: Popular Culture, Mass Media, and Social Deviance*. Bowling Green, OH: Bowling Green State University Popular Press.

Schaffner, Nicholas. 1978. *The Beatles Forever*. New York: McGraw-Hill.

Schur, Edwin M. 1971. *Labeling Deviant Behavior: Its Sociological Implications*. New York: Harper and Row.

Sheff, David. 1981. "John Lennon and Yoko Ono-Candid Conversation." *Playboy* 28 (January):75–114; 144.

Shotton, Pete, and Nicholas Schaffner. 1983. *The Beatles, Lennon, and Me*. New York: Stein and Day.

Spector, Malcolm, and John Kitsuse. 1977. *Constructing Social Problems*. Menlo Park, CA: Cummings.

Townshend, Pete. 1985. Liner notes for *Who's Missing*. MCA-5641. Universal City, CA: MCA Records.

Vellenga, Dirk. 1988. *Elvis and the Colonel*. New York: Delacorte.

Ward, Ed, Geoffrey Stokes, and Ken Tucker. 1986. *Rock of Ages: The Rolling Stone History of Rock and Roll*. New York: Summit Books.

Weinstein, Deena. 1991. *Heavy Metal: A Cultural Sociology*. New York: Lexington Books.

Willis, Paul. 1978. *Profane Culture*. London: Routledge and Kegan Paul.

Young, Al. 1988. "The 'Sepia' Struggle." *The New York Times Book Review* (December 11):16–17.

Secular Rituals in Popular Culture: A Case for Grateful Dead Concerts and Dead Head Identity

Robert Sardiello

Introduction

The Grateful Dead are a San Francisco–based rock band who began performing in the early 1960s, gaining popularity as the house band at Ken Kesey's Acid Tests (Wolfe 1968). At these events, and others like them, experiments with mind-altering drugs combined with experiments in acoustical sound to produce a version of rock and roll unique to the Grateful Dead. Over the years, their appeal has solidified a core of supporters who refer to themselves as Dead Heads. Dead Heads have been described as cult-like members of a nomadic subcultural community who construct and maintain a sense of unity and feeling of belonging which extends beyond the concert setting (Pearson 1987; Gans and Simon 1985). This sense of unity is inextricably linked to the band as the audience becomes an extended family drawn together for a concert ritual that closely resembles a religious festival (McNally 1980; Pearson 1987). In this chapter I will use ethnographic data based on interviews and observations to analyze Grateful Dead concerts as secular rituals and describe the mythic nature of Dead Head unity in terms of the shared meanings the members of this group use to interpret reality and define their identity.

Youth Subculture, Rock Music, and the Liminoid

Youth subcultures are component parts of a complex cultural milieu. They are differentiated by social variables such as age, gender, race, social class, and rural or urban residence; and also by cultural content defined in terms of distinct languages, symbols, and styles of life related to value systems that differ from adults' (Coleman 1963, Sebald 1984, Elkin and Handel 1989, Hebdige 1979, Klapp 1969, Brake 1980). Youth subcultures are, in a sense, adaptations of dominant cultural elements that are expressed as attempts to resolve collectively experienced problems relative to their position in society (Brake 1985). They are often organized around internally structured sets of patterned social relations and a means by which members can collectively reaffirm their solidarity (Sebald 1984). Membership is, however, variable, and individual youths will often claim multiple memberships or symbolic memberships and these will influence the development of their personal and social identity (Hewitt 1989, Brake 1985).

One important factor in the creation and maintenance of these groups involves the role of music (Coleman 1963, Martin 1979). The types of music available and the ways they are used and consumed by youth groups reflect both the social and cultural divisions among these groups (Frith 1981). Gender and class differences, for example, are significant in determining certain aspects of these groups, as well as the types of music they like and how they use and consume it (Denisoff and Bridges 1983:53; Gans 1974; Frith 1981). Social markers are not, however, sufficient in themselves to establish the boundaries of these groups (Peterson and DiMaggio 1975; Lull 1987a, 1987b; Lewis 1982, 1987).

The boundaries of youth subcultures are also identified by cultural content, and music is a symbolic form of communication that embodies aspects of this content. Music is meaningfully interpreted by social actors in a way that helps to define or reaffirm their social worlds (Lewis 1987; Martin 1979). Music, especially rock music after World War II, has been an important outlet for the expression of youth solidarity. Indeed, the history of rock and roll can be seen in relation to different generations, or groups, of youth attempting to acquire exclusiveness through different symbolic representations of in-group membership (Clarke 1976; Hebdige 1976, 1979). Rock performers become musical prophets (Lewis 1987) or cultural heroes (Dotter 1987), and concerts become the ritual occasions for celebrating group solidarity (Montague and Morais 1976; Martin 1979).

Rituals are a very important part of contemporary social life. Unfortunately, there is little or no consensus on the nature or definition of ritual. This is partly due to the explorations of early anthropologists who studied rituals in a total, or more homogeneous, social setting. Contemporary studies deal with a different social environment. The heterogeneity of modern social life has created a host of problems for the study of ritual activity. There are, however, a number of criteria which may be extracted from traditional definitions. Miracle (1986) noted that these would include that "it is explained by mythology; it involves attributes of the sacred; it evinces the three stages of ritual identified by Van Gennep (i.e., separation, liminality, and reincorporation); it involves the use of symbols; it is structured; it is stereotyped and repetitive; and it elicits neurophysiological effects similar to those associated with many other ritual formats."

Rituals, whether secular or religious, deal with symbolic representations of sacred collective values that are often incorporated in myths.[1] Myth themes reflect the constructions of sacred reality and allow for the meaningful integration of human communities through, or because of, a common understanding or interpretation of experiences in the world (Durkheim 1915, Geertz 1973). Modern heterogeneous societies, therefore, contain pockets of groups, or in this case, youth subcultures, identified by different ritual activities and myth themes, that heighten status boundaries and reinforce the webs of significance that provide for meaningful interaction (Geertz 1973:5).

Individuals in ritual settings are separated or released, to some degree, from routine roles and statuses. Turner (1969) called this condition of separation and release "liminality." Turner's (1969) concept of liminality is based on an extension of Van Gennep's analysis of rites of passage. Van Gennep identified three stages in these rites that characterize status transformations usually associated with the life course. The middle stage in this process is liminal, according to Turner, because it is in between the structured social positions associated with the other two stages of childhood and adulthood. Puberty rites, for example, involve the transformation of boys and girls into men and women. The rituals which mark such transformations include a dimension in which the individuals are neither boys and girls, nor men and women. This time and space, in between recognized structured cultural categories, is liminal. It is antistructure, not in the sense that it opposes structure, although it can, but because it is outside of structure (Turner 1969). According to Turner:

> Ritual's liminal phase, then, approximates to the "subjunctive mood" of sociocultural action. It is, quintessentially, a time and place lodged between all times and spaces defined and governed in any specific biocultural ecosystem . . . , by the rules of law, politics, and religion, and by economic necessity. Here the cognitive schemata that give sense and order to everyday life no longer apply, but are, as it were, suspended—in ritual symbolism perhaps even shown as destroyed or dissolved. (Turner 1982;84)

In a state of liminality, experience contrasts structure such that the interaction among equals, or liminars, may foster a special type of social relationship, which Turner defined as "communitas" (Turner 1969). These interstitial roles and experiences promote a feeling of spontaneous integration or connection similar to what Csikszentmihalyi (1975a) described as "flow."[2] Liminal communitas may also be prolonged due to the particular nature of individual ritual events and this may lead to an attempt to preserve communitas by imposing normative or ideological standards. Communitas can become normative then, similar to the way Weber described the routinization of charisma (Turner 1977a, 1978). Routinized or normative communitas is a variation associated with an extended or more permanent type of marginality or liminality, such as during a pilgrimage or among groups such as monks (Turner 1973, 1977a).

Turner's (1982) continued interest in liminal phenomena led him to differentiate liminality, which is a condition found primarily in preindustrial societies, from the liminoid, which he argued was the functional equivalent in post-industrial types of societies. Liminal phenomena, therefore, tend to be centrally integrated into the total social process, and function as Durkheim described, as collective representations under a condition of mechanical solidarity, whereas liminoid phenomena flourish in societies with organic solidarity. Both types of phenomena do, in fact, coexist in modern societies, but the liminoid are more fragmented in terms of total social involvement. They are more a matter of choice, not obligation. The voluntary nature of participation in liminoid activities, often associated with the leisure genres, makes them susceptible to commodification and institutionalization, but this does not detract from their significant social and psychological functions (Frey and Dickens 1990). The interstitial quality of liminoid phenomena is functionally equivalent to liminal phenomena, but more prevalent in structurally more complex societies because there are more cracks to fall between. Secular rituals therefore provide a setting for, or frame, liminoid experiences, which are outside of, or in between, structured social life, and these experiences offer an opportunity for communitas.

My point, thus far, has been to illustrate the integrative importance of secular rituals for a group of people who are themselves liminoid by social definition. Adolescents and youths occupy a liminoid position relative to the social structure and, therefore, actively seek membership in groups that provide a sense of belonging and basis for identity (Brake 1980, 1985; Hebdige 1979). These groups construct meaningful interpretations of their life experiences, and one very important outlet for these expressions involves participation in secular concert rituals (Montague and Morais 1976).

In this paper, I will examine how concerts by the rock group the Grateful Dead function as secular rituals. Most rock concerts can be seen as rituals (Martin 1979), but the Grateful Dead are particularly interesting because their core of fans, who are commonly referred to as Dead Heads, are extremely loyal followers. These fans construct meaning out of participation in concert events and this unifies them under a system of belief that shapes their interpretations of their social worlds.

Dead Heads create and maintain a sense of solidarity based on what Pearson (1987) called a shared acceptance of interpretive rules. My initial investigation into the dimensions of these interpretive rules began with an understanding that my interpretations would be from the symbolic inside out (Hill 1975, Glaser and Strauss 1965). I wanted to unravel the layers of constructions which create these interpretive rules (Geertz 1973). This led to a series of interviews in which I directly asked Dead Heads what it meant to be a Dead Head, how one could identify a Dead Head, and if there were different types of Dead Heads. I was also curious about band-specific iconography and other popular symbols that have come to be associated with the band, so I probed for an understanding of their meaning. I treated song lyrics peripherally and placed greater emphasis on trademark designs, such as the "Steal Your Face" skull and skeleton and roses symbols.

I interviewed a total of forty-five white concert-goers in and around the parking lots of the Capitol Centre in Washington, D.C., on September 2 and 3, 1988, and on the streets outside Madison Square Garden, in New York City, between September 15 and September 24, 1988. These nonrandom interviews were based on opportunity and accessibility but generally reflected the demographic composition of this group.

The twenty-six male and nineteen female respondents ranged in age from 16 to 60 with an average age of 23.6 years. Most of the respondents were under 25 years of age and half were students, either in high school or college. Dead Heads appear diverse in terms of age, which is probably due to the length of time the band has been together, but they seem to be similar on other demographic characteristics, such as race and class background. The students, for example, came from families with parents whose occupations would be classified as middle class. The other half of the respondents were distributed in occupations that would similarly be classified as middle class. They ranged from accounting clerks to lawyers; a few were self-employed vendors, selling such popular items as T-shirts, jewelry, drugs, and Guatemalan clothes. Dead Heads also have a tendency to see more than one show on a tour. This, combined with the longevity of the band, has made it possible for some to have seen the band more than 100 times. Several of my respondents were in this category.

After completing this stage of data collection, I began to understand the importance of the concert as a focal point for reinforcing their interpretive rules. I then went back into the field as a research assistant on a team studying the Grateful Dead subculture.[3] My duties enabled me sufficient time to collect observational data at eight concert sites between July 1 and July 20, 1989. The sites included Foxborough, Massachusetts; Buffalo; Philadelphia; East Rutherford, New Jersey; Deer Creek, Indiana; and Alpine Valley, Wisconsin.

Dead Head Identity

Dead Heads are often described in the popular press as some contemporary derivation of the stereotypical hippie from the sixties. This stereotype is an idealized conception, and as such, can be seen as a model, complete with many of the lifestyle values and themes associated with the bohemian youth movements of the sixties (Schechter 1983). According to Brake (1980) these themes included passive resistance, particularly in the political arena; movement, both physical and existential; dissociation from the material comforts of their middle class origin; expressivity and subjectivity as opposed to conformity and deferred gratification; and individualism.

Over the years, however, as these themes have faded in the broader social context, they have solidified around the Grateful Dead concert experience. Dead Heads have adopted these themes and values and have creatively applied them as the basis for a sophisticated network of interactive rules incorporated in a mythic system of belief. Myths, in general, are collective representations that encode values relevant to shared experiences. They are, in a sense, what Doty (1986) referred to as "projective psychic models," in that they ". . . have a way of disclosing us to ourselves, either as we are or as we might be—and as we might be in either a negative or a positive light" (xviii).

Most of my respondents recognized some of the thematic elements of this mythic model as part of Dead Head identity, especially in regard to the sense of unity one has with others who share a similar view. One respondent, for example, stated:

> I try to be more like I am at shows or more like everybody is at shows everywhere. You know, be an example. . . . 'cause there's a certain philosophy in it, in the scene. It's just there's a real community spirit, it's a brotherhood. There's a lack of ego there definitely, not everyone's out for themselves. It's a big together thing and that's really neat, that's something I have yet to find anywhere else, especially on that kind of scale.

The philosophy that this respondent is referring to is an important part of Dead Head identity and provides for social recognition beyond a simple appreciation of the music. An appreciation of the music is, however, the most elementary ingredient of Dead Head identity. This may seem simplistic, but I later discovered that it is an important distinguishing feature separating people who share similar values but who do not necessarily like the music of the Grateful Dead.[4]

The strong appeal of the themes contained in this mythic model forms the basis for a system of belief with spiritual connotations. In fact, Jerry Garcia, guitarist and vocalist with the Grateful Dead, said in a recent interview with *Rolling Stone*, ". . . as they [Dead Heads] elucidate the relationship between what the Dead does and what they do, we start to see ourselves as part of this complex something else. Which I think is the real substance of the sixties. For me, the lame part of the sixties was the political part, the social part. The real part was the spiritual part" (Goodman 1989). This aspect of spirituality stems from the history of the band in the sixties and from their use of drugs, particularly hallucinogenic drugs.

Some clinical studies have indicated that LSD experiences decrease interest in material possessions and produce peak sensations similar to mystical states of consciousness which induce greater feelings of self-confidence and a deeper sense of meaning and purpose (Grof 1977, Irwin 1977, Willis 1976, Savage et al. 1966). In the sixties, experiments with mind-altering drugs such as LSD combined with experiments in music to produce acid rock. The Grateful Dead were at the forefront of this trend, living in the Haight-Ashbury district of San Francisco, which came to be known as the acid center of the world (Brake 1980). The band's participation in the Acid Tests and the Tripps Festival exemplified the ritual nature of events that combined drug use and music and can be seen as focal points in the hippie subculture.

"Dosing," or ingesting LSD, is still popular at Grateful Dead concert events. It is often sold openly in the parking lots before concerts and is the source of most confrontations with police. Not surprisingly, drug arrests often increase at local venues when the Grateful Dead are in town.

The use of hallucinogenic drugs at Grateful Dead concerts ties into the mythic model in two ways. One version of the model stems from the Ken Kesey style of drug use perhaps best described in Tom Wolfe's *The Electric Kool-Aid Acid Test*. This tradition advocates a free spirited, do-your-own-thing approach to the drug experience. The other tradition stems from the Timothy Leary style of drug use. Leary advocated a more introspective, spiritual use of hallucinogens which became a tool for self-actualization (Leary et al. 1964). Individuals at concert events enter the drug experience relatively unaware of these models and learn to define the experience based on interactions with people around them. In other words, people must learn the appropriate rules to interpret the drug experience (Becker 1953).

Evidence of each model can be observed at Grateful Dead concerts. I have seen Dead Heads who appear "crazy," urinate wherever they feel like it, or masturbate openly in the parking lot. I have also seen Dead Heads who appear more introspective or spiritual, particularly during the concert. Different individuals react differently to the drug experience depending on their own particular predisposition, but those who are inclined toward the spiritual use of this drug tend to refer to their connection to the Dead Head community in a spiritual way. One of my respondents expressed her feelings succinctly.

> When you're at a Grateful Dead show you get a definite feeling of oneness and belongingness that people in general are much nicer to you, much more open, much more trusting. . . . They'll smile at you openly without

> knowing you. And it just is a really intense feeling of belongingness that you fit in and you don't stand out.

Another respondent went even further:

> . . . It's almost a cleansing for me. I'm not religious, but it's a spiritual experience. It's a cleansing, you know it cleans me out, it opens me up, it lets me get a lot of things out of my system, you know, if I want to cry at a show, even though the music is fantastic, you know, suddenly I'll just let it out. . . .

My observations of Dead Heads lead me to believe that this form of spirituality is functionally equivalent to religious belief. This does not imply that Dead Heads are a religious group, but it does distinguish an interpretation of social reality that is given a sacred quality. Dead Heads create and believe in a system of values which reinforces their individual and group identities. This is, once again, related to the origins of the band and the search for alternative expressions of symbolic integration among the different elements of the counterculture (Hardwick 1973)[5].

I have further discovered that the mythic model surrounding this system of values is the basis for interpreting band iconography. Totemic symbols which stem from specific band iconography often deviate in form as they are recreated or recombined on T-shirts, bumper stickers, or posters, but they retain their symbolic significance. Three of the most popular symbols include the "steal your face" skull, the skeleton and roses, and tie-dye.

The "steal your face" skull is perhaps the most common Grateful Dead symbol. It first appeared on the *Steal Your Face* album released in 1968 and has become one of the most popular totemic representations of Dead Head identity. The whole symbol is encapsulated within a circle, inside of which is a skull with a circular cranium. This inner circle is divided into a red and a blue side by a white lightning bolt.

Initially, the color scheme struck me as an interesting reflection of the American origins of this phenomenon, but none of my respondents picked up on its symbolic relevance. They tended instead to focus on the lightning bolt as a symbol of power. Some associated it with the power behind loud music, but others associated it with the power of self-determination, emphasizing individual autonomy or self-actualization. These claims were based on the position of the lightning bolt inside the cranium. Power, in this sense, was seen as internal, not external.

One of my respondents carried this interpretation a step further, noting that, ". . . it's like life and death, the yin and the yang . . . there's always two opposing forces in the world. . . ." In this sense, the power of the lightning bolt was associated with spiritual enlightenment. This form of enlightenment stems specifically from the Chinese philosophy of yin and yang. The unity represented by the inner circle apparently carries the weight of this oriental philosophy with it. The symbolic unity inherent in this philosophy balances dualistically opposing categories, such as life and death, good and evil, or the sacred and the profane. The ambiguity of categories adds to the potency of this representation of unity because all oppositions are seen as a whole.

Another aspect of this unity reflects what one of my respondents referred to as the divisions in Dead Heads' social identity:

> A lot of Dead Heads have two lives . . . they are part of society and have jobs like doctors and make money and provide for their families, but they always have that red side, that carefree side that wants to go and give up everything and go with the Grateful Dead.

Here again, the emphasis is on unity. In sociological terms, this unity involves an integration of social roles leading to status consistency, or a balance of social obligations. But this may also be symbolic of a common unity underlying all social distinctions. This is implied in the name of this symbol, because when you steal someone's face, you symbolically steal his or her identity. Without the distinguishing characteristics of identity, one is stripped of structured social distinctions and this may reinforce an ideal state of unity. Therefore, the skull may be seen as a common trait underlying the social and physical diversity of the human species, or at least of Dead Heads.

The skeleton and roses symbol adds a new dimension to this interpretation. According to Dennis McNally,[6] publicist for the band, the design is a derivation of an eighteenth-century print which appeared on the *Skeleton and Roses* album released in 1971. On this album cover, the full-bodied skeleton was surrounded with red roses, some of which intertwined around the skull to form a crown. No relationship between the crown of thorns and the crown of roses is apparent, but the image was acknowledged by one of my respondents who referred to it in reference to "the Jesus Christ archetype."

This is not too farfetched when one takes into account a view of the red rose as a sign of life, beauty, and love. Love is an important part of the emotional content of the Dead Head community and is expressed in many ways. During the concert ritual, Dead Heads can often be observed hugging each other and saying "I love you." Dead Heads also express feelings of "brotherhood" or "sisterhood" they feel they share with each other. These familial expressions are not uncommon and may themselves imply a sibling-type relationship among the audience under the parental guidance and love of the band. As another one of my respondents stated, "The most important thing about being a Dead Head is that we all love the music . . . and we love each other. It's one big happy family." Love reinforces and solidifies Dead Head identity and is another aspect of the mythic model.

Tie-dye is yet another symbolic representation commonly found in this ritual setting. Its origins are difficult to trace, but it became a very popular form of expression within the hippie subculture (Perry 1984). Currently, at Grateful Dead concerts, it is seen on most articles of clothing, but particularly on T-shirts. The designs are very colorful and are often the background for other artistic derivations of Grateful Dead symbols, such as the "steal your face" skull or skeleton and roses.

The totemic characteristics of tie-dye as a sign of membership are underscored by the wide variety of designs. The many variations of tie-dye allow for individual expressions and creative invention while conforming to a recognizable form. Or, as one of my respondents noted, "Every single person is different. Every tie-dye is different, and every Grateful Dead show is different. So it's kind of like a microcosm of the whole thing."

Currently tie-dyes have become very popular outside of the Dead Head subculture. The diffusion of this symbol into other cultural fields may imply a broader significance, but among Dead Heads it is a representation of their membership within a community that shares a particular set of values encoded in a mythic model. This model symbolically incorporates elements of humanist philosophy and Eastern religious doctrines, resulting in a system of belief that combines values associated with self-fulfillment and enlightenment, and values that recognize human potential and creativity to form an encompassing worldview. This is symbolically reinforced and maintained by Dead Head interaction at each concert ritual.

The Structure of Grateful Dead Concert Rituals

Grateful Dead concert rituals are structured events which frame and enhance a liminoid atmosphere that symbolically separates individuals in both space and time from their ordinary social lives. At concert sites, individuals are separated from their previous social positions as delineated by obligations associated with their role-sets, status-sets, and as members of particular social groups. Initially, the pilgrimage to the event separates individuals from their previous social context of home or work and this may be prolonged depending on the number of concerts one plans to attend. This separation may be further marked by a change in apparel. It also includes a level of detachment from the role responsibilities of the previous social context.

Dead Heads themselves sometimes refer to this as an "escape from reality." One of my respondents said, "It's like two hours of nonreality . . . that's why I like to go to concerts, because I forget about everything. Hopefully, I will forget about everything and just get away from it all and have fun." Concert dates may, in fact, coincide with other days of ritual observance, such as Halloween or New Year's Eve, and this adds to the liminoid dimension of the concert ritual.

The structure of Grateful Dead concert rituals generally follows an internal pattern comprised of two musical sets. The more experienced Dead Heads recognize that Jerry Garcia, lead guitarist, and Bob Weir, rhythm guitarist, alternate songs so that whoever starts the first set begins the pattern of alternating song selection for the rest of the concert. They also alternate this starting role by show, so that Jerry Garcia begins one night and Bob Weir begins the next night. Dead Heads often label these alternating shows as "Jerry's night" or "Bobby's night."[7]

The first set is separated from the second set by a brief intermission or "break" that allows members of the audience to wander around and seek out friends with whom to share first-set experiences. Band trivia and set lists are often exchanged at this time as well as after the show. This trivia is one means of establishing in-group identity. Drugs are often taken or retaken at this time.[8] Marijuana is generally smoked throughout the concert, but during intermission, more intimate rites of exchange develop around the sharing of this drug. LSD may also be taken or retaken at this time in preparation for the second set, which is generally regarded as the highlight of the ritual performance.

Hallucinogenic drugs combine with musical improvisation and enhance the liminoid characteristics of these concert rituals. Music, according to Dobkin de Rios (1984), acts like a "jungle gym" for the consciousness during drug states and ". . . may be a very important part of the hallucinogenic experience in that the jungle gym is built up, torn down, and rearranged, in a sort of 'block-building' of consciousness to serve specific cultural goals" (Dobkin de Rios 1984:209).

Participation in the concert ritual culminates during the second set, which reestablishes rapport through longer, more improvisationally oriented songs. It is not uncommon for these songs to blend together for twenty to thirty minutes, leading into a drum duet and free-form jam referred to as the "drums/space" part of the show. During this part of the show, my respondents tended to express their connection with each other and with the music. One stated that, ". . . it sort of feels like they take that nerve that's in the back of your head . . . and someone just sort of reaches in and takes it and jiggles it and this complete euphoria comes over you."

These feelings are also expressed through dancing. Dancing is, in fact, the most common form of participation in the concert ritual. The more enthusiastic dancers usually meet on the periphery where there is more room for elaborate body movements. Dancing occurs in crowded areas too, although it is restricted to upper-body movements due to a lack of space. This improvisational dance follows the improvisational form of the music and allows for active participation in the ritual performance.

Dancing also induces a flow experience that is shared and collectively expressed as a form of communitas (Csikszentmihalyi and Hendin 1975). The whole concert ritual, in fact, frames and enhances the liminoid in such a way as to provide an atmosphere that allows for communitas. Liminoid settings in themselves do not create communitas, but provide an atmosphere that allows for such a reconstruction of social relationships. During the actual concert performance, communitas may be generated more or less spontaneously, particularly during the second set, and those who experience it often attribute sacred qualities to it (Farwell 1976; Turner 1969). Rituals allow individuals to communicate these sentiments and, in this way, they facilitate the suspension of structured social relations and allow for a more basic, generic type of social interaction or communion (Turner 1969, 1973, 1975, 1982, Doty 1986, Black 1972, Campbell 1988, Hill 1975, Bird 1980).

The Functions of Grateful Dead Concert Rituals

Economically, Grateful Dead concerts operate as part of the entertainment industry that profits from the production and consumption of this commodity in a market economy (Frith 1981). Grateful Dead concerts are part of this industry, but profits are not the only motivation for continued concert performances. Together, the band and the audience symbolically channel and focus collective sentiments through the concert ritual. Over time, these stylized forms of expression have become entrusted with meaning derived from a particular system of beliefs, and the concert ritual has become the medium for communicating and expressing these beliefs.

Grateful Dead concert rituals function primarily as occasions for celebrating the values and beliefs central to Dead

Head identity. They channel and focus emotionally charged sentiments relative to these beliefs, and symbolically foster attachments to a social group that provides a source, or at least a partial source, of personal and collective identification. Dead Heads express their identification through dress, behavior, and attitude, even against the resistance of others in the larger social context.

In fact, the Dead Head community has been responsive to larger cultural changes, particularly the more conservative climate of the 1980s, which may be seen to have helped solidify the Dead Head community. This, combined with the near fatal drug overdose of Jerry Garcia and the subsequent release of the very popular 1987 album *In the Dark*, actually created a surge in the Dead Head population. New and younger people were beginning to join the community.

Repetition of concert events promotes opportunities for continued interaction and allows new members to learn the appropriate forms of expression relative to the interpretive rules Dead Heads use to understand reality. The generational transmission of this cultural information is adaptive to historical circumstance and is an important component in the survival of the concert phenomenon.

Grateful Dead concert rituals serve different functions for different individuals at different times. For some of the newer, younger Dead Heads, concert rituals may be seen as a rite of passage into the Dead Head community. For others, the concert ritual may be an occasion for celebrating or reaffirming their membership in the Dead Head community. In a spiritual sense, this may resemble purification rites or cleansing rituals, or it may be a simple communion with one's conception of the sacred.

Dead Heads integrate these values and sentiments into their lives in varying degrees and therefore express different levels of commitment and identification with the Dead Head community. But, as one respondent noted:

> I think everybody has it in them, it's just a matter of bringing it out and you need a place that's secure that you have reinforcement, that finally brings it out. That brings you to a point where you can say . . . this is what I believe and that doesn't mean that going along with the crowd is

> always right, but if you have a hunch to begin with, then that's what you believe in and you go and you check it out and you find other people that believe in it too.

Most Dead Heads share parts of the mythic ideal, but not all people who share this ideal are Dead Heads. The concert experience is, therefore, meaningful on different levels for different individuals, and may even be different for the same individual at different times.

Conclusion

In this paper I have argued that Dead Heads are a particular type of youth subculture with a collective identity that is based on more than a simple appreciation of the music of the Grateful Dead, but which revolves primarily around the concert ritual. Dead Heads draw on the unique history of the band to meaningfully interpret the concert experience and, in this way, they actively create and maintain a sense of identity and adapt to modern social life.

Dead Head identity is more than a reflection of the hippie rebellion against the underlying values of the status quo—middle class morality, the hard work ethic, the success image, and conventional religion (Klapp 1970). Although Dead Heads tend to reflect the demographic composition of their hippie predecessors, at least in terms of race and social class, they are more diverse in terms of age due to the longevity of the concert ritual experience. Dead Head identity is, therefore, more of a contemporary adaptation encoded in a mythic model that establishes a basis for meaning and belief.

Myths, in general, are collective projections or externalizations of shared internal experiences. As such, they provide the members of a believing community with a library of scripts upon which individuals may inspire, judge, or critique the internal drama of their multiple identities (Bruner 1960:281). Myths are, in this sense, collective psychic models for interpreting everyday experience and making sense out of the world and one's place in it (Doty 1986).

The Dead Head mythic model is dramatically enacted at concert rituals, which provide the stage for collectively sharing and reinforcing the values central to the model. Concert rituals promote a liminoid atmosphere which symbolically separates individual participants from ordinary social life so that they may more fully participate in the dramatic enactment. This separation is marked by a change in apparel and includes a level of detachment from the role responsibilities of previous social contexts. Drugs, particularly LSD, facilitate this separation and enhance the qualities of the liminoid.

The liminoid dimension of Grateful Dead concert rituals frames the symbolic expressions of sacred collective sentiments. These are manifest and preserved as a type of communitas (Turner 1969). Communitas exists in a kind of "figure-ground" relationship with social structure insofar as they are defined by contact or comparison with the other (Turner 1982). Communitas contrasts structure and allows individuals to interact without the burdens of socially structured divisions. In so doing, it provides a mechanism for the periodic evaluation of both the social structure and the more philosophical conditions of human interconnectedness. Ironically, groups who experience communitas often impose normative or ideological constraints upon it so that these groups separate themselves as symbolic in-groups within the larger social context (Turner 1977a). In large, modern, heterogeneous societies, this bricolage can be seen as the product of a series of adaptive responses by participating individuals to meaningfully interpret the variety of their life experiences within the dominant sociocultural system (Levi-Strauss 1966).

Youth subcultures develop, in this respect, as an adaptive response to identity pressures originating from their culturally defined position in the life course (Brake 1985; Coleman 1963; Klapp 1969). Social divisions and cultural beliefs separate youth subcultures as different in-groups. Music plays an important role in establishing and maintaining these divisions because it embodies and reflects aspects of these divisions (Lewis 1982, 1987; Frith 1981; Martin 1979). Participation in concert rituals, therefore, enhances feelings of solidarity and empowerment, and maintains the boundaries between different youth groups. These groups then compete for membership and legitimacy in the broader social and cultural marketplace.

Musical tastes, in themselves, do not create youth subcultures; they are a reflection of them. Music, in this case, is a function of the life-styles and mythologies of youth groups, and must be consistent with, and adapt to, those life-styles and mythologies in order to be appropriated by the group (Weinstein 1991:99). In this paper I have described Dead Head subculture, outlining some of the beliefs that influence Dead Head behavior and their relationship to the concert ritual. Other subcultures can be seen reflected by the musical tastes of rap (Rose 1989) and heavy metal (Weinstein 1991; Gaines 1990). These groups share a ritual format that revolves around live concert performances.

This raises interesting questions, in a broader sense, about identity salience and the degree to which someone may claim multiple or overlapping group memberships (Brake 1985). This line of empirical questioning should also address the differences between being a member of a subculture and being a member of an audience with limited or no subcultural ties (Weinstein 1991:98). In other words, to what degree is someone a member of a particular subculture? These considerations should be the basis for further investigations into the constructions of youth subcultures and the comparative nature and role of music in the lives of adolescents and youths.

NOTES

1. I view both secular and religious rituals in terms of the sacred, which is socially constructed and, therefore, historically and culturally variable. This conception allows for a broader interpretation of ritual activity than the traditional model based solely on religious and secular distinctions. See Moore and Myerhoff (1977) for more information on this fourfold classification.

2. Flow is a holistic sensation present when we act with total involvement. Flow experiences are tied to intrinsically rewarding activities which are often, but not solely, associated with leisure or play.

See Csikszentmihalyi (1975) for a more detailed outline of flow experiences.

3. Special thanks to the Department of Continuing Education at the University of North Carolina at Greensboro and to Rebecca Adams.

4. Some of my respondents mentioned the Rainbow Family in this respect. They are a group of communalists who gather every year in early July to celebrate their interpretation of these lifestyle values.

5. According to Hardwick, "symbolic integration is . . . that set of meanings, purposes, and ideals, celebrated in cult and ritual and enacted in everyday life, by means of which a society and thus the individuals in it, articulate their social solidarity and understand the vicissitudes of historical, social, and personal life" (Hardwick 1973:290). This definition is historically based on a functionalist interpretation of religion, but is broad enough to include secular equivalents. See also Peter Berger, *The Sacred Canopy: Elements of a Sociological Theory of Religion*. Garden City, NY: Doubleday, 1967.

6. Dennis McNally made himself available for questioning in Buffalo and at Alpine Valley in 1989 during the second stage of data collection for this project. His cooperation was greatly appreciated.

7. Song selection is important to Dead Heads. Many keep track of set lists that date back to the early years of the band. These have been compiled into a collection called *Dead Base IV* (Scott et al. 1990). Statistical information concerning the frequency of songs played, where they are located in each set, and when they have been played, are also available in this volume. Knowledge of set lists may also be seen as a form of cultural capital. Fiske (1992) borrows this term from Bourdieu (1984) but applies it to fans in popular culture, rather than in high culture. By extension, this can be seen to establish status among Dead Heads.

The band also allows their concerts to be taped and special taper sections are usually designated just behind the sound board. Tapes are verifiable evidence of song selection and exchanging them builds social networks and preserves the live concert experience.

8. It should be noted here that not all Dead Heads consume drugs. In fact, there are a group of Dead Heads called the Wharf Rats who do not use drugs and meet during intermission to encourage each other's sobriety (Epstein and Sardiello 1990).

REFERENCES

Becker, Howard. 1953. "Becoming a Marihuana User." *American Journal of Sociology* 59:235–242.

Berger, Peter, and Thomas Luckmann. 1966. *The Social Construction of Reality: A Treatise in the Sociology of Knowledge.* New York: Anchor.

Bird, Frederick. 1980. "The Contemporary Ritual Milieu." Pp. 19–35 in *Rituals and Ceremonies in Popular Culture,* ed. Ray Browne. Bowling Green, OH: Bowling Green University Popular Press.

Black, Mary. 1972. "Belief Systems." Pp. 509–577 in *Handbook of Social and Cultural Anthropology,* ed. J.J. Honigmann. Chicago: Rand McNally Co.

Bourdieu, Pierre. 1984. *Distinction: A Social Critique of the Judgement of Taste.* Cambridge: Harvard University Press.

Brake, Mike. 1980. *The Sociology of Youth Culture and Youth Subculture: Sex and Drugs and Rock 'n' Roll.* Boston: Routledge and Kegan Paul.

———. 1985. *Comparative Youth Culture: The Sociology of Youth Cultures and Youth Subcultures in America, Britain, and Canada.* Boston: Routledge and Kegan Paul.

Bruner, Jerome S. 1960. "Myth and Identity." Pp. 276–287 in *Myth and Mythmaking,* ed. Henry A. Murray. New York: George Braziller.

Campbell, Joseph. 1988. *The Power of Myth/Joseph Campbell with Bill Moyers.* Ed. Betty Sue Flowers. New York: Doubleday.

Clarke, J. 1976. "The Skinheads and the Magical Recovery of Community." Pp. 99–102 in *Resistance Through Ritual: Youth Subcultures in Post-War Britain,* ed. Stuart Hall and Tony Jefferson. London: Hutchinson.

Coleman, James. 1963. *The Adolescent Society.* New York: The Free Press.

Csikszentmihalyi, Mihaly. 1975. "Play and Intrinsic Rewards." *Journal of Humanistic Psychology* 15 (3):41–63.

Csikszentmihalyi, Mihaly and Judy Hendin. 1975. "Measuring the Flow Experience in Rock Dancing." Pp. 102–122 in *Beyond Boredom and Anxiety,* ed. Mihaly Cskszentmihalyi. San Francisco: Jossey-Bas.

Denisoff, R. Serge, and John Bridges. 1983. "The Sociology of Popular Music: A Review." *Popular Music and Society* 9(1):51–62.

Dobkin de Rios, Marlene. 1984. *Hallucinogens: Cross-Cultural Perspectives.* Albuquerque: University of New Mexico Press.

Dotter, Daniel. 1987. "Growing Up Is Hard to Do: Rock and Roll Performers as Cultural Heroes." *Sociological Spectrum* 7:25–44.

Doty, William G. 1986. *Mythography: A Study of Myths and Rituals*. Tuscaloosa: The University of Alabama Press.

Durkheim, Emile. 1915. *The Elementary Forms of Religious Life*. Trans. J.W. Swain. New York: The Free Press.

Elkin, Frederick, and Gerald Handel. 1989. *The Child and Society: The Process of Socialization*. New York: Random House.

Epstein, Jonathon, and Robert Sardiello. 1990. "The Wharf Rats: A Preliminary Examination of Alcoholics Anonymous and the Grateful Dead Head Phenomena." *Deviant Behavior* 11:245–257.

Farwell, L. J. 1976. *Betwixt and Between: The Anthropological Contributions of Mary Douglas and Victor Turner Toward a Renewal of Roman Catholic Ritual*. Ann Arbor, MI: University Microfilms.

Fiske, John. 1992. "The Cultural Economy of Fandom." Pp.30–49 in *The Adoring Audience: Fan Culture and Popular Media*, ed. Lisa A. Lewis. New York: Routledge.

Frey, James H., and David R. Dickens. 1990. "Leisure as a Primary Institution." *Sociological Inquiry* 60(3):264–273.

Frith, Simon. 1981. *Sound Effects: Youth, Leisure, and the Politics of Rock 'n' Roll*. New York: Pantheon Books.

Gaines, Donna. 1990. *Teenage Wasteland: Suburbia's Dead End Kids*. New York: Harper Perennial.

Gans, David and P. Simon. 1985. *Playing in the Band*. New York: St. Martin's.

Gans, Herbert. 1974. *Popular Culture and High Culture: An Analysis and Evaluation of Taste*. New York: Basic Books.

Geertz, Clifford. 1973. *The Interpretation of Culture*. New York: Basic Books.

Glaser, Barney G., and Anselm L. Strauss. 1965. "The Discovery of Substantive Theory: A Basic Strategy Underlying Qualitative Research." *The American Behavioral Scientist* 8(6):5–12.

Goodman, Fred. 1989. "The Rolling Stone Interview." *Rolling Stone* (November 30): 66–74.

Grof, Stanislav. 1977. "The Implications of Psychedelic Research for Anthropology: Observations from LSD Psychotherapy." Pp. 141–173 in *Symbols and Sentiments*, ed. Ioan. Lewis. New York: Academic Press.

Hardwick, Charley D. 1973. "The Counter-Culture as Religion: On the Identification of Religion." *Soundings* 56(3): 287–311.

Hebdige, Dick. 1976. "The Meaning of Mod." Pp. 87–96 in *Resistance Through Ritual: Youth Subcultures in Post-War Britain*, ed. Stuart. Hall and Tony. Jefferson. London: Hutchinson.

———. 1979. *Subculture: The Meaning of Style*. New York: Methuen.

Hewitt, John. 1989. *Dilemmas of the American Self.* Philadelphia: Temple University Press.

Hill, Carole E. 1975. *Symbols and Society: Essays on Belief Systems in Action*. Athens: University of Georgia Press.

Irwin, John. 1977. *Scenes*. Beverly Hills: Sage Publications.

Klapp, Orin E. 1969. *Collective Search for Identity*. New York: Holt, Rinehart and Winston.

———. 1970. "Style Rebellion and Identity Crisis." Pp. 69–80 in *Human Nature and Collective Behavior*, ed. Tamotsu Shibutani. Englewood Cliffs, NJ: Prentice-Hall.

Leary, Timothy, Ralph Metzner, and Richard Alpert. 1964. *The Psychedelic Experience: A Manual Based on the Tibetan Book of the Dead.* New Hyde Park, NY: University Books.

Levi-Strauss, Claude. 1966. *The Savage Mind*. Chicago: The University of Chicago Press.

Lewis, George. 1982. "Popular Music: Symbolic Resource and Transformer of Meaning in Society." *International Review of the Aesthetics and Sociology of Music* 13:183–189.

———. 1987. "Patterns of Meaning and Choice: Taste Cultures in Popular Music." Pp. 198–211 in *Popular Music and Communication*, ed. James Lull. Beverly Hills: Sage Publications.

Lull, James. 1987a. "Listeners' Communicative Uses of Popular Music." Pp. 140–174 in *Popular Music and Communication*, ed. James Lull. Beverly Hills: Sage Publications.

———. 1987b. "Popular Music and Communication: An Introduction." Pp. 10–35 in *Popular Music and Communication*, ed. James Lull. Beverly Hills: Sage Publications.

McNally, Dennis. 1980. "Meditations on the Grateful Dead." *San Francisco Sunday Examiner and Chronicle*, 28 September.

Martin, Bernice. 1979. "The Sacrilization of Disorder: Symbolism in Rock Music." *Sociological Analysis* 40(2):87–124.

Miracle, Andrew W., Jr. 1986. "Voluntary Ritual as Recreational Therapy: A Study of the Baths at Hot Springs Arkansas." Pp.

164–171 in *The Many Faces of Play*, ed. Kendall Blanchard. Illinois: Human Kinetics Publishers Inc.

Montague, Susan P., and Robert Morais. 1976. "Football Games and Rock Concerts: The Ritual Enactment." Pp. 33–52 in *The American Dimension: Cultural Myths and Social Realities*, ed. William Arens and Susan P. Montague. Sherman Oaks, CA: Alfred Publishing Co.

Moore, Sally, and Barbara Myerhoff. 1977. *Secular Ritual*. Asson, The Netherlands: Van Gorcum.

Munn, Nancy D. 1972. "Symbolism in a Ritual Context: Aspects of Symbolic Action." Pp. 579–612 in *Handbook of Symbolic and Cultural Anthropology*, ed. J.J. Honigmann. Chicago: Rand McNally Co.

Pearson, Anthony. 1987. "The Grateful Dead Phenomenon: An Ethnomethodological Approach." *Youth and Society* 18(4):418–432.

Perry, Charles. 1984. *The Haight-Ashbury*. New York: Random House.

Peterson, Richard. A., and Paul Di Maggio. 1975. "From Region to Class: The Changing Locus of Country Music." *Social Forces* 53:497–506.

Rose, Tricia. 1989. "Orality and Technology: Rap Music and Afro-American Cultural Resistance." *Popular Music and Society* 13(4):35–44.

Savage, Charles, James Fadiman, Robert Mogar and Mary H. Allen. 1966. "The Effects of Psychedelic (LSD) Therapy on Values, Personality, and Behavior." *International Journal of Neuropsychiatry* 2(3):241–254.

Schechter, Harold. 1983. "The Myth of the Eternal Child in Sixties' America." Pp. 81–95 in *The Popular Culture Reader*, ed. Christopher D. Geist and Jack Nachbar. Bowling Green, OH: Bowling Green University Popular Press.

Scott, John. W., Mike Dolgushkin, and Stu Nixon. 1990. *Dead Base IV: The Complete Guide to Grateful Dead Song Lists*. Hanover, NH.

Sebald, Hans. 1984. *Adolescences: A Social Psychological Analysis*. Englewood Cliffs, NJ: Prentice-Hall.

Turner, Victor. 1968. "Myth and Symbol." *International Encyclopedia of the Social Sciences* 10:576–582.

———. 1969. *The Ritual Process: Structure and Anti-Structure*. Chicago: Aldine.

———. 1973. "The Center Out There: The Pilgrim's Goal." *History of Religion* 12(3):191–230.

———. 1975. "Ritual as Communication and Potency: A Ndembu Case Study." Pp. 58–81 in *Symbols and Society: Essays on Belief Systems in Action*, ed. Carole E. Hill. Athens: University of Georgia Press.

———. 1977a. "Variations on a Theme of Liminality." Pp. 36–52 in *Secular Ritual*, ed. Sally F. Moore and Barbara G. Myerhoff. The Netherlands: Van Gorcum.

———. 1977b. "Symbols in African Ritual." Pp. 183–194 in *Symbolic Anthropology: A Reader in the Study of Symbols and Meanings*, ed. D. Kemnitzer, J. Dolgin, and D. Schneider. New York: Columbia University Press.

———. 1978. "Comments and Conclusions." Pp. 276–296 in *The Reversible World*, ed. B. Bobcock. Ithaca, New York: Cornell University Press.

———. 1982. *From Ritual to Theatre: The Human Seriousness of Play*. New York: Performing Arts Journal Publications.

Van Gennep, Arnold. 1960. *The Rites of Passage*, trans. Monika B. Bizedom and Gabrielle L. Coffee. Chicago: University of Chicago Press.

Weinstein, Deena. 1991. *Heavy Metal: A Cultural Sociology*. New York: Lexington Books.

Willis, P. 1976. "The Cultural Meaning of Drug Use." Pp. 106–118 in *Resistance Through Ritual: Youth Subculture in Post-War Britain*, ed. Stuart Hall and Tony Jefferson. London: Hutchinson.

Wolfe, Tom. 1968. *The Electric Kool-Aid Acid Test*. New York: Bantam Books.

The Postmodernization of Rock and Roll Music: The Case of Metallica

Joseph A. Kotarba

I have been a Metallica fan since 1988, when they issued their breakthrough album, *... And Justice for All*. Although I had been aware of this group's exhilarating speed metal music for several years, there was something very special about this album and what it had to say about the state of rock and roll at the end of the decade. Metallica gained considerable notoriety within the rock industry for selling over one million copies of *... And Justice for All*, in spite of the fact that it received very little radio airplay (Fricke 1989). And the rock and roll press was replete with stories about the way Metallica enhanced speed metal's—and consequently its parental musical style, heavy metal's—credibility and respectability with politically attuned songs such as the title track and "Blackened," a warning about the pending environmental disaster (see Weinstein 1992, pp. 50–51).

These observations suggest that *... And Justice for All* is special because of the way speed metal progressed under Metallica's creative tutelage. This rock and roll genre had been long identified as loud, fast, mindless, pubescent, sometimes satanic, and always raucous—neatly personified by the Ozzy Osbournes, David Lee Roths, and other sleazes of the rock world. But now, speed heavy metal had become almost, well, an art form!

I don't buy any of this romanticized conjecture. My sense of specialness is gut level, or shall I say ear and eye level. As a fan, I feel that Metallica and their music are special because of a certain primitiveness they render, not any linear and modernist movement towards artistic perfection. This primitiveness defines the essence of the relationship between Metallica and its fans, a relationship in which Metallica's music resonates with the deepest feelings and thoughts of its audience. As a sociologist, I am drawn to the dynamics by which Metallica serves as a primary cultural resource for many of its audience members. This cultural resource provides viable meanings for life, its problems and its possibilities. The purpose of this essay is to describe the ways this relationship marks Metallica analytically and artistically as a prototypical rock and roll band of the contemporary 1990s period.

My perception of the special relationship between Metallica and its fans originated in an ethnographic study of the delivery of emergency medical services at large rock music festivals (Kotarba and Hurt 1993). The first stage of the study took place at Rice University Stadium on a hot July day in 1988. Approximately 45,000 heavy metal fans braved the summer sun to witness the Monsters of Rock tour. The concert featured an all-star lineup of bands, including Kingdom Come, the Scorpions, Dokken, Metallica and the headliners, Van Halen, with their new lead singer, Sammy Hagar.

As a sociologist of health, I was interested in examining the strategies by which teams of paramedic workers creatively adapt traditional emergency health care procedures to the specific problems incurred in a hostile environment. I analyzed this form of health care metaphorically, as if it were battlefield medicine. Much of our work involved retrieving heat-exhausted kids from the pit over a five-foot-high wooden security fence (with the help of numerous 250-pound security guards); loading them onto twenty-five folding canvas cots lined up in a triage area that would make Florence Nightingale proud, located under the massive stage; cooling them down with ice packs; filling them up with Gatorade to restore electrolytes and fluids; and sending them back into battle.

At approximately 5:00 P.M., Metallica came onstage. I was down in the moat between the stage and the fence observing two guards on the perimeter of the stage delivering preventive health care (i.e., hosing down the kids caught up in the slam dancing pit before they could overheat). I was in a spot to observe a distinct change in the temperament and flow of the crowd. To this point, the kids had been very much in a party mood, enjoying the music, the event, and the excitement. When Metallica began their set, bodies ceased to move and everyone's attention seemed to shift to the *stories* being told. Thousands of fourteen-, fifteen-, and sixteen-year-old kids, mostly boys, almost all attired in appropriate black T-shirt, did not so much sing along with Metallica as they *spoke* along. Song after song, the kids moved their lips in sync as they collectively tuned into another reality. This reality was not predicated by drugs, alcohol, or sensuality but by the ability of the narrative to collectively conceptualize individual experiences of growing up.

I witnessed a similar collective narrative at the Guns n' Roses concert held in the Summit in early 1992. During the break between the leadoff group (Kings' X) and the headliners, the stadium sound people played the expected four or five stadium rock songs as fans took time out for a beer and a trip to the men's or women's room. When the first few distinctive chords of Metallica's anthem "Enter Sandman" came over the public address system, the kids issued the expected deafening applause for a top MTV heavy metal hit song. Yet, when James Hetfield began singing the words, the kids spoke along at a level of volume and bravado that seemed to proclaim defiantly to a real world populated by parents, teachers, and other adults: "We may not care to know the words to your commandments and your grammars, but, believe it or not, we know the words to 'Enter Sandman'!"

A sociological reading of Metallica involves a discussion of their particularly intense relationship with fans, the centrality of lyrical narrative to this relationship, and the band's reflection of the state of rock and roll in the 1990s. Moreover, an adequate reading of Metallica requires a conceptual apparatus that accounts for the fact that this phenomenon is occurring in the postmodern cultural period marked by flux and paradox, openness and diversity. I will argue Metallica is not only archetypical of heavy metal music, but also of all rock and roll, which is an essential feature of and the very soundtrack to American culture. This admittedly broad claim is plausible to the degree we can liberate ourselves from conventional ways of conceptualizing rock and roll as a form of adolescent or youth culture, and an exclusive possession of youth.

Journalistic and Sociological Criticism of Heavy Metal

The cover of the August 13, 1987 issue of *Rolling Stone* magazine carries a picture of Mötley Crüe, one of the most popular heavy metal bands, with the following appropriate headline: "HEAVY METAL: It's Loud, It's Ugly, It Won't Go Away." Heavy metal is a style of very loud, very fast, guitar-driven rock music. Arriving at a more precise definition of heavy metal is difficult because, as Deena Weinstein notes in her ground-breaking sociological examination of the genre (1991, p.5), it is more of a bricolage than any unified musical style of subculture. Varieties or subgenres of heavy metal include light metal, cheese metal, pop metal, death metal, Christian metal, and the subgenre of special interest in this chapter, speed metal.

The specific roots of heavy metal have been traced to the late 1960s and early 1970s white British, blues-inspired bands such as the Yardbirds and Led Zeppelin (Russell 1983). Current popular bands include AC/DC, Van Halen, Poison, Megadeth, and Iron Maiden, among many others. Only with exceptions, such as Living Colour, heavy metal bands are comprised exclusively of male musicians, commonly attired in outfits ranging from black-on-black to spandex but with universally accepted and desired long hair.

Heavy metal is extremely popular, perhaps the single most popular style of rock today. Heavy metal is rarely played on mainstream FM rock radio stations, which ordinarily prefer more mainstream pop or power pop bands such as U2, Genesis, and R.E.M. Syndicated heavy metal programming designated as "Z-Rock" has emerged from Dallas, Texas, over the past few years to satisfy the apparent market demand. Yet this programming is often broadcast over low-power AM stations, as has been the case in Houston. Only recently has the great popularity of heavy metal been formally acknowledged. In May 1991, *Billboard* magazine, the traditional monitor of pop music consumption, responded to years of criticism by changing its method for gauging record sales. Instead of relying on a questionably representative sampling of retail outlets, the new system, known as Soundscan, attempts to measure all record sales. In any event, the new system quickly highlighted the true marketing power of heavy metal. After several years of chart dominance by dance music and rap, *Billboard*'s album chart was now led by Skid Row, Van Halen, Guns n' Roses and, most recently, Metallica (Powis 1992).

In spite of (or perhaps because of) high record sales and concert attendance, rock music critics have been merciless in their condemnation of heavy metal music and its fans. Ironically, the most telling attacks have come from both the religious right and the liberal-left rock critics (Weinstein 1992, p. 3). The former generally base their attacks on moral grounds, whereas the latter are especially significant for the present discussion because they invoke aesthetic criteria. Quite frequently, the critics pan heavy metal albums and concert performances because of or in terms of heavy metal fans. The argument is that heavy metal can't amount to much artistically since it attracts an audience (allegedly) comprised almost totally of fifteen- and sixteen-year-old, working-class males who believe their aspirations to masculine adulthood can be fulfilled by means of Eddie Van Halen's meteoric guitar work. In addition, the critics view heavy metal as commercial, banal, sexist, violent and—perhaps worst of all—excessively loud.

In summary, the critics have traditionally panned heavy metal music on aesthetic grounds. Either the music or the audience (or both) are distasteful to the critics. These assessments are usually made without lending credence to or paying much attention to the audience's appreciation for the music. The social class standing of an audience is clearly more relevant to the critical enterprise than audience taste. A good current example of this elitism is the surprisingly warm reception critics have been giving to grunge metal groups. This variety of hard rock (or heavy metal, if you will) involves extremely loud and ferocious music, sometimes almost devoid of melody. Grunge rockers have replaced traditional black-jeans-and-spandex metal garb with flannel shirts and ratty jeans.

Major groups in this genre include Helmet, Soundgarden, Hole, and Nirvana. Although one would be hard pressed to say that grunge is somehow "better" than traditional heavy metal artistically or any other way, the critics generally like it. The missing piece of this puzzle is the demographic profile of the audience: middle-class, college-oriented, and otherwise socially respectable and desirable kids with whom critics prefer to identify. Heavy metal magically becomes respectable when it and its audience is placed under the rubric "alternative" (see Azerrad 1992).

In spite of the overall lack of enthusiasm shown to it by critics, the gatekeepers of the rock culture cannot readily dismiss heavy metal music anymore. Even the Grammy Awards have deigned to provide heavy metal with the recognition of its own prize category. Even Michael Jackson has incorporated metal styles and touches into his recent pop-dance-video-tribal musical stew/extravaganza, *Dangerous*.

Given the dramatic presence of heavy metal on the American cultural landscape, this genre should certainly be of interest to sociologists, and it is. In general, sociologists haven't devoted enormous attention to heavy metal music. The available literature does, however, portray heavy metal through three analytical frameworks. First, some academic observers (e.g., Cashmore, 1987) have agreed with their counterparts in the mass media, whom Weinstein (1992, p. 240) refers to as the "progressive critics," that heavy metal is a banal, sexist, and apolitical, if not conservative, rock style in contrast to other styles such as punk and progressive rock. Second, some sociologists do not address heavy metal directly, but instead invoke a classic, modernist, if you will, perspective to view heavy metal as an *indicator* of some underlying structural feature of society. For example, heavy metal is viewed as an indicator of the alienation of working-class youth who perceive their occupational and personal futures as problematic as best (e.g., Gaines 1991). Third, and most recently, some sociologists have come to appreciate heavy metal in its own right, to celebrate it as a legitimate art form to be defended. Deena Weinstein's work (1992) is most notable in this regard. Although passionately committed to the heavy metal genre and its fans, she coolly and objectively describes the historical and musical roots of heavy metal. She attempts to defuse the negative and often moralistic critics of heavy metal by reading its overall imagery as a form of music that affirms life, not destruction. Perhaps most relevant to the present study is the fact that Weinstein conducts her analysis with open appreciation for the perceptions, experiences and feelings of the heavy metal audience. She tempers the strong and appealing attraction sociologists feel when they are tempted to serve in the comfortable if speculative role of rock critic (see Kotarba 1989).

Two very important questions about heavy metal music escape current sociological thinking. First, what is the relationship between heavy metal music and the rock and roll phenomenon in general? Critics largely discuss this issue in terms of relative quality among rock genres, the musicological genealogy of rock genres, and so forth. The bigger-picture issue is the effect heavy metal has on the totality of the rock enterprise, especially the impact it has on the very definition of what rock and roll is in the 1990s. Second, what is the relationship between heavy metal music and the broader American culture? The big picture issue here is the relative centrality of heavy metal to our culture. Is heavy metal simply one of several musical possessions of youth, or does it "belong to" all generations by impacting the cultural experiences of all generations? In order to address these issues, I will invoke the postmodernist model of social/cultural analysis.

Heavy Metal Music as a Feature of Postmodern Culture

Various ideas, ways of speaking, and statements of problems which fall under the rubric "postmodernism" have been enjoying increasing presence within the sociological enterprise over the past few years. Postmodernism may in fact turn out to be the single most influential new theoretical development in our discipline since ethnomethodology introduced us to realities like accounts, indexicality, and reflexivity in the late 1960s. Invoking a postmodernist viewpoint as a method for analyzing cultural phenomena can, however, be like jumping into an intellectual snakepit. Postmodernism is a word that has taken on a life of its own over the past few years, meaning lots of different things to lots of different people. As Dick Hebdige (1988:181–182), who is otherwise quite sympathetic to the postmodern impulse, cynically observes, postmodernism has become a buzzword used to "designate a plethora of incommensurable objects, tendencies, emergencies." Risking the wrath of purists who abhor naively oversimplified efforts to generate textbook definitions for this rather sacred term, I offer the following as a practical effort to move my discussion along (see Kotarba 1989).

The term "postmodernism" originated in the fields of architecture, art, and literary criticism, and has been used two different ways in those disciplines as well as in sociology. First, it refers to a particular period in Western civilization, the contemporary period, in which traditional modernist culture has been eroded by the mass media (Jameson 1984). Modern culture, coinciding with the industrial age, stood independent of, reflected, made reference to, conceptualized, criticized, promoted, and was based upon the assumption of the existence of an underlying reality. In the postmodern period, culture *is* reality. Images presented by the all-pervasive mass media proliferate and constantly reproduce themselves. As Jean Baudrillard (1983) has argued, contemporary reality is *hyperreality*, a state in which images, illusions, phantasms, logics, illogics, signs, and signals all take on a life of their own and are able to coexist fairly comfortably. These elements of culture require no universal criteria of truthfulness in order to gain plausibility and taken-for-granted acceptability by their audiences.

Second, postmodernism refers to a particular style—or more accurately, styles—of studying, analyzing, and theorizing about our contemporary social and cultural condition. The postmodern project treats social and cultural phenomena as texts, to be read, interpreted, and deconstructed. There is no one ultimate or master reading of any phenomenon. Ideally, the postmodernist observer is careful not to portray his or her reading as truth, but merely as one observer's statement emerging from a particular—and not necessarily privileged—biographical, epistemological, and historical perspective. The work of the postmodernist sociologist becomes proximate to that of the literary or art critic. Of all the different features of social life available for study (e.g., structural features such as social classes and institutions), the postmodernist sociologist chooses to study culture. Or, the postmodernist sociologist chooses to conceptualize or "see" the topic of interest in cultural terms (Kotarba 1991; see also Clifford 1988).

Although both definitions of postmodernism are relevant to the present work, the former definition is critical because of my claim that Metallica is a prime example of a postmodern rock and roll band. Steven Connor (1989) correctly notes that the examination of rock music as a form of postmodern culture uncovers more paradox than simple clarification. For example, postmodern rock supports and even fosters plurality of style and cultural identities. Musical styles which would ordinarily lie at the margins of modern, hegemonic capitalistic culture are given a voice in the media. Connor cites Caribbean reggae and Chicano music; rap might be a more current example. Yet the performers who are cited as examples of this process, by sheer reason of their visibility and availability to serve as examples for arguments like this, are themselves capitalistic success stories!

Connor suggests that the major problem facing the application of the postmodern viewpoint to rock and roll is that of historical scope. Is all rock and roll postmodern, or are certain songs or performances occurring at certain times in the history of rock postmodern? Given that rock and roll emerged following World War II concurrently with the youth culture, the first postulate is supported. From the days of Little Richard, Buddy Holly, Carl Perkins, and Chuck Berry, rock and roll always fulfilled postmodernism's principles of parody and pastiche. Nevertheless, major writings on the topic have singled out particular bands and music as postmodern in a field of either modernistic rock or no rock at all, assuming the analytical "death" of rock and roll in the early 1970s. I'll give two of the better examples of these writings, and then I'll suggest a third position that incorporates the audience's experience of rock and roll into a postmodernist analysis.

Lawrence Grossberg (1983) introduced one of the most powerful ideas in the scholarly discussion of rock and roll when he located rock's essence in its ability to empower its audiences through the production of affective alliances. These alliances are "organization(s) of concrete material practices and events, cultural forms and social experience which both opens and structures the space of our affective investments in the world" (105). I interpret Grossberg to mean that rock and roll is most powerful and useful to its audiences when it forges links between otherwise disparate groups or cultures. For example, youth were empowered to coalesce as a social, cultural, economic, and, at least during the late 1960s, political force when white suburban kids could "get into" inner-city, Mississippi-bred, electrified black blues. The power of both blacks and whites was enhanced through this cultural melding. The magic of rock and roll lies in its ability to separate youth from the hegemonic adult world.

Grossberg, like many other lay and professional observers, is cynical about the role of rock music in the contemporary world. He fears that rock and roll has been co-opted, that the commercialization of rock by the adult, late capitalistic economy has taken away what was perhaps its greatest gift to kids: their ability to be different from adults and adult culture. The punk movement of the late 1970s was rock's last large-scale attempt to celebrate itself. Groups such as The Clash and the Sex Pistols mark a postmodern moment of opposition to the cultural—and, therefore, political—structures of everyday life. Punk deconstructs the hegemonic greater world by deconstructing its own family—the world of rock and roll itself—and exposing rock's loss of its historical and critical cutting edge. Grossberg locates a glimmer of hope for rock and roll in certain performers who create contemporary music with the oppositional power of early rock and roll, performers such as Laurie Anderson, Bruce Springsteen and Echo and the Bunnymen.

Ann Kaplan (1987) presents us with an elegant reading of music television (MTV), beginning with a description of MTV as a commercial institution (which is becoming increasingly commercial), and ending with the conclusion that the contradictory aspects of MTV make it a truly postmodern phenomenon. In between, Kaplan identifies five distinct types of videos, largely on the basis of stylistic differences: romantic, socially conscious, nihilist, classical, and postmodernist. Again, Kaplan praises those videos in her postmodernist category that are avant-garde, such as those by the Talking Heads and Art of Noise, and satisfy adult aesthetic wants. Postmodernist videos are most notably marked by a melding of otherwise disparate elements, such as black and white with color, video with film, and old with new. Kaplan places heavy metal in her nihilist category. She argues that it is "anti-narrative," which I interpret to mean it not only does not convey a meaningful story of sorts, but opposes the telling of meaningful stories. Furthermore,

> In nihilist videos, the love theme turns from a relatively mild narcissism and a focus on the pain of separation, to sadism, masochism, androgyny, and homoeroticism; while the anti-authority theme moves from mere unresolved Oedipal conflicts to explicit hate, nihilism, anarchy, destruction. (Kaplan 1987, p. 61)

As Bill and Ted, and Wayne and Garth—four popular idolaters of heavy metal—would put it: "Strong stuff, dude!"

The issue of whether the entirety of the rock and roll phenomenon is postmodern, or whether specific rock performances at specific historical times are postmodern, is not an efficient way to frame the problem of rock and roll. To say that all rock and roll is postmodern runs counter to the spirit of postmodern analysis. This argument reifies rock and roll by anchoring it to a discrete historical period with an arbitrary and discrete beginning point (i.e., the end of World War II). This argument also ignores the very significant changes that have occurred within rock and roll over the years, such as the expansion of the ownership of rock and roll to all generations. For example, rock and roll increasingly belongs to young children through vehicles such as the Hammer Saturday morning cartoon show and the Teenage Mutant Ninja Turtle rock concert tour. Rock and roll also increasingly belongs to middle-aged adults through vehicles such as the Lovin' Feelin's nostalgia concert tour and the lasting popularity of oldies radio.

The argument that certain rock music performances are postmodern reduces the postmodern to merely a style. Yet, by definition, styles are always subject to change. This argument also diminishes the value of postmodernism as a comprehensive theory of culture. If we are truly living in a distinctively postmodern historical period, which I believe we are, then Amy Grant's Christian pop, Whitney Houston's heartfelt ballads, the Ghetto Boyz' gangster rap, and even Michael Jackson's musical flirtations are all part of that period. One should be able to see the postmodern or some feature of the postmodern in all rock music phenomena. In terms of specific genres like heavy metal, one should also be able to see the impact of the genre on a range of individuals who populate the historical period in question, not just the immediate subpopulation of fans. Everyone in American society may not be a Metallica fan, but everyone is affected to some degree by the presence of Metallica in our culture.

Metallica and the Postmodernization of Rock and Roll

It makes great sense to portray postmodernity as a dynamic process: the postmodernization of cultural phenomena. Heavy metal music represents the power of the process by which rock and roll increasingly becomes the soundtrack of American life, and not simply the possession and mirror reflection of a particular social or cultural class. Metallica is at the forefront of this process, not because it is in any substantive way "progressive," as is often said about alternative rock music, but because the band displays clearly and dramatically the high point of the postmodernization of rock and roll, a high point which by definition is always the present.

As rock and roll music becomes the preeminent form of popular music in American culture, heavy metal music becomes the preeminent form of rock and roll in the postmodern period. If we examine rock music internationally, we could almost equate heavy metal with rock music. Heavy metal music is *culturally pervasive* to the degree it increasingly functions to define situations not inherently or necessarily predicated by rock phenomena nor populated by rock music fans as (for example):

- *Adventurous.* For the past ten years or so, the Armed Forces have produced television recruitment advertisements containing a heavy metal guitar solo as the musical soundtrack. These ads have been broadcast during sports events and rock music programming ranging from "Nightflight" on the USA network to "Saturday Night Live" on NBC. The ads display fast-paced, combat-related action. The heavy metal guitar usually plays a melody like the Marine hymn, but at up-tempo. The guitar work serves to help create a feeling of adrenaline-driven adventure. The ads' audience may well include heavy metal fans, but the ads would also get the point across to those likely recruits who prefer country music or rap.
- *Sophisticated and calm.* During the winter season in 1991–92, the Houston Symphony broadcast a television advertisement that opened with an actor costumed to look like Alice Cooper (e.g., grotesque facial makeup, long prickly black hair, and a spandex body suit open at the chest). The character was surrounded by eerie smoke, and he looked like a demon. The story line claimed that heavy metal was a poor alternative to classical music, because the former was noise and the latter was calming and soothing. The audience for this commercial would not likely include traditional heavy metal fans.
- *Evil.* A number of late-night/early-morning public service announcements have been produced by the Centers for Disease Control and the National Institute on Drug Abuse. These spots attempt to show the evils of drug abuse and adolescent suicide. Heavy metal music is used to create a foreboding atmosphere and context for the message. The intended as well as actual audiences for these spots are not limited to traditional heavy metal fans.
- *Absurd.* The recent film *Honey, I Blew Up the Kids* portrays a little toddler who grows to gargantuan size as a result of his bumbling father's scientific misadventures. As the child is marching down a major thoroughfare in Las Vegas, Godzilla-style, he grabs the neon guitar from the roof of the local Hard Rock Cafe. Watching this little kid play at playing heavy metal

guitar (with a heavy metal audio background) reinforces the absurdity and thus the humor of the film's pretext.

As heavy metal increases its overall preeminence and presence as a cultural form in American society, it simultaneously displays and clarifies a number of conceptual features of the postmodernist era. These conceptual features serve to illustrate the essence of paradox that marks all of postmodern culture. The following is an inventory of these features as highlighted by their visibility in the Metallica phenomenon.

- *Heavy metal no longer references only the subpopulation of working-class teenagers.* As Jameson (1984) and others have noted, culture in the postmodern era no longer refers to, indexes, or belongs to specific social groups. Culture and its audiences are fragmented, just as culture is separated from social and economic life. Similarly, restrictive social structural boundaries no longer chart the demarcations of the heavy metal audience. It has become a respectable musical genre increasingly marketed to and appreciated by middle-class kids, as witnessed by the grunge rock movement discussed above. This is not in any way to deny that adolescent kids have a special affection for Metallica. Although teenage boys comprise the bulk of heavy metal's material consumer group, specific social class and age are not requisites for membership. For example, I attended the Metallica/Guns n' Roses concert on September 10, 1992, in the Houston Astrodome. Among other reasons, I was there to continue my research on rock concert paramedic work. I also got a chance to talk to approximately fifty of the estimated 45,000 fans present. The crowd was peppered with young and middle-aged adults as well as preadolescents skipping school to attend the 4:00 P.M. Friday afternoon concert.

- *Heavy metal no longer references only boys.* Rock and roll music has always been ambiguous towards women. Girls have been allowed to be passive consumers of rock and roll, either as dates or dancers. Women who have tried to enter the inner circles of rock have usually been stigmatized with labels such as "groupies." Few women have achieved much success as rock performers. Those who have made it are usually dismissed as merely mimicking tough and swaggeringly male styles and attitudes (e.g., Pat Benatar and Patti Smith). Most female performers who achieve success do so in the unthreatening realm of "pop" music (cf. Weinstein 1991, pp. 66–69).

Heavy metal music marks a bit of a change in this situation. Although there are really very few successful female heavy metal groups, performers like L7, Lita Ford, Surrea, and Hole create a distinctly female and even feminist version of metal. Yet the most theoretically interesting gender-related phenomenon in metal is the emergence of a male, morally discreditable equivalent of the traditionally female groupie: the "poseur." Poseurs are male metalheads who are not musicians themselves, but try desperately to achieve the identity of heavy metal musicians (Kotarba and Wells 1987). This identity consists primarily of hair (i.e., long and curly), shirt (i.e., open at the chest), pants (i.e., spandex), boots, and attitude. The value of this identity lies in its attactiveness to girls. True musicians, male fans, and female fans who catch on to the scam all look down on and make fun of poseurs. Their presence in the heavy metal scene provides girls the opportunity to exercise moral judgment, instead of always being the recipients of moral judgment.

The distribution of Metallica fans by gender is largely a function of the range of fans by age. At least in terms of concert attendance, the younger fans are generally male. The cohort of older fans, the young adults in the audience, are almost evenly split by gender. Metallica is a rock group that can be comfortably appreciated by couples. My interviews with concertgoers, however, strongly suggest that the men still exert more authority in determining which performers to see in concert (cf. Gaines 1991, pp. 62–67).

- *The heavy metal experience is intergenerational.* Within the postmodern world, all social structural apparatus that traditionally function to demarcate cultural experiences, including generational boundaries, are subject to dismissal. Adults can be Metallica fans, as noted above. While occupying the role of parent, they also can use Metallica as a medium for positive and supportive as well as negative and sanctioning interaction. As Grossberg (1986) has observed, rock and roll no longer necessarily serves to distance children from adults. Many parents create the possibility for their children to experience heavy metal through allowances, the giving of tapes and CDs as birthday and Christmas gifts, and so forth. At the Metallica concert in Houston, promoters set up a special drop-off point for parents. All afternoon, there was a long and steady stream of cars and minivans dropping kids off as if the Astrodome were a suburban high school!

Paradox again emerges when considering the role of parents in their kids' heavy metal experiences. Again and again, I heard kids say that their parents didn't like Metallica at all, yet allowed their kids to experience the band. Frank is a sixteen-year-old suburban kid whose mother recently got a divorce. We had the following exchange in the box seat area of the Astrodome between sets:

> J: What does your mother think of Metallica?
> F: She hates 'em. She hates all my music. She says that music is the reason I'm doing so shitty in school.
> J: How were you able to get here today, then?
> F: Oh, my mother bought me tickets for my birthday.

Some parents use heavy metal as a medium for expressing their fears about their children's welfare, and for constructing explanations for evil that occurs either in their children's own lives or in the world in general. Frequently, parents aren't sure what their feelings about heavy metal are. One such parent wrote a very elegant letter to the editor of the *Houston Chronicle* immediately following the Metallica show in the Astrodome. The parent is a fifty-year-old assistant U.S. attorney in Houston. When he accompanied his fifteen-year-old daughter to the concert, he was appalled at how:

> these young folks act autistic and angry at a music concert. . . . There was no laughter, no joy in the Astrodome. Surely everyone was happy to be there, but no one smiled. . . . In solitary dance, they jerked their heads violently, punched the sky and yelled obscenities. . . . What did we do to these kids? . . .

Bless his heart, this dad was oblivious to the most obvious answer to his question. What was *he* doing there? Did his daughter head bang and punch the sky? Did he bother to ask his daughter what was the basis for her attraction to Metallica? This dad clearly illustrates both the emotional diversity and ambiguity parents display towards heavy metal.

- *Heavy metal is marked by an open horizon of meaning.* In the postmodern world, the meaning of cultural objects is flexible and malleable. The meanings attributed to any particular object can be consistent or contradictory. Furthermore, meanings can function either as explanations for events, or as motives or drivers for action (see also Lyman and Scott 1970). Heavy metal music is perhaps the most semantically open-ended of all popular music forms, as illustrated by the great variation in the way audience members interpret lyrics perceived as relevant to suicide. Many conservative critics of heavy metal are quick to locate lyrics that either implicitly or explicitly discuss suicide. The common interpretation offered by groups such as the Parents' Music Resource Center is that these lyrics function to suggest if not support suicidal thoughts and tendencies among vulnerable teenagers (Weinstein 1991, pp. 250–256). When we investigate audience members' interpretation and use of these lyrics, however, we find great variety. Metallica fans identify two songs specifically related to suicide: "Fade to Black" and "Ride the Lightning." They may use these songs the following ways in their own lives: to make sense of friends' and acquaintances' suicidal attempts; to make sense of their own thoughts and feelings about suicide; to make sense of their own general feelings of meaninglessness and hopelessness. In my interviews with fans, I rarely heard any mention of music like this suggesting suicide. On the contrary, the kids often talked about the way heavy metal music in general and Metallica in particular serves to prevent suicidal attempts by providing some viable meaning for an otherwise depressing life (cf. Gaines 1991, pp. 203–205).
- *Heavy metal illustrates the integration of and ambiguity towards good and evil in the postmodern period.* In the modern world, morality was a game played out in arenas such as the court, the tribunal, and the text on moral philosophy. In the postmodern world, morality becomes a game largely played out in the mass media. Moral issues drown in the morass of ideology, politics, and sound bites, three perceptual frameworks conducive to the logic of the mass media (see Altheide and Snow

1991). It's tough to tell the good guy from the bad guy anymore. In an earlier ethnographic analysis of an all-ages, rock and roll club in Houston (Kotarba and Wells 1987), I was intrigued by the common audience shared by satanic heavy metal and Christian heavy metal. I routinely observed the same kids present at Roma's on Friday night grooving to Helstar, and at the Summit the following evening grooving to Stryper. When questioned about this apparent contradiction in moral commitment, the kids replied in perfectly postmodern sense that they had no problem identifying with a band whose greatest notoriety was a public condemnation from the Roman Catholic archdiocese of Houston, and a band famous for playing gigs in Japan for thousands of screaming Japanese kids who had no idea why band members were throwing Bibles out to the crowd.

Metallica displays moral ambiguity both in its music and in the management of its image. In a recent interview in *Parade* magazine (Minton 1992), the band was asked to account for the presence of their lyrics at a successful teenage suicide, and certain questionable songs they perform such as "Fade to Black" and "Creeping Death." While defending their music by arguing that kids make what they want out of their music, Metallica ended the interview by having James Hetfield claim, as if they were now modeling themselves after car dealers or insurance salespersons, that: "I don't want Parade readers to think we're know-it-alls about everything. I want them to know that we care."

- *Heavy metal's open horizon of meaning creates the possibility for composing it, performing it, interpreting it, and applying it to everyday life as a form of children's culture.* As I mentioned earlier, traditional analysis of rock and roll posits it as a form of youth culture. Within the postmodern world, it makes much more sense to frame it as a form of children's culture. Metallica's artistically brilliant and commercially successful single and video, "Enter Sandman," is the example in point. When rock and roll is tied to the youth culture, the range of cultural substance available to it is limited by the nature of adolescence in our society. Songs about teenagers usually include only other teenagers, and an occasional if potentially malevolent adult such as a parent or a teacher. When rock and roll is based upon the experiences and perceptions of children, or others who are allowed by the music to act as if they were children again, the range of available others increases to include all the people relevant to children. Old people—such as grandparents, bogeymen and sandmen—are significantly more relevant to children than to adolescents in our culture.

During 1991–92, I served as principal investigator for a federally funded, community-based study of homeless adolescents in Houston (Kotarba 1993). The goal of this project was to gain an understanding of the everyday lives of these kids in order to generate effective strategies for reducing the risk of HIV infection among them. To understand these kids requires an appreciation for the centrality rock and roll, specifically heavy metal, has in their lives. Hands down, Metallica is their favorite group. In order to peer into the intimate if not sacred relationship between the two, I would routinely ask the kids who the old guys were in the "Enter Sandman" and the "Unforgiven" videos. Answers ranged from the sandman to the bogeyman to someone's grandfather to just an old guy whom the kids themselves will be like when they get old. However, the open horizon of meaning of Metallica became fascinating when the kids talked about what the nightmare portrayed in "Enter Sandman" was all about. I generally received one kind of account. The homeless kids would talk about how the video reminded them that their own lives were living nightmares, as a result of abuse at home, drug problems, and so forth. When I got the opportunity later to pose the same question to middle-class kids, I generally received another kind of account. They were able to talk about the video as just a nightmare with which they could not personally relate. It was just like a Freddy Krueger movie, a passing and inconsequential fright.

Heavy metal music's open horizon of meaning means that any particular song or performance can function in numerous ways as a cultural resource for its youthful fans. During the above-mentioned study, I interviewed a sixteen-year-old boy one day who started crying ten minutes into the interview when I asked him about his relationship with his mother. He told me that he called his mother on the phone that past Tuesday, hoping that his estranged mother would at least wish him a happy sixteenth birthday. Instead, his mother screamed at him that he was a terrible person and that she never wanted to see him again. I ended the interview at that point and proceeded to drive him back to the neighborhood where he street-hustles. Without thinking, I put on the most recent Metallica tape, and watched in wonder as the boy's face lit up and he began to *speak* along with the song, just like the kids at the Guns n' Roses concert and just like the kids at the Monsters of Rock concert. I asked him where Never Never Land, as mentioned in the song, was. I heard a homeless kid's philosophy of life in his answer: "It's where you go when you have no place to go."

Conclusion

In this chapter, I have conducted a sociological reading of one of the most popular heavy metal rock bands in the United States: Metallica. This reading was informed by ideas derived from the postmodernist movement in sociology and other intellectual disciplines. My reading occurred at two levels. The first level involved seeing Metallica specifically and heavy metal music in general as cultural forms. In the postmodern era, heavy metal music pervades our culture and the mass media, to the point that it can deliver various messages to many different people. Heavy metal can portray evil, absurdity, adventure, and youthfulness to audiences that are not composed of fans. Heavy metal also illustrates the shape of postmodern culture, in which ties between culture and social structure are ambiguous at best, and in which cultural variation is no longer necessarily tied to variance in gender and generation.

The second level involved reading the audience's experience of Metallica. Kids love Metallica because the band is fun, as are many other rock and roll bands, but also because the band serves as a rich source of meanings for life and the problems of growing up. Kids get to play with good and evil, hope and hopelessness, youth and aging in Metallica's music.

The sympathetic reader, the person who is a fan of heavy metal music in particular or rock and roll music in general, could undoubtedly come up with viable, alternative nominations for the role of *the* postmodern band. My case study was obviously chosen on the basis of less-than-totally-objective criteria. Scholars who study culture have a natural and predictable tendency to focus on artists, performers, genres, and styles to which they are personally attracted—and I obviously like Metallica a lot.

Yet both my personal and scholarly interests in Metallica are based upon the band's primitiveness and commonness. Recent critics from within the heavy metal genre, including kids, argue that Metallica "sold out" to commercialism with recent work. Their evidence is that Metallica now appeals to a mass audience denoted by a Top-40 mentality and the need for three-minute videos and melodies. I would argue the opposite, that Metallica became postmodern just at that point when the band became common to culture. Rock fans from *many* persuasions must now talk about whether or not they like Metallica, whether or not they think Metallica sold out, and so forth. People who are not even rock fans will use Metallica as a criterion for assessing the aesthetics or morality of rock music, and as a resource for constructing ideas and conversations about kids, sex, drugs, and rock and roll. And thus the particular logic of heavy metal music, which we can denote analytically as postmodern, becomes the logic of rock and roll.

NOTE

I want to thank David Klinger, Jan Lin, William Simon, and Lisa Sullivan for their thoughtful reading of an earlier draft of this essay.

REFERENCES

Altheide, David, and Robert P. Snow. 1991. *Media Worlds in the Postjournalism Era*. New York: Aldine de Gruyter.

Azerrad, Michael. 1992. "Big Boom in Industrial Metal." *Rolling Stone* 637:15; 64.

Baudrillard, Jean. 1983. *Simulations*. New York: Semiotext(e), Foreign Agent Press.

Cashmore, E. Ellis. 1987. "Shades of Black, Shades of White." In *Popular Music and Communication*, James Lull (ed.). Newbury Park, CA.: Sage.

Clifford, James. 1988. *The Predicament of Culture: Twentieth Century Ethnography, Literature and Art*. Cambridge, MA: Harvard University Press.

Connor, Steven. 1989. *Postmodern Culture: An Introduction to Theories of the Contemporary*. Cambridge, MA: Blackwell.

Fricke, David. 1989. "Heavy Metal Justice." *Rolling Stone* 543:44–49.

Gaines, Donna. 1991. *Teenage Wasteland: Suburbia's Dead End Kids*. New York: Harper.

Grossberg, Lawrence. 1986. "The Politics of Youth Culture: Some Observations on Rock and Roll in American Culture." *Social Texts* 8 (Winter): 104–126.

Hebdige, Dick. 1988. *Hiding in the Light*. London: Routledge.

Jameson, Fredric. 1984. "Postmodernism, or the Cultural Logic of Late Capitalism." *New Left Review* 146:52–92.

Kaplan, Ann E. 1987. *Rocking Around the Clock: Music Television, Postmodernism, and Consumer Culture*. New York: Routledge.

Kotarba, Joseph A. 1989. "A Critique of Postmodernism and Everyday Life: The Case of Heavy Metal Rock and Roll." Paper presented at the Annual Meeting of the Gregory Stone Symposium, Tempe, Arizona (March).

———. 1991. "Postmodernism, Ethnography, and Culture." *Studies in Symbolic Interaction* 12:45–52.

———. 1993. "The Everyday Life of Homeless Adolescents." Bethesda, MD: The National Institute on Drug Abuse.

Kotarba, Joseph A., and Darlene Hurt. 1993. "The Integration of Institutions Servicing Children: Emergency Medical Care at Rock

Music Festivals." Presented at the Annual Meeting of the American Sociological Association, Miami, Florida (August).

Kotarba, Joseph A., and Laura Wells. 1987. "Styles of Adolescent Participation in an All-Ages, Rock 'n' Roll Nightclub: An Ethnographic Analysis." *Youth & Society* 18 (4):398–417.

Lyman, Stanford M., and Marvin B. Scott. 1970. *A Sociology of the Absurd*. New York: Appleton-Century Crofts.

Minto, Lynn. 1992. "Is Heavy Metal Dangerous?" *Parade* September 20:12–14.

Powis, Tim. 1992. ". . . And Metal for All." *Music Express* 16 (167):8–12.

Russell, Tony. 1983. *The Encyclopedia of Rock*. London: Crescent Books.

Weinstein, Deena. 1992. *Heavy Metal: A Cultural Sociology*. New York: Lexington.

Redeeming the Rap Music Experience

Venise Berry

> You know—parents are the same no matter time nor place.
> They don't understand that us kids are gonna make some mistakes.
> So to you other kids all across the land, there's no need to argue—
> PARENTS JUST DON'T UNDERSTAND!
> (DJ Jazzy Jeff and The Fresh Prince 1988)

Introduction

When rap music first appeared on the scene, music critics said it wouldn't last, record companies felt it was too harsh and black-oriented to cross over, and parents dismissed it as the latest fad. Ten years later, rap has become a powerful and controversial force in American popular culture. Rap music has grown significantly from its humble street beginnings in Harlem and the South Bronx. It now encompasses a dominant media paradigm through traditional music vehicles like cassettes and CDs, as well as television coverage in videos and talk shows, rappers as actors, film themes, concerts, advertising, and other promotional components.

On *Billboard*'s top 200 album list on January 18, 1992, rappers were found as high as #3 and as low as #184. Despite, or maybe because of, the controversies, groups such as Hammer, Public Enemy, Ice Cube, Ghetto Boyz, Salt 'N Pepa, 2 Live Crew,

NWA, Tone Loc, and Queen Latifah have reached mainstream popularity, and each success pushes the rap genre into new directions. Rap music is constantly testing the boundaries of commercialism, sexism, radicalism, feminism, and realism, and a growing concern over the music's disrespect for traditional boundaries keeps it on the cutting edge.

Current literature on rap music has taken varied approaches, from content analyses which analyze and critique images and messages, to trade articles which offer promotional information on the artists and their music. One of the most important, yet least explored, areas in this discourse is the relationship between the music and its fans; particularly those whom it represents: black urban youths.

This chapter will explore three controversial issues in rap music: sex, violence, and racism, in relation to the social, cultural, and historical reality of urban black American youth. My analysis will draw on both secondary and primary sources. It will incorporate related articles and previous literature, as well as worksheet responses collected from black high school participants in the Upward Bound Program at Huston-Tillotson College in Austin, Texas, between 1987 and 1989 and personal comments from an October 17, 1990, discussion group with twenty-four of the Upward Bound juniors and seniors.

In developing a conceptual framework for this examination of rap music experience, it is necessary to distinguish between the pop-cultural and pop-crossover domains. The pop-cultural domain involves rap music, which, despite its popularity, maintains a black cultural focus in its message and style. For example, rap groups like NWA, Ice T, KRS One, Public Enemy, Ice Cube, and Queen Latifah are popular rappers with messages and styles that reflect an overt black consciousness.

In contrast, the pop-crossover domain involves rap music which follows a more commercialized format. The message and style of these rap songs are more generalizable and acceptable to mainstream audiences. Hammer, Salt N' Pepa, DJ Jazzy Jeff and the Fresh Prince, Tone Loc, and Kid and Play are examples of pop-crossover rap artists. The distinction between these two rap domains is important in recognition of their place in the American popular culture movement. The popularity of one helps to fuel the popularity of the other, just as the acceptable nature of one limits the acceptable nature of the other.

This research evolves from a broad sociocultural ideology, focusing on the wish to understand the meaning and place assigned to popular culture in the experience of a particular group in society—the young, black, urban minority. It supports the pluralist approach, which considers rap music an example of how media systems, despite their attempt to control, are basically nondominant and open to change, and can be used effectively to present alternative views. Gurevitch (1982) has examined pluralism as a component of democracy and emancipatory media. Their work advocates the idea of media as public vehicles used for enhancing and encouraging self-expression and self-consciousness by a culture. As this chapter will highlight, cultural rap is just such a vehicle.

Black Music as Cultural Communication

In the work of Standifer (1980), the musical behaviors of black society are explained as "movement with existence." From spirituals to rap, black music style is a communicative process interwoven deep within the black American experience. For example, the spiritual served as an underground form of communication and a mechanism for emotional release. Natural words and phrases had secret meanings for slave communities. According to Cone (1972), words and phrases which seemed harmless were filled with latent meanings, such as, "De promise land on the other side of Jordan," which meant "freedom north" and later "Canada," rather than "heaven" as slave owners were led to believe.

B.B. King has told the story of how blues evolved from the unanswered prayers of slaves. He explained that slaves sang to God, but remained oppressed. As a result they began to lose at least part of their faith, and started to sing what was on their minds: the blues. Walton (1972) agrees, defining the blues as a composition grounded in individual experience and one with which the audience tends to identify.

When avant-garde jazz emerged, it was in protest to mainstream-appropriated music styles such as ragtime and boogie-woogie. Kofsky (1970) explains that the revolutionary jazz style used the piano as a distraction, abandoning the traditional diatonic scale, and incorporating an atonal key structure in direct opposition to Western music form. He says the harsh and abrasive music represented the dissatisfaction of Black Americans with what they had been promised, but ultimately denied: a chance to have the American dream.

Soul music in the 1960s and 1970s presented itself as a blatantly rebellious black musical genre. It created for black American culture a sense of heightened black consciousness, unity and pride. Soul music, ultimately, served as a powerful catalyst for protest and social change during the civil rights and black power movements (Maultsby, 1983).

Finally, today's rap music style reflects the distinct experience of urban black culture. Black slang, street attitude, and fashion are reflected in powerful spoken song. Name-brand tennis shoes, sweatsuits, and an exorbitant display of gold chains and rings create a sense of appropriated success. The heavy beat, incessant scratching, aggressive delivery, and lyrical storyline present a message of anger and frustration from urban existence.

Just as socially, culturally, and historically music has always been essential to the evolution of the black American experience, an essential part of contemporary black culture is the urban environment which manifests itself within the context of rap music. Several scholars have discussed the power of rap music as a mechanism of communication involving the struggle for a recognized black cultural empowerment.

Dyson (1991) examines performance, protest, and prophecy in the culture of hip hop. He suggests that it is difficult for a society that maintains social arrangements, economic conditions, and political choices so that it can create and reproduce poverty, racism, sexism, classism, and violence to appreciate a music that contests and scandalizes such problems. He fears that the pop success of rap artists often means mainstream dilution; the sanitizing of rap's expression of urban realities, resulting in sterile hip hop devoid of its original fire and offensive to no one.

The communicative power of rap music is traced back to an African tradition called "nommo" by Stephens (1991). Nommo refers to the supernatural power of the spoken word. The rhyme and rhythm which are part of African-American speech, literature, music, and dance are essential elements of nommo. He says it is believed in Africa that nommo can create changes in attitude. It can evoke unity, identity, and an atmosphere where everyone can relate.

Perkins (1991) explains how the ideology of the Nation of Islam has become an important element of rap music's message. Perkins feels that rap artists such as Public Enemy and KRS One are social revolutionaries and their role is to carry the black nationalist tradition forward by heightening awareness, stimulating thought, and provoking the true knowledge of self.

The messages in rap music have also been compared to the messages in blues by Nelson (1991). She contrasts themes such as poverty and despair that appear in both and discusses how both musical forms are based on truth and reality. Dixon (1989) speaks about the context of rap music as truth. He feels rap music ". . . unites the listeners of the music into a common group with clear and readily identifiable racial, cultural, economic, and political/sexual shared concerns and emerges as the voice of its adherents."

Finally, the issue of rap as historical account is raised by Shusterman (1991). He says, "Many rappers have taken their place as insightful inquirers into reality and teachers of truth, particularly those aspects of reality and truth which get neglected or distorted by establishment history books and contemporary media coverage." Shusterman attributes the audible voice of rap music in popular culture to its commercial success in the mass media, which has enabled renewed artistic investment as an undeniable source of black cultural pride.

Rap Music, Urban Reality, and Popular Culture

Popular culture is made by subordinated peoples in their own interests out of resources that also, contradictorily, serve the economic interests of the dominant. Popular culture is made from within and below, not imposed from without and above as mass cultural theorists would have it. There is always an element of popular culture that lies outside of social control, that escapes or opposes hegemonic forces (Fiske, 1989).

The power and promise of rap music rests in the bosom of urban America; an environment where one out of twenty-two black males will be killed by violent crimes, where the black high-school dropout rate is as high as 72 percent and where 86 percent of black children grow up in poverty. Years of degradation, welfare handouts, institutional racism, and discrimination have created a community where little hope, low self-esteem and frequent failure translate into drugs, teen pregnancy, and gang violence. These are the social, cultural, and economic conditions which have spurred rap's paradoxical position within American popular culture.

The relationship between low socioeconomic status and the negative self-evaluation of black urban youth results in problems of low self-esteem. These feelings are prominent because of limited opportunities, unsatisfied needs, instability, estrangement, racial prejudice, and discrimination (Hulbary, 1975). As these youth struggle with questions of independence and control in their environment, they embrace a sense of powerlessness. Mainstream society tends to view the lifestyles of low-income communities as deviant. The poor are believed to be perpetuating their own poverty because of their nonconforming attitudes and unconventional behavior (Gladwin, 1967). Poussaint and Atkinson (1972) suggest that the stereotypes of deviance, a lack of motivation, and limited educational achievements ultimately become a part of their identity.

The youth movement which is evident in popular culture has, therefore, brought about only illusions for many urban American youth. The term "youth," which came to mean a specific attitude including pleasure, excitement, hope, power, and invincibility, was not experienced by these kids. Their future was mangled by racism, prejudice, discrimination, and economic and educational stagnation. As Bernard (1991) suggests, they found themselves in a gloomy darkness without friendship, trust, or hope; backed into a corner where life is all about self.

As a product of the black urban community, rap music is indisputably entangled with the struggle for black identity and legitimacy within mainstream society. Although rap music is undergoing significant changes, much of it remains true to its aesthetic purpose of bringing to the forefront the problematic nature of urban American experience.

Cultural rap music is, therefore, often seen in a negative light. The "culture of rap music" has been characterized as a "culture of attitude" by Adler (1990), who suggests that attitude is something civilized society abhors and likes to keep under control. He concludes that the end of attitude is nihilism, which by definition leads nowhere, and that the culture of attitude is repulsive, mostly empty of political content.

Costello and Wallace (1990), in *Signifying Rappers*, say that vitalists have argued for forty years that postwar art's ultimate expression will be a kind of enormous psychosocial excrement and the real aesthetic (conscious or otherwise) of today's best serious rap may be nothing but the first wave of this great peristalsis.

Negative images of rap are dominant in the news. The 2 Live Crew controversy in Florida concerning sexually explicit lyrics made big headlines, along with the charity basketball game by rap artists in New York which resulted in nine kids being trampled to death. Violence has also been reported at movies where rap themes are prominent. And, the music of defiant rap groups like NWA (Niggas with Attitude) have been considered radical and extremist. They made history as the first musical group to receive a warning from the FBI about the negative content of their song, "Fuck the Police," which encourages a lack of respect for the system.

Urban black American culture exists within a large infrastructure, segmented by various negative individual and situational environments. The relationship between the rap fan and his or her music, therefore, involves the larger contextual environment of the urban street. At the same time, it is important to recognize how the mainstream success of the rap genre has made urban language, style, dance, and attitude viable components of popular cultural form.

The Issue of Sex

The 2 Live Crew appeared in the public eye in 1986 with their first album, *The 2 Live Crew Is What We Are.* Their most successful hit, which is now considered tame, was entitled, "Hey, We Want Some Pussy." It sold a half-million copies without the backing of a major record company. The Crew's next album took sexual rap to a new level. *Move Something* sold more than a million copies and included songs like, "Head," "Booty and Cock," and "Me so Horny."

It was their third album, *As Nasty as We Wanna Be,* which made the group a household name. On June 6, 1990, U.S. District Judge Jose Gonzales, Jr., said the album was "utterly without any redeeming social value." The obscenity issue created a media bonanza for 2 Live Crew and boosted the sale of their album to more than two million copies.

Luther Campbell, leader of the group, has been on a number of talk shows and in many articles defending his right to produce sexually explicit rap music. In an interview in *Black Beat* magazine, he called the lyrics funny. "The stuff on our X-rated albums is meant to be funny. We sit down and laugh about our lyrics. We don't talk about raping women or committing violence against them or anything like that" (Henderson, February 1990).

An analysis by Peterson-Lewis (1991) presents a different perspective: ". . . their lyrics lack the wit and strategic use of subtle social commentary necessary for effective satire; thus they do not so much debunk myths as create new ones, the major one being that in interacting with black women 'anything goes.' Their lyrics not only fail to satirize the myth of the hypersexual black, they also commit the moral blunder of sexualizing the victimization of women, black women in particular."

Campbell adds that the group's lyrics are a reflection of life in America's black neighborhoods. Yet he admits he won't let his seven-year-old daughter listen to such music. While 2 Live Crew served as the thrust of the controversy, the negative images of women in this society have been a concern of feminists for many years, through various media forms.

Peterson-Lewis goes on to question the extent of the ethical and moral responsibilities of artists to their audiences and the larger public. She focuses her argument on the constitutionality and racially motivated persecution and prosecution of 2 Live Crew, which she feels overshadowed the real criticism—the sexually explicit nature of their lyrics and their portrayal of women as objects for sexual assault.

Frankel (1990) agrees that the 2 Live Crew situation took away the real focus. She says the attack on the 2 Live Crew group made it an issue of censorship, racism, and free speech, rather than an issue of disgust at how women are portrayed, especially since an act like Andrew Dice Clay, who also promotes women and sex from a negative perspective, has not been sanctioned by the law.

Even though the controversy about sexually explicit lyrics in rap music has become a heated issue, out of a list of the top fifty rap groups, only about 10 percent can actually be identified as using truly obscene and violent lyrics in relation to women. An analysis of the number of more generally negative images of females as loose and whorish would probably double that percentage.

In a discussion on the subject of sex in rap with a group of Upward Bound high school juniors and seniors, there was a split on the 2 Live Crew issue. Bené said their records contain too much profanity and are obscene, so maybe they should be sold in X-rated stores. Steve felt that fifteen- and sixteen-year-olds are able to drive, and if they can be trusted with their lives in a car, why not be trusted to select their own music? Tamara compared the group's lyrics to the Playboy channel or magazine, and wondered why access to 2 Live Crew's music is not limited as well. Marty said that teenagers are still going to get the album if they want it, despite warning labels. Finally, Dewan explained that the warning labels can't stop the sexual things teens think in their minds.

When asked about record censorship, most of them felt that some kind of censorship was acceptable for kids ages twelve and under. But they also cited television, movies, and magazines as the places where they usually receive new sexual information, rather than music.

Female rappers like Salt 'N Pepa, Queen Latifah, Yo Yo, and MC Lyte have stepped forward to dispel many of the negative images of women with their own lyrical rhetoric and aggressive performance style. Yo Yo, a popular nineteen-year-old female rapper, says that she got into rap to help improve women's self-esteem because a lot of black women don't believe in themselves. She has created an organization for teenage women called the Intelligent Black Women's Coalition (IBWC), which speaks on issues of social concern.

In direct opposition to positive female rappers are the controversial groups, Bytches wit' Problems and Hoes wit' Attitude. According to Lyndah and Michelle of Bytches wit' Problems, "There's a little bitch in all women, and even some men . . . and we're just the bitches to say it" (October 1991). Lyndah and Michelle's new album, *B.Y.T.C.H.E.S.*, reflects another side of black urban reality. They feel they can say what they want just like men do, which is evident from their songs "Two Minute Brother," "Fuck a Man," and "Is the Pussy still Good." Their definition of a bitch is "a powerful woman in control of her life, going after what she wants and saying what's on her mind" (October 1991).

The female trio, Hoes wit' Attitude, has been called the raunchiest all-girl rap group. With hit songs like "Eat This," "Little Dick," and "Livin' in a Hoe House," they constantly test their motto, "If men can do it we can too." The girls, 2 Jazzy, Baby Girl, and D. Diva, argue that "hoein' is the oldest profession, whether you're sellin' your body or something else. A hoe is a business woman. We're in business, the business of selling records."

When asked about their perceptions of such aggressive female images, the discussion group of Upward Bound students again split. Lanietra said, "All women are not like that and the words they use to describe themselves are not necessary." Louis felt rappers don't actually use the lyrics they sing about as a personal thing with another person, they are using the lyrics to warn people about the females and males of today. Tonje added concern that such rap music makes females seem like sex objects that can only be used to satisfy a man's needs.

These youth easily identified specific popular songs which had messages that were positive and negative in relation to to sex. The top three songs named as "good for moral thinking" were "Let's Wait Awhile" by Janet Jackson; "Growing Up" by Whodini; and "I Need Love" by L L Cool J. The top three songs listed as "bad for moral thinking about sex" were "Hey, We Want some Pussy" by the 2 Live Crew; "I Want Your Sex" by George Michael; and "Kanday" by L L Cool J.

The Issue of Violence

Another prominent issue which seems to follow the rap music phenomenon is violence. On December 28, 1991, nine youths were trampled to death at a charity basketball game with rap artists at City College in New York. On July 12, 1991, Alejandra Phillips, a supermarket clerk, was shot outside a theater showing of *Boyz N' the Hood*. Cultural rap is often connected with such negative images of the black underclass. Pictures of pimps, drug dealers, and gang members riding around with rap music blasting loudly are prevalent in the media. Scholars like Jon Spencer have questioned the link between rap and rape made by Tipper Gore's editorial in *The Washington Post*, "Hate, Rape, and Rap" and the juxtapositioning of the 2 Live Crew's lyrics with the rape of a New York jogger in Central Park. Spencer suggests that when people see the word "rap" they read the word "rape," and they often view "rappists" as rapists.

One of the groups most publicized when exploring violence are NWA (Niggas with Attitude). NWA consists of five L.A. rappers whose controversial lyrics include topics like gang banging, drive-by shootings, and police confrontations. MTV refused to air their video, "Straight Outta Compton," because they said it "glorified violence." The ex-leader of the group, Ice Cube, says the group's lyrics deal with reality and violence is their reality. "Our goals are to show the audience the raw reality of life. When they come out the other end they gonna say, 'damn, it's like that for real?' And, we're gonna make money" (Hochman 1989).

Williams (1990) disagrees that rap images and music are representative of the beliefs and ethics of black communities. He says when women are treated like sex slaves and ideas like "materialism is God" are put forth, they are not true visions of black America or black culture, but a slice of the worst of a small element of black culture that is not emblematic of the black community at large.

The positive efforts of black rappers to eliminate violence in their music and neighborhoods have not received as much publicity as the negative. For example, various popular rap stars from the West Coast such as NWA, Hammer, Young MC, and Digital Underground came together to record a single entitled "We're All in the Same Gang." It was a rap song that spoke out against the senseless violence of gangs.

The East Coast's "Stop the Violence" campaign raised more than $300,000 for youth-oriented community programs in New York. More than a dozen rappers, like Ice T, Tone Loc, and King Tee participated in the "Self Destruction" record and video which addressed the need to end black-on-black crime. The powerful lyrics and images of the song brought a new positive black urban consciousness into focus. As the song points out:

> Back in the sixties our brothers and sisters
> were hanged, how could you gangbang?
> I never ran from the Ku Klux Klan, and I shouldn't have to
> run from a black man.
> 'Cause that's self-destruction, self-destruction, you're
> headed for self-destruction.

Kids are forced to learn from the rhythm of life around them. Rap songs often include graphic images of drug dealers. The drug dealer is a very real personality in low-income neighborhoods. When asked to write down three questions they would include on a drug survey, Tamara asked, "Why do they (adults, authorities) allow the pushers to sell drugs on the corner by my school?" She later told me that it was very obvious what happens on that corner, but nobody bothers to do anything about it, so kids come to accept it too.

There is an obvious struggle going on in these kids' lives that links them to the conflict-oriented nature of cultural rap. The violent urban environment which is a prominent theme in rap music is also a prominent reality. One example of that reality came from a worksheet concerning a rap tune called "Wild Wild West" by Kool Moe Dee. In the song, Kool Moe Dee raps about how he and his buddies stop others (including gangs) from coming into their neighborhoods and terrorizing people. He talks about taking control of his environment in a fashion appropriate to the Old West. In response to the song, Mary said she could relate to it because in her neighborhood, people are always getting into other people's personal business. Tim also knew what Kool Moe Dee was talking about because he and his homeboys (friends) were always scuffling (fighting) with somebody for respect. Michael said the song means that kids are growing up too hard in the streets. He added, "My school and neighborhood are a lot like that." Finally, James said he had a friend who got shot at a party "because of the way he looked at a guy and that's just how it is."

On a more positive side, several of the kids have come to understand and change these negatives through their own raps. The Get It Girl Crew, four young ladies who love to rap, wrote the rap below as a testimony of their spirit and hope for the future.

> Tricky B, Lady J, Lady Love and Kiddy B from up above,
> we're the Get it Girl Crew and we're doing the do.
> And, yes when we're on the mic we're talking to you,
> homeboys and homegirls, with your jheri curls,
> we'll blow you away, knock out those curls.
> This is a rap for World Wide peace,
> listen to my rhyme while my beat's released.
> White and black, we're not the same color,
> but in this world we're sisters and brothers.
> I'll say this rhyme till my dying day,
> I'd rather be dead, dead in my grave.
> You talk about me and put my name down,
> but when I take revenge I put your face in the ground.
> This is Baby Rock in the place to be,
> throwing a def rap on the M. I. C.
> The Get it Girl Crew, there is none finer,
> 'cause we're the freshest and we're on fire.
> We're the Get it Girl Crew with strength from above
> We need peace, unity and love!

The Issue of Racism

The issue of race in America is not a silent one today. Separate ideologies of black power and white supremacy are prominent and dividing the nation even further as indicated by an ex-KKK leader, David Duke, running for public office, the travesty of Rodney King's beating and trial in Los Angeles that ignited riots, and the powerful slogan of Malcolm X, "By any means necessary," as reemerging popular black ideology.

According to Pareles (1992), rap often sounds like a young black man shouting about how angry he is and how he's going to hurt people. Pareles says, "Rap's internal troubles reflect the poverty, violence, lack of education, frustration and rage of the ghetto. . . . Hating rap can be a synonym for hating and fearing young black men who are also the stars of rap."

Samuels (1991) voices concern about the acceptance of racism in this country through rap. He writes, "Gangster and racist raps foster a voyeurism and tolerance of racism in which black and white are both complicit, particularly when whites treat gangster raps as a window into ghetto life."

Until recently, Public Enemy was the rap group who seemed to be in the middle of the racist controversy. In response to the negative environment in the United States concerning race relations, rapper Chuck D (1990) of Public Enemy makes statements such as "a black person is better off dealing with a Klansman than a liberal." He goes on to quote Neely Fuller, Jr.'s, definition of a white liberal: "a white person who speaks and/or acts to maintain, expand and/or refine the practice of white supremacy (racism) by very skillfully pretending not to do so." Public Enemy has also called for the reorganization of the Black Panther party, a group considered radical in the 1960s that advocated violence and racism.

Public Enemy emerged into the headlines as racist when an ex-member, Professor Griff, made several statements that were considered anti-Semitic in a speech. Griff's comment involved his belief that Jews financed the slave trade and are responsible for apartheid in South Africa. He went on to ask, "Is it a coincidence that Jews run the jewelry business and it's named jew-elry?" (Dougherty, 1990.)

After firing Professor Griff, Chuck D responded to his comments in *Billboard* magazine. "We aren't anti-Jewish. We're pro-black," he said. "We're pro-culture, we're pro-human race. You can't talk about attacking racism and be racist" (Newman, 1989). According to Chuck D, the group is not here to offend anyone, but to fight the system which works against blacks twenty-four hours a day, 365 days a year. He adds, "We're not racists, we're nationalists, people who have pride and want to build a sense of unity amongst our own" (Newman, 1989).

Ice Cube is the second most prominent rapper to be labelled racist because of several controversial songs on his hit album, *Death Certificate*. He calls Koreans "Oriental one-penny motherfuckers" and lambasts members of his old group, NWA, about their Jewish manager. He raps, "Get rid of that Devil, real simple, put a bullet in his temple, 'cause you can't be the nigger for life crew, with a white Jew telling you what to do." In response to the criticism, Ice Cube says people need to pay heed to the frustration as they [black men] demand respect.

Ideology from the Nation of Islam, which is often called racist, is a major part of the controversy. Many rappers are reviving the words of black leaders like Elijah Muhammad and Louis Farrakhan, calling the white society devils and snakes, and advocating a new black solidarity. Several popular rappers are actually emerging from the Nation of Islam calling themselves "The 5 Percenters." These artists base their raps on the Islamic belief that only about 5 percent of the black nation knows that the black man *is* God and it's their duty to teach others.

Finally, racism is sometimes attributed to the Afrocentric voice; the pro-black attitude. The controversial KRS-One (Knowledge Reigns Supreme over Nearly Everyone) condemns gang violence, poor educational systems, and drug use, but his attack on the "white system" has been called racially motivated. At fourteen, KRS One was a homeless runaway sleeping on steaming New York City sidewalk grates. At twenty-four, he has become a popular, positive rap star and educator. Queen Latifah is one of the most positive and powerful black female rappers. Her albums are rich in African cultural ideology and images as she dresses in African garb and tells kids that all black men and women are kings and queens. Queen Latifah believes that the only way to fight bigotry is to teach black children their history.

Cultural rap is so direct and angry that it can be frightening to those who don't understand the frustration of these storytellers. For example, the decision not to honor the birthday of Martin Luther King, Jr., as a holiday in Arizona brought forth a rap from NWA with the theme "Gonna find a way to make the state pay" and the video portrayed the violent murders of several Arizona officials. Militant rapper Paris, on his album debut, *The Devil Made Me Do It*, presents a powerful, hard-edged commentary on the murder of Yousuf Hawkins in Bensonhurst called "The Hate that Hate Made." And the logo of Public Enemy shows the black male youth as a hunted animal with the motto "Kill or Be Killed." The image of a black silhouette is chilling within the crosshairs of a gun.

When Upward Bound students were asked to respond to the worksheet question, "How has growing up black, in your opinion, made a difference in your life?" a theme ran through the responses: the need to struggle or fight. Carlos, for instance, said being black causes him to struggle more for what he wants. He said, "At school, on TV, everywhere, other people get the things they want, but not me." Titus and Karon felt they had to fight a lot because of the color of their skin. "Fighting," according to Titus, "not only with people of other races." Damon explained, "Color really doesn't matter, but just because I'm black people expect me to be able to play sports and fight." When Damon went on to list the things which he felt might hinder him in his future success, his list included skin color, money, and friends.

As a whole, the group split on the issue of whether or not they felt their skin color would affect their future. About half agreed with the statement "In the past, my skin color would have hindered my success, but that is not true today," and the other half disagreed.

When asked if they see Public Enemy, NWA, and other black-conscious rappers as role models and heroes, the group said yes unanimously. As William explained, "They say what's going on in their hearts and that's what needs to be said." John added, "When brothers keep the pain inside they explode and that happens a lot around here." Nichole says she owns all of

Public Enemy's tapes and she feels their music is important to help white people understand how black people feel about what's happening in black communities.

Conclusion

The history of black music is a history of adaptation, rebellion, acculturation, and assimilation. An essential part of black music rests inherently in black experience. As we look closely, we realize that black music has always been a communicative response to the pressures and challenges within black American society.

The cultural rap music experience exists within the realm of specific environmental contexts. For the black urban adolescent, the environment manifests itself through their most popular music choice: rap. As they listen, they construct both shared and personal realities. Rappers rising from this context are empowering storytellers. Their oral wit and unique street style create a purposeful presence for inner-city ideology. Rap music has become the champion of an otherwise ignored and forgotten reality. Through critical spoken song, rappers are forcing cultural realities into the public arena. Rap music, therefore, serves not only as a mirror to this problematic community, but as a catalyst for it, providing legitimacy and hope.

Within popular culture, rap music has increased the sense of awareness outside urban black America and interrupted normal flow of the commercialization process with a large dose of substance. Cultural musics, such as rap, often get caught in a repetitive cycle of acculturation, and are gradually absorbed into the pop mode. But, in opposition to pop-crossover rap, cultural rap has somehow managed to maintain elements which lie outside of social control, and escape the oppressive hegemonic forces.

Fiske's (1989) observations about such resistance and popular culture can be applied to the rap phenomenon. "The resistances of popular culture are not just evasive or semiotic; they do have a social dimension at the micro-level. And at this micro-level, they may well act as a constant erosive force upon the macro, weakening the system from within so that it is more amenable to change at the structural level." This is the power and promise of cultural rap.

The negative climate toward rap has been challenged by various scholars as inaccurate and inadequate. Spencer (1991) believes that the current emergence of rap is a by-product of the "emergency of black." He connects rap ideology to the racial concerns of scholar Manning Marable, saying, "This emergency still involves the dilemma of the racial color-line, but it is complicated by the threat of racial genocide, the obliteration of all black institutions, the political separation of the black elite from the black working class, and the benign decimation of the 'ghetto poor,' who are perceived as nonproduction and therefore dispensable."

Dyson (1991) views rap music as a form of profound musical, cultural, and social creativity. He says, "It expresses the desire of young black people to reclaim their history, reactivate forms of black radicalism, and contest the powers of despair, hopelessness, and genocide that presently besiege the black community. . . . It should be promoted as a worthy form of artistic expression and cultural projection, and as an enabling source of community solidarity."

Finally, Stephens (1991) sees rap music as a "crossroad to a new transnational culture." He believes that "by conceptualizing rap as an intercultural communication crossroads located on a racial frontier, we can conceive how rap's non-black constituents use this artform as an interracial bridge, even as many blacks by defining it as 'only black' attempt to use it as a source of power and exclusive identity formation."

In considering such a transnational culture, the source of rap's popularity for white youth is then, less difficult to ascertain. It is obvious, however, that the rebellious nature of rap in many way parallels the rebellious nature of original rock and roll. Grossberg (1987), in discussing rock and roll today, says that the practice of critical encapsulation divides the cultural world into Us and Them. "While being a rock and roll fan," he goes on to explain, "sometimes does entail having a visible and self-conscious identity (such as punks, hippies, or mods), it more often does not appear visibly, on the surface of a fan's life, or even as a primary way in which most fans would define themselves."

Rap is also seen as an icon of resentment to the white status quo. According to Spencer, as in any situation where an icon such as rap is attacked, there is always the potential that the attention will grant the music even further symbolic potency and, as a result, increase the population of listeners who subscribe to its newly broadened symbolism of protest.

As rock music sinks deeper into the mainstream, cultural rap music has risen as a new rebellious youth movement. Self-understanding and practice are important elements in the cultural mirror of rap music style and it has fostered a liberating transcultural understanding. This rap experience becomes an all-encompassing one, which includes the outward projection and acceptance of rebellious identity and beliefs for all who listen.

I believe that through rap music, low-income black youth are able to develop empowering values and ideologies, strengthen cultural interaction and establish positive identities. Rap music acts as a distinguishing mechanism as well as an informative cultural force for the mainstream system, similar to other cultural musics such as heavy metal and punk. As an integral part of the urban experience, the rap genre serves as a bridge from favorite songs and artists to personal and social realities. It is easy to see why mainstream society would feel uncomfortable with the sudden popularity of traditionally negative images like dope dealers, pimps, and prostitutes in rap music. Yet these are very real images and messages in the everyday world of the rapper and his original fan: the black urban youth.

Rap music offers itself up as a unique and cohesive component of urban black culture and is a positive struggle for black signification within popular culture. While there remain conflicts between negative and positive, right and wrong, good and bad, the rap dynamic is an explicit means of cultural communication fostering a crucial awareness of a reawakening urban reality.

REFERENCES

Adler, Jerry, "The Rap Attitude," *Newsweek*, March 19, 1990, p. 59.

Bernard, James, "Bitches and Money," *The Source*. November 1991, p. 8.

Berry, Venise, "The Complex Relationship between Pop Music and Low-Income Black Adolescents: A Qualitative Approach," Dissertation, The University of Texas at Austin, May 1989.

Chuck D, "Black II Black," *SPIN*, 6, October 1990, pp. 67–68.

Cocks, Jay, "A Nasty Jolt for the Top Pops," *Time*, July 1, 1991, p. 78.

Cone, James, *The Spirituals and the Blues*, New York: Seabury Press, 1972.

Costello, Mark, and David Foster Wallace, *Signifying Rappers: Rap and Race in the Urban Present*, New York: The Ecco Press, 1990.

Dixon, Wheeler, "Urban Black American Music in the Late 1980s: The 'Word' as Cultural Signifier," *The Midwest Quarterly*, 30, Winter 1989, pp. 229–241.

Dougherty, Steve, "Charges of Anti-Semitism Give Public Enemy a Rep That's Tough to Rap Away," *People Weekly*, 33, March 5, 1990, pp. 40–41.

Dyson, Michael, "Performance, Protest and Prophecy in the Culture of Hip Hop," *Black Sacred Music: A Journal of Theomusicology*, 5, Spring 1991, p. 24.

Fiske, John, *Reading the Popular*, Boston: Unwin Hyman, 1989.

Frankel, Martha, "2 Live Doo Doo," *SPIN*, 6, October 1990, p. 62.

Garland, Phyl, *The Sound and Soul: Story of Black Music*, New York: Simon and Schuster, 1971.

Gates, David, "Decoding Rap Music," *Newsweek*, March 19, 1990, pp. 60–63.

Gladwin, Thomas, *Poverty U.S.A.*, Boston: Little, Brown, 1967.

Green, Kim, "Sisters Stompin' in the Tradition," *Young Sisters and Brothers*, November 1991, pp. 51–53.

———, "The Naked Truth," *The Source*, November 1991, pp. 33–36.

Grossberg, Lawrence, "Rock and Roll in Search of an Audience," in *Popular Music and Communication*, Ed. James Lull, Beverly Hills: Sage Publishing, 1987, pp. 175–198.

Gurevitch, Michael, *Culture, Society and the Media*, London: Methuen, 1982.

Haring, Bruce, "Lyric Concerns Escalate," *Billboard*, 101, November 11, 1989, p. 1.

Henderson, Alex, "New Rap Pack: Public Enemy," *Black Beat*, 20, January 1989, p. 44.

———, "2 Live Crew," *Black Beat*, 21, February 1990, p. 15–16.

———, "LA Rap All Stars: We're All in the Same Gang," *Black Beat*, 21, December 1990, p. 16.

Hochman, Steve, "NWA Cops an Attitude," *Rolling Stone*, 555, June 29, 1989, p. 24.

Hulbary, William, "Race, Deprivation and Adolescent Self-Images," *Social Science Quarterly*, 56, June 1975, pp. 105–114.

Kofsky, Frank, *Black Nationalism and the Revolution in Music*, New York: Pathfinder Press, 1970.

Kot, Greg, "Rap Offers a Soundtrack of Afro-American Experience," *Chicago Sunday Times*, February 16, 1992, Section 13, pp. 5, 24–25.

Leland, John, "Cube on Thin Ice," *Newsweek*, December 2, 1991, p. 69.

Levine, David, "Good Business, Bad Messages," *American Health*, May 1991, p. 16.

Logan, Andy, "Around City Hall," *The New Yorker*, January 27, 1992, pp. 64–65.

Lyndah and Michelle (Bytches wit' Problems), "A Bitch is a Badge of Honor for Us," *Rappages*, 1, October 1991, p. 46.

Maultsby, Portia, "Soul Music: Its Sociological and Political Significance in American Popular Culture," *Journal of Popular Culture*, 17, Fall 1983, pp. 51–60.

Miller, Trudy, "'91 Holiday-Week Biz 3.7% Jollier than '90," *Billboard*, February 1, 1992, p. 46.

Mills, David, "The Obscenity Case: Criminalizing Black Culture," *Washington Post*, June 17, 1990, pp. G1, G8–G9.

———, "Five Percent Revolution," *Washington Post*, January 6, 1991, pp. G-1, G-6.

Nelson, Angela, "Theology in the Hip Hop of Public Enemy and Kool Moe Dee," *Black Sacred Music: A Journal of Theomusicology*, 5, Spring 1991, pp. 51–60.

Newman, Melinda, "Public Enemy Ousts Member over Remarks," *Billboard*, 101, July 1, 1989, pp. 1, 87.

"Paralyzed Man Files Suit over Boyz N' the Hood," *Jet*, 18, April 20, 1992, p. 61.

Pareles, Jon, "Fear and Loathing Along Pop's Outlaw Trail," *New York Times*, February 2, 1992, pp. 1, 23.

Perkins, William, "Nation of Islam Ideology in the Rap of Public Enemy," *Black Sacred Music: A Journal of Theomusicology*, 5, Spring, 1991, pp. 41–51.

Peterson-Lewis, Sonja, "A Feminist Analysis of the Defenses of Obscene Rap Lyrics," *Black Sacred Music: A Journal of Theomusicology*, 5, Spring 1991, pp. 68–80.

Poussaint, Alvin, and Carolyn Atkinson, "Black Youth and Motivation," in *Black Self Concept*, Ed. James Banks and Jean Grambs, New York" McGraw-Hill, 1972, pp. 55–69.

Riley, Norman, "Footnotes of a Culture at Ris:," *The Crisis*, 93, March 1986, p. 24.

Roberts-Thomas, K., "Say It Loud I'm Pissed and I'm Proud," *Eight Rock*, 1, Summer 1990, pp. 28–31.

Rogers, Charles, "New Age Rappers with a Conscience," *Black Beat*, 20, April 1989, pp. 41, 75.

Royster, Phillip, "The Rapper as Shaman for a Band of Dancers of the Spirit: 'U Can't Touch This'," *Black Sacred Music: A Journal of Theomusicology*, 5, Spring 1991, pp. 60–68.

Samuels, David, "The Rap on Rap," *The New Republic*, 205, November 11, 1991, pp. 24–26.

Shusterman, Richard, "The Fine Art of Rap," *New Literary History*, 22, Summer 1991, pp. 613–632.

Singletary, Sharon, "Livin' in a Hoe House?" *Rappages*, 1, October 1991, p. 60.

Spencer, Jon Michael, "The Emergency of Black and the Emergence of Rap: Preface," *Black Sacred Music: A Journal of Theomusicology*, 5, Spring 1991, pp. v–vii.

Standifer, James, "Music Behavior of Blacks in American Society," *Black Music Research Journal*, 1, 1980, pp. 51–62.

Stephens, Gregory, "Rap Music's Double Voiced Discourse: A Crossroads for Interracial Communication," *Journal of Communication Inquiry*, 15, Summer 1991, p. 72.

Stephens, Ronald, "Three Waves of Contemporary Rap Music," in *Black Sacred Music: A Journal of Theomusicology*, 5, Spring 1991, pp. 25–41.

"Top 200 Albums," *Billboard*, January 18, 1992, p. 86.

Walton, Ortiz, *Music Black, White and Blue,* New York: William Morrow and Co., 1972.

Williams, Juan, "The Real Crime: Making Heroes of Hate Mongers," *Washington Post*, June 17, 1990, pp G-1, G-8.

Guerrilla Music: Avant-Garde Voice as Oppositional Discourse

Thaddeus Coreno

> Art cannot change the world, but it can contribute to . . . changing the consciousness and drives of the men and women . . . who could change the world.
>
> Herbert Marcuse
> *The Aesthetic Dimension*, pp. 32–33

Introduction

The social and political conditions of the last fifteen years have spawned many loosely connected conservative groups trying to limit or overturn the perceived liberal agendas that they claim have contributed to the moral degeneration of American society. Overlapping historical trends provoked a sense of crisis in dominant institutions in the late 1970s and early 1980s. By the end of the 1970s social and political forces were playing themselves out on the nightly news: high inflation, gradually worsening opportunities for mobility, chronically high unemployment, the permanent reality of poverty, the progressively deteriorating standard of living for much of the work force, and, of course, the distressing Iranian hostage crisis. In many quarters, indicators of the slowly eroding American value system (usually referring to some version of a middle-class value structure) were rampant. Drug abuse, pornography, changing gender roles, abortion, homosexuality, and, increasingly, some brands of rock music were characterized as evidence of a generic decline of the moral commitments of Americans. The social and political climate was shifting from moderate tolerance to an oftentimes reactionary conservatism.

Many right-wing groups mobilized in order to slay the demons unleashed by liberals and secular humanists. Perhaps the most popular conservative organization to emerge from this historical context was Jerry Falwell's religious group the Moral Majority. Boasting of a huge following and tremendous financial support, the Moral Majority used all varieties of media to counter the liberal trends they portrayed as a secular humanist plot to destroy traditional religious (Christian) values. Similarly, the "700 Club" television program continues to serve as a beacon for Pat Robertson's interpretation of conservative religious and political views. The secular and religious organizations that formed the network of a conservative backlash against the "liberal establishment" have become known as the New (Christian) Right. (Several failed runs for president by New Right leaders along with sex and financial scandals have partially defused the power of the Christian New Right.) Even at its peak in the mid-1980s the New Right was not totally successful in converting mainstream institutions to their more orthodox ideologies. However, a certain impact apparently had been absorbed in the culture-at-large. Three very conservative, "born-again" presidents were elected; many economically conservative policies shaped business practices in the 1980s; public funding for artists became threatened because of the "immoral" nature of a few of the recipients; calls for less government intervention in the affairs of business and more tax breaks for wealthy Americans saturated the political rhetoric; finally, military intervention (Panama, Grenada, Nicaragua, Persian Gulf) became fashionable again. All the while, support for fascistic dictatorships around the world continued.

While it is difficult to make a case for the *total* dominance in important institutions by the New Right ideologues, inroads have been made in most of them. Many voluntary associations emerged or reappeared and functioned as conservative buffer groups in the ongoing campaigns against liberal excesses.

Antiabortion and antidrug groups were reactivated and attracted new recruits. One intriguing model example of this is the development in 1985 of the Parents' Music Resource Center (PMRC). Tipper Gore and friends established this nonprofit group as a counteroffensive against violent and sexually explicit lyrics in some rock music. Gore and her supporters organized the PMRC in order to protect children from the "twisted tyranny of explicitness in the public domain" (Gore, 1987:12). Most of their attention was drawn to the lyrics, album covers, stage performances, and videos of heavy metal bands such as Venom and WASP. Two recurring lyrical themes that especially concern the PMRC are satanism and suicide. Gore considers the obsession with Satan and the occult as "the ultimate form of rebellion" (Gore, 1987: 90).

It is not difficult to situate the response of a group like the PMRC in the mid-1980s within the tide of reactionary social forces that were flowing across America for at least five years by the time of their Senate hearing on rock lyrics on September 19, 1985. As the social and political climate shifted away from toleration it became easier for groups with conservative agendas to grab the spotlight by claiming to beat back the wild hordes. Moral crusades, while never disappearing completely from the American scene, were on center stage in the 1980s. Not only were adolescents encouraged to "just say no" to drugs but now, depending upon whom you were listening to, abortion, sex, and some rock music were also added to the "no" list.

I have introduced the PMRC and placed it in historical perspective in order to better understand the political nature (or, as I argue in this chapter, the lack of a politically motivated form) of rock music. I have not written this chapter with the intention of exposing the PMRC as a sham. The interested reader can pursue the onslaught of offensives and counteroffensives by each side. For me, the emergence of the PMRC is less interesting (especially since it was so predictable!) than the content of the music it was opposing. Popular music has consistently been under attack by groups who consider it a threat to sacred moral or social traditions (Gray, 1989). Instead, I am intrigued by the lack of a genuinely threatening popular music. I do not share the PMRC's view that the music they have indicted is diabolical. It seems to me the music they condemn offends a middle-class sensibility about certain moral codes but really offers very little oppositional substance. I want to be clear about my purpose: I am more interested in this essay with the *absence of politically threatening music* than with the political motives of groups like the PMRC. I will reiterate the many reasons most rock music *does not* offer a viable oppositional discourse for youth. In other words, I will catalogue the reasons *most* rock music poses no threat to any social institution, tradition, or political practice in America.[1] In addition, I will portray avant-garde music as an authentic source of cultural power for its listeners (of all ages).

This entire chapter is framed by the logic of the critical pedagogy project (Giroux, 1983). Critical pedagogy is a fusion of critical social theory with educational criticism (Giroux, 1983). The theoretical assumptions of critical pedagogy presume the hegemonic influence of a dominant ideology in educational discourses. These discourses usually privilege educational curricula that reproduce the values, opinions, methods, rationales, morals, and goals of the dominant classes in American society. Instead of portraying education as a nonproblematic encounter with objective knowledge, the critical pedagogists tease out the social class foundations of ideas and values congealed in the school curriculum. Because of the dominant class bias of educational formats, students of color or those who belong to working-class families often find their own groups' histories and lifestyles excluded or even degraded in the classroom. The critical pedagogists offer a strategy of resistance to the dominant educational ideology by countering it with an oppositional discourse which promises emancipation from biased, oppressive, or incomplete educational agendas. In order to provide students with real insights into the hierarchical nature of power relationships, the socially constructed nature of their everyday lives, and political manipulations that deny an emancipated citizenship, I will offer the sounds and rhythm of the avant-garde as an authentic weapon in the cultural resistance to the dominant discourse in music and education.

The Critical Pedagogy Project: Establishing the Technology of Critique

Giroux's 1983 book *Theory and Resistance in Education* serves as one manifesto in the effort by radical educators to establish an evolving model for theorizing about, as well as practicing, an emancipatory pedagogy. Giroux's writings are excellent distillations of theory and research exploring the barriers and hidden passages woven into the curricula of educational institutions in America and England. (I will use Giroux (1983) as a basis for much of my discussion in this section.) The perspective of students whose social origins qualify them for membership in excluded groups (race, class, gender) frames the analyses and strategies of critical pedagogy. The foundation of a "pedagogy for the opposition" is rooted in the suffering caused by living and trying to learn within the confines of cultural and material deprivations consolidated in the relationships between subordinates and members of dominant groups. Critical pedagogy shares a goal with the Frankfurt school of utilizing theory in order to assist in the transformation of human consciousness as well as the material relations governing social life. This "transformation" is intended to liberate those who are denied access to the corridors of opportunity because of their subordinate position in hierarchies of power and privilege. Theory, then, is deliberately constructed with the purpose of exposing the social underpinnings of the matrices of domination.

Educational emancipation requires several essential conditions to be introduced into the discourse about schooling before real empowerment and liberation for all students can become a basic goal of the curriculum. First, the existing school system must be reconceptualized in order to pinpoint the intrusions of dominant group interests, influences, and agendas into the curriculum. Schools have always functioned, in part, to assist in the reproduction of class relations by providing various groups with differential skills and experiences to fulfill particular positions in the division of labor. Radical knowledge informs oppressed groups about the architects of power who designed and erected a particular division of labor within a specific configuration of political and social institutions. The logic of domination is traced historically to situate the ongoing role of dominant groups in determining what kind of discourse is permitted in schools. Giroux (1983) expounds about the hidden curriculum or the tacit ideologies that frame the educational experience. Ideologies of instrumental reason, technocratic rationalism, competition, conformity, discipline, individualism, and the perceived inevitability of status quo social and political arrangements serve the interest of capital accumulation. Many social practices within the school must be understood as a reflection of dominant groups' attempts to structure the content of knowledge transmitted in school as well as the contexts wherein learning takes place. Consequently, schools cannot be severed from their links to the class structure nor from the political functions they serve for dominant group interests.

The second component in a discourse highlighting emancipatory pedagogy is the role ideology plays in fostering hegemony by a dominant class. Ideologies are secreted by dominant cultural institutions like mass media, churches, governments and, of course, schools. Cultural institutions try to impose a set of social practices. Ideologies emerge from these cultural fields in the form of rationales, rules, values, ideas, and commonsense assumptions. Ultimately, ideology should be understood as the creation of meaning. "Ideology, as used here, refers to the production, interpretation and effectivity of meaning" (Giroux, 1983:66). Critical pedagogy must locate the cultural forces that manufacture ideologies and probe the ways they become deposited in the consciousness (and unconscious) of individuals and groups. This involves sensitivity to the actual everyday experiences of students who become acquainted with ideological messages, consider them, and then absorb, accommodate, or resist them. Radical pedagogy's exegesis uncovers the embedded social routines, their accompanying rationales, and the commonsense assumptions that prop up existing relations of domination and subordination.

Emphasis on the dominant discourse provides insights into cultural reproduction. Culture is refracted in the institutional arrangements, knowledge, and social practices consolidating the interests of the dominant class. "In addition, it represents the attempt on the part of the dominant groups to penetrate the cultures of subordinate classes in order to win their consent to the existing order" (Giroux 1983:164). Dominant ideologies are never completely absorbed. Dissecting the discourses while attending to the alliances students exhibit with dominant ideologies provides an indication of the degree of penetration of hegemonic messages. More importantly, it encourages educators to look for and respect oppositional discourses produced by students because at the interstices of failed hegemonic efforts lies the potential for resistance and oppositional strategies that reflect the suspension of reproduction. Moments of resistance introduce the possibility for freedom. Critical pedagogy provides students with the sociological critique, enabling them to identify and interrogate the social forces involved in the production of history while forging new ideologies and cultural forms from their own lived experiences. "If students are to understand how the dominant culture bears down on them, they will have to grasp how it reaches into the logic of their own resistance" (Giroux, 1983:167). Avant-garde music is one cultural tool for learning and producing oppositional discourses, new strategies, and exotic logics which can creatively shape social transformation.

The last component of a radical pedagogy to be discussed here is a theory of resistance. Giroux (1983) and most radical pedagogists will not accept a portrayal of domination as complete. In fact, schools are depicted as sites of struggle where members of oppressed groups may absorb some of the dominant ideology but are just as likely to resist or oppose it. Students can align themselves with the governing rationality if their oppositional behavior fails to critically and self-reflectively unmask the social and political forces of domination. In this case, what appears to be resistance is actually a type of conformity. I maintain most rock music is merely entertaining or so closely tied to and supportive of the dominant ideology that it is unable to consistently offer students the necessary critical foundation of an emancipatory rationality. Most rock music desperately conforms to the governing rationales and ideologies that undergird the structures of domination. Postures of rebelliousness by members of "controversial" bands like Guns n' Roses or Skid Row reveal no oppositional strategies whatsoever. There is not even a hint of an understanding of domination. (There are some exceptions, of course. Queensrÿche's album *Operation Mindcrime* reads like a Marxist sociologist's account of ideological hegemony.) An authentic oppositional strategy must include a critique exposing the social and political forces that structure the material conditions and ideological ground rules of a society at a particular historical period. Resistance involves refusing to submit to oppressive conditions and logics.

> Thus, central to analyzing any act of resistance would be a concern with uncovering the degree to which it speaks to a form of refusal that highlights, either implicitly or explicitly, the need to struggle against the social nexus of domination and submission. In other words, resistance must have a revealing function, one that contains a critique of domination and provides theoretical opportunities for self-reflection and for struggle in the interest of self-emancipation and social emancipation. (Giroux, 1983:108–109)

Giroux's remarks highlight the preconditions for freeing education from the logic of domination by first unveiling the mechanics behind its organizational dynamics, class origins, and capacity to penetrate the needs and desires of individuals living in a postindustrial capitalist society. I believe music provides one opportunity for a self-reflective critique of domination. However, not just any music will provide the necessary conceptual or formal resources to explore successfully the veneer of legitimacy tethered to the dominant discourse. Later, I will briefly show why this is the case. Instead, the avant-garde will be offered as a revolutionary voice, a voice of the subaltern others. It is a voice shattering the pretenses of our assumptions concerning society in general and music in particular.

Forging an Alliance with Postmodern Strategies[2]

Aronowitz and Giroux (1991) pursue insights and critiques used by postmodern writers in order to pinpoint the oppressive features of dominant discourses. Their interest centers on the role of the canon in high schools and universities. Hegemonic canons invariably exclude the histories, experiences, and values of female and nonwhite, lower-class groups in their determination of what qualifies as important knowledge. Postmodernism interrogates the biases of Western values constituting ruling dogmas. Aronowitz and Giroux encourage the close scrutiny of claims made by bearers of the dominant canons to transcendental truth, wisdom, and objectivity. Like most postmodernists, the authors call for a rejection of an uncritical acceptance of a total, essential, and firmly grounded narrative that serves as an exclusive foundation for judgment and evaluation. Lyotard (1988) calls the exclusionary practices and compulsory consensus imposed by grand narratives as a kind of terrorism. The appropriate response to the coercive authorization of a dominant canon is the introduction of a new language capable of deconstructing the arrogant sanctity of the old paradigm.

Control over the dominant discourses amounts to control over language, meaning, and interpretation in the classroom. Yet schools are sites where teachers and students struggle to define and interpret the meaning of texts. Radical pedagogists must offer students the space to manifest their own histories, experiences, and desires. New formulas for the oppositional voice of students must be worked into the curriculum. These "new voices" will deconstruct the wisdom of exclusionary knowledge domains in favor of more democratic and pluralistic truths. "Oppositional paradigms offer new languages by attempting to deconstruct and challenge dominant relations of power and knowledge legitimated through traditional forms of discourse" (Aronowitz and Giroux, 1991:90–91). Aronowitz and Giroux summon an original reconstruction of knowledge that discloses the links between power, ideology, and knowledge. Western traditions and values come to be viewed as one discourse amid a universe of contradictory languages and paradigms. They deserve no special status as an exceptional or transcendent foundation.

Instead of remaining content with merely criticizing dominant discourses, Aronowitz and Giroux propose counter texts as channels offering an encounter with the voice of the other. These voices emerge from the borders of socially constructed barriers excluding students of color, women, and those from lower-class backgrounds. Border pedagogy refuses the dominant discourse to hold sway in a privileged position. New texts and discourses—that is, new voices—will actively decenter privileged canons. Central to border pedagogy informed by postmodern criticism is the need to point to ways in which those narratives based on white, patriarchal, class-specific versions of the world can be challenged and deterritorialized. That is, by offering a theoretical language for establishing new boundaries with respect to knowledge most often associated with the periphery of the culturally dominant, postmodern discourses open up the possibility for incorporating into the curriculum a notion of border pedagogy in which cultural and social practices need no longer be mapped or referenced solely on the basis of the dominant models of Western culture. Knowledge will be debated on a new decentered and "deterritorialized terrain"—one that accepts and encourages the ongoing process of producing meaning in a liberated learning zone. The histories, knowledge, and values produced around the borders of the categories of the excluded others are permitted to reserve a space in the school curriculum. This space echoes with their subaltern voices previously blotted out by the writers of ruling class history.

The Sounds of Music as Countertext

Music offers radical educators an opportunity to teach students how to shatter the veneer of the dominant discourse. Teachers can introduce music because it is an important part of adolescent experience. Furthermore, they can use critical thinking to interrogate the styles and messages of music (Shumway, 1989). The tools of radical pedagogy spelled out by

Giroux (1983) and Aronowitz and Giroux (1991) can be used to shape a space for the opposition. The content and style of music could provide oppositional themes to be used as reinforcement for the larger pedagogical efforts of chipping away at dominant ideologies. Shumway (1989) calls for an educational curriculum incorporating rock music as a teaching resource with the capacity to provoke students to question the norms and routines that structure their school experience. "Rock 'n' roll should be brought into schooling precisely because it can challenge some of what is most repressive about schooling itself" (Shumway, 1989: 226). In the next section I will catalogue some of the reasons most rock music is incapable of this task and provide an alternative. Nevertheless, treating music critically in the classroom can enlighten students about their roles as consumers of cultural products, and about the power of media conglomerates to screen, fashion, and sell a type of music. Such an approach can also give students the chance to examine the lyrics and styles of songs (Shumway, 1989). Because adolescents identify so strongly with their music, the radical educator is presented with an opportunity to extract its oppositional spirit and use it to challenge the hegemony of ruling dogmas constituting the educational curriculum.

Music will be unable to function as a cultural source of critical thought and reflection in the classroom unless it is presented to students from a revolutionary perspective. One of the purest alternative traditions available today is the avant-garde. Smith and Zantiotis (1989) call for an avant-garde consciousness and educational curriculum that teachers can bring to the classroom. An avant-garde education entails a commitment to the emancipatory claims of democratic liberation movements. Smith and Zantiotis propose a teaching strategy of insurrection against the rationales of domination, describing the two discourses as follows: ". . . the dominant discourse is the taken-for-granted, the 'normal,' and the established, whereas the avant-garde has a relativizing and estranging effect, is subversive of normality, and is heterodox" (1989:109). Teachers are hailed as "resisting intellectuals" who ethically act against any dominant discourse that produces subjugated groups. An avant-garde agenda for the classroom seeks to transform students into citizens armed with the technologies of critique.

Several complementary intentions cohere in the lesson plans of avant-garde teachers: education should be decidedly moral and ethical as it creates a discourse for the victims of history; education should accent the social and political foundations of school dynamics; finally, teachers should actively transform the language of conquest and legitimation inherent in the dominant ideology into a discourse of creativity and possibility for all students (Smith and Zantiotis, 1989). If music enters the classroom as a subject channelled through an avant-garde teaching agenda then a genuine possibility exists for imparting the technologies of critique capable of revealing the material and ideal structures of domination. Music is a particularly effective topic because of the emotional attachments adolescents make with their favorite groups. Adolescence is also a period of some experimentation with new life-styles and philosophies. These conditions provide inroads towards penetrating the everyday experiences of adolescents. In these spaces the boundaries of old discourses can be redrawn while new ones establish foundations of possibility, community, and justice.

The Pocket of Resistance

Although I have been critical of rock music's potential as a source of radical knowledge, there are several popular artists who have consciously called for social change. You can probably come up with the names of several bands or individual artists who reflect a social consciousness. Peter Gabriel, R.E.M., Bruce Cockburn, Sinead O'Connor, The Clash, John Mellencamp, Bruce Springsteen, and others have consistently included themes of social activism in their music, oftentimes with a call for change. These types of groups form the "pocket of resistance" in contemporary rock music. The typical content of this kind of music does offer teachers the chance to instruct adolescents about domination. Resistance to domination usually takes the form of a protest against some sociopolitical injustice like the decimation of the Brazilian rain forest, apartheid, U.S.-backed Central American death squad governments, poverty, imposed paralysis of the American working class, or British occupation of Northern Ireland. Music brings these issues to adolescents as symbolic and emotional messages (Lull, 1985).

Students can be taught *alternatives* by exploring protest music. Possibilities exist for an expansion of their awareness of other people's as well as their own histories, cultural resources, and political struggles. Music carries messages not only cognitively but also physically as well as emotionally. "Music appeals to and facilitates basic desires to socialize, dance, speak in contemporary codes, and to have a constant audio backdrop for other activities" (Lull, 1985:368). Teachers can create a public sphere in the classroom wherein students can experience music that exposes the painful consequences of living in a stratified social universe. Although music helps to socialize youth (Lull, 1985) it does not indoctrinate them (Lemming, 1987). Adolescents carry with them evolving value structures formed by multiple agents of socialization and use those values to filter the messages of music (Lemming, 1987). Teachers can provide additional input as a socializing force encouraging students to be critically engaged with their music. Music emanating from the pocket of resistance can betray the socially constructed nature of domination and subordination. Its unique character grabs adolescents' attention, their thoughts, and bodies. "Music has a unique and striking material relation to the human body itself, invading it, enfolding it within its own rhythms and textures" (Grossberg, 1987:187). Even the fun, excitement, and excesses of apolitical rock music can be construed as a protest, albeit a mild one, against the pretentious seriousness and boredom of everyday life in an industrial society (Grossberg, 1987). Less serious rock music confronts established values and traditions with playful, spontaneous and sometimes outrageous attitudes which refuse total indoctrination by dominant ideologies secreted by the family, school, and mass media. This type of music, though to a very limited degree as I will show in the next section, helps students carve out some space for their own experience of pleasure not usually condoned by authority and assists in the formation of unique identities (Wicke, 1987).

Just Another Brick in the Hierarchy: Why Most Rock Music Fails to Produce an Oppositional Discourse

Several impediments converge in America's capitalist society to form barriers against the development of an authentically radical music. Wicke (1987) shows that the role rock music has played throughout most of its history has been to provide postwar teenagers with entertainment alternatives that enhance their leisure activities. By the 1950s, teenagers had become consumers equipped with radios and dreams of mobility. Leisure had supplanted a rewarding occupation as a high priority in the lives of high school and college students (Wicke, 1987). The vast majority of jobs that promised fulfillment were quickly disappearing by the 1960s (Wicke, 1987). Except for a few special occupational titles that promised real creativity and input at work, most labor entailed filling some slot arranged by the technocratic rationales that drove capital accumulation (Wicke, 1987). Rock 'n' roll in the fifties did collide with the oppressive conservatism permeating the high schools, but it never threatened the social and political arrangements outside that environment.

> Only the final acceptance of the norms of family, home, and school make possible the leisure world which has arisen as an alternative to these, but which in its function is not nearly as alternative as it was thought. It simply provides a context in which the behaviour models which have been raised to the status of norms are made acceptable to young people so that ultimately these can also be adopted. . . . However rebellious and provocative rock 'n' roll appeared and however much it conflicted with the conservative and conformist pressure in the high schools at the time, it was nothing more than the cultural form in which teenagers in fifties America accepted their real conditions of life. (Wicke, 1987:47)

This quotation should not be read as a dismissal of the claims to originality, energy, and sensuality made by rock critics and performers alike. Instead, rock music is being portrayed as a cultural product that soothes the transition of a new generation of youth facing different problems of adjusting to existing conditions than their parents did. Music permits common identification of sentiments, styles, and values which may conflict with parental preferences but do not really call for an overhaul of the status quo. Somewhere within that status quo most rock listeners are trying desperately to find a niche characterized by a special style and taste.

By the 1960s rock music had become sensitized to the social predicaments that would characterize the entire decade. Facing a world of work offering increasingly routinized and meaningless drudgery as a fundamental aspect of everyday labor (even for many college graduates) and an equally senseless and brutal war in Vietnam, the youth protested. However, if a close examination is made of messages transmitted by major rock figures of the sixties it becomes evident that while a social consciousness had definitely blossomed in the music, the solutions, and hence, an understanding of the "problem," were oftentimes portrayed in overly subjective and individualistic terms ("all you need is love"). Wicke (1987) believes this was inevitable because the music business is a capitalist enterprise permitting social criticism and absorbing protest music as long as it sells, but never promoting authentic counterideologies. Even though rock music *appears* to be rebelling we must understand the consequences of cultural forms produced within the logic of capital accumulation.

> The ideology inherent in rock only apparently contradicts this, for it is precisely the individualism on which it is based which is the functional element linking it to the economic and ideological interests of capital. . . . The more marked the musician's individualism, the more convincingly the capitalist order appears as the true basis of individual self-realisation and the more convincing the motive for purchasing his record as an expression of the consumer's same individualism. (Wicke, 1987:115)

The extended matrix of interdependent business interests linked to recording companies typically remains as an apparently innocuous influence on the "free" expression of themes in rock music. Yet as Wicke (1987) claims, the consistently apolitical or even mildly reformist lyrics of most bands usually boast a very consistent ideology of individualism and, indirectly, consumerism (buy our record!). Because of these reasons most rock music fails to offer students authentic counterideologies in lyrical content, musical form, or performance style. Music is more typically used by youth to fill up leisure time and assist in the formation of uniquely styled identities and ways of life within a capitalist society (Wicke, 1987).

But what about music that appears so extreme that subcultures of youth grow around their identification with the bands? Heavy metal and punk[3] certainly reflect rebelliousness to their young working-class followers who copy their styles. Right? Actually, even these ostensibly rebellious styles are better depicted as crude or immoderate reactions to growing up in a class-stratified industrial society and not as a voice of insurrection against it or a call for a new more democratic arrangement. Wicke pinpoints these different styles of musical expression as a manifestation of cultural differentiation within capitalism. "The process gives expression to the social problems of life *in* the capitalist system but not to a political protest against it" (1987:81). These evolving cultural forms are embedded within the networks that constitute the mass media. The messages transmitted by the media, especially the recording industry, help to reproduce the existing state of relations between dominant and subordinate groups. Each new form of music produced by cultural differentiation becomes a source for the mass media to claim as an additional justification of capital accumulation. Although some of the lyrics may describe the struggles of living in a class-divided, industrial society dominated by technocratic rationality, most of the musical themes and styles fail to substitute current conditions with plans of action or visions of new social arrangements.

> With its concentration on media and mass culture for the achievement of its ideological and economic interests, capitalism uses nothing other than the legitimacy of cultural development processes which, in spite of all autonomy, still remain a form of reproduction of material production. And it achieves these so successfully, remaining unchallenged in the field, because it rarely comes across any alternatives which need to be taken seriously. (Wicke, 1987:180)

Rock music offers adolescents not critically informed observations about the logic of domination, but a rough outline for steering youth through their often difficult psychosocial rites of passage. "Rock provides some measure of stability and comfort in the midst of family problems, peer pressure, school tensions and the like" (Schultze, et al., 1991:154). Lull also notes the role rock music plays in the routinized rebellion of adolescents. "Rock music's primary audience, youth, is expected to quarrel with institutional forces such as parents, teachers, and bosses. Songs that describe philosophical conflict from the point of view of youth are common in rock music" (1987:14). Rock music has become a normative expression of adolescent adjustment. Although there are groups with more politicized styles that constitute a pocket of resistance, most rock music barely seems conscious of either the historical or institutional forces framing the social milieus that gave birth to the music and audience.

Another less obvious consequence of apolitical or innocuously rebellious music is the channelling of oppositional adolescent energy away from organized political activity towards domesticated leisure rituals.

> In retrospect, it can be said that rock fell short of inspiring the sort of political and social change it seemed to be calling for. Instead, rock became a safety valve for the anger, rebellion, and violence that seemed to lurk just beneath the relatively civilized facade of the American youth culture. Rock music may have served, and may still serve, to channel social unrest and latent violence in the direction of political passivity. . . . In other words, adversarial and nihilist rock became an effective opiate, at once providing a safe and ultimately inconsequential outlet for protest and filling the deep pockets of the opportunistic captains of the recording industry. (Schultze, et al., 1991:170–171)

Imagine the rebellious posturing of a band like Guns n' Roses. Align this image with the innocuous messages adolescents receive from their music. Messages that do not challenge but merely entertain with a predictable hard rock musical form backed up by lyrical themes tethered to the status quo. Axl Rose and Co. are a crude embodiment of the American dream guided by ideologies of machismo and individualism packaged in an uncritical rock aesthetic.

Yet, even though it is piped in through the conduit of capitalist mass media, rock music is important for youth because it reflects their experiences of living and manufactures meaning as they come together and share in the pleasures it celebrates. Most of it is not very important as a source for radical education because it produces few tools for critique and reconstruction.

The Voice of Insurgency

The European and American avant-garde art movements have impacted the evolution of a new form of music. The sounds of this music emerge from exotic methods and strategies birthed by a new wave of artists who have explicitly rejected the role of art in capitalist (bourgeoisie) society. Burger (1984) has documented the essential qualities of avant-garde art and its self-conscious attempts to fashion a new way of realizing creative practice. Avant-garde artists maintain that art has become disengaged from any socially relevant part of everyday life (Burger, 1984). In a capitalist society art really only serves as a self-reflection of the conditions of bourgeoisie existence channelled through the aristocratic values of the artist. "The avant-gardistes view its dissociation from the praxis of life as the dominant characteristic of art in bourgeoisie society" (Burger, 1984:49). This apartness from social life produces a shallow art lacking any purpose other than offering the bourgeoisie a representation of their own values. This style of art caters to aesthetic criteria reflected in the standards deemed important by the upper classes. Art does not provide liberation within these social arrangements but, instead, mirrors the values of capitalist society back to the individual recipient of a piece of work. Additionally, the themes inhering in artwork usually display ideal conditions of truth or community that have been demolished in the competitive exchange relationships guided by instrumental rationality. Burger uses Marcuse's insights for his description.

> All those needs that cannot be satisfied in everyday life, because the principle of competition pervades all spheres, can find a home in art, because art is removed from the praxis of life. Values such as humanity, joy, truth, solidarity are extruded from life as it were, and preserved in art. (Burger, 1984:50)

This kind of art does not expose the architecture of domination but instead creates images guided by the values permitting the bourgeoisie to experience beauty and joy without having to confront the debilitating contradictions rampant in capitalist society. The artwork becomes an object for sale—a thing to be bought and displayed as a symbol of status and distinction. It is judged as a "great" or significant work to the extent that it fulfills aesthetic requirements. Art, in bourgeoisie society, exists for art's sake only and for *no* other social or political reason. This "apartness" was abhorred by avant-gardistes who sought to detonate the reification of aesthetic criteria by integrating art into everyday life.

The avant-gardistes' response to this segregation of art and life was to initiate a strategy of complete rejection of aesthetic criteria. By withdrawing from traditional standards of artistic taste, art would be returned to the everyday world. A chasm between the avant-garde and bourgeoisie artists was intentionally carved out by the former. In order to resist the contaminating influence of bourgeoisie aestheticism, a radically novel artistic practice was developed apart from any concern about standards. "Only an art the contents of whose individual works is wholly distinct from the (bad) praxis of the existing society can be the center that can be the starting point for the organization of a new life praxis" (Burger, 1984:50). The new artistic practice would expose aesthetic standards as an elitist ploy to exclude those who refuse to accept their arbitrary distinctions. The myth of individual authorship is also attacked since it deceptively sets up the artist as superior to and above the "common folk" who lack talent or are incapable of grasping true genius. The sacredness of the art object itself is demolished by displays of profane objects (urinals, soup cans, montages of disparate images) as art. Finally, the qualifications designating an "authentic" work of art undergo a radical democratizing.

Artistic practice can genuinely depict domination when it uncovers the arbitrary nature of ranked positions in social hierarchies. Avant-garde art absolutely refuses to use traditional motifs because these have historically propped up the capitalist social order from which the artist has become alienated. In order to pierce the veneer of legitimacy the avant-gardistes mount an all-out assault on our senses, assumptions, logic, rationales, and expectations. By refusing to participate in *normal* artistic practice they challenge its legitimacy.

The avant-garde practice guerrilla artistic techniques in order to expose the brutality of a society predicated upon relations of domination and subordination. Their art constantly reveals the lack of freedom existing in systems of hierarchically ranked groups. In this way, their project parallels the critical theorists who also seek to expose the "unfreedom" residing in domination. Marcuse (1978) calls for art that expresses a new aesthetic of liberation from a social order that fails to ensure freedom for all. This type of art must be "subversive, of perception and understanding" in order to puncture the womb of the dominant ideology. Art should accuse the existing class-stratified social reality of failing miserably in its response to individual needs while simultaneously offering a glimpse of the possible.

> I shall submit the following thesis: the radical qualities of art, that is to say, its indictment of the established reality and its invocation of the beautiful image (*schöner schein*) of liberation are grounded precisely in the dimensions where art *transcends* its social determination and emancipates itself from the given universe of discourse and behavior while preserving its overwhelming presence. (Marcuse, 1978:6)

Revolutionary art forms confront a static citizenry with representations of an ossified class structure and its destructive consequences. Avant-garde art and music is unrelenting in its refusal to speak a familiar language or produce popular tones and timbres because they would depict a false harmony. This form of emancipatory art literally sabotages language because it represents the dominant discourse. As a consequence, a vocabulary of critique can be injected into the cracks of the umbrella of technical rationality by an art form which will not recognize the prevailing aesthetic models that uncritically echo justifications for bourgeoisie dominance.

Music can divulge the logic of domination in two ways. One possibility is a music that uses traditional styles but lyrically exposes the oppressive features of society. Several popular recording acts mentioned earlier use rock music to *sing* about social problems. Another alternative, the avant-garde option, actually subverts traditional forms of music by practicing strategies which intentionally demolish our expectations concerning sound, melody, harmony, and noise. Avant-garde music is actively disruptive of the traditional musical order. Rock music has become politically impotent as long as it remains nestled among its corporate sponsors. In other words, merely using a rock music format does not guarantee a rebellious music. Rather than use a musical style so tethered to the legitimation process wielded by elites to protect social order, avant-garde music mounts an insurrection against the *sounds* of domination. By doing this the listener is forcibly confronted with the inequities and irrationalities that exist in everyday life. Most avant-garde music does not defer to any bourgeoisie traditions or musical style. Styles and traditions, when uncritically received and used, reproduce the conditions necessary for the continuing domination of ruling elites. "If the liberation of human beings and nature is to be possible at all, then the social nexus of destruction and submission must be broken" (Marcuse, 1978:13). In order to fulfill the commitment to a liberating art, avant-garde music refuses to participate in the continued use of instrumental rationality. Everyday life must be rescued from the contaminating impact of rationales that transform interactions between human beings into exchange relationships. "What most strongly conflicts with the means-ends rationality of bourgeois society is to become life's organizing principle" (Burger, 1984:34). Several strategies are used to expose the pervasiveness of means-ends rationality used by elites to forge alienating and constraining social arrangements.

Avant-garde methodology systematically deconstructs the sound of music. Their tactics involve decontextualizing all sound contained in music produced by instruments or voice.

Furthermore, the entire universe of sound emanating from nonmusical origins is granted equal status with other sources. No privilege is granted to any distinct style or form. Sound is often removed from its context and then aligned with other orphaned sonants. The "new" product may appear meaningless within the confines of instrumental logic, but this is precisely the intention of avant-garde music. Means-ends rationality has produced a system of domination and, consequently, a false harmony. Emancipatory music that flows from this kind of society should not reproduce sounds of a fabricated consensus.

In order to resist the rationales of domination, avant-gardistes embrace strategies counteracting subordination to means-ends logic. Freedom resides, in the cultural sphere at least, in art or music opposed to the reduction of human lives to market relationships. Halley (1991) sketches several avant-garde tactics used by the Dadaists to delegitimate the existing social order. Dadaism was an artistic practice originating in several European cities such as Zurich, Berlin, and Paris around 1916. Dadaists intentionally sought to destroy bourgeois institutions and styles by practicing art in a nonsensical or grotesque way. Avant-garde music was born in these early experiments with different media. Avant-garde literature, music, and clothing styles were launched at the Cabaret Voltaire in order to topple the social order by first destroying its claim to cultural dominance. These artistic practices were linked to leftist political parties and philosophies seeking social change in a society responsible for generating a repressive class structure and the savagery of the First World War (Halley, 1991).

Like Dada, avant-garde music accomplishes its sonar insurgency by pursuing several defiant assaults on existing cultural forms. Halley (1991) extracts four methods of inflicting anarchy: particularization, disruption of linear time, randomization, and pursuing a subjective sensitivity. Particularization is an artistic practice that levels or negates all hierarchies by isolating words and behavior from their assigned contexts in the social order. By ripping words away from their socially designated relationships meaning can no longer be assumed and the power to define has been usurped. Avant-garde music frequently employs this strategy of decontextualizing cultural voices. Sound collages of politicians, preachers, advertisements, charlatans, and any other voices are often played simultaneously or randomly patched together. All voices are equally important or equally ridiculous. When pieces are lifted from their functional connections to other defined elements, questions arise as to the relative nature of language and its power to control. No one final meaning can be construed from a sound collage. There is no longer an author, just a jumbled concoction of voices vying to be heard above the din.

There is no overall unity to avant-garde music because there is no consensus or foundation in society from which such a predictable and patterned sound might emerge. "The avant-gardiste work neither creates a total impression that would permit an interpretation of its meaning nor can whatever impression may be created be accounted for by recourse to the individual parts, for they are no longer subordinated to a pervasive intent" (Burger, 1989:80). By freeing sound from a dominating grand design the listener must question the taken-for-granted rationalizations applied to the construction of reality as it stands. When music flowing from the dominant order no longer sounds harmonious and familiar, the listener becomes conscious of the disordered and fractured conditions that actually endure in the existing social arrangements. By particularizing voices and sounds the illusion of the inevitability of a hierarchically structured society begins to wither. It becomes obvious that voices and sounds, and hence, people, are situated and ranked according to the logic and interests of a controlling and powerful group.

Listening to avant-garde sound collages removes the fixity of meaning by freeing up other voices. It denudes socially prominent voices (preachers, politicians, media personnel, business spokespersons, and other professionals) of their status and privilege by aligning their voices with the discourse of criminals, social outcasts or "common" people. Nonverbal sounds also refuse to stay in their allocated niches. Any type of sound can appear at any moment because order has been suspended. The rearrangement of voices and sound returns musical creation to anyone who chooses to practice the deconstruction. In this way, art is returned to the praxis of everyday life. People living within the contradiction of a class-stratified society can now detonate the ideologies upholding the structures of domination and submission.

Disrupting linear time removes the rhythm of the day from the clutch of the machine, factory, and bureaucracy and returns it to people creating their lives without agendas and timetables established by governing elites. Time does not move inevitably forward in avant-garde music. There is no beginning and end to a piece of music. There are frequent stops and starts, moments of silence, and periods of repeated tones. Time in an avant-garde work does not lead to some preordained musical goal. The use of time in the piece is not ordered by any musical resolution involving chord sequences or patterns required by particular styles such as blues, rock, or jazz. The artist interrupts the sounds or extends them without recourse to aesthetic considerations. The present is stressed along with simultaneous resonances pouring out of the constructed and material environments. Cyclical time is preferred in repetition without a resolution, the point being that time should be used to satisfy human needs, not to control people's movement. Avant-garde music can last a few seconds or more than an hour. This is decided by the artist without deferring to prevailing taste.

A typical avant-garde work usually delivers a blow upon the dominant ideology by experimenting with chance or random sound events. Predictability in an environment ordered by instrumental logic is impossible without coercively organized institutional arrangements. Consequently, a liberating musical form must allow chance to produce the music as much as possible. Randomly arranged sounds often have a disorienting effect—all the better from the avant-garde perspective. Allowing events to unravel in their own way opposes the instrumental logic of control and dominance over humans and nature. Protest against this regimentation takes the form of allowing sound to find its own temporary niche in a piece. "The regression to a passive attitude of expectation, in other words, must be understood as stemming from the total opposition to society as it is" (Burger, 1984:66). When chance is permitted to guide the direction of musical instruments, voices, and any other rescued sounds, the progressive unravelling of a liberated chorus can make an appearance without appealing to some logically necessary style. The evolving wave of sound is thus free from domination. This act of encouraging chance music to play itself out is an act of opposition in its withdrawal from concern about order. Rigid predictability is replaced with spontaneity (Burger, 1984). Randomly generated timbres disconnect the listener from mechanically programmed causality in the sound environment by cultivating a sensitivity for synchronicity in social life (Halley, 1991). The imagination, as opposed to instrumental reason, is given the chance to direct the flow of sound. Now, all possibilities are available to both the artist and listener. The consequence of assaulting the listener with these delegitimating techniques is the opening of a channel to a subjectivity outside the territory claimed by means-ends rationality. "The possibility of an alliance between 'the people' and art presupposes that the men and women administered by monopoly capitalism unlearn the language, concepts, and images of this administration, that they experience the dimension of qualitative change, that they reclaim their subjectivity, their inwardness" (Marcuse, 1978:37). Avant-garde music helps the listener to "unlearn" by literally annihilating her language and rearranging the vocal and sonic environment to the extent that it *sounds* confused, meaningless, or fractured. Embedded within this chaos is the space to carve out a new version of reality, a reenchanted one free of hierarchically administered domination.

Particularization of voice combined with the randomization of sound produces musical *chatter* (Halley, 1984). Chatter is meaningless and socially useless but in losing its function it also can no longer be used to dominate. Particularized voices rearranged by chance are dissociated from power relations and delivered immediately to the listener. Halley's exegesis of Dadaism reveals the attempt by the artists to directly communicate with the audience in a new deconstructed language. "For the Dadaists, in particularizing language, it becomes emptied of its reified implications of cultural domination, and rediscovers its raw intensity and immediateness" (1981:237). Randomizing voice and sound blocks reason from screening music. When reason cannot "make sense" of sound, a portal is created within the void shaped by the suspension of the familiar. A new transcendent power is seized when the illegitimate force of means-ends rationality has been destroyed. Avant-garde music invites the listener into that portal in order to experience the infinite possibilities of imagination in a reenchanted world (Halley, 1991). Everything is possible since the old foundations have been abandoned. The actual discourse of domination has been detonated into a million pieces from which emerges a new emancipated unity. This is the practice of cultural politics by the avant-garde musicians. Referring to Dadaism, Halley makes the following observation, "It is the first moment of rebellion, one that raises the problem and vitiates the order of reason as domination. This is its political significance" (1991:241). The existing system of meanings has been invalidated. Music is partly responsible for this condition. But it does not stop there. Avant-garde music creates a new reality from the scattered sounds of the old order. Avant-garde music as a cultural form contains an exceptionally effective delegitimating counterideology because it interrupts the flow of the industrial soundscape. A music liberated from domination negates the use of time and space for instrumental functions. Avant-garde music refuses to be contained by the structural limits imposed by bureaucratic institutions that reproduce the conditions necessary for the domination of social relations by industrial capitalism.

Music communicates its messages symbolically. Music, like other symbols, arises from the collective expression of people who designate meaning with words and sound to situations (Shepherd, 1991). In order to link music to its social foundations it is imperative to sketch the social forces impacting the shape of composition. Society, in part, is mirrored in music. "Music stands in the same relationship to society as consciousness: society is creatively 'in' each musical event and articulated by it" (Shepherd, 1991:83). The sonic charges assaulting the ears emanate from a sociocultural province partially determining their contours. Music has meaning because it carries in it the timbre of social life (Shepherd, 1991). The texture of sound is homologous to the rhythm of social interaction taking place under the scaffolding of social and cultural structures.

Shepherd (1991) portrays functional tonality as the musical illustration of industrial capitalist domination. The structure of music reflects the existing sociopolitical arrangements because it was generated within those forces.

> Functional tonality creates a hierarchy of fundamentals, all of which, through the various levels of the hierarchy, finally and ultimately relate back to one note. The architectonicism of the functional tonal structure articulates the dominant world sense of industrial societies. It is a structure having one central viewpoint (that of the keynote) that is the focus of a single, unified sound sense involving a high degree of distancing. . . . The analysis of functional tonal music often concerns itself with "showing" how the final satisfying effect of stating the tonic chord is "due" to previously created harmonic tension. (Shepherd, 1991:122–124)

Shepherd (1991) has connected the internal configuration of musical composition to external social forces. Seen in this light, music is intimately political. Today it continues to represent the collective expression of people who live during a particular historical epoch within the matrix of capitalist social structures. The experience of living as a member of either a dominant or subordinate group is secreted in the symbols people use to communicate. Music is no exception. Its construction is not immune to the ideologies that shape the parameters of cultural conflict. Functional tonality is the essence of the dominant musical discourse. The arrangement of musical structures in functional tonality generates a hierarchically ordered edifice of fundamentals tied to the keynote. The chord sequences create a tension which comes to a complete harmonious resolution. "Functional tonality is about the creation and resolution of harmonic tensions—the articulation through harmonic progressions of explicit and complex arguments which come to a firm and satisfying conclusion on the keynote" (Shepherd, 1991:130). The dominance of the keynote directing the resolution of harmonic tensions mimics the dominance of capitalist institutions attempting to control hierarchically ordered individuals grouped into social classes.

The surface appearance of capitalist relations is one of order. Capitalist relations, like the music they generate, appear functional. Conflicts are worked out without the system being threatened. Like capitalist relations, the tensions in social relations are resolved in functional tonality by deferring to the dominance in the musical schemata of the keynote. The logic of functional tonality is similar to technocratic rationality.

> The framework has one note, the keynote, which is more important than other notes. These other notes, in their turn, have an order of importance. This hierarchy of fundamental notes (or "fundamentals") parallels the materially and intellectually hierarchical nature of industrial capitalist societies. (Shepherd, 1991:133)

The structure of the major-minor scale system imposes a certain conformity upon the direction of a series of notes (Shepherd, 1991). Marginalized notes yield to the central authority of the keynote in order to manufacture a harmonious rhythmic product. Dominated people, like dominated notes, remain submerged under the scaffolding of ideologies that assign their rank in a hierarchy while masking the coercive political forces involved in perpetuating such an arrangement. The keynote arrives as a consequence of the measured performances of rhythm and pitch complimented by pure timbres (Shepherd, 1991). The harmony manufactured by functional tonality remains ostensibly an expression of liberation.

> The keynote in functional tonal music thus articulates a false sense of freedom and "democracy," because the attainment of the final keynote can only be achieved by controlling others and alienating them from their full power to exist in the world. (Shepherd, 1991:140)

Music embedded in the structures of functional tonality is alienating because it distances hierarchically arranged notes from each other. These notes are not linked in a free or natural fashion. Instead, they remain subservient to the dominance of keys and scales. Within that subordinate posture they are used to serve the dominant tonal order instead of finding their own place. Like workers who lack control and direction over their creative activity, atomized notes created by functional tonality are coercively implanted into musical templates. The harmony that emerges from a functional uniformity is best characterized as the consequence of an imposed order.

African and African-influenced music offer a respite from the ossified hierarchies of functional tonality. Both styles deviate from the formulaic requirements impinging on rhythm, pitch, and timbre. Blues, jazz, and rock are partially dislodged from the calculating strategies of classical music. These brands practice unique styles that include changing the beat, inflecting or bending notes in a melody, and improvising pitch in compositions (Shepherd, 1991). Overall, African-influenced music is more intimate and emotional since it reclaims some of the creative spontaneity denied in industrial capitalism. Jazz and blues evolved as a reaction against the white power structure cohering in class-stratified urban centers (Shepherd, 1991). Rock, too, is able to loosen itself from the confines of an elitist musical schema by experimenting with its basic elements in order to capture the emotional-expressive components of a creative involvement with the social environment. True liberating moments arrive, according to Shepherd (1991), when musical forms reflect a conscious rejection of inherited designs. This is a partial turning away, also, from the social structures that spawned the original musical templates.

Although African-influenced American styles are capable of rewriting the musical scripts prescribed by functional tonality in opposition to their oppressive features, they remain tethered to its logic. A certain degree of subjective expressivity is brought into being but is still contained within the fabric of functional harmony. An authentic transcendence is never complete if the dominant ideology perpetuated by the ruling class has been partially internalized (Shepherd, 1991). The music flowing from subordinate groups will not provide an authentic cultural liberation if it must cater to the rationales of domination implicit in the sound of their compositions. "However much the harmonic-rhythmic framework is stretched, suspended, reordered, and dismembered as part of a creative, interpretive act, African-American and Afro-American-influenced musics seldom approach a true transcendence and dissolution of that framework" (Shepherd, 1991:164). One approach to musical transcendence involves really breaking free from the dependence upon a hierarchically ordered system of notes. Shepherd (1991) believes avant-garde jazz represents a revolutionary offensive against the dominant musical-political structures. I maintain the avant-garde tactics discussed so far also deliver a salvo against the imposed order of stratified musical relationships that inhere in functional tonality. Independence from functional relationships provides an occasion to enter an alternative field of sound beyond the influence of exploitive alliances. This new space resonates with nonhierarchical sound reflecting the creative imagination's capacity to liberate the listener from instrumental ideologies. Living within a musical field free from domination invites the free play of subjective experience. A community of sound is evolved by a subjective consciousness in touch with musical vocabularies capable of deconstructing instrumental logic. The resulting compositions reflect more genuine human encounters of the social and personal fields.

The avant-garde alternative desegregates a stratified social universe by levelling the imposed order of industrial political culture. A liberated music of temporarily assembled sound produces a less alienated condition since this type of creative activity has not yet been commodified. Most avant-garde music exists on the margins of or in tension with market forces. Consequently, a less administered sound is generated. It does not direct the listener (or performer) towards a specific goal but *away from* organized coercion. All different styles of avant-garde music usually encourage this type of transcendence. This account helps explain the various avant-garde musics. It is impossible to account for the entire range of different sounds produced by the avant-garde. Sometimes industrial-inspired drones are manipulated to induce paranoia. Atonal or dissonant timbres typically collide in a spontaneous orgy of noise. Fragments of recognizable musical instrumentation are introduced and then withdrawn. Beautifully melodic tones oftentimes arrive as a consequence of a restrained control over mechanically created auras. The use of industrial textures to establish a mood acknowledges the continued dominance of the machine in the postmodern age. The industrial milieu of contemporary class-divided societies frames the contours of structural inequities (Kinloch, 1989). Sound bites from different media sources or naturally occurring human voices are woven into the fabric of a composition. As mentioned above, all of the sounds and voices tend to be particularized or decontextualized. In this way, they find a new territory to inhabit. Denuding them from their assigned position in the industrial order liberates them to freely assemble in an emancipated environment. Oftentimes the atonal dissonance of drones reflects the ugliness and alienation of industrial culture. This kind of sonic assault tries to bring to consciousness an awareness in the listener of the painful emanation of industrial waste (material and sonic) into the natural environment. An onslaught of noise can also be cathartic as the musician and listener release the tension built up by living within an alienating social and physical environment.

As a counterpoint to noise many avant-gardistes have embraced the musical strategies of nonindustrialized cultures. Functional tonality can be effectively replaced by music produced in less stratified tribal communities. Incorporating the instrumentation or vocal styles of nonindustrialized cultures is a celebration of the decay of technocratic rationality. Synthesizing these various tactics of musical transformation provides an antidote capable of transcending the sounds of domination. An appreciation of tribal/folk music brings with it an intensified experiential quality found in oral/aural societies (Shepherd, 1991). The sounds emanating from tribal/folk communities, where codes have not yet become colonized as a sacrosanct reflection of elite superiority, reflects the fluid nature of personal and social interaction (Shepherd, 1983). Dominant groups always attempt to control the written word. They attempt to translate their claims of authority in a discourse that excludes the victims of their conquest. Subordinates use their own oppositional discourses to combat this dominance. So it is with music. Avant-garde voice, like the tribal/folk music it borrows, cannot be transcribed into a codified system. Consequently, it cannot be ordered in hierarchical schemas. It is free. Music is most threatening when it refuses to reproduce the dominant logics of industrial society. Music from nonindustrialized countries reflects the intimate nature of interpersonal communication. By providing an experience of immediacy in a face-to-face context, tribal music enhances awareness of the shifting transience of social life (Shepherd, 1991). Interactions are built up and then dissolved. Unlike the written word, music is unrestrained when it exists outside dominant rationalities.

Finally, sound produced by playing recorded music or voice backwards sometimes fills the compositions of avant-garde musicians. To generate sound by apparently irrational methods mocks the means-end logic of a mechanistic society. Creative transformations of sound occur *outside* the framework of cause and effect rationales. Consequently, music that does not pay homage to the inviolate hierarchical divisions of industrial societies is suspect.

> Music has always posed a problem for scribal elites. Sound, the "raw material" out of which music is comprised, is fluid, dynamic and evanescent. A sound only exists as it is going out of existence, and, as such its "shape" and "tonal characteristics" are constantly shifting. Music, therefore, has always been well suited to encode the flux and continuity of internal personal experience and external social interaction. (Shepherd, 1991:37)

Music that refuses to be condensed in mathematically arranged notations is threatening music. Assembled sounds at the margins of the dominant discourse point beyond the object relations of industrial capitalism. A music of immediacy produced not for the market but for reflexive involvement by the listener does not reduce human interaction to exchange relationships. Instead, it invites the self to move away from the concocted sounds of manipulation towards a spontaneous, immediate, and dynamic encounter with the sonic environment. Avant-garde music celebrates the transitory qualities of social life by emancipating the notes, pitches, rhythms, and timbres of sounds, then summoning them to reappear in a zone free of dominating discourses. In this way, stratified relationships are overcome as the field of sound is liberated. Refusing to reproduce the music flowing from oppressive social structures stands as an insurrection. Producing a new ensemble from the emancipated elements is a step in the direction of authentic freedom. All of the strategies used by the avant-garde directly or indirectly lead towards this goal.

Some Avant-Garde Options

Pristine forms of avant-garde music remain close to the core of the emancipatory project presented in this chapter. Although the artists mentioned here reflect my preferences they also make up at least a tiny sample of contemporary musicians who continue to employ avant-garde strategies in order to mount an insurgency against the rationales cohering in the dominant discourses erected by ruling groups. Many of these names may be unfamiliar to you yet they have been producing music with an avant-garde agenda for at least the last ten years. Some of these groups/artists are Throbbing Gristle, Illusion of Safety, the Hafler Trio, Zoviet-France, Nocturnal Emissions, Negativland, the Tape-beatles, Randy Greif, and John Duncan. Classical composers who shattered musical barriers by experimenting with sound such as Edgard Varese, John Cage, and David Tudor, as well as contemporary performer Laurie Anderson, may sound more familiar. I mention these names because I am familiar with their music but a seemingly infinite number of different artists with unique styles are currently practicing guerrilla music. Avant-garde music is reviewed in a network of lesser known publications and distributed by independent record companies. *Option* and the *Alternative Press* are two periodicals that review and explore avant-garde music. These magazines provide additional sources of information concerning different artists, journals, and record distributors.

Some Final Thoughts

I have introduced an alternative music as a potential oppositional and emancipatory cultural form. Of course, many examples of musical resistance using a traditional rock format can be found. A few that come to mind are the Marxist-influenced, post-punk band Gang of Four and the early music of Cabaret Voltaire, especially the album *The Voice of America*. Therefore, I do not mean to imply that all rock music is politically impotent. Clearly it is not. It continues to play a fundamental cultural role in mass movements (Garofalo, 1992). Avant-garde music offers additional cultural resources for a radical critique of domination that may be lacking in more familiar musical formats. Avant-garde music bursts assumptions and denies uncritical acceptance of the rationales constituting the dominant discourses of a class-divided industrial society. Consequently, this kind of music provides an opportunity to invent new discourses free of domination. Because of this it deserves our attention. Critical pedagogists can use avant-garde music to expose the architecture of domination sometimes barely audible in the musical discourses of most rock music. In order to practice as "resisting intellectuals," we must expose the inherent injustice of a class-divided social universe. The music presented here assists in that practice in so far as it delivers an unrelenting assault on the scaffolding of domination. It does this from the margins of the music world so that a new consciousness might emerge. This awakening is intended to usher in a sensitivity to the need for human liberation, for ". . . art represents the ultimate goal of all revolutions: the freedom and happiness of the individual" (Marcuse, 1978:69). As teachers we are provided with a rich pool of cultural resources that can help students *hear* the sounds of liberation.

NOTES

1. Some rap music uses very atypical musical formats and is intentionally political. The music of Public Enemy is perhaps the most original and explosively political music to come along since punk rock. My critique is aimed mostly at mainstream rock and heavy metal music.

2. I am aware of the countless variations of postmodern theory currently filling the bookshelves. I will not enter into the many theoretical twists and turns of the postmodernism debate. For an excellent review of this morass, see Rosenau (1992).

3. There are some avant-garde influences on early punk rock (Hebdige, 1979). Also, many bands emerging from this period, such as

the Dead Kennedys and The Clash, were intensely political. Again, I am focusing on mainstream rock music.

References

Aronowitz, Stanley, and Henry Giroux. 1991. *Postmodern Education*. Minneapolis: University of Minnesota Press.

Burger, Peter. 1984. *Theory of the Avant-Garde*. Minneapolis: University of Minnesota Press.

Garofalo, Reebee. 1992. *Rockin' the Boat*. Boston: South End Press.

Giroux, Henry. 1983. *Theory and Resistance in Education*. New York: Bergin and Garvey.

Gore, Tipper. 1987. *Raising PG Kids in an X-Rated Society*. New York: Bantam Books.

Gray, Herman. 1989. "Popular Music as a Social Problem: A Social History of Claims Against Popular Music." Pp. 143–158 in *Images of Issues: Typifying Contemporary Social Problems*. New York: Aldine de Gruyter.

Grossberg, Lawrence. 1987. "Rock and Roll in Search of an Audience." Pp. 175–197 in *Popular Music and Communication*, edited by James Lull. Newbury Park, CA: Sage.

Halley, Jeffrey A. 1991. "Cultural Resistance to Rationalization: A Study of an Art Avant-Garde." Pp.227–244 in *The Renascence of Sociological Theory*, edited by Henry Etzkowitz and Ronald M. Glassman. Itasca, MN: F.E. Peacock.

Hebdige, Dick. 1979. *Subculture*. New York: Routledge.

Kinloch, Graham C. 1989. *Society as Power*. Englewood Cliffs, NJ: Prentice Hall.

Lemming, James S. 1987. "Rock Music and the Socialization of Moral Values in Early Adolescence." *Youth and Society* 18:363–383.

Lull, James. 1987. *Popular Music and Communication*. Newbury Park, CA: Sage.

Lyotard, Jean François. 1988. *The Postmodern Condition*. Minneapolis: University of Minnesota Press.

Marcuse, Herbert. 1978. *The Aesthetic Dimension*. Boston: Beacon Press.

Rosenau, Pauline Marie. 1992. *Post-Modernism and the Social Sciences*. Princeton, NJ: Princeton University Press.

Schultze, Quentin J., and Roy M. Anker, James D. Bratt, William Romanowski, John W. Worst, Lambert Zuidervaart. 1991. *Dancing in the Dark*. Grand Rapids, MI: William Eerdmans.

Shepherd, John. 1991. *Music as Social Text*. Cambridge, MA: Polity Press.

Shumway, David. 1989. "Reading Rock 'n' Roll in the Classroom: A Critical Pedagogy." Pp. 222–235 in *Critical Pedagogy, the State, and Cultural Struggle*, edited by Henry Giroux and Peter McLaren. Albany: State University of New York.

Smith, Richard, and Anna Zantiotis. 1989. "Practical Teacher Education and the Avant-Garde." Pp. 105–122 in *Critical Pedagogy, the State, and Cultural Struggle*, edited by Henry Giroux and Peter McLaren. Albany: State University of New York.

Wicke, Peter. 1987. *Rock Music*. New York: Cambridge University Press.

Does Love Really Stink?: The "Mean World" of Love and Sex in Popular Music of the 1980s

Emily D. Edwards

Background

Media and Relationships in the 1980s

The 1980s was a decade characterized as selfish and excessive from global economics to interpersonal relations, but it seems to have been a particularly tough decade for love, marriage, and relationships. Peaking at 38th in April of 1980, a song by the J. Geils Band, "Love Stinks," seemed to be the romantic forecast for the upcoming decade. A casual look at news reports and other media of the period shows the 1980s to be the decade of divorce, ever more frightening venereal diseases, the discovery of AIDS, sexual harassment, high rates of teenage pregnancy, and date rape. While divorces declined slightly toward the end of the decade, divorces per year still numbered about half of the marriages (Johnson, 1990). During the 1980s the FBI estimated that at least 25 million women were sexually abused by their husbands each year (Wilkin-Lanoil, 1987). Articles in popular magazines suggested that men and women continued to have different expectations of relationships (Leo, 1987; Warshaw, 1988; Seligmann, 1984), creating social tensions that led to difficulties in interpersonal rapport between men and women, failed relationships, sexual harassment, and date rape. As the 1990s began, the issue of sexual relations and interpersonal behavior between men and women gained national prominence as the rape trials of William Kennedy Smith and Mike Tyson and the Supreme Court nomination hearings for Clarence Thomas brought into the public forum the issue of what is appropriate between couples.

If the decade was excessive for adults, it was even more immoderate for teenagers, particularly in the area of sexual relationships. A recent survey of seventh graders found that 34 percent of a Greensboro, North Carolina, sample had been sexually active, while 75 percent of high school seniors had been sexually active (Doolittle, 1992). Teenage pregnancy rates in the United States were among the highest in developed nations (Manning, 1988). Research on date rape and sexual aggression showed perceptions about dating behaviors and miscommunication are among variables that appear to be risk factors in date rape (Muehlenhard and Linton, 1987). Other research found that callous sexual attitudes are prevalent among young men who committed sexual crimes (McDonald, 1988), attitudes that may have been formed as early as sixth grade, where 51 percent of boys in a survey of sixth through ninth graders said it was okay for a man to rape a woman he had dated for six months (Blair, 1990).

Distressed by what appeared to be unprecedented problems of teenage promiscuity, venereal disease, and sexual aggression contributing to the increasing challenge of health care for teenagers, physicians looked to the role of media as a contributor to the construction of teenagers' ideas about love and sexual relations that might ultimately affect their behavior. Brown and Hendee (1989) believed physicians who treat adolescents need a better understanding of the sociocultural environment that influences teenagers as they struggle to become adults. They recognized that music is a powerful medium for teenagers and could serve as a clue to the emotional, mental, and physical health of the adolescent patient. The Committee on Communications for the American Academy of Pediatrics (Mendelson, 1989) called for more research on the impact of rock music on adolescents. Semanticist Sheila Davis

(1985) called for semanticists, journalists and sociologists to give serious attention to the content of popular music lyrics to evaluate what lyrics say as well as what they may be contributing to the construction of the social environment.

Media, Music, and Social Construction

Many scholars believe that meanings and interpretations of reality are socially constructed. The works of Burke, Meade, Goffman, and Blumer emphasize the importance in social life of definitions: definitions of character, rank, role, norms, and situation. All are definitions in which communication is vital. It is believed that audiences use mass media as one communication source in defining and validating the suitability of behavior. Mass media messages may be one means thorugh which people construct a perception or interpretation of their physical and social world. The classic work by Walter Lippmann (1922) presented the concept that people's expectations are often derived from media accounts that emphasize certain aspects of social life, altering people's perceptions of reality and, therefore, affecting behavior. Similarly, Defleur (1966) noted that media contribute to public perception of cultural norms through selection and emphasis of topics.

Drawing from the idea that media help shape perceptions, George Gerbner and his associates developed the cultivation theory of media effects (Gerbner, 1972; Gerbner and Gross, 1976; Gerbner et al., 1986). Cultivation theory suggests that if similar messages are repeated often enough, in different contexts, over a significant period of time, the aggregate message will be "learned" by its audience, shaping audience perception of norms (Potter, 1986). Cultivation theory is concerned with the totality of messages communicated by a medium over time rather than a specific content of a specific media product. For example, the message that "the world is a violent place" can be viewed as a consistent message of network television, which emphasizes violence in programming. Gerbner's (1976) studies of cultivation effects have largely been concerned with the violent perception of the world developed in heavy viewers of television, exaggerating fears about crime and personal risk. However,

Gerbner (1981) also believed that television cultivates the perception of norms for sexual behavior. In a survey of high school students, Singletary and his associates (1990) found a positive and significant relationship between TV use and the perception that friends engaged in premarital sex. This relationship increased if subjects were high in exposure to those TV programs identified as "sexy." Research examining several cultural pressures on adolescents, including music, found the combination of media and other cultural pressures is extremely compelling (Janus and Janus, 1984). The general conclusion is that if messages about love and sex are consistent in popular media attended to by young adults, then popular media can help shape expectations about love, the success of relationships, and appropriate dating behavior.

Mass media provided numerous portrayals of romantic and sexual relationships in the 1980s. Women's magazines, such as *Glamour, Redbook,* and *Cosmopolitan* continued to carry advice for women on how to attract men and interpret their behavior. Television continued to portray love affairs in genres from soap opera to sitcom. The 1980s provided a new medium for the depiction of relationships in music video through MTV, and relationships continued to be a staple item in film. While love and sex were important subjects for print and electronic media, as thematic content the subjects of love and sex dominated popular music (Sicoli, 1986). Popular music, more than any other medium, is a constant companion and soundtrack for the activities of adolescents and young adults (Edwards and Singletary, 1989).

As adolescent interests and activities take young people away from home, TV viewing declines (Selnow and Reynolds, 1984), but the portability of popular music makes music not only an easy accompaniment, but also difficult to escape, an ever-present part of the environment in cars, on beaches, at parties, and in shopping malls. Even as MTV and other music video outlets weakened in television ratings toward the end of the 1980s, popular music continued to be a staple item in the mass media diet of younger audiences.

Research shows that the teenage environment is steeped with their interest in popular music. Popular music provides young people with social stimulation and core values (Brake, 1980; Frith, 1981; Deihi, 1983; Lull, 1985a, 1985b). Along with clothes, language, and leisure activities, music is one element that functions to define youth culture as separate from adult society (Gantz et al., 1978; Grossberg, 1986). Teenagers between the seventh and twelfth grades listen to thousands of hours of music, only slightly less than the number of hours spent in the classroom from kindergarten through high school (Avery, 1979). In fact, Roe (1987) stated that because of the sheer amount of time devoted to popular music and the meaning it assumes, it was hard to escape the conclusion that music, not television, is the primary medium for adolescents.

While research on cultivation theory has largely dealt with television, a medium as pervasive as popular music may also exhibit cultivation effects for its primary audience. That is, just as high amounts of violence on television are expected to generate a "mean world" perception among heavy viewers, expectations about love, sex and relationships may be as easily cultivated in popular music if a consistent enough message is presented in popular songs. The shaping of expectations should also be greater for adolescents who listen a lot than for those who spend little or no time listening. If messages presented in popular music are consistent with messages presented in other media on the same topic, the cultivation effect of that message is strengthened. The concern of this research is to determine if there is an aggregate message or a consistent portrait of relationships presented in popular music of the 1980s.

Lyrics, Music, and Messages

There has been an unfailing concern for the sociological implications of the epistemological content of popular music and a persistent faith that popular music may provide social guidance for young people. In the 1960s it appeared that young people were looking to popular music for political leadership as well as diversion. The political right worried that popular music had become a lethal weapon in a revolution designed to destroy traditional values, while the political left regarded rock and roll as a voice for social change. Carey (1969) found that rock had indeed moved away from traditional values. In the 1970s, research found significant associations between political orientation and music preferences of college students (Fox and Williams, 1974). Fuller (1981) associated listening to rock music with a general nihilism, which he believed was a primary aspect of hard rock. In a historical analysis of the censorship of music lyrics, McDonald (1988) examined the attempt to suppress sexually explicit lyrics and noted that since the 1940s there have been attempts to control messages in popular songs.

While concerned groups continue to scrutinize popular music for hidden messages or advocate the use of warning labels, the worry about what young people learn from the beat and lyrics of specific popular songs may be unfounded. Numerous studies show that young listeners are more interested in the sound of a particular song than in its meaning (Edwards and Singletary, 1985; Robinson and Hirsch, 1972; Roe, 1985). Research also indicates that the meaning of lyrics may be idiosyncratically created by listeners from words and phrases that are vague enough to allow listeners to construct the message from their own physical and metaphysical experience (Murphey, 1989).

However, the worry about the influences of messages contained in the melodies and lyrics of popular music on young people's perceptions is a hard one to dismiss. Additional research has shown that while young people interpret lyrics literally or have a superficial understanding of what lyrics may mean, popular music lyrics may still have important symbolic meanings for audiences (Prinsky & Rosenbaum, 1987). It can't be denied that lyrics are important to the popularity of a song. As Albert (1978) noted, few instrumentals become national hits. Love appears to be a theme that teenagers are often able to identify (Rosenbaum and Prinsky, 1987). Hyden and McCandless (1983) investigated music lyrics as sex-role stereotypes and suggested that some messages, such as sex-role messages, may be more clear and less complex than other types of messages. An experimental study of the effects of music lyrics and rock music videos found that while lyrics are often misunderstood, comprehension develops with age. The study also showed that music videos provide less stimulation to the imagination and are enjoyed less than the songs alone (Greenfield et al., 1987). If a similar message is repeated in a large number of popular songs, young people are likely to pick up the message and a general attitude toward the subject, even if they are not able to decipher the meaning of the lyrics of a specific song.

Research on popular music and radio has found increasing homogenization and lack of diversity in the music industry (Rothanbuhler and Dimmick, 1982). Some of this lack of diversity, both musically and with regard to subject matter, may be due to a tendency in the popular arts to repeat styles and content that have proven successful with audiences. Repetitive patterns of style and message are central to the concept of cultivation. It is clear that the topics of love and sex are repetitive in popular music. Sicoli (1991) noted that even as the original rock audiences age, mid-life issues—such as the joys and trials of parenting—go unsung in favor of themes of love, sex, and relationships. But some question remains about the cumulative message presented about love and sex in popular music. Early research examining the portrayals of courtship in popular music asserted that the lyrics of popular songs supplied the script for teenagers' romantic interludes (Horton, 1957). Research in the early 1980s traced a shift away from romantic love to physical love in the lyrics of popular music (Fedler et al., 1982). As Brown and Hendee (1989) noted, even the words "rock and roll" carry strong sexual connotations, with music of the 1980s being particularly explicit in songs such as Prince's "Darling Nikki," which coarsely depicts masturbation. Davis (1985) observed that along with casual sex, popular music openly expresses hard-core themes of fellatio and incest. However, later research has also found that popular music depicts casual sex as a road to unhappiness (Lemming, 1987). An analysis of music videos found that along with traditional scripts for love and romance, themes of toughness, domination, and bad romance occur (Bennett & Ferrell, 1987). A laboratory experiment studying the effects of music television found that seventh and tenth graders are more likely to approve of premarital sex after watching an hour of selected music videos in comparison with a control group of adolescents (Greeson and Williams, 1986).

Some research has observed consistency in the portrayal of women in popular music lyrics. Rodnitsky (1975) noted that popular music offers unvarying portraits of women in a limited number of roles as love objects, mothers, tramps, bitches, babies, and pets. Analysis of popular music between 1972 and 1982 found women to be portrayed as dependent and emotional or dangerous and seductive (Hyden & McCandless, 1983). Research on the portrayal of women in music videos observed sexism and depiction of traditional roles (Vincent et al., 1987). Studies of music videos have also been concerned with presentation of sex and violence (Aufderheide, 1986; Baxter et al., 1985).

Following the stabbing death of a fourteen-year-old girl by her troubled boyfriend, one concerned citizen wrote the *Greensboro News and Record* blaming popular media: "Youth today spend all their adolescence trying to find that perfect love. They look at all the ads on television to see what they're supposed to look like. Then they listen to the radio and hear the music describe that perfect love" (Cruise, 1992, A6). This research provides an analysis of that musical description.

Methods

To discover if a consistency of messages exists, a content analysis of popular music lyrics was undertaken. The top 20 songs per year from 1980 to 1989 were investigated, reasoning that the most popular songs were the most likely to have been attended to by young audiences. These were songs listed by *Billboard* magazine as having the top 20 year-end national ratings for each year. While this list does not include music from all the various musical genres young people listen to, it was reasoned that these songs would have the greatest exposure. A total of 200 songs were investigated to obtain a profile of romance and sexual relations as presented in 1980s popular music.

Songs were categorized according to whether the artist was a male vocalist or group, female vocalist or group, or a mixed male/female duet or group. In each case the vocalist was considered to be describing his or her own situation.

Songs with lyrics about love or sex were then analyzed for both manifest and latent content. Each song was categorized according to whether a relationship was the predominant theme, secondary theme, or not a concern of the song at all. If it was determined that the primary theme of the song was about a relationship, each phrase of a lyric was examined for statements or implications about that relationship. Phrases were counted and grouped according to whether they were optimistic, pessimistic, physical, or emotional. A phrase was considered optimistic if it described or characterized the relationship as meaningful, giving, happy, enduring, or joyful or if partners were praised as loving, thoughtful, kind, sweet, or faithful. A phrase was counted as negative if it described the relationship as doomed to failure or in terms of loss, heartache, or addiction, or if the vocalist characterized his or her partner as greedy, selfish, or cheating.

A phrase was counted as physical if it concerned the body, movement, actions, and connections with material things. For example, phrases that concerned holding, kissing, touching, watching, dancing, or rolling in designer sheets were coded as physical. Phrases were counted as emotional if they concerned feelings or sentiments such as love, hate, joy, sorrow, affection, devotion, dislike, loyalty, or disgust. A phrase might be counted in more than one category. For example, the phrase, "I want to hold you in my arms forevermore," would be counted once as physical and once as optimistic. Repetitive phrases were counted as often as they were repeated. Results were collapsed into categories for analysis: none (no phrases contained this descriptor), low (contained one to five phrases with this descriptor), moderate (contained five to ten phrases with this descriptor), high (contained eleven or more phrases with this descriptor). Songs that fell in the high category were generally songs in which the descriptive phrase was repeated in the refrain.

Songs were additionally coded as to whether or not they clearly depicted a relationship between two people in a narrative manner. If the lyrics did tell a story, coders attempted to determine the stage of the relationship: beginning, if partners had recently met; established, if the partners had known each other for a while; or the end, if the relationship was over or breaking up. A fourth category marked "hoped for" or illusory relationships, if the singer dreamed of unachieved possibilities. When the stage of the relationship was unclear, coders placed it in a "stage unknown" category.

Coders also examined the roles played by the male and female characters in narrative lyrics, whether as partner, friend, seducer, aggressor, resistant, spurning, indifferent, victim, object, dependent, or independent.

Results

Love and Sex as Themes in 1980s Popular Music

Of the 200 songs examined, 14.5 percent had no references to romantic or sexual relationships. These included songs such as "Another Brick in the Wall" by Pink Floyd (1980), "9 to 5" by Dolly Parton (1981), "Down Under" by Men at Work (1983), "Flashdance" by Irene Cara (1983), "Ghostbusters" by Ray Parker, Jr. (1984), "We Are the World" by USA for Africa (1985), "Walk Like an Egyptian" by the Bangles (1986), and "Rock Me Amadeus" by Falco (1986). Other songs, such as "Funkytown," by Lipps, Inc. (1980) or "Celebration" by Kool and the Gang (1981) might be interpreted by some as having sexual implications but phrases were too ambiguous to be coded this way and were placed in the no references category. For 8.5 percent of the songs, lyrics contained only minor references to love or sexual relationships between couples.

Seventy-two percent (N=144) of the songs examined contained the dominant theme of love or sexual relationships. Of these, 64 percent were presented by a male vocalist or male group; 27 percent were presented by a female vocalist or female group; and 9 percent were presented by a mixed group. The songs that made it to the top twenty each year included a variety of musical types, but many music subgenres were excluded, including heavy metal, rap, punk, hip hop and jazz. Not surprisingly, most of the songs investigated were ones that would be at home on an adult contemporary, urban contemporary, or contemporary hit radio format, and classic or album-oriented rock stations. Of the songs examined, 91 percent peaked at number one for at least one week or more during a year, with 19 percent of those songs remaining at number one for four weeks or more. The remaining 9 percent peaked at number two.

Most of the songs that created such a stir among parents and critics did not make it into the top 20 for the year. For example, "Sister" (Prince, 1984), a song about incest, didn't chart (Whitburn, 1991). However some music, such as "She Bop" (Cyndi Lauper, 1984), about autoeroticism (Davis, 1985) made it into the *Billboard* top 40, ranking 28th for 1984. "I Want Your Sex" (George Michael, 1987) was ranked 35th for 1987. "Relax" (Frankie Goes to Hollywood, 1984) peaked at 67th in 1984 and was rereleased in 1985, where it peaked at number 10, not high enough or long enough to make it into the top 20 for the year.

Sex, Love, and Optimism

An investigation of the songs that had love or sexual relationships as predominant themes found that 33 percent of the songs had nothing optimistic to say about the relationships they described. Twenty-three percent carried one to five negative phrases. Nineteen percent had six to ten negative phrases. And another nineteen percent had eleven to fifteen negative phrases. Eighteen percent of the songs carried more than sixteen negative phrases about a relationship. Examples of negative phrases about relationships included statements like "what's love but a secondhand emotion," "broken hearts lie all around me," and "the beauty is there, but a beast is in her heart." There was a moderate positive association between emotional statements and negative statements, while a larger number of statements about feelings were correlated with pessimistic or negative phrases. ($r = .598, p > .001$)

However, optimism was also prevalent in many of the songs, with statements like: "I'm your knight in shining armor and I love you," and "we both know our love will grow." Eight percent of the songs made more than sixteen optimistic statements. Twelve percent had eleven to fifteen optimistic phrases, seventeen percent had six to ten, and thirty-three percent had one to five. Twenty-three percent of the songs were completely optimistic, with no pessimistic or negative phrases about the relationships they described.

Negative statements predominated in the lyrics. While many songs carried both optimistic and pessimistic phrases, 77 percent of the songs contained one or more negative statements compared to the 67 percent that carried one or more optimistic statements. Lyrics sung by female voices were not as likely to emphasize negative or pessimistic phrases (see Table 1). The amount of negativism in the music lyrics remained consistent throughout the decade; there was no significant increase or decrease in pessimistic statements as the decade progressed. Lyrics that contained only physical descriptions of relationships (21 percent, N=31) occurred nearly as often as music lyrics that contained only emotional descriptions of relationships (22 percent, N=32).

Stages of a Relationship

Twenty-nine percent of the songs clearly dealt with the beginning of a relationship. Twenty-six percent described established relationships. Eighteen percent of the songs dealt with the end of relationships. Twenty-seven percent of the songs dealing with the theme of relationships could not be identified as describing a distinct stage. These included songs that were about imaginary or longed-for love affairs and songs that made philosophical statements about relationships in general.

Taken together, popular music of the 1980s traced the narrative path of a relationship, characterizing distinct stages in the life of a couple. The story is predictable. The couple meet, they have a relationship, they experience a brief happiness and, finally, the couple inevitably and painfully break apart. As shown in Table 2, a moderate negative correlation was found between the stage of a relationship and the number of positive statements about the relationship; fewer positive statements occurred in lyrics describing established relationships or relationships that were ending ($r = -.367$, $p > .001$).

Table 1: Pessimistic Statements about Relationships in Music Lyrics by Male, Female, and Mixed Voices

	Voice			
	Male	Female	Mixed	Total
Negative or pessimistic phrases				
None	19	9	5	33
Low	16	13	5	34
Medium	24	8	2	34
High	31	8	4	43
Total	90	38	16	144

Table 2: Negative Statements by Stage of Relationship in Popular Music Lyrics

	Negative or Pessimistic Statements			
	None	Low	Moderate	High
Stage of relations				
Beginning	8	15	12	7
Middle	5	15	12	9
End	0	0	4	22
Other	20	7	6	5
Total	33	34	34	43

In picturing the first stage of a relationship, lyrics will often depict the couple's meeting and initial attraction to each other. Examples of this stage are reflected in songs like Joan Jett's (1982) "I Love Rock and Roll," in which the artist describes noticing a seventeen-year-old dancing by the record machine and asking the dancer for his name and a dance. Shortly afterward she describes taking the young man home. The implications of this song are wholly sexual. There are no hints of a long-lasting relationship in the offing. The refrain, "I love rock and roll," has sexual suggestions in the context of this song. Similarly, Madonna's (1985) "Crazy for You" also emphasizes the sexual attraction of the first (and—in the case of a one-night affair—perhaps only) stage of a relationship. Madonna doesn't bother to ask for the name of her prospective lover, "I walk over to where you are . . . eye to eye, we need no words at all." Gregory Abbott (1987) shares essentially the same message in "Shake You Down," in which the artist watched a girl "from so far across the floor" and she "picked up on my telepathy."

Some songs about this first stage of a relationship deal with the complications of past romances. One example is the hesitancy expressed in Jack Wagner's (1984) "All I Need," where the artist vents uncertainty about an involvement in a romantic relationship because past relationships have been painful. The theme of failing and starting over is repeated in Foreigner's "Waiting for a Girl Like You" (1981): "This heart of mine has been hurt before/This time I want to be sure." "I Want to Know What Love Is" (Foreigner, 1985) also expresses this idea of heartache from past relationships clouding the start of a new one, but optimistically states "I want to know what love is/I know you can show me/I've got nowhere left to hide/It looks like love has finally found me." This same idea is also evident in Whitesnake's (1987) "Here I Go Again."

The next stage deals with an established relationship. A number of songs dealing with relationships at this stage are joyous: sexual relations are described as magic, and romantic declarations of "no one else but you" and "no other love like ours" abound. Examples of these optimistic songs are "Truly" (Lionel Ritchie, 1982), "Endless Love" (Diana Ross and Lionel Ritchie, 1981), "Lady" (Kenny Rogers, 1980), and "Heaven Is a Place on Earth" (Belinda Carlisle, 1987). However, some of the songs in this category also express the notion that this ecstatic love is "too good to be true," reminiscent of the old adage about bargains, "If it's too good to be true, then it probably is," and a forewarning of the bad times to come. While the message about the relationship is still generally positive in "Cool It Now" (New Edition 1984) and "Kiss on My List" (Hall and Oates 1981), these songs also suggest that the couple's friends are interfering.

Other songs at this stage picture a bumpier relationship. For example, "Out of Touch" (1984) by Hall and Oates repeats the phrases "You're out of touch, I'm out of time, but I'm out of my head when you're not around." "With or Without You"

(1987) by U2 again expresses the conflicting emotions and trials of this stage of a relationship: "I can't live with or without you." In "Broken Wings" (Mr. Mister, 1986), the artist suggests "Baby, I think tonight we can take what was wrong and make it right." Some music lyrics suggest the struggle to communicate: "How about some information please?" (Paula Abdul, "Straight Up," 1989). Prince ("When Doves Cry," 1984) sings "Maybe I'm just too demanding, maybe I'm just like my father, too bold/Maybe you're just like my mother, she's never satisfied. Why do we scream at each other?" "Stuck With You" (Huey Lewis and the News, 1986) describes a relationship where the couple "thought about breakin' up—now we know it's much too late . . ./we are bound by all the rest/like the same phone number . . ./and the same address"; however, the male vocalist claims to be "happy to be stuck with you."

Money problems emerged in some lyrics about established relationships. Examples include songs like "The Way It Is" (Bruce Hornsby/Range, 1986), "Don't You Want Me?" (Human League, 1982), "Everything She Wants" (George Michael, 1984). For example, "Electric Avenue" (Eddie Grant, 1983) contains the lines "workin' so hard like a soldier and can't afford a thing on TV./Deep in my heart I abhor ya—can't get food for the kid./Good God." Some lyrics make the more optimistic statement that love can endure on very low finances. For example, "My baby may not be rich, he watches every dime./But he loves me, loves me, loves me. We always have a real good time" ("Let's Hear It for the Boy," Deneice Williams, 1984) and "He works from nine to five and then . . ./[he]works all day to earn his pay so we can play all night" ("Morning Train," Sheena Easton, 1981). One bittersweet message repeated in songs describing this stage is the notion of couples as a refuge for one another in a cruel world. In Bon Jovi's (1987) "Livin' On A Prayer," a couple weather the tough times together. In Starship's (1987) "Nothing's Gonna Stop Us Now," the couple plan to stay together even if "this world runs out of lovers."

Dorothy Parker once stated, "scratch a lover, and find a foe." However, rather than presenting enmity, lyrics of popular music usually present the end of relationships as a type of consumption in which the patient inevitably dies. "On My Own"

(Patti LaBelle and Michael McDonald, 1986) expresses the regrets of love that would "often talk in divorce, and we weren't even married." "Missing You" (John Waite, 1984) also presents the regrets of failed love. In "Careless Whisper" (George Michael, 1985), the end of the relationship is guilt-ridden. Some relationships simply end, as in Human League's "Don't You Want Me," or the artist is looking for a way out, as in "I Just Died in Your Arms Tonight" (Cutting Crew, 1987). In a few songs the hope of a reunification is presented at the end of the relationship. These included "Hard to Say I'm Sorry" (Chicago, 1982), "Separate Lives" (Phil Collins and Marilyn Martin, 1985) and "The Boys of Summer" (Don Henley, 1984). A song that made it to the top 40, "C'est La Vie" (Robbie Nevil, 1987), makes the statement that life is a boring, confusing routine and getting dumped is just part of it.

More male voices than female voices sang about the end of relationships. Fifteen percent of the songs about the end of relationships were sung by male voices. One percent of the songs about the end of relationships were sung by women.

Rather than present one of the stages in a relationship, some of the lyrics describe a longed-for or fantasy relationship. In "Alone," by Heart (1987), there is an attraction, but the relationship doesn't move forward because the attraction is either one-sided or kept a secret. Disappointment in a former high school crush is expressed in "Centerfold" (J. Geils Band, 1982), when the artist finds a picture of her in a girlie magazine. He fantasizes about taking her to a motel room, but for now, he buys the magazine. In some lyrics the artist expresses what would be the ideal in looking for or in beginning a new relationship. Stevie Winwood (1986) does this in "Higher Love," in which he yearns for a superior relationship in comparison to past ones. Whitney Houston (1987) expresses a similar yearning in "I Wanna Dance With Somebody." She asks for a "man who'd take a chance on a love that burns hot enough to last," since in previous relationships "sooner or later the fever ends and I wind up feeling down." Some lyrics were philosophical about love in general. "Shame on the Moon" (Bob Seger, 1983) relates the observation that "Once inside a woman's heart a man must keep his head . . ./some men go crazy; some men go slow;/some men go just where they want;/some men never go."

Roles of Lovers

A clear role could not be established for males in 27 percent of the relationships described by music lyrics. The role of the woman could not be established in 30 percent of the songs. The most clear and frequent descriptions that emerged for males were as seducer (18 percent), victim (17 percent), caring and intimate partner (15 percent), acquaintance/friend (6 percent), rejecting (6 percent), object (5 percent), and indifferent (4 percent). The most frequent descriptions of women in the relationships of music lyrics were as rejecting (17 percent), nurturing partner (16 percent), seducer (11 percent), victim (10 percent), vicious and/or corrupt (5 percent), and as an object (5 percent). Women in music lyrics were also often described in association with money. They "marry for the money," ("Gloria," Laura Branigan, 1982), "money's a matter" for them ("Maneater," Hall and Oates, 1983), they demand it of men ("Everything She Wants," George Michael, 1984), and they can be bought like a commodity or given away, "chicks for free" ("Money for Nothing," Dire Straits, 1985).

Conclusion

Clearly, the responsibility for failure between couples cannot be left at the door of popular music. Popular music is a human construct, the result of human decisions and social pressures. Lyrics are as much a result of social behavior as its cause. Making music choices, listening to, and interpreting the meaning of music is a complex process that must also take into account the needs of young listeners and what is happening in their lives. Additionally, the sound of the music itself, the rhythm of the drums, whine of the guitar, and thc joyful shout of the horns shapes the message; even repetitive negative phrases can be restrained by an upbeat tempo. It is also important to recognize that different music subgenres may present more optimistic or more negative portraits in either music or lyrics or both. Music critic and sometime *Rolling Stone* editor Parke Puterbaugh (1992) noted the splintering of rock into various subgenres: metal, rap, rave, techno, world beat, grunge, jangle, and other esoteric spinoffs that seem to have little in common with one another. Adolescents devoted to a particular type of music may be exposed to a different portrait of social life (Robinson and Fink, 1986). However, one thing that both optimistic and negative rock-lyric portraits of relationships share is the use of superlatives in describing the relationship. Whether good or bad, the relationship is obsessive, excessive, and extreme, presenting the greatest joy or the worst sorrow. Passions are all-consuming. According to popular music lyrics, love relationships never calmly fit into daily life, enhancing and supporting family and work. Even optimistic love relationships are generally all-consuming, monopolizing, and disruptive.

Music is an important agent of teenage socialization in the United States and one aspect of a larger environment in which young people establish impressions about the human experience and social life. Where observations of real-life behavior may be limited, as in the case of private, interpersonal relationships, it seems safe to assert that music, in addition to other popular media, may be responsible for cultivating adolescent expectations about love and sexual relationships. The extent to which popular music echoes the story of the couple as presented in other media and the extent to which high users of popular music agree with the portrait music presents may lend support for the concept of cultivation: that music is not only a consequence of private, personal experience, but can help to shape it.

The annual top 20 popular music lyrics of the 1980s did not depict an aggregate message of the perfect love that Cruise (1992) suspected they did, setting an ideal standard for relationships existing in a imperfect world. While many of the most optimistic songs do present a notion of flawless love, the more frequent image of romantic relationships in popular music is not ideal, wholesome, or lasting. There is little stability in a sexual relationship, and romantic love is frequently portrayed as unnatural and equated with mental illness, addiction, black magic, regret, and heartache. Popular music is not the only medium in which the lover's world is often pictured as a mean place. News media, television dramas, soap operas, magazine features, novels, and films have all carried accounts of love gone bad. But popular music, more than any other medium, is central to the lives of young people who are beginning romantic encounters, and the story of the young couple has always been a central theme in American popular music.

Marriage as the possible goal of a relationship is rarely mentioned. The few times marriage is directly referred to it is never as desirable or intended. For example, in "Papa Don't Preach" (1986), Madonna sings about possible outcomes for an unplanned pregnancy: "He says that he's gonna marry me—we can raise a little family—/maybe we'll be all right/it's a sacrifice."

Sexual abstinence as possible behavior within a relationship is also never clearly mentioned. A line from Billy Ocean's "There Will Be Sad Songs" (1986) might suggest abstinence to some: "You're the one I care for—the one that I will wait for." George Michael's "Faith" (1987) suggests waiting for "something more" than a physical relationship when he sings: ". . . And when that love comes down/without devotion,/well it takes a strong man, baby,/but I'm showing you the door." However, these lines were about as close or as clear as any lyric came to suggesting any kind of sexual sobriety. Interestingly, in an age of AIDS, the lyrics of popular songs rarely expressed any hesitancy about entering into a sexual relationship. It was a romantic relationship that created uncertainty; there was more concern about broken hearts than disease or pregnancy. Sexual relationships were frequently presented as fun and fulfilling; at least for the moment, it "hurts so good."

Depictions of characters and situations in music are a product of their own time. The love songs of the 1980s, while they have their soft and tender moments, are also tough and materialistic, depicting relationships that are not expected to last. However, this may not be unique to the 1980s. One of the more popular songs of the Civil War era, "Tom Dooley" (1886) tells the story of a man who murders his girlfriend, then hangs. As the struggle to meet, mate, and build a life together are a central part of the human condition, its most startling examples of success and failure and its most dramatic moments will probably always be a part of popular music and popular culture.

Lacking firsthand experience, when an adolescent encounters emotionally burdened, consistent, and negative depictions of relationships in popular music, the lessons learned may contribute to a cynical world view, diminishing the capacity to be optimistic, to risk more than a superficial relationship. Optimism is the characteristic that unites individuals in the belief that problems can be solved. As Lionel Tiger (1984) suggested, optimism may be the essential attribute that enables people to cope with problems, conflicts, and difficulties intrinsic to all life. When perception of the world becomes too pessimistic, too negative, too insurmountable, a young person may "lock the heart and throw away the key." Similarly, where the more positive portraits of love are so superlatively optimistic as to be unrealistic, a young person observing the imperfections in her own relationship or the relationships of friends may be encouraged to view the world through pessimistic lenses. In either case, the message about "true love" is that such a relationship should be an all-consuming physical or emotional passion, whether the relationship is the greatest of pleasures or the worst of addictions. Clearly, repetition and similarity of messages about relationships exists in popular music. Survey research of adolescents can determine if those repetitive messages in popular music help cultivate a young person's expectations.

REFERENCES

Albert, W.G. (1978). "Dimensions of Perceived Violence in Rock." *Popular Music and Society*, 6:27–38.

Aufderheide, P. (1986). "Music Videos: The Look of the Sound." *Journal of Communication*, 36:57–77.

Avery, R. (1979). "Adolescents' Use of Mass Media." *American Behavorial Scientist*, 23:53–70.

Baxter, R.L., C. De Riemer, A. Landini, L. Leslie, and M.W. Singletary. (1985). "A Content Analysis of Music Videos." *Journal of Broadcasting and Electronic Media*, 29:333–340.

Bennett, H.S., and J. Ferrell. (1987). "Music Videos and Epistemic Socialization." *Youth and Society*, 18(4):344–362.

Blair, S.D. (Spring, 1990). "When a Date Becomes a Crime." *Cross and Crescent*, 5–9.

Brake, M. (1980). *The Sociology of Youth Culture and Youth Subculture*. London: Routledge and Kegan Paul.

Brown, E., and W.R. Hendee. (1989). "Adolescents and Their Music: Insights into the Health of Adolescents." *Journal of the American Medical Association*, 262:1659–1663.

Carey, J.T. (1969). "The Ideology of Autonomy in Popular Lyrics: A Content Analysis." *Psychiatry*, 32:150–164.

Christensen, P., P. De Benedittes, and T. Lundloff. (1985). "Children's Use of Audio Media." *Communication Research*, 12:327–343.

Clarke, P. (1973). "Teenager's Co-orientation and Information-Seeking about Pop Music." *American Behavorial Scientist*, 16:551–566.

Cruise, K. (March 9, 1992). "Troubled Teens Looking for Love." *The Greensboro News and Record:* A6.

Davis, S. (1985). "Pop Lyrics: A Mirror and Molder of Society." *Et Cetera*, 167–169.

Defleur, M. (1966). *Theories of Mass Communication*. New York: McKay. Pp. 145–146.

Deihl, E.R., M.J. Schneider, and K. Petress, K. (1983). "Dimensions of Music Preference: A Factor Analytic Study." *Popular Music and Society*, 9(3):41–43.

Doolittle, R.P. "School Health Advisory Council Survey." (July 1, 1992). A Report to Duke University Medical Staff.

Edwards, E.D., and M.W. Singletary (1985). "Mass Media Images in Popular Music: An Examination of Media Images in Student Music Collections and Student Attitudes toward Media Performance." *Popular Music and Society*, 9:17–26.

———. (1989). "Life's Soundtracks: Relationships between Radio Music Subcultures and Listener Belief Systems." *The Southern Communication Journal*, 54(2):144–158. Reprinted (1990) in *The National Academy of Recording Arts and Sciences Journal*, 1:34–50.

Fedler, F., J. Hall, and L. Tanzi. (1982). "Analysis of Popular Music Reveals Emphasis on Sex, De-emphasis on Romance." Presented at the annual meeting of the Association for Education in Journalism and Mass Communication, Athens, OH.

Fox, W.S., and J. Williams. (1974). "Political Orientation and Music Preference among College Students." *Public Opinion Quarterly,* 38:352–371.

Francesconi, R. (1986). "Free Jazz and Black Nationalism: A Rhetoric of Musical Style." *Critical Studies in Mass Communication,* 3:36–49.

Frith, S. (1981). *Sound Effects: Youth, Leisure, and Politics of Rock and Roll.* New York: Pantheon.

Fuller, J.G. (1981). *Are the Kids All Right? The Rock Generation and Its Hidden Death Wish.* New York: Times Books.

Gantz, W., H.M. Gartenberg, M.L. Pearson, and S.O. Shiller. (1978). "Gratifications and Expectations Associated with Pop Music Among Adolescents." *Popular Music and Society,* 6:81–89.

Gerbner, G. (1972). "Violence in Television Drama: Trends in Symbolic Functions." Pp. 28–187 in George A. Comstock and Eli Rubenstein (eds.), *Television and Social Behavior, Vol. 1: Media Content and Control.* Washington, DC: U.S. Government Printing Office.

———. (1981). "Sex on Television and What Viewers Learn from It." Paper presented to the National Association of Television Program Executives Annual Conference, San Francisco, CA.

Gerbner, G., and L. Gross. (1976). "Living with TV: The Violence Profile." *Journal of Communication,* 26(2):172–199.

Gerbner, G., L. Gross, M. Morgan, and N. Signorielli. (1986). "Living with Television: The Dynamics of the Cultivation Process." Pp. 17–39 in Jennings Bryant and Dolf Zillman (eds.), *Perspectives on Media Effects.* Hillsdale, NJ: Lawrence Erlbaum Associates.

Greenfield, P.M., L. Bruzzone, K. Koyamatsu, W. Satuloff, W. Nixon, M. Brodie, and David Kingsdale. (1987). "What Is Rock Music Doing to the Minds of Our Youth? A First Experimental Look at the Effects of Rock Music Lyrics and Music Videos." *Journal of Early Adolescence,* 7(3):315–329.

Greeson, L.E., and R.A. Williams. (1986). "Social Implications of Music Videos for Youth: An Analysis of the Contents and Effects of MTV." *Youth and Society,* 18:177–189.

Grossberg, L. (1986). "Is There Rock after Punk?" *Critical Studies in Mass Communication,* 3:50–74.

Horton, D. (1957). "The Dialogue of Courtship in Popular Songs." *American Journal of Sociology*, 17:569–578.

Hyden, C., and N.J. McCandless. (1983). "Men and Women as Portrayed in the Lyrics of Contemporary Music." *Popular Music and Society*, 9:19–25.

Janus, S.S., and C.L. Janus. (1984). "Children, Sex, Peers, Culture: 1973–1983." Paper presented to the Seventh Annual Convention of the International Psychological Association, Graduate Center, City University of New York, June 15.

Johnson, O. (1990). "U.S. Statistics/Marriage and Divorce." *The 1991 Information Please Almanac.* Boston: Houghton Mifflin Company, 809.

Lemming, J.S. (1987). "Rock Music and the Socialization of Moral Values in Early Adolescence." *Youth and Society.* 18(4):363–383.

Leo, J. (March 23, 1987). "When Date Turns to Rape." *Time*:77.

Lippmann, W. (1922). *Public Opinion*. New York: Macmillian.

Lull, J. (1985a). "On the Communicative Properties of Music." *Communication Research*, 12:363–372.

———. (1985b). "The Naturalistic Study of Media Use and Youth Culture." Pp. 212–230 in K.E. Rosengren, L. A. Wenner, and P. Palmgreen (eds.), *Media Gratification Research.* Beverly Hills, CA: Sage.

———. (1987). "Listeners' Communicative Uses of Popular Music." Pp. 212–230 in Lull J. (ed.), *Popular Music and Communication.* Beverly Hills, CA: Sage.

Manning, A. (October 3, 1988). "Teens and Sex in the Age of AIDS." *USA Today*:1.

McDonald, J. (1988). "Censoring Rock Lyrics: A Historical Analysis of the Debate." *Youth and Society*, 3:294–313.

McDonald, K. (1988). "Male Students Who Commit 'Date Rape' Found to Have Callous Sexual Attitudes." *Chronicle of Higher Education*, 34(18):A35.

Mendelson, R.A., chair , and the Committee on Communications, American Academy of Pediatrics. (1989). "The Impact of Rock Lyrics and Music Videos on Children and Youth." *Pediatrics*, 83:314–315.

Muehlehard, C.L., and M.A. Linton. (1987). "Date Rape and Sexual Aggression in Dating Situations: Incidence and Risk Factors." *Journal of Counseling Psychology*, 34(2):186–196.

Murphey, T. (1989). "The When, Where and Who of Pop Lyrics: The Listener's Perogative." *Popular Music and Society*, 8:185–193.

Potter, J.W. (1986). "Perceived Reality and the Cultivation Hypothesis." *Journal of Broadcasting & Electronic Media*, 30(2): 159–74.

Prinsky, L., and J.L. Rosenbaum. (1987). "'Leer-ics' or Lyrics: Teenage Impressions of Rock 'n' Roll." *Youth and Society*, 18:384–397.

Puterbaugh, P. (October 23, 1992). "Time to Roll Over Rock and Roll and Tell Elvis the News." *Weekend: Greensboro News and Record*:4.

Robinson, J.P., and P. Hirsch. (1972). "Teenage Response to Rock and Roll Protest Songs." Pp. 222–231 in *The Sounds of Social Change*. Chicago: Rand McNally.

Robinson, J.P., and E.L. Fink. (1986). "Beyond Mass Culture and Class Culture: Subcultural Differences in the Structure of Music Preferences." Pp. 226–239 in Sandra J. Ball-Rokeach and Muriel G. Cantor (eds.), *Media Audience and Social Structure*. Beverly Hills, CA: Sage.

Rodnitsky, J.L. (1975). "Songs of Sisterhood: Music of Women's Liberation." *Popular Music and Society*, 1:77–85.

Roe, K. (1985). "Swedish Youth and Music: Listening Patterns and Motivations." *Communication Research*, 12(3):352–362.

———. (1987). "The School and Music in Adolescent Socialization." Pp. 212–230 in James Lull (ed.), *Popular Music and Communication*. Newbury Park, CA: Sage.

Rosenbaum, J., and L. Prinsky. (1987). "Sex, Violence and Rock 'n' Roll: Youth's Perceptions of Popular Music." *Popular Music and Society*, 11(2):79–90.

Rothenbuhler, E.W., and J.W. Dimmick. (1982). "Popular Music: Concentration and Diversity in the Industry, 1974–1980." *Journal of Communication*, 32:143–149.

Seligmann, J., J. Huck, N. Joseph, T. Namuth, L. Prout, T. Robinson, and A. McDaniel. (March 23, 1984). "The Date Who Rapes." *Newsweek*:91–92.

Selnow, G.W., and H. Reynolds. (1984). "Some Opportunity Costs of Television Viewing." *Journal of Broadcasting*, 28(3):315–322.

Sicoli, M.L. (1986). "The Music is the Message: Male-Female Relationships as Portrayed in Popular Music." Paper presented at American Culture Association/Popular Culture Association annual convention in Atlanta.

———. (1991). "Mid-Life Music: Mid-Life Message." *Popluar Music and Society,* 15(1):69–80.

Singletary, M., D. Ziegler, K. Reid, C. Milbourne. (1990). "Media Use and High School Students' Perception of Sexual Behavior: A Cultivation Analysis." Paper presented to the Mass Communications Division of the International Communications Association. Dublin, Ireland.

Tiger, L. (April 5–6,1984). "The Danger Vitamin." Paper presented at the Morbid Curiosity and Mass Media Symposium, sponsored by the University of Tennessee and the Gannett Foundation, Knoxville, TN.

Vincent, R.C., D.K. Davis, and L.A. Boruszkowski. (1987). "Sexism on MTV: The Portrayal of Women in Rock Videos." *Journalism Quarterly,* 64:750–755, 941.

Warshaw, R. (1988). "The Hidden Plague of Acquaintance Rape." *Utne Reader,* 30:110–111.

Whitburn, J. (1991). *Top Pop Singles.* Menomonee Falls, WI: Record Research Inc.

Wilkin-Lanoil, G. (1987). "Emotional Best: Too Close to Home." *Health,* 19(6):71.

Crowd Crushes at Two Rock Concerts: A Value-Added Analysis

Jerry M. Lewis

Introduction

Rock concerts are very much a part of the life of young people in the United States. Most of these concerts are conducted with little or no trouble. A few arrests here and there demonstrate some of the difficulties faced by spectators and police. But, as illustrated by the research in this chapter, this may be luck. The risk of injury and death is present at almost all large, sold-out rock concerts because of the potential for crowd crushes. The causes of the crowd crushes lie in the actions of young and eager music fans. In attempting to get access to the hall or stage where the stars of the concert are performing, they create crush conditions.

This chapter has four parts. First, I review Neil J. Smelser's (1962) "value-added" model of collective behavior. This interpretation is based on an analysis I developed, with Michael Kelsey, of the 1989 Hillsborough soccer crowd crush in England (Lewis and Kelsey, 1990). Second, in the narrative section I describe the events of two rock concerts where deaths and serious injuries occurred: The Who concert (1979) in Cincinnati and the AC/DC concert (1991) in Salt Lake City. Third, the essay analyzes the rock concert crushes using the value-added model combined with notions of triangulation based on my research on English and European soccer crowds (Lewis, 1986). Fourth, the essay concludes with some policy suggestions for preventing rock concert crowd crushes.

Theoretical Considerations[1]

Most crowd violence has been treated as mobs or what Smelser terms a hostile outburst. I see rock concert crushes differently. These events are not hostile outbursts or panics, which Smelser defines as "collective flight based on a hysterical belief" (1962:131). Instead, in this study, I examine two events as entertainment crowd crushes drawing on Smelser's views of crowd actions as craze behavior.

Smelser defines a craze as "mobilization for action based on a positive wish-fulfillment belief" (1962:171). It seems ironic to explain a crowd crush using a theoretical model based on a positive set of feelings, but a case can be made that that is exactly what happens at rock concerts. This is behavior based on wish fulfillment. This behavior is labeled an entertainment craze leading to a crowd crush. Goode (1992:222–223) refers to this behavior as a stampede, a term which I see as denoting that crowds are crazy. The notion of crowds as "crazy entities" has been resisted by collective behavior scholars since the 1960s.

The Smelser Model

Smelser's model is divided into five determinants, each with a set of subdeterminants. The determinants are: (1) structural conduciveness, (2) structural strain, (3) growth of a generalized belief, (4) mobilization for action, and (5) social control. The precipitating event which some versions of the Smelser model use is treated under the growth of generalized belief (Lewis, 1989). The discussion begins with structural conduciveness.

Structural Conduciveness

This determinant refers to social structure. It describes structural possibilities for an incident of collective behavior to happen. Structural conduciveness describes the parameters and constraints for the other components of the model, particularly structural strain. The model (Smelser, 1962:175–176), relates conduciveness to three subdeterminants: a differentiated setting, a reward-cost relationship which generates action, and a generalized medium of exchange.

An economically differentiated market develops independently from other social institutions such as the polity, the family or religion. In a differentiated economic system the analyst would expect to observe competition for scarce and desired commodities based on the value of the commodities per se. In highly desired rock concerts there is a differentiated market of fans who generate competition for access to the event.

A defined reward/cost calculation for an entertainment craze is the weighing of access to the performance against costs. These include money, time, individual discomfort, and personal energy. In the area of the manipulation of resources, the person involved in an entertainment craze can opt to continue or stop his or her participation with these resources. Lastly, the ticket becomes a crucial medium of exchange as an entertainment craze develops.

It is argued that for the United States access to rock concerts has a differentiated economy that is conducive for the development of entertainment craze behavior. This craze behavior has the possibility of leading to an entertainment crowd crush.

Structural Strain

Structural strain occurs within the parameters of conduciveness. The model requires that the researcher look for strain in terms of ambiguity that is defined as anxiety generated by uncertainty. Strain increases as uncertainty increases about the allocation of resources as well as the profit and loss from other actions. For example, the occurrence of an important entertainment event automatically creates strain through ambiguity about whether access to the event will be possible. Therefore, the uncertainty or lack of predictable outcomes increases anxiety. Thus, alternate choices begin to be considered such as music television (MTV) coverage or listening to a recording or reading about the event (see Figure 1 later in the chapter). The actor must decide if these choices equal participating in the entertainment event. Additional strain occurs when location in the concert hall becomes a factor in the choice situation (see Figure 2 later in the chapter).

Growth of a Generalized Belief

Smelser's model instructs the analyst to look for beliefs which guide action. Wish-fulfillment beliefs are "rooted in ambiguity stemming from situations of strain" (Smelser, 1962:94). But, in contrast to hysteria, wish-fulfillment beliefs are *positive*. Persons guided by wish-fulfillment beliefs are seeking something positive and have become convinced that what they seek is scarce. Thus, in an entertainment craze, the belief is that an experience that is highly desired is scarce. Ironically, these positive feelings can lead to tragedy.

The precipitating event is considered a subdeterminant of the generalized belief. It serves to focus the belief on specific events. In a sense the precipitating event combines with the belief to propose a solution for the ambiguity found in the strain conditions.

Mobilization for Action

Here I look at the subdeterminants of an entertainment craze which includes leadership, the initial and derived phases of the craze, and the turning point. People and/or events provide leadership that shapes the craze. This is labelled "keynoting." Most incidents of collective behavior change during the flow of events. Smelser refers to this as the process of moving from the initial and derived phases. In an entertainment craze I examine the initial response to the entertainment event and how it changes into the derived phase as speculation begins. Lastly, the "turning point" refers to the slowing of activity in the speculation phase.

Social Control

The Smelser model proposes that the investigator look at several dimensions of social control that shape a craze and prevent it from getting out of hand. The first of these is labeled "normative regulations" (Smelser, 1962:218) and influences structural conduciveness. Normative regulations in an economic craze reduce or eliminate conditions of structural conduciveness in the market (Smelser, 1962:218) by restricting the possibility of speculations in commodities. In an entertainment craze, both ticket producers and consumers engage in speculation. A producer speculates that people will want to buy a certain amount of tickets to an event, which will generate revenue which exceeds the costs. Consumers speculate as they try to decide whether an entertainment event will be so valuable that a ticket and location should be sought despite the time, money, effort, or discomfort involved.

Social control also occurs through leadership; leaders can discourage interest in speculation. In an entertainment craze, leaders or peer pressure can increase or decrease demand for an event through the level of interest they generate. Thus, leader communication influences interest, need, and speculation.

Lastly, information serves as social control by providing accurate facts on commodity status. For example, in an entertainment craze, the important information would be an accurate account of the actual amount of seating capacity available to concert fans.

Triangulation and the Description of Rock Concert Crushes

Triangulation was the method used for collecting data in this research. The strategy of triangulation was based on a procedure developed in my (Lewis, 1986) study of English soccer crowds. There are two types of triangulations. The first uses primary data, in which the researcher records observations and carries out personal interviews. The other way is through the use of secondary data which the researcher obtains by collecting information from sources such as newspaper and magazine articles. Damon Lewis (1991) has analyzed the sources of data that can be used to develop information about rock concert events. My discussion is based on his analysis.

Data Sources

Researchers have various ways of collecting data for the studies they conduct. Five sources of data can be used to investigate rock concert crowds: site visits, personal interviews, newspaper accounts, photographs, and police documents.

Site Visits

A researcher is rarely present at the scene of a rock concert riot; he or she must reconstruct the riot behavior. The researcher should visit a site both when the crowd is present and when the site is empty. Site visits help capture the conditions that may have led to the violence. They also allow the researcher to achieve the point of view of the fans, police, ushers, and performers.

Personal Interviews

Obvious candidates for interviews are violent and nonviolent concert fans, police, ushers, and ticket takers. Ushers and security guards are closest to the fans and can provide an unique perspective on fan concert behavior. There are two types of interviews: one that the scholar completes personally, and one that he or she obtains from secondary sources.

Newspaper Accounts

Journalists are often present when violence occurs. They provide information about the riots that occur before, during, or after the concert. They are helpful in describing the size of the crowd. *Rolling Stone* was used often in this research. Its stories are long and consequently there are many excellent first person quotes available to the scholar.

Photographs

Photographs can be used to provide clues about the reactions of the fans. They provide evidence about the types of behavior that occurs at rock concerts. In a few cases, the researcher is also able to obtain films.

Police Documents

Police documents are helpful in informing a researcher about the amount and location of officers, how many arrests were made, and the types of violence that occurred. Table 1 classifies the data sources used to analyze the two crowd crushes studied in this article.

Table 1: Data Sources Related to Rock Concert Crushes

	Concerts	
	The Who	AC/DC
Data Sources		
Site Visits	No	No
Personal Interviews*	Yes	Yes
Newspaper Accounts	Yes	Yes
Photographs	Yes	Yes
Police Documents	Yes	No

*All the personal interviews were obtained from secondary sources.

Narratives—Two Case Histories of Rock Concert Crowd Crushes[2]

The Who

On December 3, 1979, eleven persons, ten of them teenagers, were trampled to death and twenty-three injured in the crowd crush of rock and roll fans in Cincinnati's Riverfront Coliseum. The injured fans were taken to five area hospitals. The youngest of the fans was reported to be only four years old.

Causes of the deaths ranged from suffocation due to insufficient oxygen to physical crushing of bodies and broken bones. Dr. Frank Cleveland Hamilton, county coroner, said that "the asphyxiation resulted from the victims' bodies being compressed by the weight of the others on top of them" (*Daily Kent Stater*, December 6, 1979:15). Dr. Alex Trott, an emergency room supervisor at Cincinnati General Hospital, reported that the victims all displayed multiple bruises and that "there was some evidence of footprint-like injuries" (*The Plain Dealer*, December 4, 1979:1). The crowd was pressed together so tightly that it took police twenty-four minutes to fight through the mass to attempt to rescue the victims.

The persons involved were awaiting first-come first-serve seating to The Who concert that was to begin at 8:00 P.M. that evening. This was the Ohio leg of The Who's nationwide promotional "farewell" tour. The tour was promoting the band's newly released film "Quadrophenia." Approximately 20 percent of the 18,000 available tickets were numbered and reserved, leaving 80 percent of the tickets available on a first-come first-serve basis. The people with the numbered reserved tickets were let in before the people with the unnumbered tickets; they were to be let in only minutes before the concert began.

The band arrived late and personnel at the coliseum were instructed to not let the fans with the unnumbered tickets in until the group had had sufficient opportunity to warm up. Most reports show that The Who did not arrive until 8:30 P.M., although there is considerable dispute about this. However, the crowd pressure had begun building around 6:15 P.M., since the official time to open the doors was 7:05 P.M. (Flippo, 1980:12).

The band began to warm up with one of its most popular songs, "Quadrophenia." At this point members of the waiting crowd began pushing even harder to get in, first breaking in glass doors, and eventually breaking them down completely. One witness, a forty-nine-year-old usher, reported that "first they threw a bottle through the window in the door, then they pushed through the hole" (*The Guardian,* 1979:1). John Limoli, Jr., had been knocked down during the pushing and shoving. Luckily, he made it back to his feet during the skirmish. He reported that "there was a girl beneath my right shoulder" and "she was screaming 'I want my husband' and then she started screaming she was pregnant. She was hysterical" (Diemer and Kermisch, 1979:1). Dale Stevens, a veteran concert attender, called the people involved in the crush "animals" and reported that "I had come to see a concert" and "in reality, I had been to a funeral" (Kay, 1979:1). Michael Jordan, aged seventeen, said, "I was in the middle. It was crazy. You had to fight to save your life" (*The Plain Dealer,* December 4, 1979:10–A).

Many reports blamed the incident on the unreserved seating which caused fans to trample each other to get seats as close as possible to their idolized musicians. In addition, only two of the coliseum's admission gates were opened to let in the fans. Police officials reported that the reason that only two doors were open was because "there were no more ticket takers available" (*The Plain Dealer,* December 5, 1979:17–A). Apparently only twenty-five ticket takers were on duty for the concert.

The concert began, despite the tragedy, with more music from the film "Quadrophenia." The Who and most of the fans were unaware of the crush events. The band's personal manager, Bill Curbishley, reported that "we decided that there was no reason to stop the concert and give the people any reason to make more trouble" (*Daily Kent Stater,* December 5, 1979:1). Later, Roger Daltrey, the band's lead singer, said to a crowd at Buffalo's Memorial Auditorium that "there's nothing we can do about it" and "the band is totally shattered. But life goes on and this show's for them." He also said that the band was not in charge of crowd control and that "I'm a performer" (Kay, 1979:1).

AC/DC

On January 18, 1991, three teenagers were killed at an AC/DC concert at the Salt Palace in Salt Lake City, Utah. Two of the victims were only fourteen years of age while the third was nineteen. The three fans were trampled, dying of suffocation as surging fans attempted to get near the stage as the band was beginning the concert. Seating was first-come first-serve, also known as "festival seating," which denotes that seats in front of the stage, also known as "floor tickets," are sold as general admission. This type of seating practice had already been tied to the deaths of eleven fans at The Who concert.

The total attendance of the AC/DC concert was only a little below the capacity of the Palace's 13,920 persons. There were 4,450 floor tickets allotted and they sold out almost immediately. The group that runs the Salt Palace, Spectator Management Group, reported that the actual attendance of the concert was 13,294 and that crowd control efforts were more than adequate.

AC/DC started the concert around 9:15 P.M. with "Thunderstruck." As the band began to play, there was an immediate dash to the stage by eager fans. A Salt Palace security guard reported that "someone just took a wrong turn and caused everyone to topple" (Light, 1991:19). Despite the catastrophe, AC/DC continued to play during the initial happenings and finally ceased playing approximately forty-five minutes into the concert. Some fans reported yelling "Stop the concert" when the trampling began. AC/DC later went on record denying allegations that they "continued to play with callous disregard for the safety of the audience." Their statement insisted instead that "once the gravity of the situation was communicated to the band, they immediately stopped performing" (Light, 1991:99).

The concert was eventually halted for approximately forty-five minutes as the victims were carried out of the Palace. The band then finished the concert "with the house lights still up" (Light, 1991:99). AC/DC decided to finish the concert after consulting the fire marshal. It was agreed to be safer to continue the concert than to cancel the remainder of it.

Wayne Hammond, a twenty-two-year-old University of Utah student, described the events that took place:

> The floor was full but no rowdier than usual. General admission is always a kind of push and shove. And there was no way you could have heard the crowd if they were screaming. Normally there's an even row of heads across the floor but in one spot I noticed there was a gap. Once the problem became evident, the biggest gap seemed to be getting the lights on. (Light, 1991:99)

A Brigham Young University student reported that he and his roommate were at the bottom of at least thirty people and that:

> I was just trying to reach my hands up out of all the people. . . . they were laying all over our faces. It was too hard to pull because I had so much weight on me. There was nothing they could do to get me out. People were landing on top of me, and I was saying "Please, God, let me live." (Light, 1991:99).

The student then became unconscious and was taken to a local hospital and treated for minor injuries.

Scott Neil, seventeen, reported that "it was chaotic. It was hell. People were screaming. After they started another song, people started chanting, 'Stop the concert, stop the concert,' until it echoed, but they wouldn't" (*New York Times*, 1991:A3).

Analysis of Rock Concert Crowd Crushes

This analysis uses Smelser's model, both determinants and subdeterminants, as well as triangulation to order and explain the data about rock concert entertainment crowd crushes. The analysis begins with structural conduciveness.

Structural Conduciveness

What conditions were generated by the social structure that facilitated the rock concert crowd crushes? The social elements creating the possibilities for collective behavior are analyzed as an entertainment craze using three subdeterminants: differential setting, reward/costs, and the general medium of exchange.

Differential Setting

The differential setting sets the condition where rock concert fans make decisions about the event independently of other factors such as family, work, religion, or other recreational activities. Participating in the rock concert involves a variety of choices and decisions that may lead to an entertainment craze. Figure 1 illustrates the decision flow of the differentiated setting. Whether one decides to be involved or not is the first decision and this pertains to the importance or interest in the event. Young people eagerly await a rock concert. If no involvement is the choice, there are other decisions, but wanting to be a participant leads to other levels of decisions.

Wanting to be involved, the next step is to decide whether to go or not go to the concert. Going to the concert creates a condition of ambiguity which is predicated upon access. Deciding not to go enables the participant to choose alternate ways of being involved, such as reading about the concert or listening to a recording, and, in a few cases, watching the concert on television.

I now use each of the subdeterminants to examine crushes at the Who concert, (from now on, "The Who"), and the AC/DC concert (from now on, "AC/DC"). I begin with The Who.

The Who. The Who hit the rock scene in America in the mid-60s, becoming an extremely popular group among teenagers. Advertisements on the radio and in the newspaper hyped this concert as part of The Who's farewell tour. The fact that the group was very popular, combined with the possibility of never again seeing or hearing the group, created among some fans a very strong desire to attend the concert. When the concert was announced, immediately there was a large population of fans who wanted to attend the concert. There were 14,770 festival seating (general admission) tickets available and 3578 reserved seats (Flippo, 1980:1). While no data is available on this, it is likely that the tickets were quickly sold.

Figure 1: Decision Flow Diagram of Differential Setting for a Rock Concert

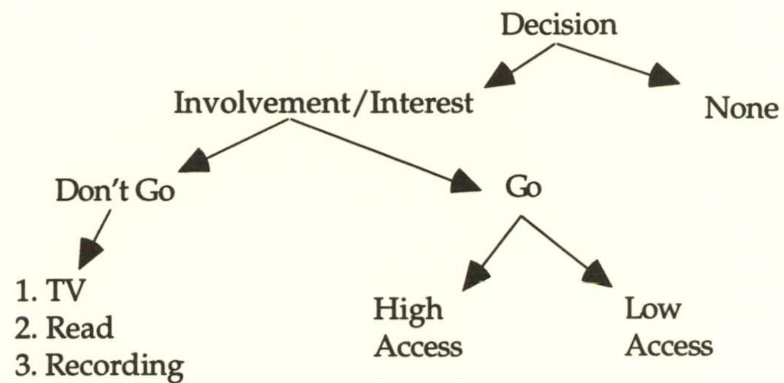

AC/DC. This group is a very popular band in today's rock culture. The pressure of being a farewell concert was not present for the AC/DC performance. Nevertheless fans many fans of AC/DC wanted to be at the concert.

For both concerts a choice situation was present, which facilitated the eventual collective behavior situation. That is, for many young people, participating as an audience member at the concerts was the only way to have a satisfying experience.

Reward/Cost Ratio

Participating in a highly desired event, especially one perceived by fans as being a onetime event, is the reward or benefit of attending. The rewards for participating are balanced against its costs. Costs can vary depending upon individual tastes. They include not only the cost of tickets but all expenses related to the concert, such as transportation, food, T-shirts, and other rock concert souvenirs. In addition to financial costs, there are addtional costs, including personal energy which involves the effort expended to get to the concert, to enjoy the concert, and to make the return trip home. There is also risk-taking. The excitement of the concert is, in part, based on the physical contact between fans—although death or serious injury is probably not a factor that most rock concert fans consider. Lastly, there is physical discomfort. This is related to the energy expended and to the conditions of the concert itself, such as overcrowding or waiting in long lines for several hours.

The Who. The festival seating tickets cost ten dollars apiece, and reserved seating tickets cost eleven dollars each (Flippo, 1980:1). The estimate of costs beyond the actual ticket costs is difficult to quantify, but can be evaluated qualitatively. It would include transportation, food, and The Who souvenirs. But there were other costs as well. It is likely that fans traveled considerable distances to the concert from Ohio, Indiana, and Kentucky. Thus, travel time and organizational activities for travel must be considered. Lastly, there must have been considerable personal discomfort as well. Johnson (1987:165) reports that some fans began arriving at the coliseum as early as six hours before the concert was to begin. As the crowd began to build up, another type of personal discomfort was noted by Johnson. Drawing on police reports, he writes, "The crowd density became so great that one person reported he could not raise his arm to scratch his head and another said that he could not reach to his pocket for his wallet." The award/costs ratio was becoming clear to The Who fans, but most persisted in their quest to get into the concert.

AC/DC. The same type of cost/ratio described for The Who concert was present at AC/DC. The physical problems facing the audience in front of the stage might even have been greater. As the earlier narrative described, one fan noted that general admission is always "push and shove." The noise level in front of the stage also brings some risks as well. AC/DC clearly presented cost to some of their fans. Yet few, if any, thought the risks involved loss of life.

The analysis for both concerts suggests that there were cost/reward conditions that contributed to the structural conduciveness of the concert environment.

General Medium of Exchange

A ticket not only serves as the medium of exchange for access but is also a variable of social control. Having a ticket does not automatically guarantee that concert attenders will have a good seat in the house. Most concerts have two problems related to location in the concert hall. First, some tickets are for festival seating. This means that the holder has a ticket which allows access to the hall, but not to a particular, reserved, seat. Second, the ticket holder may want to be closer to the stage. If so, after gaining access to the hall, he or she tries to get as close as possible to the stage where the performers are playing.

The Who. Both conditions were present in Cincinnati. There was festival seating for at least half the crowd. The norm for The Who concert was moving to the front to be close to the performers.

AC/DC. The seating for this concert also used the festival format on the main floor. This was done in part because the Salt Palace had lost money on broken chairs in the past (Evensen, 1992:B1). But in contrast to The Who concert, all AC/DC ticketholders attenders got into the Salt Palace. The entertainment crush began after music started with the rush to the stage.

In summary, all the conditions for the structural conduciveness of an entertainment crowd crush were met at the Who and AC/DC rock concerts. There were differential settings which shaped various decisions; rewards and costs associated with attending the event were evident; the general medium of exchange was a festival-seat concert ticket. The existence of all three subdeterminants at these particular concerts suggests that these factors are likely to be present at most rock concerts.

Structural Strain

Smelser's model indicates that strain is ambiguous as defined by the presence of uncertainty. Structural conduciveness sets the parameters in which strain can be present. Structural strain is the ambiguity that exists within the social structure.

In considering the structural strain of an entertainment craze, most ambiguity would be related to the anxiety generated by the uncertainty associated directly with the concert event. There are three major dimensions of uncertainty for rock concert fans. One, ticket availability for the concert. Two, being able to hear the complete concert. Three, access to attractive locations within the concert hall. Thus, at the start of concerts there are four types of fans based on two factors: reserved versus festival seating, and motivation to get physically close to the artists.

Figure 2: Types of Rock Concert Attenders (I, II, III, IV)

	Ticket Format	
	Reserved	Festival
Close to Stage		
Yes	I	II
No	III	IV

These two dimensions classify four types of fans. Type I are those who hold reserved seats and desire to be close to the stage. Type II are those who hold festival tickets and desire to be close to the performers. Type III are those who hold reserved tickets and do not desire to be close to the performers. Type IV are those fans who hold festival tickets and do not want to be close to the performers.

The Who. For many members of the crowd gathering outside the coliseum, there were two types of heightened strain when The Who began to play "Quadrophenia." First was the chance that they would miss some of the music The Who was performing. Obviously the drama and excitement of a live concert can never be captured by alternate media. The fans wanted to be there for the entire event. Second, those fans wanting and seeking attractive locations in the hall defined themselves as disadvantaged when the music began and they were still outside the coliseum. Both factors contributed to the strain as well as the willingness of those on the outside to begin pushing and shoving to get inside the hall. It is likely that those fans sensing the greatest strain were Type II's—those with festival tickets desiring to be close to the stage. It is not possible to know empirically the number of the Type II's in the plaza, but there were enough to begin the pushing and shoving that led to the crush.

AC/DC. Although the seats at this concert were general admission, there were two places for fans to sit: the main floor and the balcony. Most popular were the 4,450 floor tickets, which sold out immediately after they went on sale (Light, 1991:19). This was because of the access to the stage that main floor tickets provided. Thus, the main floor situation was similar to that of The Who concert.

In summary, the conditions of strain were present for both concerts. Strain was based on the uncertainty and anxiety of missing the full concert and/or reaching a desired location in the hall.

Generalized Belief

The generalized belief directs the behavior of the fans by preparing them for action. In an entertainment craze, wish-fulfillment is the conviction that action will help participants obtain desired results. Beliefs create a "common culture" (Smelser, 1962:82) for participants in an episode of collective behavior. Generalized beliefs can be observed at both the individual and social level. At the individual level it is necessary to learn how feelings of ambiguity and anxiety emerge to chart the development of beliefs. At the social level it is necessary to investigate the degree to which these beliefs become shared. Using the Smelser value-added model can be difficult at this point because, lacking interview or direct observational data, it is not always easy to determine the individual feelings or the extent of generalization and sharing of those caught up in an episode of collective behavior.

The Who. However, it is possible to suggest three basic beliefs that were likely present at The Who concert. The first was that the concert was a very attractive music event that might not happen again—at least not in Cincinnati. Being able to be part of this onetime event was the motivation of the supporters. Thus, the concert attenders saw themselves as part of a historical music event. The importance of the occasion was being shared as the young people gathered on the plaza outside the coliseum.

Along with the belief in the importance of the event, two others were developing on the plaza also. These can be treated in combination. The second belief was that the concert was starting, and the third was that it would be difficult for fans to reach a desired location. These beliefs began to be shared with other nearby Who fans. It is likely that there were pockets of Type I's scattered all over the plaza. When the music began, it is likely that the generalizing of belief also began.

AC/DC. As with The Who concert there were two basic beliefs operating. One was the feeling that the concert would be missed if fans did not aggressively try to get into the hall. Second was the thought that the concert experience would be better if the fans were close to the artists on the main floor.

Clearly the most important belief for many fans was the thinking that the enjoyment of the concert would be enhanced by being as close to the stage as possible. When the concert began there was quick movement toward the band. The generalized belief had likely prepared the way for this to happen.

In summary the same process of developing generalized beliefs occurred at both crushes. While the specific content of the beliefs varied with each concert, the general content was that the concert was a highly desired event that would be enhanced by being close to the performers. It is likely that these generalized beliefs were factors leading to the crowd crushes.

Mobilization for Action

Mobilization for action in the Smelser model specifies that the analyst look at the actual behavior of the music fans involved in the crush. It involves three subdeterminants including leadership, the initial and derived phases, and the turning point.

Leadership

Leadership for the entertainment craze comes from three sources: the promoters of the concert, the media, and peers of rock concert fans.

The Who. The promoter for The Who concert was Larry Magid and his company Electric Factory Concerts. Magid was a major promoter of rock concerts (Flippo,1980:12). His promotions regularly used festival and general seating formats. He had received warning from one of his former employees that festival seating was dangerous. Nonetheless Magid, as an experienced promoter, effectively used advertisements to generate interest in the concert.

For the young people there was considerable peer interest in the concert. This is supported by the arrival of a large crowd on the plaza several hours before the concert was to begin. Fuller reports the experience of Jeff Waddle, a journalism student from the University of Cincinnati, which illustrates, in a microcosm, the power of peers. Fuller (1981:156) writes that about 6:30 P.M.:

> . . . Jeff noticed a half-dozen school kids near them [he was with a date], jostling and pushing each other. But they were in good spirits, and singing The Who favorite "Can You See The Real Me?" A few minutes later, someone started a chant: "Who! Who! Who! Who!" It was harmless enough, but for some reason it was a little scary for Jeff. He could feel a spontaneous energy rising from the crowd, and began to read an intense restlessness in the eyes of the people surrounding him.

It is likely that this vignette was played out often that evening as the fans got ready for The Who concert.

AC/DC. The concert was promoted by J.C. McNeil, an experienced promoter in the western states. The hype for the concert was the radio and newspaper advertisements.

Lastly, the main peer pressure was on the floor of the Salt Palace. It involved the definition of the situation of some fans that the concert would be enhanced if they were closer to the performing artists.

Initial and Derived Phases

The second aspect of mobilization in the value-added model involves the initial versus the derived phase of the collective behavior episode. Smelser argues that in all types of crazes, ranging from economic to religious, the analyst can locate two district phases, the initial and the derived. These phases are particularly important because social control is interpreted in the initial and derived dimensions of an entertainment crowd crush.

The Who. The initial phase at The Who concert began six hours before show time, when the concert attenders began arriving. The groups were likely Type II (See Figure 2) people who did not have reserved seats. The derived phase of the crowd crush began with the crowd buildup, around 6:15 P.M. anticipating the opening of the doors at 7:05 P.M. Because The Who arrived late, that meant that the warmup began after the scheduled start of the concert. This led fans (particularly Type II's) to the conclusion that they were going to miss some music. There was also the possibility of not achieving an attractive seat (location) in the hall.

The experience of Richard Kloop (Flippo, 1980:12) is instructive. Kloop, a Ph.D. candidate, arrived at the plaza with his wife at 2:30 P.M., ". . . because he wanted to be sure they got good seats." The buildup began around 6:15 P.M. Then he was separated from his wife and knocked to the concrete. Someone helped him up, but he was still in the crush. "At one point he was within five feet of the closed door, but he had no control over his movement [Kloop is 6′ 2″ and weighs over 200 pounds]. At times his feet were off the ground. Despite the cold, he was drenched in sweat. He could not breathe" (Flippo, 1980:12). Kloop estimated that the crush went on until at least 7:45 P.M. The first report of a death to the police was at 7:54 P.M. (Johnson, 1987:165). Kloop was eventually reunited with his wife inside the coliseum.

AC/DC. It is easy to pinpoint the initial phase of this crowd crush. It was the period of time leading to the opening number of AC/DC. While the crowd had been boisterous before the opening set, it had moved into the hall in an orderly way. However, without seats, the fans thought they had the right to move around at will. The derived phase began when AC/DC began playing "Thunderstruck." Alan Light describes the scene in the Salt Palace as the music began:

> There was an immediate surge of fans toward the stage, and according to one Salt Palace security guard, "someone just took a wrong turn and caused everyone to tumble. . . . AC/DC continued to play during the initial surge as the hall's security staff unsuccessfully tried to fight its way through the audience to the fallen bodies. The band

> eventually stopped playing after forty-five minutes. (1991:19, 99)

As noted earlier, however, there is some dispute about how soon the band stopped playing.

For both crushes, The Who and AC/DC, what seems to have occurred was that a portion of the rock music fans defined the situation as one that required movement toward the area where the performers were playing or getting ready to play. Portions of the fans began pushing and shoving each other to reach a point closer to the stage. When resistance was met, they continued to shove and push even harder. From the point of view of the actors doing this, the behavior was rational in that they were trying to achieve valued goals of either getting into the concert or placing themselves in a desired location. But from the point of view of those trapped in the crush, the actions of unknown others were highly irrational. There is a synergistic effect of rational actions leading to socially irrational consequences of deaths and injuries.

The Turning Point

The value-added model predicts that every craze has a turning point. This means that there is a moment when activity slows. It may be a rapid or gradual slowing of activity. In the entertainment crowd crush it is usually rapid. This typically happens when the crowd members become aware of the fact that there have been serious injuries or deaths.

The Who. The turning point in this crush was about 7:55 P.M. Many members in the crowd were, by this time, getting into the coliseum. Secondly, there was realization that injuries had occurred. Members of the crowd were helping each other as were the police and other security agents.

AC/DC. At this concert the turning point came when it became clear to the band that there was a problem from crowd pressure on those at the front of the stage. When this happened is not clear. Some reports say it was about halfway into the concert, others suggest that it happened after AC/DC had played just two songs. The lead singer of AC/DC, Brian Johnson, learning of the problems from its security staff stopped the band and told the crowd to step back. He also instructed the staff to turn on the house lights. The bodies were removed and the concert was continued after fifteen minutes (Light, 1991:99).

In summary, the two crushes followed the patterns suggested by the Smelser model for mobilization for action. All had leadership, initial and derived phases, and turning points.

Social Control

In the value-added model, social control is a counter-determinant, and classifies normative regulations (norms) as a preventive measure in dealing with structural conduciveness and strain. In an entertainment craze leading to a crush, there is a breakdown or lack of social control in three areas of control: normative regulation, leadership, and information (Smelser, 1962:218–219). All three mechanisms need to be analyzed in terms of the initial and derived phases, where mobilization occurs. The initial phase of an entertainment crowd crush is that period of time before the point that members of the crowd begin putting pressure on others (derived phase) to gain a desired location in the concert hall. It is, in economic terms, the speculative aspect of an entertainment crowd crush. For each crush in this study, the analysis focuses primarily on the social control mechanisms during the derived phases. However, social control can take place anywhere in the value-added process.

The Who. The crowd had been gathering since early afternoon on the plaza. Type II people, having a festival ticket and a goal of being close to the stage, used the ineffective gate control by ushers to attempt to enter the concert. The stimulus for this was the thinking that the music that the people heard outside the coliseum was the beginning of the concert.

There was clearly a *normative* breakdown among those fans who were pushing hard to get into the coliseum to get access to the concert in a favorable location. However, one cannot be totally critical of all fans. This is true for two reasons. First, it is likely that most fans were unaware of the fact that people in front them (or behind) were being crushed. Second, and more importantly, Johnson reports that there was considerable helping behavior. He (1987:167) states that 40 percent of the people in his case histories reported experiencing all three types of helping behavior during the crush—giving, receiving, and observing. When these indicators are grouped together, 75 percent of the people in the case histories reported at least one form of prosocial behavior. Thus, while some people in the crowd were pushing and shoving trying to get into the concert, others began helping when the crush started. It is likely some people displayed both anti-and prosocial behavior.

With so much helping behavior, why were there so many deaths and injuries? This is difficult to answer. But one response might be that without the helping behavior there might have been even more deaths and injuries to The Who fans.

For *leadership*, the analyst looks first to formal agents of social control. In The Who concert this is the security staff and the police. The first issue to consider is why so few gates were open for the fans to use. This is not as simple a question as it seems. One of the problems was the fact that the young people were killed and injured because the flow of the crowd was slowed by the lobby filling so rapidly. The ticket takers could not work fast enough to relieve the pressure on those in the lobby and behind. It was not just the doors, but also the physical structure of the coliseum that shaped the development of the crush. Second, the coliseum staff as social control agents should have attempted to transform Type II Who fans to Type IV (those who accept the condition of having to be in a "poor" location in the coliseum). The mechanisms of social control could have reduced speculative pressure on the gates. However, communication conditions were very difficult, making it virtually impossible to inform the crowd that the crush was going on.

The media would be an example of how *information,* or a lack of information, contributed to the initial phase of mobilization. Promoting the concert contributed to the tremendous demand. After a sellout was assured, the media could have distributed information which instructed fans about appropriate behavior at the coliseum.

Social control broke down at The Who concert in terms of normative regulation, leadership and information. When the derived phase began at the coliseum, social control activities should have tried to eliminate speculation. All three mechanisms of control should have been used to change Type II spectators to Type IVs as reflected in the typology. Increasing the amount of people who passively accepted their condition would have resulted in reduced strain.

AC/DC. In this concert the derived phase began when the music started and the fans on the main floor began rushing the stage. There was *normative* breakdown as the fans on the main floor were trying to get close to the stage and the crush began. The police and security people were unable to control the actions of the AC/DC fans who wanted to get close to the stage.

The social control mechanisms of *leadership* and *information* can be analytically combined for this crowd crush. AC/DC did act as leaders when they stopped playing and encouraged the crowd to move away from the front of the stage. Unfortunately, the information that a crush was happening was received too late to prevent the deaths and injuries.

As in The Who concert, social control broke down for two reasons. First, some fans wanted to get close to AC/DC and were willing to take risks and create problems to do so. Second, after the crush had begun, communication became difficult. Crowd conditions were such that authorities had problems communicating with others as well as the audience.

In summary, when one looks at The Who and AC/DC crushes a similar pattern can be seen which is illuminated by the Smelser model of crowd crushes. First and foremost, in each case antisocial behavior occurred when some fans attempted to get closer access to the performers. Second, for a good part of the time, many people who were causing the crush did not know it was going on or that they were causing it. Therefore, it became, in each case, difficult to stop because fans were unaware that their individual actions (pushing and shoving) were causing harm. Third, the crushes in all three cases lasted a short time. Yet in that time, deaths and serious injuries occurred.

Policy Implications

There are five issues that warrant discussion in developing the policy implications of the analysis of the two crushes. First, there are promoter and artist ethical practices. Second, positive rock music fan behavior, particularly altruistic behavior, needs to encouraged. Third, the actions of social control agents need to be evaluated. Fourth, the media's responsibility for informing and educating the rock concert community needs to be established. Fifth, the scholarly community of sociologists needs to include the study of rock concert crowds as part of its general program of research. I begin with promoter and artist ethics.

Ethics

The ethics of promoting involves evaluating the continuing and persistent dangers associated with festival (general admission) seating. It is hard to imagine, after reading these case histories, why festival seating still exists. One of the reasons for its continued existence is economic, in that it is cheaper than other forms. Another reason is that rock concert fans expect it as part of the concert experience.

An ethical question tied to the promotion of concerts is the issue of the "hype." Promoters are constantly creating the aura that the concert is so unique that it will never happen again. This is what happened in The Who concert. It is done to ensure a sold-out house. Promoters should not promote false "farewells" or "one-time-only" events. The Who "farewell" concert was an example of a "rare" event that was not so rare.

Rock performers need to look to their own actions, which encourage the pressure to get close to them. They create the values of the rock concert culture that encourages close contact with rock performers. Crowd diving is a good example of a behavior that clearly motivates some fans to want to get very close to the action on the stage.

Fan Culture

First and foremost, fans must develop a sense that concert enjoyment can be achieved in any location in the hall. This will be difficult. As I just stated, values of the rock culture combined with actions of some performers encourage movement toward the stage. Second, the rock culture has failed to develop ways to encourage its community to develop a sense of responsibility toward each other. In particular, rock audiences need to begin to think in ways that develop audience safety as well as helping behavior. Research (Johnson, 1987) has shown us that the latent potential of crowd members to help each other is clearly present. Artists, promoters, and social control agents need to think through ways to develop and enhance the helping behavior potentialities of rock concert fans.

Social Control Agents

In the cases presented here, the social control agents, particularly the police and emergency services, responded well once the crush had run its course. This probably resulted in lives being saved. But one has the sense that some problems could have been anticipated. Certainly in the case of The Who there were serious breakdowns in communication between the various agencies responsible for social control. It seems to me that police and emergency service personnel need more training in the dynamics of crowd behavior. Too many people in charge rely on practical experience alone, not recognizing the fact that there is a body of "collective behavior" theory and empirical studies about the issues under consideration in this analysis. This is recognized in the United Kingdom where, for example, a conference in York, England, in 1992 focussed on the place of crowd dynamics in natural and social disasters (Lewis, 1992).

The Mass Media

First, the media need to take some responsibility for their participation in the hype associated with the "rare event" aspects of many rock concerts. While I am not calling for the censorship of advertisements, my concern is that the media buy into the scarcity argument of promoters. Also, the media need to do more to encourage responsible concert fan behavior. Drawing on the work of Johnson (1987), it can be said that the potential for helping behavior is present in any rock concert crowd. The media could do wonders in encouraging responsible fan behavior. Lastly, the media need to inform and educate rock concert fans that a valuable musical experience can be achieved without being in the arms of the rock artist as he or she dives off the stage.

The Scholarly Community

It has been proposed that sociologists should study rock concert crowds (Aguirre, 1992: private communication). These events are very important to the lives of our students. We in the collective behavior community have a responsibility to comment on these experiences. I would add that it is one of the places where our students consistently place themselves under physical risk.

There are several issues that need study. First, there is a need to work on rock concert crowds that do not have violence associated with the performance. We need to know more about the successes of helping fan behavior and effective social control. Second, studies need to be conducted on the actual behavior of the fans in crowds. What is "collective" about their behavior should be studied. The work of Clark McPhail (Lewis et al., 1993) would be a useful starting point here. We need research on the behavior of concert fans toward each other, the artists and police. It is essential that those in charge of safety as well as the fans themselves understand the differences between "normal" concert behavior and the structure of crushes.

Conclusion

Neil J. Smelser has developed a general model of collective behavior which I applied to two well-known cases of crowd crushes. All five determinants—structural conduciveness, structural strain, growth of a generalized belief, mobilization for action, and social control—are necessary for the entertainment craze crush to occur. The entertainment craze that occurred at The Who and AC/DC concerts contained all the elements of Smelser's model of collective behavior.

Rock music is deeply embedded in the life of America's youth. I have tried to show, using the Typology of Rock Fans, how ambiguity related to participating in a complete concert combined with access to favorable locations in the halls produces four types of spectators. These conditions can lead to entertainment crowd crushes. In order to help prevent further crushes, I have concluded with a discussion of policy issues related to the research.

NOTES

1. The theoretical discussion as well as some the analyses follow an earlier paper (Lewis and Kelsey, 1990) that dealt with the Hillsborough soccer tragedy in England. This is because the crushes at the rock concerts parallel, in many aspects, the crush at Hillsbourough.

2. The narratives were initially developed by Scott A. Reid using case materials collected by the author for The Who concert and by Scott Webb for the AC/DC concert.

ACKNOWLEDGMENTS

I thank Jon Epstein for the invitation to write this chapter. In addition, Diane L. Lewis, Damon M. Lewis, Scott A. Reid, Marion Voase, and Scott Webb have been very helpful with the research on this chapter.

REFERENCES

General

Aguirre, E. 1992. Private communication.

Lewis, Damon M., 1991. "The Use of the Triangulation Method of Data Collection for Rock Concert Violence," Undergraduate Collective Behavior Seminar, Kent State University.

Lewis, Jerry M. 1986. "A Protocol for the Comparative Analysis of Sports Crowd Violence," *Mass Emergencies and Disasters*, 4 (2):211–225.

———. 1989. "A Value-Added Analysis of the Heysel Stadium Soccer Riot," *Current Psychology*, 8:15–29.

———. 1992. "Theories of the Crowd: Some Cross Cultural Perspectives," *Easingwold Papers #4*, Emergency Planning College, York, England. 8–15.

Lewis, Jerry M., and Michael Kelsey. 1990. "The Crowd Crush at Hillsborough: A Study in Collective Behavior," paper presented at North Central Sociological Association meetings, March 1990, in Louisville, Kentucky.

Lewis, Jerry M., Damon M. Lewis, and Marion Voase. 1993. "Observing Rock Concert Crowds Using the McPhail Categories," Unpublished paper.

Smelser, Neil J. 1962. *Theory of Collective Behavior*. New York: The Free Press.

The Who

Brummer, Alex. 1979. "Drugs a Cause of Panic Which Killed Who Fans," *The Guardian* (England), 12/5:1 and back.

Daily Kent Stater. 1979. "Eleven Die in Stampede at Cincy Concert," Kent State University, 12/5:1.

———. "Eleven Died of Asphyxiation at Concert," Kent State University, 12/6:13.

Diemer, Thomas K., and Amos A. Kermisch. 1979. "Seating Plan Blamed in Fatal Rush," *The Plain Dealer*, 12/5:1, 18–A.

Flippo, Chet. 1980. "Rock and Roll Tragedy," *Rolling Stone*, January 24:1, 10, 12, 22–24.

Fuller, John G. 1981. *Are The Kids All Right?* New York: Times Books, 155–189.

Johnson, Norris R. 1987. "Panic at 'The Who Concert Stampede': An Empirical Assessment," *Social Problems*, 34 (4):162–173.

Kay, Joe. 1979. "Rock Crowd called 'Animals,'"*Cleveland Press*, 12/5:1, A–4.

Kermisch, Amos A., and Thomas K. Diemer. 1979. "'They Opened Three Doors. Everyone was Pushing,'" *The Plain Dealer*, 12/5:17–A.

Krieger, Dave. 1980. "Police Report Sheds Light on Cincinnati Tragedy," *Rolling Stone* 3/20:25–26.

The Plain Dealer. 1979. "Eleven Killed in Crush at Cincy Rock Concert," 12/4:1, 10–A.

Report of the Task Force on Crowd Control and Safety. 1980. *Crowd Management*, City of Cincinnati, Reproduction and Printing Division, Cincinnati, Ohio.

AC/DC

Evensen, Jay 1991. "Festival Seating Became Official in '88," *Deseret News*, Salt Lake City, Utah, 1/26:B1–B2.

Jarrel, Tom. 1991. "Fatal Frenzy," *20/20*, ABC News, New York, 4/26: second segment.

Light, Alan. 1991. "Three Fans Die at AC/DC Show," *Rolling Stone*, 3/7:19, 99.

New York Times. 1991. "Reports Vary on How Band Acted as 3 Fans Were Killed," 1/23:A3.

Roberson, Kenneth S., and Brooke Adams. 1991. "Concert Stampede Claims BYU Student as 3rd Victim," *Deseret News*, Salt Lake City, Utah, 1/22:B1, B6.

Voase, Marion. 1991. "The Use of Triangulation in Research on the AC/DC Concert Riot," Undergraduate Collective Behavior Seminar, Kent State University.

Popular Music as a "Social Cement": A Content Analysis of Social Criticism and Alienation in Alternative-Music Song Titles

Amy B. Mohan
Jean Malone

For musicologist Theodor Adorno (1941:39) the strength of popular music lies in its ability to act as a "social cement," creating a feeling of identification in each listener and making him feel part of a common group. He described popular songs as social products created within a fairly standardized format and designed to arouse the listener's emotions. A pop song, therefore, has its greatest effect when it expresses emotions the listener is unable to express himself because of personal repression or social taboos (Adorno, 1976). For this reason, Adorno feels that popular music must be studied in terms of its effect on the listener rather than for its musical content.

Adorno is not alone in this view. Other sociologists have recognized the importance of the audience in the study of music. Sorokin defined different types of music according to the different attitudes evoked in listeners (Etzkorn, 1989). In her 1991 book *Teenage Wasteland,* sociologist Donna Gaines states that among the teenagers in her sample, "subcultural affiliations are expressed through clothing and music, coded in signs" (92). In other words, the music and its attendant clothing styles serve as Adorno's "social cement" and help to integrate the teenagers into a community of like-minded companions. In addition, Frith (1987) suggests that choosing which records to buy constitutes cultural expression for those whose access to other avenues of expression may be blocked.

The concept of "social cement" can be further clarified by examining the value structures of various kinds of music. For example, country and western and R&B are two distinct styles of music which nevertheless employ an identical pop music format. However, the two styles of music are radically different and have separate audiences. Following Adorno, we would expect that the feelings of identification created in the audiences of these musical styles are determined by the values inherent in the lyrical content of the songs. Thus, when pop music acts as a "social cement," it is working to communicate a value system to its audience.

The purpose of the present research is to describe an emerging musical category, alternative, in terms of the value system it communicates to its audience. In the last three years an alternative music community has become increasingly recognizable in the United States and in Europe. Alternative music has its origins in the underground music of the 1960s and in British punk of the 1970s, the lyrics of which stressed pessimism, alienation, and intellectual criticism of commonly held social values. Because of these origins, alternative music genres, while stylistically diverse, adhere to a common value system which revolves around social criticism and alienation.

This study will use the method of content analysis to determine the extent of social criticism in alternative music. It will also examine a variety of other values to measure the extent of alienation. For comparison, the extent of social criticism and alienation will also be measured in a sample of songs from the pop mainstream. The expectation is that alternative music will contain more social criticism than mainstream pop, as well as more negative themes in general. The findings can then be used to describe the value systems communicated to the audiences of each category. The results of the study should confirm the existence of a distinct alternative community with a discernible value system.

This study will also attempt to develop a relatively new method of content analysis for use in the study of popular songs. It will address some of the reliability problems inherent in analysis of latent content of song lyrics by changing the focus of the analysis from song lyrics to song titles.

In the past, content analyses have focused on latent content in song lyrics; however, the purpose of this study is to examine the way in which songs actually communicate to an audience, rather than to examine the intentions of the songwriters themselves. On radio, the main instrument of dissemination for pop music, the song title communicates more directly to the audience than do song lyrics, which often cannot be understood. This study, therefore, will focus on the manifest content of song titles.

Before describing the methods employed in this study, however, it is necessary to document the emergence of the alternative community, which is presently growing in size and media recognition. The growth of the alternative community indicates that the value system communicated by alternative music is becoming increasingly influential in Western culture. It will also be necessary to relate something of the history of alternative music. Such an account will support the existence of the values of social criticism and alienation in this musical category.

The Alternative Community

The term "alternative music" is used by the music media and the recording industry to categorize the work of musical groups with one or a combination of the following characteristics: unique musical styles, affiliation with independent or noncorporate record labels, and exposure through college radio and local venues rather than mainstream radio.

The most common characteristics of alternative artists are local origins and representation by independent record labels. Analysis of 151 new alternative releases listed in the June 1992 issue of *Alternative Press* magazine shows that 85 percent were released by independent record labels or small subsidiaries of major corporate labels, 9 percent were released by independent labels with the support of major labels, and 6 percent were released by major corporate labels alone. These figures indicate that the majority of alternative music is the product of small, independent, locally run labels.

Record sales confirm that alternative music is serving the needs of an increasingly recognizable community. In the past, even the most successful alternative bands were lucky to sell over 250,000 copies of a recording (Mason, 1992); however, in 1991 and 1992, Nirvana, a Seattle-based group making its major-label debut, sold an unprecedented four million copies of its album *Nevermind*. The Red Hot Chili Peppers, from Los Angeles, sold three million copies of their album *Blood Sugar Sex Magik*. Another indication of the growth of a distinct alternative community is the record crowds of young people attending "Lollapalooza," a concert tour of seven alternative bands that sold out shows around the country during the summer and fall of 1992. Tickets for one date near New York sold out entirely on the first day of sales (Watrous, 1992).

The music media are reflecting the emergence of this community as well. *Alternative Press: New Music Now* is one of at least six nationally circulated magazines that report on the alternative music community. During the last three years, *Alternative Press* has had sufficient interest to warrant a full-time staff and regular monthly publication (Banks, 1992). In 1989, *Billboard,* the music industry trade weekly, added "Modern Rock Tracks," a weekly listing of the top 30 songs on college radio, to its regular collection of music charts. This indicates that the staff at *Billboard* view the alternative community in the same way that they view the audiences of country and western, R&B, or rap. They view the audience of alternative music as a distinct demographic group.

Alternative music is clearly becoming a strong "social cement" for an increasingly recognizable community of listeners. It is thus a worthy object of sociological study; however, little sociological literature has considered the subject. McDonald (1987) has analyzed the content of hardcore punk songs, but hardcore is only one genre of many in the alternative community. Consequently, no generalizations about the larger alternative community can be made.

The purpose of this study is to examine the value system communicated and maintained for the alternative community by alternative music. The method of content analysis will be used to describe the values communicated by this music, comparing them with those communicated by mainstream popular music. The results should support the existence of the alternative community as a socially critical group that feels alienated from mainstream society.

The high value placed on social criticism and expressions of alienation by alternative music and its audience can be traced to underground music of the 1960s and British punk of the 1970s.

The History of Alternative Music

Alternative outlooks and musical styles are not new in pop music. The community of musicians and music businesspeople today labelled "alternative" continues musical and lyrical themes begun in the 1960s by bands such as The Who, The Kinks, The Doors, The Velvet Underground, and The Stooges, who expressed, sometimes violently, the theme of alienation from society. While the theme of societal alienation was common in the music of the 1960s, the tone of the alienation expressed by these bands was different from the typical protest song. Instead of writing songs that expressed hope for the future and supported the idea of positive change, these bands wrote songs that were dark, pessimistic, and intellectually cynical.

The most important antecedent of today's alternative genres was British punk of the mid-seventies. This genre "[rejected] a sense of melody or instrument virtuosity in favor of simple, three-chord guitar parts" and "steady, rapid rhythm pounded on drums with a shouted vocal" (Dixon, 1980:211). It began as an expression of rage and rebellion on the part of unemployed, working-class youth and evolved into a distinct musical style, as well as a worldview and way of life for some.

Much has been written about the punks, and a few students of popular music have attempted to analyze their impact on the music world. Dancis (1978:59) characterizes punk as "a manifestation of cultural despair and decadence, featuring nihilism, sexism, a glorification of violence and fascist imagery, sadomasochism, and musical incompetence." Dixon (1980:211) states that British punk was an "angry political railing against the ills of established society" which "[screamed] resentment against the status quo."

Although the alternative community is musically diverse, it is also unified in its devotion to values derived from punk: social criticism and alienation from mainstream values. The purpose of the present study is to use the method of content analysis to determine the extent to which alternative music contains these values. It will also attempt to determine the extent of these values in mainstream pop music for the purpose of comparison.

The results of the content analysis will then be used to suggest the existence of an alternative community with values different from those of the mainstream of American youth culture. If alternative music does contain more of the values of social criticism and alienation than mainstream popular music, it will then be possible to define the alternative community as dissatisfied with the status quo and conventional social values.

Content Analysis in the Study of Popular Music

Content analysis is the most popular method employed by social scientists in the study of popular songs (Lewis, 1977, Denisoff and Bridges, 1983). Frith (1987) and Denisoff and Bridges (1983) point out that the first published content analysis of popular songs was conducted in Germany as early as 1943, by Roland Warren. The 1960s saw a surge of studies using the content analysis of popular songs to understand the youth culture of the time (Frith, 1987). Few content analyses since the 1960s have strayed beyond the music of that time, however, with the exception of analyses of country and western music (Singletary, 1983, Armstrong, 1986). A study by McDonald (1987), which analyzed the lyrics of hardcore punk songs, is unusual in that it deals with a genre of alternative music.

Students of popular culture have criticized content analysis as a means of studying mass communication because often the question of "who, exactly, is being communicated with" is left unanswered (Lewis, 1977:23). Adorno and Sorokin believed this question could be answered through analysis of the social needs fulfilled by the music.

This study will examine popular songs in terms of the audience to which they communicate. It will also attempt to maximize the reliability of content analysis in the study of popular songs. The most difficult dilemma which has arisen in past content analyses of popular songs is that of striking a balance between the coding of manifest and latent content in song lyrics. Babbie (1989:298) describes this dilemma as a "fundamental choice between depth and specificity of understanding." In the past, many content analyses have focused on coding of latent, or underlying, content of lyrics rather than manifest, or explicit, content.

The most important difficulty that arises in the coding of latent content is that of reliability. Since coding of latent content involves a subjective interpretation, one coder will not necessarily make the same interpretation as another. In past content analysis, reliability has not been a major concern.

A much-cited analysis by Horton (1957) focuses only on the latent content of song lyrics. Horton provides no support for the reliability of his categories—we do not even know if Horton tested for reliability. A similar method was employed by Carey (1969). This study also focuses entirely on the latent content of lyrics without raising the question of reliability. A content analysis published by Richard Cole in 1971, however, does address the problem of reliability by using two coders.

All three of these widely cited studies share common problems: they are exploratory in nature but try to force this exploration into a quantitative format, they are too broad in scope, and they examine song lyrics that contain too many different images for clear conclusions to be drawn. Song lyrics are a worthy subject for qualitative exploration of communication, and any content analysis contains a subjective element, but a more quantitative approach is possible.

Sedlack and Stanley (1992) suggest that interpretive training of coders might eliminate some of the subjectivity problems inherent in the coding of latent content, but not all such problems. They suggest that the way to conduct content analysis, therefore, is to code manifest content alone. In their view, assuring the reliability of the study takes precedence over assuring the validity of the study. Babbie (1989), on the other hand, feels that the problems of validity that arise when one only codes manifest content are serious. He suggests a compromise between the two perspectives. This study will attempt to achieve such a compromise.

The present research will approach the content analysis of popular songs in a way which allows the number of cases included in a sample to be greatly expanded: by analyzing song titles. This approach reduces the number of different images under consideration from many per song to one or two. This approach is especially useful in the analysis of alternative songs, the lyrics of which are often unintelligible on recordings and seldom found in printed form anywhere, because it eliminates the need for time-consuming transcription of lyrics.

Focusing on song titles allows for the effective coding of both manifest and latent content. Because a song title presents only one or two images, the amount of latent content is decreased. There is less opportunity for inter-coder disagreement. At the same time, categories can be designed that focus mostly on the manifest content of the communication.

The title of the song is the principal way in which the intent of the song is communicated to its audience. It appears on the CD cover, it is uttered by the DJ; in short, it is the ID tag of the song. A songwriter's decision as to title is a social communication in itself, summarizing images from the song that hold the most impact for him/her and broadcasting these priorities to a generalized listener. In this way the song title acts as a kind of poetic signpost, directing the listener's mind toward specific themes and emotions, piquing his curiosity, or confusing him, if the songwriter so desires.

Methods

This study focused on song titles from 1990 to 1992. The sampling frame consisted of issues of the music industry weekly *Billboard* published from January 6, 1990, to October 3, 1992. Song titles were taken from the "Modern Rock Tracks" chart, a top 30 listing for alternative music, and the "Hot 100" chart, a mainstream chart. While the "Hot 100" chart tracks retail sales and airplay for pop songs, the "Modern Rock Tracks" chart is compiled solely from college radio airplay.

The sample of song titles was taken from "Modern Rock Tracks" and "Hot 100" charts for twelve different weeks in 1990, 1991, and 1992. Four issues from each year were sampled, spaced approximately three months apart in order to give the charts time to change completely. Because ample time was given for the titles on the charts to change, it was possible to sample the entire "Modern Rock Tracks" chart for each week of the twelve weeks with little repetition of titles. For each list of thirty alternative titles, the first thirty titles from the corresponding "Hot 100" chart were also selected. The completed alternative and mainstream title lists, therefore, reflect only the most popular song titles in the two categories for the weeks included. A total of 343 alternative and 345 mainstream titles were included in the sample.

Limitations of the Sample

There are several inherent problems in using *Billboard* charts as a sampling frame. The first problem is that of probability. Since certain songs are more popular and stay on the charts longer, some song titles have a greater probability of being sampled than others. Certain songs repeated themselves on the charts even after the three-month interval. Since this study deals with the way the song communicates to the audience, it is important to realize that these repetitions occur. Songs that are over-sampled may communicate more effectively to an audience than other songs. A total of twelve alternative and eighteen mainstream titles repeated themselves on the charts in this way, but the recurrences were eliminated from the total sample and the titles were coded only once.

It is also necessary to note that because these charts list only those songs receiving the greatest amount of radio airplay, the songs of certain very popular artists may also be over-sampled. Artists on major record labels are able to release two or three different singles in a given year. Frequent airplay for such singles is fairly automatic, at least for a time. Less well-known artists have to release a particularly effective song to get similar airplay, something which, for those lacking a wide following or major-label support, may happen only once. The generalizations that can be made from samples taken from *Billboard* are thus limited in that popular appeal is not always created by the song itself.

It is also important to note that certain songs are popular with both audiences and may appear on both charts. Seventeen titles were eligible for coding on both the alternative and the mainstream list. Songs that occur on both charts are particularly interesting and were coded on both the alternative and the mainstream list.

To eliminate possible coder bias that might arise from the connotations of the words "alternative" and "mainstream," the titles were given identification numbers, "one" for the alternative list and "two" for the mainstream list. The two lists were then combined and alphabetized. Coders had no access to the identification number during coding. The titles were coded by three independent coders into ten categories, following written coding guidelines. The categories appear in Appendix A at the end of the paper.

The expectations of the study were that alternative song titles would be high in themes of social commentary since they serve as a "social cement" for those dissatisfied with conventional values. In addition, these titles might be expected to be high in negative themes, since pessimism, cynicism, and alienation have long been prevalent themes in underground music.

Findings

The findings of the content analysis are summarized in Table 1. As expected, alternative titles rated higher in the "social commentary" category than the mainstream titles. The mainstream titles rated much higher in the "love/romance" category. While alternative titles rated higher in the "negative event" category, as expected, they also rated the same as the mainstream titles in the "positive event" category, contrary to expectations. The difference in the distribution of titles into categories on the two lists was significant (x^2=77.89, df=9, p<.000).

Table 1: Value Content of Song Titles in Percentages

	Alternative (n = 343)	Mainstream (n = 345)	Difference
Negative Event	30.6%	18.8%	+11.8
Social Commentary	17.2	7.0	+10.2
Miscellaneous	15.5	14.5	+ 1.0
Positive Event	20.7	20.0	+ .7
Violence	1.7	1.2	+ .5
Humor	.6	.3	+ .3
Imperatives	2.9	4.6	- 1.7
Sex	1.2	4.9	- 3.7
Music/Dancing	2.0	5.8	- 3.8
Love/Romance	7.6	22.9	-15.3
Total	100.0%	100.0%	

Reliability

One of the goals of this study was to address the problems of reliability which often arise in the content analysis of popular songs. Analysis of inter-coder agreement shows two of the three coders reaching a 61 percent agreement. The overall kappa was

.55, which indicates a moderate agreement beyond chance, and an acceptable level of reliability for the categories.

Agreement between all three coders was more problematic, only reaching 36 percent. This level of agreement indicates that subjectivity remains a serious difficulty even when the amount of latent content under consideration is decreased.

Discussion

The purpose of this study was to examine the values that alternative music communicates to its audience. The expectation of the study was that a content analysis of song titles from the alternative category would confirm the existence of the alternative community as a group with different values from mainstream society. Social criticism and alienation were expected to be greater in the titles of alternative songs than in the titles of mainstream popular songs.

The results of the content analysis show that social criticism is indeed greater in alternative song titles than in mainstream song titles. Alternative song titles, 17.2 percent of the time, contained some element of social commentary, as opposed to 7 percent of mainstream pop titles. Pessimism was more evident in the alternative titles, as 30.6 percent dealt with some kind of negative event or image. By contrast, only 18.8 percent of the mainstream titles referred to negative events outside of those occurring in romances. The mainstream titles were much more concerned with all aspects of love and relationships, scoring 22.9 percent in this category. When combined with specific references to sex, the score rises to 27.8 percent. The combined score for the "love/romance" category and the "sex" category on the alternative list, however, was only 8.8 percent.

The only result not in line with expectations was the "positive event" category. References to positive events and images were similar on both lists: 20.7 percent for the alternative titles and 20 percent for the mainstream titles. This may be due to a problem with confounding of the "positive/negative event" categories and the "love/romance" category. On both lists, some of the titles containing references to positive and negative events also referred to love or romance in some way. Because of the higher scores for "love/romance" on the mainstream list, it is possible that this confounding may have affected the coding of titles on the mainstream list more often than on the alternative list.

It is possible, however, to eliminate the effects of this confounding by separating the titles from the "love/romance" category into positive and negative groups. On the alternative list, 5.6 percent of the titles were about positive aspects of love, while 2 percent were about negative love. On the mainstream list, 17.1 percent of titles were about positive love, while 5.8 percent were about negative love. A useful comparison of the "positive/ negative event" categories may be made by combining negative love with negative events and positive love with positive events on both lists and comparing the results.

When positive romance is added to the "positive event" category, the combined scores are 26.3 percent for the alternative list and 37.1 percent for the mainstream list. When negative romance is added to the "negative event" category, the combined scores are 32.6 percent for the alternative list and 24.6 percent for the mainstream list. Thus, alternative song titles refer to positive events and images less often.

Another value of alternative music discussed in this study is that of alienation. While there was no reliable way to make a category for alienation, the combined scores for "social commentary," "violence," and "negative events" ought to yield a fairly good measure of alienation themes. The combined scores for these categories on the alternative list was 49.5 percent, while for the mainstream list the score was 27 percent. Clearly, alienation is expressed in alternative song titles much more often than in mainstream titles.

These results are in line with expectations and generally support the idea that alternative music contains a greater amount of the values of social criticism and alienation than does mainstream music. These results are much less compelling than expected, however. A pilot study conducted for the purpose of category formulation indicated that levels of social commentary, violence, and humor would be much higher in the alternative titles than this study shows. It also indicated that scores for "love/romance" would be much lower on the alternative list.

The explanation for this difference between expectations and actual results lies in the method by which the pilot study was conducted. Titles for the preliminary sample were collected from the backs of CDs in the alternative section of a local record store. The differing frequencies of themes in the record-store titles and the music-chart titles suggests that the most popular songs in any category are not the best measure of themes in the category as a whole. It may be that in order to appeal to the widest range of listeners and receive more airplay, artists must employ more traditional themes. This accounts for the wide difference between music-chart alternative song titles and record-store alternative song titles.

These differing theme frequencies lessen somewhat the support that this study provides for the existence of a unified alternative community dedicated to the values of social criticism and alienation. While these themes are more prevalent in alternative titles than in mainstream titles, the results of the study indicate that ultimately the alternative audience differs from the mainstream audience only mildly. However, the alternative titles sampled may not be representative of all alternative music.

Conclusion

This study has developed a method of content analysis which addresses some of the reliability problems inherent in past analyses of the latent content of song lyrics. The title of a song summarizes key images from the song and directs the listener's attention to its most important lyric elements. For this reason, the present research focused on the coding of manifest and latent content in song titles. Analysis of song titles reduces the amount of different images under consideration and increases the possible sample size. This method has proven an effective means of exploring the values communicated by alternative music to its audience.

The popular music world is divided into multiple categories which employ similar, if not identical, pop music formats. The audiences of many of these categories, however, vary in terms of their demographics and value systems. Theodor Adorno viewed popular music as a "social cement" capable of communicating and maintaining values for its audience. This concept suggests that the differing value systems of these pop audiences are reinforced through the differing thematic content of popular songs in separate musical categories.

This study has examined one such musical category, alternative, in terms of the value system it communicates to an increasingly recognizable alternative community. Results of the study show that alternative song titles express social criticism, pessimism, and alienation from society to a greater extent than mainstream song titles. Alternative music can thus be said to serve as a "social cement" for an audience dissatisfied with conventional mainstream values. The recent commercial success of groups expressing values of social criticism and alienation may indicate that dissatisfaction with the mainstream is increasing among young people in our society.

Appendix A: Categories

1. *Social Commentary:* Includes any reference to politics, religion, cities, states of nations, media figures (e.g., movie stars, sports figures), media images (e.g., movie cliches), technology (e.g., automobiles, household appliances, or their use), science fiction or fact (e.g., outer space, medicine), occultism, drug use, racial imagery, and any overtly critical message, such as one referring to the state of "the world" in any way.
2. *Violence:* Includes any reference to or imagery dealing with weapons, poison, war, blood, death, or physical acts of aggression such as hitting or shooting.

3. *Sex:* Includes references to sexual acts or sexual desire, and overt sexual innuendos.
4. *Love/Romance:* Includes references to feelings of love, hearts, heartbreak, the use of the words "baby" or "honey," (apart from the linkage of these words with a sexual or dance theme), and any general statements about being in a romantic relationship or marriage. In general, if the word "love" appears in the title, the song will be coded in this category.
5. *Humor:* Titles which include plays on words, puns, the twisting of popular catchphrases, nonsense words, and any other humorous images which contain no overt social criticism.
6. *Music/Dancing:* Includes references to rock, funk, dance crazes of the past or present, dance styles, being funky, jumping, moving, singing, grooving, grooves, or playing musical instruments.
7. *Positive Event:* Imagery about, or description of, an event or emotion positive in tone, including positive spatial relationships (e.g., "top of the world"). In addition, any references to nature, good weather, or bright colors should be considered a positive reference.
8. *Negative Event:* Imagery about, or description of, an event or image negative in tone, including negative spatial relationships (e.g., "back against the wall"). In addition, any references to illness, mental illness, or other forms of altered consciousness (e.g., "my friend delirium") should be considered a negative reference.
9. *Imperatives:* Any title with an understood "you" which indicates an attempt at communication without any indication as to the real intent of the communication (e.g., "talk to me").
10. *Miscellaneous:* Song titles which are too obscure or contain too few words to be classified. Song titles which contain personal names will be coded here if no other reference in the title indicates an attitude toward the name.

REFERENCES

Adorno, Theodor. (1941). "On Popular Music," *Studies in Philosophy and Social Science*, 9:1, 17–49.

———. (1976). *Introduction to the Sociology of Music*, New York: Seabury Press.

Armstrong, Edward G. (1986). "Country Music Sex Songs: An Ethnomusicological Account," *Journal Of Sex Research*, 22:3, 370–378

Babbie, Earl. (1989). *The Practice of Social Research*, Belmont, CA: Wadsworth Publishing Company.

Banks, Joe. (1992). Senior Editor, *Alternative Press: New Music Now*, telephone interview.

Burns, Gary. (1983). "Trends in Lyrics in the Annual Top Twenty Songs in the United States, 1963–1972," *Popular Music and Society*, 9:25–39.

Carey, James T. (1969). "The Ideology of Autonomy in Popular Lyrics: A Content Analysis," *Psychiatry*, 32: 150–164.

Clark, Donald (Ed.). (1989). *The Penguin Encyclopedia of Popular Music*, London: Viking.

Cole, Richard R. (1971). "Top Songs of the Sixties: A Content Analysis of Popular Lyrics," *American Behavioral Scientist*, 14:389–400.

Dancis, Bruce. (1978) "Saftey Pins and Class Struggle: Punk Rock and the Left," *Socialist Review*, 8:39, 58–83.

Denisoff, Serge, and John Bridges. (1983). "The Sociology of Popular Music: A Review," *Popular Music and Society*, 6:3, 210–218.

Dixon, Richard D. (1980). "The Cultural Diffusion of Punk Rock in the United States," *Popular Music and Society*, 6:3, 210–218.

Etzkorn, Peter. (1989). Introduction to Honigsheim, Paul, *Sociologists and Music*, New Brunswick, NJ: Transaction Publishers.

Frith, Simon. (1987). "Why Do Songs Have Words?" *Sociological Review Monograph*, 34:77–106.

Gaines, Donna. (1991). *Teenage Wasteland: Suburbia's Dead End Kids*, New York: Pantheon.

Horton, Donald. (1957). "The Dialogue of Courtship in Popular Songs," *American Journal of Sociology*, 62:569–578.

Kurtz, Howard. (1982). "Differences in Themes in Popular Music and Their Relationship to Deviance," *Popular Music and Society*, 8:2, 84–89.

Lewis, George H. (1977). "Social Class and Cultural Communication: An Analysis of Song Lyrics," *Popular Music and Society*, 5:1, 23–27.

———. (1988). "The Creation Of Popular Music: A Comparison of the 'Art Worlds' of American Country Music and British Punk," *International Review of the Aesthetics and Sociology of Music*, 19:1, 35–51.

Loud, Lance. (1992). "Los Angeles 1972–74: Glam Loses Its Virginity," *Details*, 11:2, 76–79.

Mason, Jack. (1992) ."Here Comes the Bride," *Spin*, 8:4, 39–40.

McDonald, James R. (1987)."Suicidal Rage: An Analysis of Hardcore Punk Lyrics," *Popular Music and Society*, 11:3, 91–102.

Miller, Richard E. (1987). "The Music of Our Sphere: Apocalyptic Visions in Popular Music of the Eighties," *Popular Music And Society*, 11:3, 75–89.

New Releases Listing, *Alternative Press: New Music Now*, 6:48, 8.

Sedlack, R. Guy, and Jay Stanley. (1992). *Social Research: Theory and Methods*, Boston: Allyn and Bacon.

Shepard, John. (1991). *Music as a Social Text*, Cambridge, MA: Polity Press.

Singletary, Michael. (1983). "Some Perceptions of the Lyrics of Three Types of Recorded Music: Rock, Country, Soul," *Popular Music and Society*, 9:51–63.

"Spinfacts: Adult Demographic Profile." (1992). Media kit, *Spin*.

Stambler, Irwin. (1989). *The Encyclopedia of Pop, Rock, and Soul*, New York: St. Martin's Press.

Sterling, Eben. (1992). "Sub Pop Guide to Crass Commercialism," *Soundchoice*, 17: 67–68.

Thompson, Dave. (1992). "Superchunk: Cut 'em Some Slack," *Alternative Press: New Music Now*, 6:47, 43–48.

Watrous, Peter. (1992). "Good Things Happen to Lollapalooza," *New York Times*, August 5, 1992, Sec. 2, p. 22.

Living on a Lighted Stage: Identity Salience, Psychological Centrality, Authenticity, and Role Behavior of Semi-Professional Rock Musicians[1]

Scott A. Reid
Jonathon S. Epstein
D.E. Benson

Introduction

The sociology of rock music has only marginally been interested in social-psychological issues of self, identity, and role behavior and has primarily focused on the relationship between the music and its audience (cf., Frith 1981; Mullen 1987; Wicke 1990). Research that has concentrated on social-psychological topics has generally dealt with very specific aspects of the musician role (e.g., Becker 1963; Bennett 1980; Dotter 1987; Frederickson and Rooney 1988; Groce 1989) and often begins with the a priori assumption that occupants of this role have a high degree of identification with the role.

This chapter adds to the sociological literature on rock music in that it is the first effort to empirically test the assumption that rock musicians identify strongly with the role. It measures the magnitude of role identification via three related sociological concepts that will be defined and discussed herein.

This research is also the first attempt to systematically examine the effects of the musician role on the occupant's definition of self using theoretically anchored measurement scales in a questionnaire format. A related groundbreaking aspect of this research that clearly sets it apart from previous social-psychological studies on the role of musicians is that it is explicitly informed by an established theory in sociological social psychology. Within sociology this theory is currently termed identity theory. Identity theory, as developed within the perspective of symbolic interactionism, argues that particular relationships exist between roles, role identities, self, and behavioral choices.

The current research is also one of the first efforts (cf., Stryker and Serpe 1992) to undertake the task of examining the constructs of identity salience and psychological centrality in terms of their impact on the role occupant's self-structure and corresponding role-related choices. This is also the first effort to include the construct of the "authenticity" of a role identity together with the constructs of identity salience and psychological centrality for an empirical assessment of their individual and combined effects on role-related choices.

As will be explicated in this chapter, identity salience and psychological centrality are two slightly differing conceptions of how identities are organized within the self as well as the effects of those differences. However, both stress that the self is partially composed of role identities held by the individual and that these identities reflect the structural positions held by the individual in the society. Role authenticity is a related construct that refers to the relationship between having a particular role identity and the extent to which the role occupant believes that identity reflects their fundamental values and beliefs.

Hypotheses addressing the relationship between these social-psychological concepts and behavior in the role are examined with data from a sample of forty-three semi-professional rock and roll musicians. The analysis presented promotes a greater understanding of the extent to which the role of semi-professional rock and roll musicians affects the self structure of its occupants. The analysis also empirically examines the role's impact on role-related choices, mainly the amount of time the role occupant has spent, currently spends, and anticipates he or she will spend in the role in the future.

Review of the Literature

The musician role was considered by Becker in his classic text *Outsiders* (1963). His research is based on field notes written during in-depth participant observation among semi-professional and regional level commercial jazz musicians in Chicago. Becker found that musicians tend to conceive of themselves as different and "better" than those outside of the professional subculture. This assertion is supported by musicians' attitudes toward idiosyncratic behavior (which is viewed as a further expression of creativity), the high esteem to which musicians regard their own sexual prowess, and musicians' low opinion of non-musicians. In short, being a musician becomes the way in which the self is defined and, in turn, affects musicians' interactional behavior. Becker's findings receive support from Mullen (1987) who partially replicated Becker's study in Aberdeen, Scotland.

Perhaps the most in-depth examination of the rock musician role was accomplished by Bennett (1980). Bennett describes the process by which individuals come to define themselves within the social world of the professional rock musician. The social world of the rock musician, particularly the small time or semi-professional level musician, is largely defined by the picture of the music business that is drawn by the promotional mechanisms of the industry itself.

The social world of the musician according to Bennett is dependent on the musician's interactions with other musicians, promoters, bar owners, technicians, club patrons, and fans. Bennett proposes that because of the extensive network of music industry personnel that the professional musician is necessarily involved with, all of whom know the musician primarily as a musician, it is not surprising that most musicians tend to define themselves as such. Bennett notes that this appears to be the case even when the individual occupies other occupational roles that would, at least partially, appear to be equally or more important than that of musician (see also Becker 1963; Mullen 1987; Groce 1989 for related discussions of this topic).

Dotter (1987) has discussed the relationship between rock and roll performers and the cultural meanings attached to the role. According to Dotter, rock musicians are best understood as cultural heroes. The construct of cultural hero refers specifically to individuals who have been set apart as symbols of youth and includes all the vague meanings couched in the term "youth" for the larger culture.

Dotter's research also demonstrates that the cultural status and high regard afforded to the rock and roll musician is, in large part, due to the promotional mechanisms of the music industry. He argues that these mechanisms also foster what have been described as "star cults" (e.g., Wicke 1990). From a music industry perspective, the creation of a star cult involves the focus of attention on a particular band or toward a specific band member—generally the vocalist. This phenomenon abets and ensures relatively stable promotional effectiveness.

As a result of the star cult, the music consumer finds himself or herself identifying with the music star and is lead to believe, quite independently of any objective evidence, that the characteristics of the musician in question resonate with his or her own interests. This is precisely because of the reflection, through music industry promotions, of the listener's interests back to the listener himself or herself. The result of this process is that the listener comes to believe that the fabricated existence of the rock star is in fact possible for himself or herself as well.

While these studies are informative and deal in some way with particular aspects of the musician role, they have not produced systematic data about how musician-related self-perceptions are associated with other aspects of self and behavioral choices regarding the role. Also important is that this body of research has yet to examine the musician role within the parameters of identity theory. As previously discussed, this chapter adds to the sociological literature on rock music in that it is the first effort to systematically examine the effects of the musician role on the occupants' definition of self using theoretically anchored measurement scales in a questionnaire format.

Theory

Identity Salience

Identity theory in sociology originates from a body of writing known collectively as symbolic interactionism. Symbolic interactionism is a micro-level approach to the explanation of social phenomena and is the foremost theory in the discipline of sociology for the study of the relationship between social structure and the self. As the name symbolic interactionism implies, this body of research concerns itself directly with humans and their ability to employ symbols in the communicative process. This is primarily because symbols are seen as the basis of meaningful communication, thus providing the necessary prerequisite for social interaction.

A second central tenet of this approach is that the self and society are mutually dependent upon one another (Mead 1934), and the self is conceptualized as a reflection of the society in that like society, its components are complex and hierarchically arranged. The self is correspondingly defined, within symbolic interactionism, as "an organized collection of identities, each of which serves to shape our behavior in social interaction where there is a choice among possible alternative behaviors" (Burke and Hoelter 1988:29). Embedded in this view is that the self is a dynamic process and is continually being created and modified during social interaction.

The sociological foundation of this conceptualization of the self cannot be overemphasized, because the identities that compose the self are not seen merely as psychological entities that individuals possess but rather as definitions of self that are due to enacted social roles, such as teacher, student, musician, mother, and daughter. A related idea is that all roles carry with them structurally determined components that impact the actor's definition of self vis-à-vis an interpretive process. Critical to this argument is that identities are seen as parts of the self that are "internalized positional designations" and "exist insofar as the person is a participant in structured role relationships" (Stryker 1980:60).

Identity theorists employ the concept of "role identity" as the link between the individual (self) and social structure primarily because role identities are defined as social objects that denote a dimension of self that is shared and socially recognized. This implies that others must recognize someone as occupying a particular position in social structure. In other words, to have a role identity of "musician," a person must not only play an instrument, but be known by others as a musician. Also important is that role identities are defined by enacting role-related behaviors that are influenced but not dictated by behavioral expectations from social structure.

It is of course conceivable that persons may have many role identities due to the fact that they occupy multiple positions in the social structure. Illustrative of this is that a person may be a musician, father, husband, and teacher. In reference to this multifaceted nature of roles, identity theorists postulate that people are confronted with structurally influenced choices about which role to play in any given situation and that the choice as to which role to enact is influenced by the individual's self-structure of role identities. A central question of identity theory is, correspondingly, "Why is one behavioral option selected over another in situations in which either is available to the person?" (Stryker and Serpe 1992:5)

As an answer to this question, Stryker posits that the behavioral option chosen (i.e., playing music versus studying for an exam) "is a function of the relative salience of the identities" (Stryker and Serpe 1992:5); in this case, musician versus student. The logic undergirding this explanation is that to Stryker, identities are arranged in a hierarchy of salience and that the higher an identity is in the hierarchy, the greater the probability that the particular identity will be elicited in a variety of interactions. Salience is correspondingly defined by Stryker as the probability of invoking a given identity in a particular setting or across a wide variety of settings.

Identity theory also allows for the possibility that a situation may invoke more than one identity, as when a father brings his wife and children to the place where he performs with his band. In this situation, it is conceptually possible for the role identities of husband, father, and musician to be invoked. For identity theory, what needs to be explained is how an individual's salience hierarchy of role identities is arranged, because it determines which identity will most likely be invoked or take precedence over potential others and, therefore, impact behavioral outcomes.

In terms of explaining or predicting behavioral outcomes, identity theory postulates that once a particular role identity is established and acquires a prominent position in the salience hierarchy, behaviors that emanate from that identity are more likely to be enacted by the social actor than behaviors flowing from another role identity. Thus, according to identity theory, a person with a highly salient role identity of musician will spend more time performing in that role than another person who has a lower salience level for the role identity.

Psychological Centrality

A related but alternative conceptualization of the arrangement of components of the self is known within the social-psychological literature as "psychological centrality." This approach originates in the writings of McCall and Simmons (1978) and Rosenberg (1979) and differs from identity salience primarily because it assumes individuals are introspective and thus aware of the identities that compose the self-structure and their relative ordering of importance. The concept of identity salience, in contrast, postulates that individuals may not be aware of the ordering of the salience hierarchy of role identities (see Stryker 1980 for a discussion of this).

While the concepts of identity salience and psychological centrality differ in their assumptions about the reflective capacities of social actors, both converge on the notion of hierarchically arranged self-components to generate theoretically anchored predictions about behavioral outcomes (Stryker and Serpe 1992). Borrowing extensively from the writings of James (1890), psychological centrality is more inclusive of the meanings attached to role identities than is identity salience when making behavioral predictions. The concept of psychological centrality also incorporates and attempts to assess the global self-esteem of role occupants (Stryker and Serpe 1992).

Role Authenticity

Recently a number of researchers (e.g., Erickson 1993; Gecas 1986, 1991; Turner and Billings 1991) have discussed a concept that is related to both identity salience and psychological centrality. The concept is termed "role authenticity" and is construed as the relationship between having a particular role identity and the extent to which the person believes the identity reflects who he or she "really is." That is, to what extent are the characteristics of the role isomorphic with one's perception of his or her own personal characteristics and system of self-meanings? In the context of the present study, the question is, to what extent do musicians perceive that the role demands of the work reflect the "kind" of person they think they are? If the role does reflect the kind of persons musicians think they are, the identity of musician can be said to be an "authentic" one. If not, the identity is "inauthentic," false, and contradictory to their own self-values.

Examining the motivational aspects of authenticity, Gecas (1991) maintains that people will attempt to avoid or escape role identities that are perceived to be inauthentic primarily because being in this position leads to feelings of self-estrangement, anomie, and depression. Thus, if people are presented with choices about various role identities, identity theory predicts that they will not incorporate inauthentic role identities into their self structure.

The construct of authenticity has seldom been utilized in empirical research (cf. Zurcher and Snow 1981; Reid, Epstein, and Benson in review) and never with musicians. Given the somewhat prestigious and reputable nature of the role of musician and the highly voluntary nature of occupying the role, it would be expected that people performing in the role of musician would feel authentic.

Hypotheses

Given the previous theoretical discussion of identity salience, psychological centrality, and authenticity, six hypotheses concerning semi-professional rock and roll musicians will be examined. The six hypotheses are:

1. the role identity of musician will be highly salient;
2. the role identity of musician will be psychologically central to musicians;
3. musicians will regard the role identity of musician as authentic;
4. the greater the salience of the musician role identity, the more time will be spent in the role of musician;
5. the more psychologically central the musician role identity, the more time will be spent in the role of musician;
6. the greater the sense of perceived role authenticity, the more time will be spent in the role of musician.

Methodology

Sample

Initially, professional rock and roll shows were attended in the greater Cleveland, Ohio, area in order to gain insight into the dynamic processes of the occupation and to discuss some of the issues of the research with professional rock and roll musicians. Access was gained to backstage areas at shows involving the professional rock and roll bands Cinderella, Judas Priest, Rush, and Rhythm Corps.

A lengthy informal interview was held with Geddy Lee of the band Rush. During this interview, philosophical issues of lyrical content and occupational matters were discussed. Extensive informal interviews were also held at several shows (n=5) with the band Rhythm Corps. The locations of the interviews were in "back region" areas, including the place of performance, the musicians' hotel rooms, on the tour bus, local restaurants, and in one case, during a tour of a local college campus (see Goffman 1959 for an elaboration of the concept of back region and Reid 1991 for a usage of it within professional rock and roll performance settings). These interviews were informative in that they provided insight into the nature of the occupational role and thus guided the researchers in the development and distribution of the questionnaire for this study.

A sample was culled from semi-professional rock and roll musicians who reside in the northeastern Ohio and western Pennsylvania areas. The researchers distributed the instruments (n=105) through liaison persons who were either in a band themselves or who had sufficient contact with musicians to distribute the instrument.[2] After the instruments had been administered, they were collected by the liaisons and returned to the researchers. While in some instances (n=7) the name of the band was known, the names of the musicians themselves were not submitted to the researchers or written anywhere on the instrument in order to safeguard anonymity. This distribution procedure resulted in a total of forty-three usable instruments.

Measures

Data for this research were gathered through the use of an instrument devised by the first author and drawn from the work of Callero (1985), Burke and Reitzes (1991), Stryker and Serpe (1992), and Trew and Benson (1993). The instrument primarily consisted of standardized scales that were designed to measure the major concepts employed in this research. The scales in their entirety may be found in Appendix A. Additional data were gathered on the sample's demographic characteristics. These characteristics included age, education, race/ethnicity, religious preference, sexual orientation, income, marital status, and length of time in the role of musician.

Role identity salience was measured by a four-item scale adapted from Callero (1985). Principal components factor analysis was used to determine whether the items represented one dimension in this sample. Results, using varimax rotation, indicated only one factor with eigenvalues over unity. All four items in this factor had loadings of .50 or above. For this population the scale has a low, but acceptable, alpha = .62. See Appendix A for a listing of the items and their loadings.

Role identity authenticity was measured using a three-item scale devised by Trew and Benson (1993) to assess the degree to which a role occupant feels that fundamental and important features of his or her sense of self are represented by the characteristics of the role. Again, principal components factor analysis with varimax rotation was used to determine whether the items represented one dimension in this sample. The results of this procedure indicated only one factor with eigenvalues over unity. All three items in this factor had loadings of .50 or above. For this population the scale has a low, but acceptable, alpha = .60. See Appendix A for a listing of the items and their loadings.

Time spent in the role of musician was measured with four separate questions: "How long have you been a musical performer?", "How many hours during a typical week, on the average, do you spend in the role of musician?", "How much of your available time do you spend in the role of musician?", and "In the near future, how much of your available time will you spend in the role of musician?" For the first two questions, the respondent was presented with four choices in years and eight choices in hours, respectively. For the last two questions, the respondent was presented with five choices in a Likert format ranging from "not very much time" to "almost all the time."

Psychological centrality was measured using the Thurstone paired comparison method. This procedure combines all possible combinations of choices for an answer and, for each choice, instructs respondents to mark which option they would choose for that pair. For this research, five major role identities for this particular population (musician, parent, spouse or boyfriend or girlfriend, student, and political party membership) were paired with each other. The respondent was asked, "Which activity is more important to how you think about yourself?" for *each* choice and asked to mark that choice. The resulting data, for each respondent, indicated which identity received the greatest number of "first choices," which received the fewest, and which were distributed within those boundaries.

Results

Sample Characteristics

Respondents (n=43) in this study had the following demographic characteristics. (For education, marital status, and race, N=42, because one respondent did not answer.) All of the respondents in the sample were male and their ages ranged from eighteen to thirty-nine with the mean age being twenty-four.[3] Levels of education were "less than high school" (n=1; 2%), "high school graduate" (n=14; 33%), "some college" (n=20; 47%), and "B.A./B.S. degree" (n=7; 16%). Results for marital status were "single" (n=34; 79%), "married" (n=3; 7%), "divorced" (n=3; 7%), "separated" (n=1; 2%), and "other" (n=1; 2%). Racial and ethnic characteristics were "white" (n=40; 93%), "black" (n=2; 5%), and "American Indian" (n=1; 2%). Results for religious preference were "Catholic" (n=15; 35%), "Protestant" (n=6; 14%), "agnostic" (n=4; 9%), "atheist" (n=2; 5%), and "other" (n=15; 35%). In terms of sexual preference, the subjects described themselves as "heterosexual" (n=39; 90%), "homosexual" (n=3; 7%), and "other" (n=1; 2%).

The respondents' income earned from being a musician ranged from under $10,000 to over $70,001 per year with 90% (n=39) of the respondents earning "under 10,000" per year, 5% (n=2) earning "$10,001 to $15,000" per year, 2% (n=1) earning "15,001 to $20,000" per year, and 2% (n=1) earning "over $70,001" per year. Most of the respondents spend between six and twenty hours per week in the role of musician and have been musicians for an average of four to six years. All of the respondents in the sample have at least one other occupation other than musician. Income earned from their other occupations ranged from under $10,000 to $70,000 per year with 70% (n=30) of the respondents earning "under 10,000" per year, 14% (n=6) earning "$10,001 to $15,000" per year, 9% (n=4) earning "15,001 to $20,000" per year, 2% (n=1) earning "$25,001 to $30,000" per year, 2% (n=1) earning "$30,001 to $40,000" per year, and 2% (n=1) earning "60,001 to $70,000" per year.

Tests of Hypotheses

The first three hypotheses posit that the role identity of musician will be highly salient (Hypothesis #1), very central in identity configuration (Hypothesis #2), and feel very authentic (Hypothesis #3) for these musicians. These hypotheses were tested by observing the mean score relative to the potential range of scores for each variable.[4]

The scale for the measurement of role identity salience may range between 0 (not salient) to 20 (maximum salience). The mean salience score for the role identity of "musician" in this sample is 17.96, indicating strong support for the first hypothesis.

The scale for the measurement of psychological centrality of the musician role may range between 1 (not central) to 5 (highly central). The mean salience score for the role identity of "musician" in this sample is 3.97, indicating clear support for the second hypothesis.

The scale for the measurement of the authenticity of the role identity of musician may range between 0 (not authentic) to 15 (highly authentic). The mean authenticity score for the role-identity of "musician" in this sample is 13.02, again showing that the third hypothesis is supported.

These data clearly provide support for the conclusion that the musicians in this sample consider the role identity of "musician" to be highly salient, psychologically central, and reflecting their core sense of "who they are." The relationship among these variables is graphically portrayed in Appendix B, Figure 1. This graph shows that, in this sample of musicians and as predicted by identity theory, the three variables are positively related to each other in linear fashion with some curvilinearity as the variables interact at the higher values.

The data regarding the last three hypotheses will now be examined. The last three hypotheses posit relationships between dimensions of identity as elucidated by identity theory, and the degree to which such dimensions can explain the behavior, or perceptions of behavior, of people playing the role of musician. These hypotheses were examined using both zero-order correlations and multiple regression techniques. The results of these equations are contained in Tables 1 and 2 respectively.

Table 1 presents the results of the zero-order relationships for the major variables of the study. As can be seen by inspection, the data reveal many significant relationships. Sense of authenticity is significantly and positively related to all of the variables except for how long the respondent has been a musical performer. The same pattern exists for psychological centrality. Identity salience is also positively related to all the variables except how many hours per week the musicians spend in the role and how long they have been in the role.

These zero-order relationships provide mixed support for Hypothesis #4 (role identity salience is positively related to being in the role). Salience is significantly and positively related to the respondents' perception of how much time they spend in the role or will spend in the future but not to their reporting of actual time spent in the role.

Hypothesis #5 (psychological centrality will be positively related to being in the role) is strongly supported by the data in Table 1. Psychological centrality is strongly correlated with all measures of being in the role except how long the performer has been in the role.

Table 1: Zero-order Correlations between Major Study Variables.

Authen	Future	How many	Time role	Psy cen	Salience	How long
Authen	0.458**	0.292*	0.417**	0.317*	0.357*	0.084
Future		0.554***	0.859***	0.552***	0.371*	0.171
How many			0.718***	0.299*	0.265	0.117
Time role				0.473**	0.328*	0.218
Psy cen					0.355*	0.020
Salience						-0.055
How long						

* = p<.05
** = p<.01
*** = p<.001

The pattern of support for Hypothesis #6 (sense of authenticity will be positively related to being in the role) found in Table 1 is much like that of Hypothesis #5. Sense of authenticity is significantly correlated with all measures of being in the role except how long the performer has been in the role. Thus, Table 1 provides considerable support for Hypotheses 4, 5, and 6; the primary exception being how long the performer has been in the role.

Table 2 contains the multiple regression equations necessary to test more stringently Hypotheses 4 through 6. As can be seen in this table, the results of the regression equations confirm some of the findings of the correlational analysis, but not others. Hypothesis #4 is not supported by the regression equations. The level of salience for the role identity of musician is not found to be predictive of any of the four measures of time spent in the role. Hypothesis #5 finds support only for the two perceptual measures of being in the role (perception of how much time is spent in the role and perception of how much time will be spent in the future). Thus, the data provide partial support for Hypothesis #5. As with the correlational data, the pattern of support for Hypothesis #6 is much like that for Hypothesis #5. Sense of authenticity is not predictive of years spent as a musician or number of hours spent in the role. It is, however, predictive of the perception of how much time will be spent in the role in the future and aids in the prediction of the perception of how much time is spent in the role ($p=<.07$). Finally, psychological centrality and sense of authenticity are good predictors of the perception of time spent in the role now (R^2 =.31) and in the future (R^2 =.41). Further analyses (not shown) indicate that these effects are enhanced by the elimination of the "salience" variable from the equations.

Table 2

Regression equations for salience of the role identity of musician, psychological centrality of the role identity of musician, and sense of authenticity of the role of musician on: number of years as a musician, number of hours in the role last week, perception of time spent in the role, and perception of how much time will be spent in the role in the future. (Standardized coefficients follow the unstandardized coefficients in parentheses.)

Variables	Years	Hours Spent	Time Spent	Future
Salience	-0.045 (-0.102)	0.096 (0.131)	0.035 (0.108)	0.035 (0.122)
Centrality	0.026 (0.020)	0.430 (0.194)	0.309 (0.350)*	0.360 (0.420)**
Authenticity	0.082 (0.114)	0.222 (0.183)	0.128 (0.267)	0.132 (0.282)*
R =	0.125	0.382	0.559	0.637
R^2 =	0.016	0.146	0.312	0.406

N = 43
* = p <.05
** = p <.01

Thus, the regression equations provide no support for the hypothesis (#4) that role identity salience is predictive of being in the role of musician. Psychological centrality is predictive of the two perceptual variables of being in the role of musician, but not the ones reporting actual time spent (#5). Similarly, sense of authenticity is predictive of future time in the role and influences the perceived amount of time spent in the role but is not related to the variables reporting actual time (#6). It is concluded that there is no support for Hypothesis #4 and some support for Hypotheses 5 and 6. These findings will be discussed below.

Limitations of the Study

Although a convenience sample of forty-three rock and roll musicians will not permit the results of the present study to be generalized to the entire population of semi-professional rock and roll musicians, it does gather exploratory data necessary to begin analyses of role-identity processes of rock and roll musicians and corresponding behavioral outcomes. A larger random sample of musicians would permit more robust testing of the hypotheses presented and allow for the investigation of outcomes while controlling the pertinent variables. Additionally, the possible differentiation between various types of semi-professional rock and roll musicians (i.e., heavy metal, R&B, and pop) and the corresponding social characteristics of the musicians has not fully been explored by the present research.

Another possible substantive limitation of the current research is that the relationship between the major variables in the study and the various levels of musicians (professional, semi-professional, and studio) has not been explored and compared. Data on the salience, psychological centrality, and authenticity of all levels of rock and roll musicians would allow for the examination and comparison of role-identity configurations and corresponding behavioral-choice measures.

Discussion and Future Research

This research was designed to clarify and test some questions concerning the relationship between participating in an entertainment occupation and that occupation's effect on the salience and centrality of that role identity. It was also intended to examine whether the role is felt to be authentic, and the individual and combined effects of salience, psychological centrality, and role authenticity on role behavior and the perception of role behavior. Below, the findings will be summarized, some of the implications of the findings discussed, and suggestions for future research offered.

Utilizing a sample of forty-three musicians, the descriptive information reveals that the role occupants are, typically, in their mid-twenties, have taken some college course work, are single, have been musicians on the average of four to six years, earn under ten thousand dollars per year as a musician, and have a high level of salience, psychological centrality, and authenticity for the role of musician. With the exception of rather low income, nothing about this profile is unusual for a male in his mid-twenties living in largely blue-collar areas of American cities.[5]

The data that resulted from testing the six hypotheses provide support for the first three, no support for the fourth, and partial support for the fifth and sixth. While the data show that the role identity of musician is salient, psychologically central, and felt to be authentic, the salience of the role identity of musician was not found to be a significant predictor of how much time the musicians perceive they spend or reportedly spend in the role. One plausible explanation for this phenomenon is that musicians perceive they are "in the role" only when they are practicing with the band or performing in front of an audience. As a result, they may not be including other important time-consuming aspects of the role as "in the role." In other words, they may not be including as "in the role" such behavior as presentation of self as a musician, reading music magazines, dealing with band management issues, hanging out with members of the band and road crew, and shopping for and purchasing equipment.

Consistent with theoretically derived predictions, the sense of "authenticity" of the role of musician was found to be a significant predictor of perceived time spent in the role but not of reported time spent. Psychological centrality or the "importance" of the role identity of musician was found to be the best predictor of perceived time spent in the role. None of the independent variables were good predictors of reported time spent in the role.

As mentioned above, the data indicate that the role identity of musician is highly salient and psychologically central (Hypotheses 1 and 3) as well as authentic (Hypothesis #2) for the musicians in this study. It is interesting that all musicians in the sample have occupations other than musician yet still rank the musician identity as highly salient and of prime importance as a self descriptor. The identity salience findings may be interpreted using the concept of commitment, and the findings for psychological centrality may be informed by the high subcultural status that the musician role holds, as well as the musical ability of the musicians.

From the work of Foote (1951), identity theory employs the concept of commitment to explain the relative ordering of the identities in a hierarchy of salience such that the higher the level of commitment to a role identity, the more likely is someone to engage in behaviors relevant to that identity, and the higher the salience level of the identity (cf McCall and Simmons 1966; Stryker 1968, 1980, 1987; and Burke and Reitzes 1991 for a further elaboration of the concept of commitment). This implies that the higher the level of commitment to the musician role identity, the more likely is the person to engage in musician-related role activity and this in turn raises the activation threshold of the role identity of musician.

Stryker delineates two types of commitment that may influence the salience level of role identities. The first type is referred to as "interactional commitment" and denotes the "extensiveness of relationships that would be foregone were one to no longer play a given role" (Stryker 1987:98). In this case, it refers to the number of persons a musician would lose contact with by giving up the musician role. The second type of commitment is referred to as "affective commitment" and refers to the "emotional costs attached to departure from a given role" (Stryker 1987:98). The resulting hypotheses are (1) the higher the interactional commitment (i.e., the more people that a musician would lose contact with by virtue of giving up the musician role identity), the higher the musician role identity will be in the salience hierarchy; (2) the higher the affective commitment (i.e., the greater the emotional cost related to losing the musician role), the higher the musician role identity will be in the salience hierarchy.

The data for this study indicate, if these hypotheses were empirically tested and supported, that both interactional and affective commitment levels would be high for musicians in that they know many people vis-à-vis the musician role and they would suffer considerable emotional cost if they were to forfeit the musician role and lose contact with these people. However, this study cannot directly address these hypotheses since data were not gathered on either of the two types of commitment levels of the musicians. Future research in this area should incorporate both commitment measures into the research design in order to arrive at a more theoretically complete explanation of the salience level of the musician role identity.

As mentioned above, the findings for psychological centrality may be explained by the high subcultural status that the musician role holds as well as the musical ability of the musicians. In terms of the latter explanation, Rosenberg (1979) writes that people focus their sense of worth on various self-components and that the self-components that they hold as psychologically central tend to be in those areas in which they excel or are extremely competent. This is done in an effort to protect or enhance the self-esteem of the individual. The resulting hypothesis for Rosenberg is that people will value those activities at which they excel and devalue those at which they do not.

In the framework of the present study, it is reasonable to contend that the musicians excel in musical ability because all are members of (semi-professional) bands that play to paying audiences. Thus, the high musical ability of the musicians may result in a high degree of self-identification with the musician role. As was true with measures of commitment, measures of musical or perceived musical ability were not gathered in this research. Future research on rock and roll musicians should include both objective and subjective measures of musical ability to explore this relationship.

As previously discussed, the musicians in this study earned, on average, less than $10,000 per year as musicians, making it unlikely that income is a strong motivational factor in the high degree of identification with the role. However, it is possible that the high subcultural value attached to the musician role also plays a paramount part in fostering high identification with it. This is supported by previous research that proposes that some of the status that is derived from the role is due to the fact that rock musicians can be considered the heroes of the youth subculture (Dotter 1987) that is itself largely defined by adolescents' use and consumption of rock culture (Frith 1981).

The rock musician role, as a subcultural status marker, is likely to cross a variety of social situations and be present within and outside of the context in which the role is directly enacted (i.e., rehearsing, recording, or playing for an audience versus presentation of self as a rock musician to any others who are not in the role). The musician role is therefore one that gains the occupant high status in a wide variety of settings in that it can easily be enacted and communicated to others via behavioral and stylistic presentations of self.

Rock musician presentation of self can be accomplished by utilizing rock music and musician jargon, talking about a particular gig or the band in general, wearing rock and roll paraphernalia, or by parroting the popular artists' appearance as seen on music television (MTV). It is also possible that the ability of the role occupant to "act" in the role in a variety of social settings fosters the ability to think about oneself mainly within the confines of the role. This implies that musicians may rarely step outside of the role even in settings where they are playing other roles such as parent or spouse; that is, they experience "role engulfment." The role occupants are therefore likely to strongly identify with the features imbedded, or thought to be imbedded, in the role.

The results of this analysis are important in that they provide information in a substantive area that has yet to be empirically researched with theoretically anchored scales in a questionnaire format. As previously discussed, no studies to date have examined the salience, psychological centrality, and authenticity of professional or semi-professional rock and roll musicians. Research that has dealt with identity and role-related issues tacitly assumes that the musicians identify highly with the role. This research provides the first empirical support for this assumption in that it substantiates that semi-professional rock and roll musicians have a high level of salience for the role identity of musician and find it to be psychologically central. They also perceive the role as having characteristics they believe to be reflective of "who they are."

While no variable was found to be an excellent predictor of time in role measures, the rock musician role is clearly important to semi-professional musicians in that it is a major role identity in comparison to the other role identities they may possess such as student, spouse or boyfriend. This suggests that there is something unique about the musician role that positions it as paramount in the way the role occupants define themselves. Again, one plausible explanation for this phenomenon is the relatively high subcultural status that the rock musician role holds and the ease with which individuals can claim and act out the role in a wide variety of social settings. In an effort to further examine this relationship, future research should include both objective and subjective measures of the rock musician status level and the extent to which musicians attempt to present themselves to others as musicians because of the status derived from this enactment. It should also empirically assess the extent to which the musician role takes precedence over other roles in the presentational and organizational aspects of the self.

Future research in this area should also gather data on the various levels of rock and roll musicians such as professional, studio, and semi-professional. This type of data would allow researchers to delineate the role-identity configurations among the various levels of rock and roll musicians and examine the relationship between the major variables in the present study and their relationship to these various skill levels.

This chapter has laid the foundation for future research to begin to discern the features of and delineate the processes attendant to the role identity structures of various levels of rock musicians. Questions concerning time in role and rewards gained from the role such as fame, income, and status can now be addressed and their individual and combined effects on identity salience and psychological centrality explored. This type of analysis will garner much needed insight into the differing nature of the occupational roles of semi-professional musicians as opposed to "famous" or professional musicians. Most importantly, the results presented in this chapter support the assertion that semi-professional musicians tend to identify strongly with the role and present the first theoretically informed analysis of the many antecedents and consequences that flow from this empirical finding.

APPENDIX A

Items and Response Categories for Major Variables

Item loadings obtained during factor analysis (principal components analysis) are presented in parentheses for those items with a score 0.40 or better on factor one.

Role Identity Salience

a. My job as a musician is something I rarely even think about. (.777)
b. I would feel a loss if I were forced to give up being a musician. (.822)
c. For me, being a musician means more than just playing music for a living. (.549)
d. Musician is an important part of who I am. (.667)

Items "b," "c," and "d" were "reverse coded." Score of "0" indicates the highest degree of identity salience. Judged on a five-point scale (1–5), from "strongly agree" to "strongly disagree"; range=5–20; mean=17.90; S.D.=3.03; alpha for scale =.63.

Role Identity Authenticity

a. Being a musician is consistent with my important values. (.826)
b. Deep down, I often feel that being a musician is not really "me." (.849)
c. Most of the time I like thinking of myself as a musician. (.522)

Items "a" and "c" were "reverse coded." Score of "1" indicates the least amount of alienation. Judged on a five-point scale (1–5), from "strongly agree" to "strongly disagree"; range=3–15; mean=13.02; S.D.=2.13; alpha for scale =.60.

APPENDIX B

Figure 1: The Relationship Between Role Identity Salience, Centrality, and Authenticity

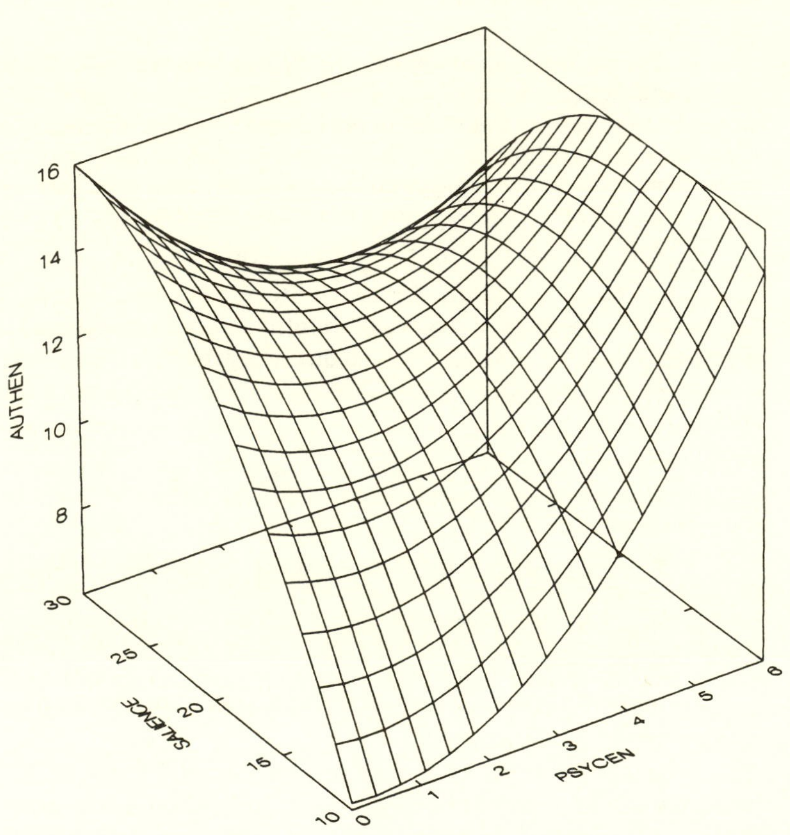

NOTES

1. The authors would like to thank Jerry M. Lewis for providing us several liaisons and Mauri L. Aven for her editorial support during the final phase of this research. Members of the bands Anger, The Awakening, Blasphemous, Cinderella, Deli Bandits, Judas Priest, Kilgore Trout, Marry Decker's Fall, Rhythm Corps, Rush, Sediki, Tempo Tantrum, and all other bands who in some way participated in this research are also deserving of our appreciation. A special note of gratitude also goes out to Geddy Lee of Rush and all members of the band Rhythm Corps for their more than hospitable nature in the backstage areas of their shows.

2. The construct of semi-professional rock and roll musician is operationalized for the purposes of this research as someone who is currently a member of and plays an instrument (vocalists are included here) in a local rock and roll band. Persons who merely play an instrument for personal pleasure are not included because the socially shared component of the role that is necessitated by identity theory may not be evident. The term "semi-professional" does not necessarily imply that the musicians *only* play in a small geographic locality, but rather denotes that they are not at the professional level touring the entire country and that *all* have at least one other occupation. This indicates that being a musician is *not* their only source of income.

3. The fact that all respondents in the sample are male is not due to a purposive component of the sampling design but rather is a sampling artifact.

4. The mean scale scores reported in this section will not be shown in tabular form.

5. Recall that the respondents' income earned from being a musician ranged from under $10,000 to over $70,001 per year with 90% (n=39) of the respondents earning "under 10,000" per year. Also, all of the respondents in the sample have at least one other occupation other than musician. Income earned from other occupations ranged from under $10,000 to $70,000 per year with 70% (n=30) of the respondents earning "under 10,000 per year."

REFERENCES

Becker, H.S. 1963. *Outsiders: Studies in the Sociology of Deviance*. New York: The Free Press.

Bennett, H.S. 1980. *On Becoming a Rock Musician*. Amherst: University of Massachusetts Press.

Burke, P. 1991. "An Identity Theory Approach to Commitment." *Social Psychology Quarterly*, 54:239–251.

Burke, P., and J.W. Hoelter. 1988. "Identity and Sex-Race Differences in Educational and Occupational Aspirations." *Social Science Research*, 17:29–47.

Burke, P., and D.C. Rietzes. 1981. "The Link Between Identity and Role Performance." *Social Psychology Quarterly*, 44:83–92.

Callero, P. 1985. "Role Identity Salience." *Social Psychology Quarterly*, 48:203–215.

Denisoff, R.S. 1975. *Solid Gold: The Popular Record Industry*. New Brunswick, NJ: Transaction Books.

Dotter, D. 1987. "Growing Up Is Hard To Do: Rock and Roll Performers as Cultural Heroes." *Sociological Spectrum*, 7:25–44.

Erickson, R. 1993. "Beyond an Identity Theory Approach to Commitment: Self-Meanings, Self-Values, and the Biographic Self." Unpublished manuscript.

Foote, N.N. 1951. "Identification as the Basis for a Theory of Motivation." *American Psychological Review*, 26:14–21.

Fredrickson, J., and J.F. Rooney. 1988. "The Freelance Musician as a Type of Non-person: An Extension of the Concept of Non-personhood." *Sociological Quarterly*, 29:221–239.

Frith, S. 1981. *Sound Effects: Youth, Leisure, and the Politics of Rock 'n' Roll*. New York: Pantheon.

Frith, S., and H. Horse. 1987. *Art Into Pop*. New York: Methuen.

Gecas, V. 1986. "The Motivational Significance of Self-Concept for Socialization Theory." Pp. 131–156 in E. Lawler (ed.), *Advances in Group Process* (Vol. 3). Greenwich, CT: JAI Press.

———. 1991. "The Self-Concept as a Basis for a Theory of Motivation." Pp. 171–187 in J. Howard and P. Callero (eds.), *The Self-Society Dynamic: Cognition, Emotion, and Action*. Cambridge: Cambridge University Press.

Goffman, E. 1959. *The Presentation of Self In Everyday Life.* New York: Doubleday & Company.

Groce, S.B. 1989. "Occupational Rhetoric and Ideology: A Comparison of Original and Copy Performers." *Qualitative Sociology,* 12:391–410.

James, W. *Principles of Psychology* (Vol.1). 1890. New York: Holt.

McCall, G.H., and J.T. Simmons. 1966. *Identities and Interaction.* New York: The Free Press.

———. 1978. *Identities and Interaction* (rev. ed.) New York: The Free Press.

Mead, G.H. 1934. *Mind, Self and Society: From the Standpoint of a Social Behaviorist.* Edited and with an introduction by Charles W. Morris. Chicago: University of Chicago Press.

Mullen, K. 1987. "Audience Orientation and the Occupational Rhetoric of Public House Performers." *Popular Music and Society,* 11:15–29.

Reid, S.A. 1991. "Uncovering the Dramaturgical Phenomenon: Dramaturgical Analyses of Rock Concerts." Paper delivered at the annual meetings of the Mid-South Sociological Association, Jackson, Mississippi.

Reid, S.A., J.S. Epstein, and D.E. Benson. In review. "Role Identity in a Devalued Occupation: The Case of Female Exotic Dancers." *Sociological Focus.*

Rosenberg, Morris. 1979. *Conceiving The Self.* New York: Basic Books.

Stryker, S. 1968. "Identity Salience and Role Performance: The Relevance of Symbolic Interaction Theory for Family Research." *Journal of Marriage and the Family,* 30:558–64.

———. 1980. *Symbolic Interactionism: A Social Structural Version.* Palo Alto, CA: Benjamin Cummings.

———. 1987. "Identity Theory: Developments and Extensions." Pp. 89–104 in K. Yardley and T. Honess (eds.), *Self and Identity: Psychosocial Perspectives.* New York: Wiley.

Stryker, S., and R.T. Serpe. 1992. "Identity Salience and Psychological Centrality: Equivalent, Redundant, or Complementary Concepts?" Paper delivered at the annual meetings of the American Sociological Association, Pittsburgh, Pennsylvania.

Trew, K., and D.E. Benson. 1993. "Dimensions of Social Identity In Northern Ireland." Paper delivered at the conference on Changing European Identities, Farnham, Surrey, England.

Turner, R.H., and V. Billings. 1991. "The Social Contexts of Self-Feeling." Pp. 103–122 in J. Howard and P. Callero (eds.), *The Self-Society Dynamic: Cognition, Emotion, and Action*. Cambridge: Cambridge University Press.

Weinstein, D. 1991. *Heavy Metal: A Cultural Sociology*. New York: Lexington Books.

Wicke, P. 1990. *Rock Music: Culture, Aesthetics and Sociology*. New York: Cambridge University Press.

Zurcher, L.A., and D.A. Snow. 1981. "Collective Behavior: Social Movements." Pp. 447–382 in M. Rosenberg and R.H. Turner (eds.), *Social Psychology: Sociological Perspectives*. New York: Basic Books.

Recent Theory and Research in the Sociology of Popular Music: A Selected and Annotated Bibliography

Stephen B. Groce
Jonathon S. Epstein

Introduction

The decade of the 1980s and the first third of the 1990s has been a time for the expansion of the hybrid enterprise known as the sociology of popular music. Since George Lewis published in *Popular Music and Society*, the first annotated bibliography on the sociology of popular music in 1979, the theoretical and research scholarship on popular music has increased in both breadth and depth. This scholarship has occurred within a generally favorable academic atmosphere created by the renaissance of cultural studies. We believe that this suggests that perhaps the sociology of popular music is now taken more seriously than ever before. It seems to be on its way to shedding its image as sociology's forgotten stepchild. While there are still only two academic journals devoted exclusively to the study of popular music (*Popular Music and Society* and *Popular Music*) the annotated bibliography that follows demonstrates that a wider range of journals—some representing what most of us would recognize as mainstream sociology—have published scholarship on popular music in the 1980s and early 1990s. Included below are articles published in *American Sociological Review, Sociological*

Inquiry, Social Forces, Symbolic Interaction, Sociological Spectrum, Sociological Quarterly, Sociological Perspectives and *Sociological Review,* to name a few. There is also evidence that the study of popular music has become a truly interdisciplinary endeavor, as indicated below by publications from the fields of communications, journalism, broadcasting, and ethnomusicology.

There are four areas of study within the sociology of popular music that seem to have experienced significant growth in the fourteen years since Lewis's annotated bibliography in the late 1970s. Along with continuing research on the inner workings of the popular music industry, the tensions between art and capitalism and analyses of song lyrics, there has been an increasing amount of work on (1) women in popular music—as performers and as other key personnel in the industry; (2) what Bennett has called small-time or local-level, aspiring artists and performers, rather than an exclusive focus on those who have attained commercial success; (3) roles other than that of performer—producers, sound engineers or mixers, radio personnel, and popular music critics; and (4) the content and impact of music videos.

Included in this annotated bibliography are what we believe to be the best and most sociologically relevant of the recent scholarly work on popular music. This annotated bibliography suffers, as does any attempt such as this, from our own sociological biases as well as from our inability to be exhaustive and inclusive. However, it is our hope that sociologists and others working in the area of popular music research, as well as those of us who teach courses on the sociology of popular music, will benefit from the compilation that follows. We have divided the annotated entries into general, and we hope sensible, sections that will allow readers to locate pertinent information quickly. These sections are Theoretical and Methodological Comments, Historical and Critical Analyses, Performers and Performances, Other Industry Roles, Audiences, Women in Popular Music, Analyses of Song Lyrics, and Analyses of Music Videos.

Theoretical and Methodological Comments

Becker, Howard S. 1989. "Ethnomusicology and sociology: A letter to Charles Seeger." *Ethnomusicology* 33: 275–285.

Becker suggests ways in which the discipline of ethnomusicology might benefit from sociological methods and insights. He speaks to both the similarities and differences between ethnomusicology and sociology and cites the works of Faulkner, Gilmore, and Bennett as exemplifying sound sociological analyses of popular music.

Denski, Stan. 1989. "One step up and two steps back: A heuristic model for popular music and communication research." Popular *Music and Society* 13: 9–21.

Denski argues that while popular music scholarship, particularly rock scholarship, has grown recently in volume, it still suffers from two major problems—an inability to discriminate between the various types of rock and pop music and a kind of pseudo-academic approach to scholarship. The article contains a model of the author's view of how to conduct research on popular music. The model emphasizes both macro and micro levels of analysis and stresses the relationships between popular music and sociological variables such as age, social class, gender, and race in the production, performance, and consumption of popular music.

Foret, Miroslav. 1991. "Some theoretical-methodological problems of the research on popular music." *Popular Music and Society* 15: 1–10.

The author argues that too much of the research in the field of popular music studies has focused on perceptions of popular music. This is to the neglect of the two other important dimensions, namely, creation and distribution. The author also argues that researchers should be more attuned to situated practices of popular music production and consumption—perceptions of music played in small clubs versus large auditoriums, music produced and consumed by adolescents versus older people, the reputations of different types of performers, and so on.

Frith, Simon. 1987. "Towards an aesthetic of popular music." Pp. 133–149 in Richard Leppert and Susan McClary (eds.), *Music and Society: The Politics of Composition, Performance and Reception*. Cambridge: Cambridge University Press.

Frith argues that the sociology of popular music makes an aesthetic theory possible rather than impossible, as is commonly believed. At the heart of his discussion is the question of how and why people make musical judgments. Popular music not only reveals certain things about people, it also constructs them. Frith outlines what he takes to be the four major functions of popular music—providing answers to questions of identity, giving us a way of managing the relationship between public and private lives, shaping popular memory, and providing something to be possessed. He concludes by discussing an aesthetics of popular music that enables popular music to fulfill its functions.

Keller, Marcello Sorce. 1986. "Sociology of music and ethnomusicology: Two disciplines in competition." *Journal of General Education* 38: 167–181.

This is a useful discussion of the similarities and differences between ethnomusicology and the sociology of music. Perhaps of most value is the author's discussion of what he sees as the four primary approaches to "musical sociology": (1) the philosophical approach, which Keller aligns with the work of Adorno; (2) the rationalistic approach, traceable to Max Weber; (3) the sociohistorical approach, which shows that musical history is not simply the history of great works—the great works exist precisely because of a "rich background" of "less timeless" music; and (4) the empirical approach, which focuses on a variety of dimensions—institutions, tastes, attendance, and the socialization of musicians. He concludes by arguing that the sociology of music and ethnomusicology—which he aligns with anthropology—are "very much in need of one another" if advances are to be made in understanding the relationship between musical and social phenomena.

Koskoff, Ellen. 1982. "The music-network: A model for the organization of music concepts." *Ethnomusicology* 26: 353–370.

The article examines cognitive structures that people use to organize music information. The author coins the concept "music-network." Music-networks display the relationship between individual and cultural meanings of music. Koskoff concludes that music-networks can be used to analyze individual and group patterns of thinking about music.

Lewis, George H. 1983. "The meaning's in the music and the music's in me: Popular music as symbolic communication." *Theory, Culture and Society* 1: 133–141.

The author discusses what he feels to be the three main approaches to the sociology of popular music: (1) historical, wherein music is treated as reflective of the social structure; (2) interactive, wherein studies focus on the creation of meaning by both performers and audiences; and (3) critical, which focuses on analyses of the commercial aspects of the popular music industry. Lewis concludes the article by applauding the recent explosion of studies in the sociology of popular music, but at the same time, he laments the lack of a strong theoretical focus within the field. He suggests the possibility of viewing popular music as a system of meaning and exploring how music is used as a symbolic resource.

Lull, James. 1985. "On the communicative properties of music." *Communication Research* 12: 363–372.

Lull argues that popular music is a strong agent of socialization, especially for adolescents. People are exposed to alternative perspectives on many issues and problems through song lyrics. They also use music to achieve personal and interpersonal goals and to establish identities. Popular music also functions to enhance adolescents' activities and social gatherings.

McDonald, James R. 1988. "Politics revisited: Metatextual implications of rock and roll criticism." *Youth and Society* 19 (4): 485–504.

McDonald argues that, counter to several recent positions, that rock music offers a wide variety of social and political messages for its listeners. The impact of these messages is on the area of listener awareness as opposed to the creation of an active political stance. Rock music offers the possibility of empowerment for its listeners yet this empowerment is generally on the level of the individual listener, not a group of listeners as a whole.

Shepherd, John. 1991. *Music as Social Text*. Cambridge, MA: Polity Press.

The first half of this book is Shepherd's criticism of the failure of the discipline of musicology to come to terms with the social nature of music. The second half is more interesting sociologically. The author establishes music as a social process and goes on to analyze the theoretical connections between music and other social processes. He concludes by arguing for a "musicology of society" that would contribute both to musicology and to the study of popular culture.

Weinstein, Deena. 1991. "The sociology of rock: An undisciplined discipline." *Theory, Culture and Society* 8 (1): 97–109.

This review article examines the state of the sociology of rock subdiscipline through the critical examination of four recent texts. Weinstein concludes that while there is outstanding work being done in the field, there is little foundational work on the level of key terminology and that the subdiscipline is in a Kuhnian preparadigmatic stage. As a result, Weinstein suggests that many studies in the sociology of rock lack methodological and theoretical rigor. She awaits the emergence of an overarching research agenda for the sociology of rock.

Historical and Critical Analyses

Attali, Jacques. 1985. *Noise: The Political Economy of Music*. Minneapolis: University of Minnesota Press.

In this book Attali offers a historical account of the relationship between music and political economy. The relationship is seen in four overlapping stages: (1) sacrifice (ritual practices); (2) representation (the performance of music as a commodity, but still primarily in live performance settings); (3) repetition (recording, music-on-demand); and (4) composition (music as yet fully realized—people making music by themselves, for themselves). Perhaps most useful for understanding our own popular music industry is Attali's discussion of the differences between composition and reproduction or repetition.

Barnes, Ken. 1988. "Top 40 radio: A fragment of the imagination." Pp. 8–50 in Simon Frith (ed.), *Facing the Music*. New York: Pantheon.

Barnes provides a detailed analysis of the development of the relationship between popular music, economics, and radio in the United States. The article is particularly useful for its attention to the wide variety of programming formats in contemporary radio (adult contemporary, album-oriented radio, country, Christian radio, new age, etc.) and its discussion of the fragmentation in popular music radio that has occurred in recent years.

Blau, Judith R. 1988. "Music as social circumstance." *Social Forces* 66: 883–902.

Blau explores the relationship between the prevalence of music and various indicators of social discontent. Her main goal is to answer the question of whether there is a link between music and social disorganization or between music and social harmony. She uses the prevalence of different kinds of music in large U.S. cities to test different theories concerning the relationship between quality of life and music. Results indicate that culture is not totally autonomous from its socioeconomic context and that cultural activities are not necessarily positive indicators of quality of life in major urban areas.

Cohen, Sarah. 1991. "Popular music and urban regeneration: The music industries of Merseyside." *Cultural Studies* 5 (3): 332–346.

Cohen's article discusses the history of the link between popular music, the music industries, and urban regeneration initiatives in Liverpool. The first part of the article outlines the background of the city of Liverpool's attempts to create and sustain a viable (and profitable) popular music scene. In the second part, Cohen examines a few of the more notable efforts, including the major attempt by the Liverpool City Council to establish a promotions and management company to identify and market local musicians. The third part of the article briefly discusses some of the research projects currently being undertaken by Liverpool University's Institute of Popular Music. Cohen argues that what is needed is a greater awareness of locality—the social and cultural situations of musicians and other producers of culture.

Curtis, Jim. 1987. *Rock Eras: Interpretations of Music and Society, 1954–1984*. Bowling Green, OH: Bowling Green State University Press.

Curtis's interest is in making specific the social and cultural contexts of the development of rock music. He sees three important periods in the development of rock: 1954–1964, 1964–1974, and 1974–1984. He applies a McLuhanesque framework of enhancement, retrieval, and obsolescence to these decades to discuss what he sees as recurring themes and patterns. The chapters on punk, hard rock, and MTV are particularly good.

Cusie, Don. 1991. "Basic differences: The British and American music industries." *Popular Music and Society* 15: 47–56.

The author compares the structure and functioning of the two music industries. He concludes, based on his analysis of fifteen reasons—ranging from geographic size to club scene to social system—that the British music industry has some distinct advantages over the American industry.

Daniels, Douglas Henry. 1985. "The significance of blues for American history." *Journal of Negro History* 70: 14–23.

The article contains a good history of the origins and development of the blues. The author also examines the attitudes and values of black musicians who created the blues, and in the process dispels some myths and stereotypes about early black performers and their music. He argues that blues music is valuable for helping people understand that they can overcome the limitations of history and society.

Dannen, Fredric. 1990. Hit Men: Power Brokers and Fast Money Inside the Music Industry. New York: Random House.

This book provides a history of the most powerful figures in the popular music industry, from record company presidents and other top executives to independent promoters. The focus is on the practices of questionable ethics that are routinely used to create hit records and generate tremendous profits. Those who figure prominently in Dannen's account are record company personnel Dick Asher (one of the few honest record company executives), Walter Yetnikoff, Morris Levy, Clive Davis, David Geffen, and Goddard Lieberson, along with independent promoters Joe Isgro and Fred DiSipio. The author at times stresses the connection between organized crime and the popular music industry.

Dasilva, Fabio, Anthony Blasi, and David Dees. 1984. *The Sociology of Music*. Notre Dame, IN: University of Notre Dame Press.

This book contains an interesting chapter on roles and music, including composers, performers, studio musicians, and dancers. The authors, however, make an Adorno-type distinction between popular music and musicians and "serious" composers and performers that detracts from an otherwise useful description of roles and role relationships. Also of interest is the chapter entitled "Illustrative Studies," which contains a good discussion of the function of costuming in musical performance.

Denisoff, R. Serge. 1986. *Tarnished Gold: The Record Industry Re-Visited*. New Brunswick, NJ: Transaction.

This is an update of *Solid Gold*, the author's 1970s analysis of the forces that drive the recording industry. It follows the inception, production and distribution of records. The book contains a good treatment of the institutional constraints placed on performers—the constant struggle of trying to "make it" and the loss of autonomy and control when they finally have. The third and fourth chapters contain a dissection of the record industry that highlights the split between art and capitalism.

Eliot, Marc. 1989. *Rockonomics: The Money Behind the Music*. New York: Franklin Watts.

Eliot writes a historical analysis of the economics of the popular music industry. The book is full of facts and figures, many of which are eye-opening and staggering in their implications. It truly exposes the popular music industry for the megabucks force in American culture that it is. While not particularly stimulating sociologically, it does present the development and practices of the industry from a perspective that many other histories do not.

Fornas, Johan. 1990. "Moving rock: Youth and pop in late modernity." *Popular Music* 9: 291–306.

This article focuses on changes within the popular music industry and how popular music creates change both inside and outside itself. It is based on two studies conducted by the author in Sweden. One was at the micro level, involving observations and interviews with twenty amateur rock musicians. The second was a macro-level study of political forms of music in Sweden. The discussion focuses on four dimensions of popular music: (1) music and the objective world; (2) music and the social world; (3) music and the subjective world; and (4) music as a cultural form.

Frith, Simon. 1981. *Sound Effects: Youth, Leisure and the Politics of Rock 'n' Roll*. New York: Pantheon.

Frith challenges the notion that capitalism has made rock music just another meaningless product for public consumption. He argues that contradictions in the nature and uses of rock, both uncontrollable and unpredictable, simultaneously resist and reproduce the system. The book is divided into three parts—rock meanings, rock production, and rock consumption. The four chapters that the comprise the second part, rock production, provide an excellent history and analysis of the process of creating and producing popular music.

Frith, Simon. 1987. "The industrialization of popular music." Pp. 53–77 in James Lull (ed.), *Popular Music and Communication*. Newbury Park, CA: Sage.

The focus of the article is on rock and roll as an evolutionary development. Frith adopts a historical perspective to analyze the popular music industry. His analysis is comprised of three considerations: (1) the effects of technological change on the popular music industry; (2) the economics of popular music; and (3) musical culture. This is a useful history and a solid analysis.

Goertzel, Ben. 1991. "The rock guitar solo: From expression to simulation." *Popular Music and Society* 15: 91–101.

This is an interesting article which examines the evolution of the rock guitar solo from a meaningful index of individual expression to a somewhat meaningless structural frill. Goertzel links this evolution to the transformation of rock music in general from a rebellious art form into a highly stylized commercial product. Discussed are the soloing techniques of 1960s artists such as Clapton, Beck, Hendrix, and Page through more modern players such as Vaughn, Satriani, Holdsworth, and Malmsteen. The author ends by locating this soloing evolution within Baudrillard's discussion of simulation and the successive phases of the image.

Gow, Joe. 1992. "The 'trouble' with digital audio tape." *Popular Music and Society* 16: 31–48.

Gow details the history of the development of digital audio tape, and more importantly, discusses the resistance to it on the part of the six multinational corporations who virtually control the popular music industry. Included are discussions of the "problem" of standardization, anticopying systems, legislative processes, and competing formats.

Gross, Robert L. 1990. "Heavy metal music: A new subculture in American society." *Journal of Popular Culture* 24: 119–130.

The author examines five dimensions of the type of popular music known as "heavy metal": the origins of heavy metal, the parameters of the music, the economics of metal, the messages of the music, and the cult or subculture of heavy metal. Gross concludes by arguing that, contrary to the assertions of certain conservative groups, heavy metal poses no serious threats to its audience. The cult or subculture that has flourished around heavy metal is no better or worse than those which have flourished around many other forms or styles of popular music.

Grossberg, Lawrence. 1986. "Is there rock after punk?" *Critical Studies in Mass Communication* 3(1): 111–123.

In this article Grossberg examines the possibility of rock remaining a viable center of affective organization for youth. He contends that rock will find new avenues of expression, possibly through video, which will allow for new strategies of expression within the postmodern condition and the socioeconomic and cultural logics which surround youth culture.

Grossberg, Lawrence. 1987. "Rock and roll in search of an audience." Pp. 175–197 in James Lull (ed.), *Popular Music and Communication*. Beverly Hills: Sage.

In this article Grossberg examines the creation of a rock "audience" by examining the career of Bruce Springsteen. This audience was built upon a series of incremental additions to his audience on three levels: the artist's image, the artist's populism, and the artist's presence as a performer. For Grossberg, the successful rock performer is one who can define him- or herself as authentic (according to the above three criteria), even in the face of overwhelming evidence that the careful machinations of the record industry are behind many rock performers' "authenticity."

Hatch, David, and Stephen Millward. 1987. *From Blues to Rock: An Analytic History of Pop Music*. Manchester, England: Manchester University Press.

The authors trace the origins and development of popular music. They highlight the cross-fertilization that has occurred between country music, blues, rock, rhythm and blues, and rock 'n' roll. The book contains a particularly good treatment and analysis of black music, an example of the authors' overall goal of locating varieties of popular music in their social and historical contexts.

Howard, Jay R. 1992. "Contemporary Christian music: Where rock meets religion." *Journal of Popular Culture* 26 (1): 123–130.

Howard examines the social and political stances of what he terms "avant-garde" contemporary Christian music. He finds that much of it offers a critique both of society and the church and its role. In the case of the former, he notes that artists such as Steve Taylor and Rez challenge both the dominant ideology of capitalist society and the right of hierarchical authority. In the case of the latter, he cites Rez, Resurrection Band, and Amos, who question the church's stance on apartheid, the arms race, the disabled, and the poor, among other issues. Howard concludes by noting that although the avant-garde artists do not currently command much attention in terms of record sales, their popularity among Christian youths is growing.

Koval, Howard. 1988. "Homogenization of culture in capitalist society." *Popular Music and Society* 12: 1–16.

An interesting study that tests empirically one of the central arguments of Horkheimer and Adorno's critical theory—that under capitalism, new cultural ideas and messages are devalued and replaced by repetitions of the same values, ideas, and messages. Koval counts numbers of new songs, length of time on the charts for these songs, and number of new artists on the charts for the time period 1958–1982. His findings demonstrate that since about 1965, fewer and fewer new artists have reached the charts, but the ones that have gotten there stay there longer. Thus, he feels that Horkheimer and Adorno's hypotheses and predictions about culture under capitalism are essentially accurate.

Lewis, Alan. 1987. "The social interpretation of modern jazz." Pp. 33–55 in Avron Levine White (ed.), *Lost in Music: Culture, Style and the Musical Event*. London: Routledge and Kegan Paul.

This article contains a brief but useful history of the development of American jazz. Lewis reviews some of the literature that identifies jazz with the sociopolitical situation of blacks in the United States. The major focus of the article, however, is to demonstrate that developments in jazz are not solely the result of black collective consciousness. Lewis argues that the development of jazz parallels the evolution of modernism in art—exploration of new techniques at a rapid pace, the disassociation of its aesthetic, and stylistic fragmentation. Thus, the development of jazz is tied to larger cultural and social realities.

Lewis, George H. 1991. "Storm blowing from paradise: Social protest and oppositional ideology in popular Hawaiian music." *Popular Music* 10: 53–67.

This article examines the reaction by Hawaiian musicians and others to the commercialization (Americanization) of Hawaiian music that occurred in the 1950s and 1960s. Lewis carefully links music with protest and social movements and their developments of ideologies of opposition. He then traces the historical development of the "Hawaiian renaissance," the movement in protest of the Westernization of Hawaiian music and the search for the cultural roots of authentic island music. The movement involved not only a celebration of the older performers who still played traditional music, but also incorporated the movement by younger performers to compose and perform new material written in the older style. The movement has been successful because of the power of music, as a set of symbols, to bolster ideologies, dominant and especially oppositional.

Lewis, George H. 1992. "La pistola y el corazon: Protest and passion in Mexican-American popular music." *Journal of Popular Culture* 26 (1): 51–67.

Lewis discusses the roots of Mexican-American music in the first part of this article. He includes in his discussion the music and dance of the Mexican Indians, European influences, and Afro-Cuban music. He also treats specific types of songs; for example, waltzes, polkas, the cancion ranchera, and corridos. The second part of the article addresses the topic of self-identity in Mexican-American music. He examines Los Lobos as a central voice for the themes and issues concerning Mexican-Americans, and discusses the East Los Angeles renaissance in general.

London, Herbert I. 1984. *Closing the Circle: A Cultural History of the Rock Revolution*. Chicago: Nelson Hall.

This book is a cultural history with a focus in rock music. The author holds that popular music is highly related to both the politics and the social life of a culture. The book is broken down into eight basic historical periods: Early Rock, the Conformist Years (both pre–1956), Accession (1957–1963), Germinal (1964), Fructidor (1965–1972), Thermidor (1973–1978), Restoration (1979–

present [1984]), and the Future. Each of these stages is treated in terms of the political possibilities that each contained. While London does not see a bright future for the revolutionary possibilities of rock he allows that, since rock music and culture seem to be circular, that there is still a possibility for music to effect social change.

Lopes, Paul D. 1992. "Innovation and diversity in the popular music industry, 1969–1990." *American Sociological Review* 57: 56–71.

Analyzing data on popular music trends from *Billboard,* Lopes argues that diversity and innovation in the popular music industry depend more on organization and the structure of markets than on degree of market concentration. This is because major record companies use an open system of development that encourages diversity and innovation as strategies for maintaining market control.

Perry, Steve. 1988. "Ain't no mountain high enough: The politics of crossover." Pp. 51–87 in Simon Frith (ed.), *Facing the Music*. New York: Pantheon.

The purposes of this essay are to describe both the contributions of black performers in the popular music industry and their simultaneous negative treatment by that same industry. The author provides a good history of black influence on the early days of rock and roll and country music. The article concludes by noting that blacks are still underrepresented in certain areas of popular music, but that the situation is better than is found in any other area of mass culture.

Pratt, Ray. 1990. *Rhythm and Resistance: Explorations in the Political Uses of Popular Music*. New York: Praeger.

This is an engaging work which traces the ways in which popular music transcends individual meaning and consumption to function as expressive and instrumental political behavior. Pratt argues that popular music has become an important vehicle for political discussions, especially when existing political institutions do not or cannot provide the means for such discussions. Especially useful are the chapters on blues, rock, and women's music.

Robinson, Deanna Campbell, Elizabeth B. Buck, and Marlene Cuthbert. 1991. *Music at the Margins: Popular Music and Global Cultural Diversity*. Newbury Park, CA: Sage.

This is an ambitious study, eight years in the making, conducted by the International Communication and Youth Consortium (ICYC). The primary research question was whether or not there is a growing homogenization of popular music in the world—the cultural imperialism hypothesis. Results indicate that there is a one-way flow of popular music around the world that tends to decrease cultural diversity. The authors call this "core music." But the flow of core music around the world has not homogenized the world's music. Thanks largely to the influence of "peripheral music," the authors claim that there are now innovative and potentially culturally boundless forms of popular music being created. This is the only full-length work I have seen that attempts to link macro and micro levels. It contains not only a thorough industry analysis (at the global level), but also case studies (interviews with local level, small-time musicians around the world) that demonstrate what the organization and functioning of the popular music industry means in the practical, musical lives of people who perform. The book concludes with a critical response written by Simon Frith.

Romanowski, William D. 1992. "Roll over Beethoven, tell Martin Luther the news: American evangelicals and rock music." *Journal of American Culture* 15 (3): 79–88.

An interesting article that briefly traces the development of contemporary Christian music (CCM) in the United States. The author describes CCM as a hybrid creation, a curious mix of sacred and secular music and ideology. The article contains a valuable discussion of how CCM was co-opted by the mainstream music recording industry.

Ryback, Timothy W. 1990. *Rock Around the Bloc: A History of Rock Music in Eastern Europe and the Soviet Union*. Oxford: Oxford University Press.

An important book, as it is one of the few really thorough treatments of the history of rock music in Eastern Europe both during and after the Cold War. Ryback's detailed accounting of the popular music scenes in the Soviet Union, Poland, Hungary, Bulgaria, and Czechoslovakia quickly debunks the common notion that rock music is somehow a new phenomenon in (now formerly) Communist-bloc countries.

Shaw, Arnold. 1986. *Black Popular Music in America*. New York: Schirmer.

This is a fairly comprehensive treatment of the growth of black popular music in the United States. The book ranges from spirituals to ragtime to soul to disco. Each chapter contains a concluding section, "The White Synthesis," which details the mainstreaming of various forms of black popular music. The chapter on blues is particularly good.

Street, John. 1986. *Rebel Rock: The Politics of Popular Music*. New York: Basil Blackwell.

An interesting book about music, money and politics. The book is divided into three parts. The first part explores the ways in which governments, political parties, and social movements have co-opted popular music for political ends. The second part deals with the popular music industry, broadcasters, and musicians as they make political choices and create the popularity of products. Important here is Street's contention that social scientists have often overlooked the tensions and conflicts within the industry over commercial products and the influences both performers and audiences exert in the creation of meaning for musical products. The third part of the book focuses on how certain songs can convey political stances while others cannot and how popular music can encourage divergent interpretations.

Szatmary, David P. 1991. *Rockin' in Time: A Social History of Rock and Roll.* Englewood Cliffs, NJ: Prentice-Hall.

This book is a social history of rock and roll that places rock music within the everchanging context of American and British history from the early 1950s to 1990. Its focus is on explaining how rock music both influenced and was influenced by the major transformations which occurred during those decades. The text's value lies in its relatively accurate historical account of the history of rock placed into a sociocultural perspective.

Vignolle, Jean-Pierre. 1980. "Mixing genres and reaching the public: The production of popular music." *Social Science Information* 19: 79–105.

This article examines the French record industry. The author discusses the mutual interdependence of major record firms and the smaller independent companies. One of the more interesting portions of the article deals with the actual production of a song in the studio. Vignolle includes a lengthy excerpt wherein the engineer, producer, arranger, technician, writer, and musicians create collectively the "perfect" sound that none of them can articulate independently. He concludes by arguing that music is a social production, which includes not only the participants mentioned above, but also the consumers or listeners.

Wallis, Roger, and Krister Malm. 1990. "Patterns of change." Pp. 160–180 in Simon Frith and Andrew Goodwin (eds.), *On Record: Rock, Pop and the Written Word*. New York: Pantheon.

This essay is excerpted from the authors' 1984 book, *Big Sounds From Small Peoples* (London: Constable). Here they examine the globalization of popular music and use popular music in four countries—Tanzania, Tunisia, Trinidad and Sweden—to summarize the changes that the transformation from local to global music has created. Three of the major areas of change are: (1) the structure and style of music; (2) government involvement in popular music and the integration of popular music into countries' economies; and (3) the uses and functions of music—for group identities, political uses, or commercial purposes. They focus on the process of transculturation wherein elements of music and technology are spread by transnational industries and become incorporated into music at local levels. The essay concludes by suggesting the possibility of a global popular music that might incorporate elements of each musical subculture the music industry has affected.

Walser, Robert. 1992. "Eruptions: Heavy metal appropriations of classical virtuosity." *Popular Music* 11 (3): 263–308.

A very interesting discussion of the relationship between heavy metal and classical music. Walser argues that, thanks largely to the early influences of Van Halen, Malmsteen, Blackmore, and others, heavy metal guitarists have not only appropriated certain scales and techniques from classical music, but also have been influenced in terms of theorizing, conceptualizing, and pedagogy. He also argues that this "combination" of styles may help to bridge the perceived gap between "art" and "entertainment" within popular music.

Ward, Ed, Geoffrey Stokes, and Ken Tucker. 1986. *Rock of Ages: The Rolling Stone History of Rock and Roll*. Englewood Cliffs, NJ: Prentice-Hall.

A thorough, comprehensive, and well-written history of rock and roll in particular and popular music in general. The book is divided into three sections, each one by a different author: the fifties and before, the sixties, and the seventies and beyond. It is filled with facts and interesting stories and insights from the development of the popular music industry. It is surprisingly coherent and flowing even though each section was written by a different author.

Weinstein, Deena. 1991. *Heavy Metal: A Cultural Sociology*. New York: Lexington.

Weinstein offers a comprehensive look at the genre of rock music called heavy metal in this substantial volume. She explores heavy metal as a structured and significant cultural phenomenon by examining both the fans of the music and the music's creators. Of particular interest is her description of the rock concert and its relationship with its fans. The volume is one of the most important books in the sociology of rock to have emerged in the past decade.

Wicke, Peter. 1990. *Rock Music: Culture, Aesthetics and Sociology*. New York: Cambridge University Press.

Wicke traces both the development and influences of rock music from Elvis Presley to the Beatles to the present. He argues that in rock music a new relationship between everyday life, creativity, and the media has emerged. Of particular value are the chapters on the ideology of rock, the rock music business, and punk rock.

The Production of Popular Music: Performers and Performances

Bastien, David T., and Todd J. Hostager. 1988. "Jazz as a process of organizational innovation." *Communication Research* 15: 582–602.

The authors treat jazz as a musical form based on individual musicians' conscious and simultaneous adaptations to each other and to the music. Using a case study of a jazz concert in which four musicians collectively produced a smooth show without the benefit of practice or sheet music, they demonstrate that the performance of jazz is dependent on musical structures (theory and song) and social practices (behavioral norms and communicative code). The overall emphasis of the article is on how individual instrumental innovation is inextricably embedded in the social situation and dependent on the other musicians.

Bastien, David T., and Todd J. Hostager. 1992. "Cooperation as communicative accomplishment: A symbolic interaction analysis of an improvised jazz concert." *Communication Studies* 43: 92–104.

Based upon the study outlined in the previous annotation, this article investigates the structure of cooperative social action. Using professional jazz musicians who have never played with each other (zero-history), and grounding the study in symbolic interactionism, the authors argue that the musicians are able to play with each other because they share a common theory of the task. The authors stress the importance of agreed-upon conventions and synchrony of individual actions in order for people to play music with each other and, indeed, to participate in any form of concerted social action.

Bennett, H. Stith. 1980. *On Becoming a Rock Musician*. Amherst: University of Massachusetts Press.

This book represents a pioneering effort in the sociology of "small-time" musicians. Bennett joined numerous bands in Colorado in the early- and mid-1970s to observe and conduct informal interviews, in addition to performing with them. The result is a highly readable description and analysis of the inner working of local-level (and in a few cases, regional-level) rock 'n' roll bands. The book is filled with well-chosen quotes from musicians Bennett talked with. The chapters on gigs (detailing the different kinds of jobs that small-time musicians typically play), practice (the social constraints surrounding practice), and group definition are especially good.

Denisoff, R. Serge, and John Bridges. 1982. "Popular music: Who are the recording artists?" *Journal of Communication* 32: 132–142.

Denisoff and Bridges give a useful demographic analysis of popular recording stars. The first part of the article introduces the authors' typology for types of bands/performers—starting bands, working performers (either barroom acts or lounge acts) and recording acts. The second part of the article uses published artist biographies from record companies to examine the age, gender, racial, and educational distributions for recording acts, according to what type of music they record. Findings indicate a strong relationship between race and musical style, a predominance of male recording acts over female recording acts, and an average age of over thirty years.

Dotter, Daniel. 1987. "Growing up is hard to do: Rock and roll performers as cultural heroes." *Sociological Spectrum* 7: 25–44.

The author traces the development of rock artists as cultural symbols from early stars like Elvis Presley, to the Beatles and Dylan, to contemporary artists such as Bruce Springsteen and Michael Jackson. One of the more interesting sections of the article is the author's discussion of how rock and roll performers can, through the process of social typing, become heroic regardless of their specific intentions. He argues that, as social types, today's stars reinforce cultural values, seduce their audiences by showing how cultural values may be broken, and may show audiences the beginnings of new cultural forms.

Finnegan, Ruth. 1989. *The Hidden Musicians: Music-Making in an English Town*. Cambridge: Cambridge University Press.

This is a study of huge proportions. Finnegan spent four years observing and interviewing musicians and bands of all varieties in an English town's churches, pubs, and other venues. The result is a rich description and analysis of the different "music worlds" in Milton Keynes. She demonstrates how musicians learn the different kinds of music they play and how it is composed and created. She has skillfully investigated rock and pop, folk, country, and classical musicians. Probably the best treatment of local-level, "small-time" popular musicians since Bennett's book.

Frederickson, Jon, and James F. Rooney. 1988. "The free-lance musician as a type of non-person: An extension of the concept of non-personhood." *The Sociological Quarterly* 29: 221–239.

This is an interesting article that examines the situation and experiences of free-lance classical musicians in Washington, D.C. Through interviews and participant observation, the authors identify four structural conditions that contribute to these freelance musicians' occupational identities as "nonpersons": (1) free-lancing as a low-status service occupation; (2) the interchangeability of free-lancers in typical job situations; (3) definitions of free-lancers as people who are to be heard but not seen; and (4) the constant separation of core and support personnel during performances. The article contains some well-chosen quotes from the musicians, as well as a section on musicians' strategies for coping with status as nonpersons—pranks, creating a private world, and role redefinition.

Gilmore, Samuel. 1987. "Coordination and convention: The organization of the concert world." *Symbolic Interaction* 10: 209–227.

The article examines how concerts are produced through the interdependent activities of composition and performance. These activities are coordinated through a set of musical conventions. The author demonstrates how the use of conventions varies according to organizational characteristics of concert collaboration and the aesthetic interests of the participants. He compares collaboration in repertory, academic, and avant-garde concert activities.

Gilmore, Samuel. 1988. "Schools of activity and innovation." *Sociological Quarterly* 29: 203–219.

The author argues that concerts are produced through the collective activity of musical specialists. Compatible collaborators are able to identify each other through "schools of activity" that represent alternative conventions. The different schools also vary according to the differences in aesthetic interests in virtuosity and innovation. The article contains some interesting quotes from interview material on the social worlds of composers and performers.

Groce, Stephen B. 1989. "Occupational rhetoric and ideology: A comparison of copy and original music performers." *Qualitative Sociology* 12: 391–410.

The author compares the ideological underpinnings of copy and original musicians. Findings indicate that copy musicians' ideology emphasizes a strong audience orientation, definitions of musicians as technically competent, and a view of themselves as entertainers rather than artists. Original musicians' ideology stresses the creative process rather than the final product, technical mastery of instruments as unnecessary, and a definition of themselves more as artists than entertainers.

Groce, Stephen B. "What's the buzz? Rethinking the meanings and uses of alcohol and other drugs among small-time rock 'n' roll musicians." Forthcoming in *Deviant Behavior*.

Drawing on in-depth interviews with thirty-five local-level performing musicians, this study investigates the relationships between the social organization of musicians' workplaces, the nature of musicians' work, and the ways musicians define and use various mind/mood-altering substances. The author also links rules and sanctions for boundaries of appropriate substance use with the process of becoming a professional musician—the musician socialization process.

Groce, Stephen B., and John A. Dowell. 1988. "A comparison of group structures and processes in two local level rock 'n' roll bands." *Popular Music and Society* 12: 21–36.

The article uses in-depth interviews and participant observation to analyze similarities and differences between bands who compose and perform their own material and bands who perform Top 40 hits, or copy music. It focuses on norms, goals, cohesiveness and differentiation within the two groups. The authors conclude that group goals are the most important characteristic defining and influencing the other structures, but that all four characteristics influence each other.

Jones, Kevin E., and Patricia Atchison Harvey. 1980. "Modeling the rock band and audience interaction." *Free Inquiry in Creative Sociology* 8: 131–134, 138.

The article's focus is on the relationships between bands, management, and audiences. The authors discuss how bands use their capacities to entertain and technical competence to elicit positive audience response. One of the more interesting aspects of this article is the authors' delineation of types of bar patrons and their relationships to performers: hustler, romancer, escaper, obliged, facilitated, converser, listener, and follower.

Kruse, Holly. 1993. "Subcultural identity in alternative music culture." *Popular Music* 12 (1): 33–41.

Kruse examines the creation and maintenance of subcultural identities within the alternative music scene. Focusing on the "indie pop" scene of Champaign, Illinois, she argues that alternative music practitioners define themselves in opposition to the "baby boomers" and their music. Of particular importance is her insistence that sociologists should spend more time examining the situated practices of local-level performing musicians in an effort to thoroughly understand their social identities.

Lewis, George H. 1984. "Beyond the reef: Role conflict and the professional musician in Hawaii." Pp. 189–198 in Richard Middleton and David Horn (eds.), *Popular Music IV: Performers and Audiences*. Cambridge: Cambridge University Press.

This is an examination of how Hawaiian professional musicians must perform for two very different types of audiences. The first is comprised of native Hawaiians and is the audience with whom the performers identify and share common values. Musicians perform the authentic Hawaiian music for this audience. The second is comprised of tourists (mostly American) and American military service personnel. The Hawaiian musicians are forced by market demands to perform watered-down "Americanized" Hawaiian songs that oftentimes demean or ridicule Hawaiians and their culture. They not only do not identify with this type of audience, but they report feeling hostile to them. Lewis concludes by noting the complex relationship between role conflict and the organization of music at the international and local levels. Performers deal with role conflict in a variety of ways that are intimately connected to performers' relationships with their audiences, musical peers, the larger community, and the structure of the music industry.

Mullen, Kenneth. 1985. "The impure performance frame of the public house entertainer." *Urban Life* 14: 181–203.

This article uses interview data and participant observation to study how performers in a public house in Aberdeen, Scotland, sustain their activities at performances in the face of a variety of threats. In the absence of stages and lighting, performers resort to bracketing activities to maintain a sense of performer-audience separation and distance. The article contains a useful discussion on performer-audience interaction that highlights the ways in which performers deal with threatening situations such as equipment failure, forgetting words or music, and drunk and obnoxious bar patrons.

Mullen, Kenneth. 1987. "Audience orientation and the occupational rhetoric of public house performers." *Popular Music and Society* 11: 15–29.

The author examines how musicians, working in different contexts, create and sustain different occupational rhetorics that they use to define themselves, their work situations, and their audiences. Using interviews with musicians performing in public houses in Aberdeen, Scotland, Mullen identifies two types of musicians with corresponding occupational rhetorics: musical entertainers and musical artists. Musical entertainers are very audience-oriented, willing to adjust their sets to accommodate requests to make sure the audience is happy; musical artists are more self-oriented, choosing to emphasize the technical aspects of the music rather than audiences' reactions.

Nye, William P. 1986. "The social organization of time in a resort band; or, 'Moments to Remember.'" *Popular Music and Society* 10: 63–71.

Nye uses his own involvement as a musician in a resort band specializing in dinner and dance music as the basis for an exploration of the features that make a successful resort band performance. He focuses on the organized, planned, and ritualized elements of performance that must be repeated night after night in order for the band to keep working. Particularly relevant is his discussion of the band's and band leader's adherence to strict norms regarding time, dress, alcohol consumption and manipulation of the audience—including procedures designed to coax the audience to dance and to stay out on the dance floor.

Prato, Paolo. 1984. "Music in the streets: The example of Washington Square Park in New York City." Pp. 151–163 in Richard Middleton and David Horn (eds.), *Popular Music IV: Performers and Audiences*. Cambridge: Cambridge University Press.

Prato analyzes how street music has reappeared in urban areas, in both new and old forms. Whereas music that is performed indoors is concerned largely with questions of time, music that is performed outdoors is concerned with space. The article focuses on informal music practices that mix with the outdoor environment of Washington Square Park—folk singers, rock bands, ethnic music groups and the like. Prato sees the reemergence of street music in urban areas as part of a socialization process reintegrating the performance of music with people in public spaces.

Salomone, Frank A. 1988. "The ritual of jazz performance." *Play and Culture* 1: 85–104.

The author emphasizes how through the use of ritual, jazz creates and renews itself and sustains an aura of being sacred. He focuses on musicians' use of symbols and rules to generate their identities as well as their jazz performances. These outcomes are made possible by the recurring elements of ritual on predictable occasions. Salomone tests his perspective by analyzing a performance by a jazz trio and a guest soloist on a television jazz show.

Seca, Jean-Marie. 1988. *Vocations Rock.* Paris: Meridiens-Klincksieck.

This article reports the results of the author's study of popular music bands in France. Seca chronicles the careers of around one hundred bands in order to investigate how musicians learn to play before audiences in live performance situations and how they take on and sustain the identity of professional musicians. The author uses two concepts to frame his study: (1) "rock minority"—how these performers locate themselves within the industry and the larger society; and (2) "acid state"—a process through which these musicians and bands acquire social recognition and approval through their public performances. This is one of a growing number of studies on aspiring small-time popular musicians.

Small, Christopher. 1987. "Performance as ritual: Sketch for an inquiry into the true nature of a symphony concert." Pp. 6–32 in Avron Levine White (ed.), *Lost in Music: Culture, Style and the Musical Event.* London: Routledge and Kegan Paul.

This essay analyzes symphony concerts as social and ritual productions. Small describes the ritual functions of audience seating, persons in secondary roles to the concert (clerks, ushers, piano tuners), entrances and exits of the performers, and dress expectations. He argues that the symphony concert is a ritual way of celebrating the history and values of the Western middle classes. The article concludes by calling for explorations into the ritual nature of all concert events.

Smith, John L. 1987. "The ethogenics of musical performance: A case study of the Glebe Live Music Club." Pp. 150–172 in Michael Pickering and Tony Green (eds.), *Everyday Culture: Popular Song and the Vernacular Milieu.* Philadelphia: Open University Press.

Smith writes a good participant observation analysis of a typical evening's performance in a folk club in Sunderland, England. The author applies Harre's ethogenic, social-psychological approach to analyze the tacit norms and rules that generate an evening's performance by four or five different musicians. This article is rich in details about the setting, the musicians, and the performer-audience relationship.

Stanton, Beverley. 1988. "Music and aging: A gerontological perspective on jazz musicians." *Gerontology Review* 1: 59–66.

This is the only article we are aware of dealing with popular musicians and the aging process. The study is based on interviews with professional jazz musicians over the age of fifty-five. Results indicate that for these musicians their continuing involvement with music is based more on intrinsic benefits than on extrinsic rewards. Above all, the respondents speak to a process of continuous adaptation to the instability of a musician's work life and tensions within families. Most felt that the increasing years had not noticeably diminished their performance skills; some even felt that they play better now than they did thirty or forty years ago.

White, Avron Levine. 1987. "A professional jazz group." Pp. 191–219 in Avron Levine White (ed.), *Lost in Music: Culture, Style and the Musical Event*. London: Routledge and Kegan Paul.

White provides a case study of a jazz band he played drums with for over two months in a Swiss club. The article is valuable for its descriptions of the norms, role differentiation, and degree of group cohesiveness sustained by the band, RJ and his Jazzmen. It also contains some good examples of interaction between band and audience members. The author is careful to link the production of live music with a variety of nonmusical social factors. He concludes by identifying conventions and constraints as the two most important factors with which performing musicians must deal.

The Production of Popular Music: Other Industry Roles

Faulkner, Robert R. 1983. *Music on Demand: Composers and Careers in the Hollywood Film Industry*. New Brunswick, NJ: Transaction.

The book provides an excellent discussion of the tensions, conflicts and general problematics of this particular niche in the popular music industry. Faulkner uses his interview material well, giving the reader a sense of the social worlds of Hollywood film score composers. Particularly good are the chapters on entry points into the occupation and patterns of interaction between composers, filmmakers, and other studio personnel.

Groce, Stephen B. 1991. "On the outside looking in: Professional socialization and the process of becoming a songwriter." *Popular Music and Society* 15:1 33–44.

The author examines songwriters and the process of songwriting itself from a sociological perspective. The most important contribution of the article is the documentation of stages of development in the social identity of songwriter. The author uses in-depth interviews with local-level songwriters to identify beginning writers, intermediate-stage writers and mature writers. These different stages are characterized by the way in which writers approach writing songs, how much time they spend writing and rewriting, how they describe or classify the songs they write, and their commitment to the identity of songwriter as measured by their contacts with the music industry.

Hennion, Antoine. 1990. "The production of success: An antimusicology of the pop song." Pp. 185–206 in Simon Frith and Andrew Goodwin (eds.), *On Record: Rock, Pop and the Written Word*. New York: Pantheon.

This is an interesting examination of producers in the popular music industry. Hennion draws on his own observations as well as interviews with producers to explore how producers, working in concert with singers and engineers, work to create that elusive combination of sounds and feelings that make hit songs. He breaks the songwriting and recording process down into identifiable steps and provides interesting interview quotes from producers at almost every step. He argues that for producers, the keys to successful songmaking are "sociosentiments," meaning just the right phrases, sounds, images, attitudes, and so on.

Kealy, Edward R. 1979. "From craft to art: The case of sound mixers and popular music." *Sociology of Work and Occupations* 6: 3–29.

This article is one of the few pieces available on sound engineers or mixers. Kealy identifies three periods in the development of sound mixers vis-a-vis the organization of the popular music industry—"modes of collaboration." The first is the craft union mode, prevalent in the World War II era, wherein mixing was a by-product of rationalization in the industry. Sound mixing was purely a craft—the mixers were not to compete with the artists they recorded, they were just to record the sound as it was produced. The entrepreneurial mode, beginning in the late 1940s and early 1950s, was characterized by recording artists and mixers working together to produce a finished product. Technological innovations allowed mixers more input into the recording process. The final mode is the art mode, characteristic of modern recording. Here mixers, thanks to the incredible innovations in digital technology and special effects, have become artists in their own right.

Lindstrom, Fred B., and Naomi Lindstrom. 1986. "Adorno encounters cu-bop: Experimental music as a task for critics and their audiences." *Sociological Perspectives* 29: 284–304.

This article examines how popular music critics write for different audiences. The authors use Adorno's typology of music listeners to investigate the responses of jazz critics to the Caribbean influenced cu-bop. They argue that Adorno's typology provides a useful framework for studying innovation in popular music and critics' responses to it.

Muikku, Jari. 1990. "On the role and tasks of a record producer." *Popular Music and Society* 14: 25–33.

The article provides a brief history of the development of the role of record producer within the popular music industry. The experiences of producers differ greatly depending on whether one is a producer for a major record company or a free-lance producer. The article also contains a discussion of the tasks of a producer, which the author has divided into three areas—economic, artistic, and social.

Porcello, Thomas. 1991. "The ethics of digital audio-sampling: Engineers' discourse." *Popular Music* 10: 69–84.

This article deals with a topic that should be of considerable interest in the years to come, ethics and the question of ownership in the age of digital sampling technology. Porcello reports the results of interviews with four studio sound engineers, focusing on four issues or themes: (1) under which conditions sampling is ethical and under which it is not; (2) where the ethical boundary lines should be drawn in practice; (3) what sound engineers should do to protect themselves from charge of copyright infringement; and (4) concern over the fate of musicians in the age of digital sampling. Even though the sample of respondents is small, the author has chosen quotation from interview material quite well.

Rothenbuhler, Eric W. 1985. "Programming decision making in popular music radio." *Communication Research* 12: 209–232.

This article uses both qualitative and quantitative data to determine whether radio stations' programming decisions are made based more on the national industry or the local community. The author studied an album-oriented radio station for nine months. His analysis is valuable because it offers a glimpse of how a station's music director, consultant, and program director interact to produce programming decisions. Results indicate that these decision makers were more attuned to the national industry than to influences within the local community.

Stratton, Jon. 1982. "Between two worlds: Art and commercialism in the record industry." *Sociological Review* 30: 267–285.

Stratton's article focuses on the role of rock music critics and their location within the popular music industry. The first part of the article discusses the tensions between aesthetics and commercialism, or art and capitalism, which define not only the popular music industry but all cultural industries as well. The second part is an interesting exploration of how music critics locally produce the criteria by which records are judged to be "good" or "bad." The conclusion is that music critics have no objective criteria for evaluating records. As a result, "liking" a record tends to make it a "good" record. Theoretically, music critics, by maintaining a supposed split between art and capitalism, are really helping to resolve a fundamental economic conflict brought about by the rationalization of art under capitalism.

Stratton, Jon. 1982. "Reconciling contradictions: The role of the Artist and Repertoire person in the British music industry." *Popular Music and Society* 8: 90–100.

Stratton investigates how Artist and Repertoire (A & R) people make sense of their roles and locations within the British popular music industry, as well as how their understandings of their roles influence how they discuss popular music. He finds that how A & R people relate to their roles is dependent on the size of the record companies they work for. A & R people in large companies have a decided capitalist orientation that the people working for smaller companies seem to lack.

Tankel, Jonathan David. 1990. "The practice of recording music: Remixing as recording." *Journal of Communication* 40: 34–46.

An interesting article that traces in some detail the development of sound recording and focuses on the sound mixer or "recordist" as an increasingly important role in the popular music industry. Tankel argues that "remix recording," where producers and sound engineers rework previously recorded material, is an original form of artistic expression. It is also a new cultural artifact that can be reissued for public consumption.

The Consumption of Popular Music: Audiences

Arnett, Jeffrey. 1991. "Adolescents and heavy metal music: From the mouths of metalheads." *Youth and Society* 23 (1): 76–98.

The article attempts to understand the heavy metal experience from the point of view of "metalheads." Through participant observation and survey methods Arnett attempts to answer several questions: What do male adolescents like about heavy metal music? What reasons do they give for liking their favorite groups and songs? To what extent are boys who like heavy metal devoted to the music? Do they own more records, go to more concerts and spend more money on music-related items than boys who listen to other forms of popular music? What kind of effect (self-reported) does the music have on the boys who listen to it? Does their enthusiasm for heavy metal define their sense of who they are and what kind of person they would like to be? Is their enthusiasm for the music related to their expectations for the future? What are the attitudes of boys who like heavy metal towards their parents, friends, school, politics, and religion? Results indicated that the boys who liked heavy metal music were not substantially different from other young adults with the exception of possessing more "libertarian" views on matters of legalization of marijuana and gun control.

Baron, Stephen. 1989. "Resistance and its consequences: The street culture of punks." *Youth and Society* 21 (2): 207–37.

This study examined the activities of the punk subculture to demonstrate how its activities both represent and are consequences of resistance. Resistance, in the case of the participants in this study, led to the adoption of marginal socioeconomic status as indicated by their living in "squats" and supporting themselves primarily through public support or petty theft. Unlike other studies in this area, Baron could not determine that all members of the subculture came from lower- or working-class backgrounds. He suggests that there has been an emergence of a "classless" youth subculture which merits further examination.

Bennett, H. Stith, and Jeff Ferrell. 1987. "Music videos and epistemic socialization." *Youth and Society* 18 (4): 344–362.

This article assumes that pop culture is deeply involved in the creation of common knowledge. The following kinds of questions were raised: What categories of knowledge are associated with contemporary electronic culture? Are different types of knowledge associated with different popular cultural forms? What are the sociological implications of the epistemological content of popular culture productions that are specifically intended for young audiences? The researchers used content analysis, deconstruction, and cultural hermeneutics applied specifically to music videos in order to answer the above questions. They found five basic portrayals of social identity presented in their sample: politics, romance, motion, conversion, and persona shift.

Berry, Venise T. 1990. "Rap music, self concept and low income black adolescents." *Popular Music and Society* 14: 89–107.

This study focuses on how rap music and its lyrics may be a rejuvenating mechanism for low income black youths that enhances their self-esteem. Using interviews, observation, and questionnaires, the author studied 115 black youths, ages thirteen to eighteen, who were participants in an Upward Bound program in Austin, Texas. The author concludes with some specific suggestions for future research.

Christenson, Peter G., and Jon Brian Peterson. 1988. "Genre and gender in the structure of musical preference." *Communication Research* 15: 282–301.

The authors analyze the popular music preferences of a sample of 239 college students. They divided popular music into twenty-six categories, ranging from mainstream pop to heavy metal to black gospel. Some significant gender differences emerged, particularly in the categories of mainstream pop, contemporary rhythm and blues, soul and late 1970s disco, where females had stronger preferences than males. Men were found to have significantly stronger preferences than women for psychedelic rock, blues, and Southern rock. The authors conclude by emphasizing that the underlying structure of music preference is multivariate in nature.

Epstein, Jonathon S., David J. Pratto, and James K. Skipper, Jr. 1990. "Teenagers, behavioral problems, and preferences for heavy metal and rap music: A case study of a Southern middle school." *Deviant Behavior* 11: 381–394.

This study explores the relationships between teenagers' musical preferences, their commitment to popular music, and behavioral problems. Results indicate that race is a strong predictor of musical preference, but neither musical preference nor commitment to popular music can predict behavioral problems.

Epstein, Jonathon S., and Robert Sardiello. 1990. "The wharf rats: A preliminary examination of Alcoholics Anonymous and the Grateful Dead Head phenomenon." *Deviant Behavior* 11: 245–257.

This article was the report on a preliminary study of the Grateful Dead Head subculture and the twelve-step groups that have sprung up within that subculture. According to the authors, twelve-step programs have become a frequent addition to the Dead Head community. This is possibly explained by that community's positive attitude toward the use of illicit substances. A follow-up study was being carried out, using Denzin's interpretive interactionism and biographical method, at the time this book went to print.

Epstein, Jonathon S., and David J. Pratto. 1990. "Heavy metal rock music, juvenile delinquency, and satanic identification." *Popular Music and Society* 14 (4): 67–76.

This article reports the findings of a pilot study carried out in the optional middle school in a mid-Southern city. The researchers engaged in participant observation at the school for a one-year period in order to determine if there was a relationship between musical preference and adolescent behavior. The researchers found no support for the contention that musical preference was a viable predictor for adolescent behavior and stated that "no firm evidence was found in this research to support anything other than a spurious connection between heavy metal and delinquency." A follow-up study was reported in *Deviant Behavior* 11: 381–394 (see above).

Fink, Edward L., John P. Robinson, and Sue Dowden. 1985. "The structure of music preference and attendance." *Communication Research* 12: 301–318.

The authors examine how people behave toward different types of popular music. They used survey data collected by the National Endowment for the Arts on 17,254 respondents. By using multidimensional scaling the authors were able to see how types of music clustered and the relationship between people's behaviors and attitudes toward types of music.

Hall, William E., and Judith Blau. 1987. "The taste for popular music: An analysis of class and cultural demand." *Popular Music and Society* 11 (1): 31–50.

This article attempts to suggest the usefulness of theories concerning subcultural tastes and taste cultures for macrosociological analysis. It is the authors' contention that popular concert events are directed towards specific groups within a culture. It is by identifying who these groups are that the sociologist can begin to identify the functions that these events fulfill in the lives of those who are attracted to them. The types of people attracted to specific concerts point to the specific shared experiences, thus allowing an explanation for the importance of critical mass, which might explain subcultural demand.

Lemming, James S. 1987. "Rock music and the socialization of moral values in early adolescence." *Youth and Society* 18 (4): 363–383.

Lemming holds that there are three hypotheses that concern the causal relationship between popular music and youth socializations. The hypotheses are that (1) music helps to tie teen peer groups together and makes them more resistant to legitimate adult authority, thereby strengthening their unique value system; (2) music creates an open and free feeling that encourages impulsiveness and makes individuals more open to suggestion; and (3) most music is listened to as a private experience. This heightens privatism and withdrawal from family and community life. It is Lemming's purpose to show how the sociologist can explain music's influence through the creation of personal and social contexts that contribute to the weakening of traditional patterns of socialization.

Rosenbaum, Jill, and Lorraine Prinsky. 1987. "Sex, violence and rock 'n' roll: Youth's perception of popular music." *Popular Music and Society* 11 (2): 79–90.

This study investigates the ability of students to interpret lyrics. Two hundred and sixty-six students were given questionnaires asking them to interpret their favorite songs. Demographic information was also collected. The final sample contained 116 females and 121 males. Results indicated that few students described songs which had questionable themes. There were 622 songs mentioned. Of these, 7 percent reported themes of satanism or sex and violence. Love was the most highly reported characteristic. Respondents were unable to explain 37 percent of the songs selected. Respondents claimed that 11 percent of the males wanted to listen to the words as opposed to 7 percent of the females. The most cited reason for listening to music was "it helps me to relax and stop thinking about things" (males 30 percent, females 34 percent). "It's good to dance to" was picked by 16 percent of the males and 35 percent of the females. "The words express how I feel" was chosen by 17 percent of the males and 24 percent of the females. The researchers concluded that if youths are influenced by negative themes in popular music, we would expect them to describe such topics in their favorite songs. However these data indicate that the students questioned hear or understand very little of the references to these topics in their favorite songs. The possibility of backmasking was discarded as unsupported by other research.

Rouner, Donna. 1990. "Rock music's use as a socializing function." *Popular Music and Society* 14: 97–107.

The author investigates how adolescents use rock music lyrics in self-socialization, and how they learn about norms, values, and interpersonal relations. A survey was administered to 175 high school students in Cleveland. Results indicate that 16 percent of the respondents named rock music lyrics as a source of information about moral values and beliefs. Another 24 percent named lyrics as a source of information about interpersonal interaction.

Snow, Robert P. 1987. "Youth, rock 'n' roll and electronic media." *Youth and Society* 18 (4): 326–343.

Snow attempts to locate an understanding of youth culture and style within a Simmelian formal sociology. The form he had in mind was the "play form." He contends that, consistent with Simmel's play form, rock music and youth culture exist within their own logic of interaction for interaction's sake. Rock and youth, therefore, are pure "play." He later concludes by stating that the relationship between youth and the electronic media is a dynamic process, linked by a solid bond, which exists for the purposes of exciting observation and enjoyable participation.

Wells, Alan. 1988. "Images of popular music artists: Do male and female audiences have different views?" *Popular Music and Society* 12: 1–17.

Wells explores the images of sixteen popular music artists as perceived by 108 male and female college students. Women and men were about equally likely to recognize the sixteen stars. But when the respondents used their own words to describe the artists, some interesting gender differences emerged. Women tended to add dimensions to their descriptions that men did not. Males seemed particularly hostile to male artists whom women respondents found sexy.

Women in Popular Music

Bayton, Mavis. 1990. "How women become musicians." Pp. 238–257 in Simon Frith and Andrew Goodwin (eds.), *On Record: Rock, Pop and the Written Word*. New York: Pantheon.

The article investigates, through in-depth interviews with female rock 'n' roll performers, the problems women encounter as they become performing popular musicians. The author focuses on such issues as dealing with amplification (instruments and microphones), learning to play together as a group, rehearsals, commitment, and the development of an identity as a musician. The quotes from the female musicians in this article are interesting and well chosen.

Becker, Audrey. 1990. "New lyrics by women: A feminist alternative." *Journal of Popular Culture* 24: 1–22.

This is a perceptive and informative article that attempts to locate the lyrics of certain contemporary female popular music artists within both the popular music industry and the feminist critique of society and the arts. Becker begins the article by reviewing literature on the narrow role of women in popular music. The main part of the article focuses on new women-centered lyrics by performers such as Tracey Thorn, Natalie Merchant of 10,000 Maniacs, and Suzanne Vega. She argues that these and other women represent a break from the traditional male-oriented world of popular music because they speak not only *in* their lyrics, but *with* them. Becker concludes by noting that these new lyrics not only challenge tradition in the popular music industry, but they also serve the feminist redefinition of the canon of poetry and art.

Groce, Stephen B., and Margaret Cooper. 1990. "Women in local level rock and roll: Just me and the boys?" *Gender & Society* 4: 220–229.

This is one of the few studies to examine the day-to-day experiences of female performers in popular music. The authors interviewed fifteen women currently performing at the local level to document that these performers are not "one of the boys in the band." Results indicate that female performers are pressured to sell sexuality, are not taken as seriously as musicians as their male counterparts, and have little say in the day-to-day workings of local-level rock and roll bands.

Keyes, Cheryl L. 1991. "We're more than a novelty, boys: Strategies of female rappers in the rap music tradition." Pp. 363–390 in Joan N. Radner (ed.), *Feminist Messages: Coding in Women's Folk Culture*. Urbana: University of Illinois Press.

This article is one of a growing number of studies on rap music and its practitioners, but one of the few on female rappers and their experiences and contributions. It contains a useful history of the development of rap, particularly the "foresisters" of rap, Moms Mabley and Millie Jackson. Keyes finds that female rappers of the 1980s have worked hard to overcome negative stereotypes. They have in their routines appropriated many of the male rappers' techniques and approaches, particularly "dissin'," but have moved beyond them, to become a force in their own right.

Lont, Cynthia M. 1992. "Women's music: No longer a small private party." Pp. 241–254 in Reebee Garofalo (ed.), *Rockin' the Boat: Mass Music and Mass Movements*. Boston: South End Press.

The author has two purposes in this article. The first is to briefly trace the history of women's music, with an emphasis on its cultural basis. The second is to examine the relationship between the early female performers and the newer performers of the 1980s and 1990s. Lont argues that while the face of women's music does not look the same as it did in the days of Chris Williamson and Holly Near, it is nonetheless a vibrant, viable music which is gaining a greater measure of mainstream acceptance—largely through the efforts of artists such as Tracy Chapman and k.d. lang.

Parsons, Patrick R. 1988. "The changing role of women executives in the recording industry." *Popular Music and Society* 12: 31–42.

The article focuses on how women have recently been able to attain executive positions in record companies, positions long dominated by men. Parsons includes a solid review of extant research on women and the popular music industry. The substance of the article is the author's analysis of questionnaires responded to by twenty female record company executives. Results indicate that women are slowly moving out of the public relations-type jobs and into positions of greater responsibility, e.g., A & R, sales, marketing. While they may still experience sexism and discrimination, Parsons's results lead him to conclude that the situation for women in the popular music industry is improving.

Pavletich, Aida. 1980. *Sirens of Song: The Popular Female Vocalist in America*. New York: De Capo.

A thorough chronicle of the history of female singers in popular music. The author pays special attention to country, folk, rock, and women's music vocalists.

Petersen, Karen E. 1987. "An investigation into women-identified music in the United States." Pp. 203–212 in Ellen Koskoff (ed.), *Women and Music in Cross-Cultural Perspective*. Westport, CT: Greenwood Press.

The article traces the development of music written by women and based on the experiences of women. Petersen locates the beginnings of women-identified music in the lesbian and feminist songs of the early 1970s. An important development was the founding of Olivia Records in 1973. Women were for the first time able to take control of the recording and production of their own music. Other companies such as Ova, Sister Sun, Sweet Alliance, and Mother of Pearl have followed. The article concludes with a critical assessment of women-identified music and calls for a musical breakthrough that goes beyond proclaiming one's lesbianism or singing about feminist ideology.

Robertson, Carol E. 1987. "Power and gender in the musical experiences of women." Pp. 225–244 in Ellen Koskoff (ed.), *Women and Music in Cross-Cultural Perspective.* Westport, CT: Greenwood Press.

Robertson explores situations in which men use music as social control and how they regulate the lives of women through coercion. She also examines some crosscultural data that document occasions and situations where women are able to act out their own conceptions of social reality through music. The article concludes with the author's suggestions for central questions about gender, music, and power around which future research might be centered.

Stewart, Alan D. 1989. "Declarations of independence: The female rock and roller comes of age." Pp. 283–298 in Cynthia M. Lont and Sheryl A. Friedley (eds.), *Beyond Boundaries: Sex and Gender Diversity in Communication.* Fairfax, VA: George Mason University Press.

The author investigates how female hard rock artists have "come of age" and are currently making, through their music, statements of independence from traditional and stereotypical expectations for women and their roles. Stewart finds that these statements may be both direct—as in lyrical content—and indirect; for example, the music itself. The study focuses on the lives and music of Chrissie Hynde, Patti Smith, Genya Raven, Marianne Faithful, and Robin Lane. For these and other female hard rock performers, rock music is a form of empowerment.

Wells, Alan. 1986. "Women in popular music: Changing fortunes from 1955 to 1984." *Popular Music and Society* 10: 73–86.

Wells measures the successes of female performers over the last three decades in terms of yearly Top 50 singles and *Rolling Stone* album charts. Despite the trend toward greater success in the industry, women are still underrepresented in both hit singles and albums.

Wood, Elizabeth. 1980. "Women in music." *Signs: Journal of Women in Culture and Society* 6: 283–297.

Wood writes a useful review of works by female musicologists, both in Europe and the United States. She reviews material from a large number of sources, both published and unpublished. She shows how female musicologists are challenging many of the traditional sexist assumptions concerning women and their historical role in the composition and performance of art music. The article concludes with a call for more rigorous scholarship and theoretical analyses that examine women's contributions in other forms of music, namely jazz, folk and oral musical traditions, and that forge a link with feminist scholarship in other academic disciplines.

Analyses of Popular Music Content: Song Lyrics, etc.

Armstrong, Edward G. 1993. "The rhetoric of violence in rap and country music." Sociological Inquiry 63 (1): 64–83.

Armstrong conducts a semiotic ethnography in which he compares the rhetoric of violence found in two supposedly divergent types of popular music—rap and country. The analysis examines lyric contents for claims about violent crimes—murder, manslaughter and assault. Armstrong finds that these supposedly incompatible forms of popular music have hidden resemblances in terms of their rhetorics of violence.

Burns, Gary. 1987. "A typology of 'hooks' in popular records." *Popular Music* 6: 1–20.

In this article Burns seeks to provide a framework of categories to facilitate the analysis of hooks in commercial music. He divides his discussion into how songwriters create hooks by manipulating rhythm, melody, harmony, and lyrics (textual elements), and how engineers and producers create hooks by manipulating tempo, dynamics, editing, mixing, and using special effects such as distortion, reverb, and flanging.

Cooper, Virginia W. 1985. "Women in popular music: A quantitative analysis of feminine images over time." *Sex Roles* 13: 499–506.

The author used content analysis to examine popular music lyrics from 1946, 1956, 1966 and 1976 for feminine images. A sample of 1,164 songs about women from those years was coded for eleven stereotypical images of women. Ninety-six percent of the songs contained at least one of the stereotypical images. There was an increase in the emphasis on women's physical characteristics and an increase in portrayals of women as powerful and harmful to men. The article concludes with a discussion of song lyrics as agents of socialization.

Enders, Kathleen L. 1984. "Sex role standards in popular music." *Journal of Popular Culture* 18: 9–18.

This study investigates the attributes, behaviors, and attitudes of men and women as portrayed in popular music lyrics. The author chose three years for examination—1960, 1970, 1980—and selected twelve songs from each year to examine. She finds that in 1960 songs displayed traditional gender role standards; by 1980, more diverse and less traditional messages about gender were conveyed by the songs. Enders attributes the change to the effect of women's increasing involvement in economics, social, and political life.

Hyden, Colleen, and N. Jane McCandless. 1985. "Men and women as portrayed in the lyrics of contemporary music." *Popular Music and Society* 9: 19–26.

This study uses a sample of 110 songs that were popular between 1972 and 1982, as determined by *Billboard* magazine. The authors generated a list of descriptive adjectives for men and women found in the songs. Findings suggest that women are most often portrayed with traditional gender stereotypes and men are not. In some cases, the same adjectives were found to describe both men and women, but in most cases different sets of adjectives were used. The authors conclude by contesting the assumption that popular music lyrics are degrading to women.

Lewis, George H. 1991. "Duellin' values: Tension, conflict and contradiction in country music." *Journal of Popular Culture* 24: 103–117.

Lewis argues that country music lyrics reflect the concerns and values of its listeners. Many times these values are riddled with tension, conflicts, and contradictions and are not at all as harmonious and interconnected as earlier research has suggested. Lewis uses the concept of axes of cultural variation to discuss the tensions and conflicts present in country music lyrics. He finds three general areas in which oppositions manifest themselves: (1) connections between the individual and society; (2) freedom or restraint; and (3) looking to the past or to the present. Lewis uses good examples from popular country songs throughout the article to illustrate his argument.

Thaxton, Lyn, and Charles Jaret. 1985. "Singers and stereotypes: The image of female recording artists." *Sociological Inquiry* 55: 239–263.

The authors use album cover photographs to study the images of female vocalists in different popular music styles. They made slides of album covers from ninety-one albums recorded between 1973 and 1981. Panels of judges then rated the slides on thirty-one different traits. The judges rated female singers positively, regardless of the singers' musical styles. The authors conclude by arguing that female singers in the popular music industry are not presented in the same traditional, stereotypical manner that women in other media are often presented.

Tunnell, Kenneth D. 1991. "Blood marks the spot where poor Ellen was found: Violent crime in bluegrass music." *Popular Music and Society* 15: 95–115.

Tunnell analyzes the images of murder and other forms of violence found in the lyrics of bluegrass songs. He concludes by discussing several competing explanations for the presence of violence in bluegrass. He suggests that the subcultural explanation is probably the best.

Tunnell, Kenneth D. 1992. "99 years is almost life: Punishment for violent crime in bluegrass music." *Journal of Popular Culture* 26 (3): 147–160.

The author analyzes the lyrics of popular bluegrass songs. He details the images of prisons and sentencing and goes on to use subcultural theory as a means of explaining the frequency of prison imagery.

Analyses of Popular Music Content: Music Videos

Abt, Dean. 1987. "Music video: Impact of the visual dimension." Pp. 96–111 in James Lull (ed.), *Popular Music and Communication*. Newbury Park, CA: Sage.

This essay describes what the author sees as the four critical issues surrounding music videos: (1) their visual styles and characteristics; (2) their inhibition of the imagination in consuming popular music; (3) their violent and sexist images; and (4) the role of videos as a new form of advertising. The article also includes results of the author's study of the relationship between music purchasing patterns and music video viewing. Using responses from 385 record buyers he concludes that viewing music videos does influence record buying by giving them something personal to connect with.

Aufderheide, Pat. 1986. "Music videos: The look of the sound." *Journal of Communication* 36: 57–78.

Aufderheide provides a brief but useful history of the development of music videos, along with their distinctive characteristics. This essay also discusses the links between videos and the larger popular music industry, particularly in terms of economics—promotion and advertising—and creating opportunities for those who would probably not otherwise have careers in popular music.

Baxter, Richard, Cynthia De Riemer, Ann Landini, Larry Leslie, and Michael W. Singletary. 1985. "A content analysis of music videos." *Journal of Broadcasting and Electronic Media* 29: 333–340.

The authors investigated sixty-two videos from MTV coded for twenty-three content categories. Results indicate that the majority of videos portray sex, violence, crime and other negative behaviors. The authors also found that 96 percent of the central characters in these videos were white males.

Brown, Jane D., and Kenneth Campbell. 1986. "Race and gender in music videos: The same beat but a different drummer." *Journal of Communication* 36: 94–106.

Using a sample of videos from MTV and "Video Soul" (Black Entertainment Television), the authors examine the gender and race of lead performers, as well as conceptual elements of the videos. Findings indicate that blacks are more likely than whites to be shown as helpful and caring people, but only on Black Entertainment Television; social protest themes are almost exclusively shown on MTV; and that males and females are equally likely to initiate aggressive behaviors. The authors conclude by noting that music television probably creates and sustains a very stereotypical worldview for its viewers.

Gow, Joe. 1992. "Making sense of music video: Research during the inaugural decade." *Journal of American Culture* 15 (3): 35–43.

This is a useful article that chronicles the significant research on music videos during the 1980s. The author divides the discussion by type of study, including historical, content analytic, audience-centered, and critical studies. He ends by noting that scholars investigating music videos need to develop a better understanding of how viewers interact with the videos, and how the aural and visual dimensions work together to become meaningful.

Gow, Joe. 1992. "Music video as communication: Popular formulas and emerging genres." *Journal of Popular Culture* 26 (2): 41–70.

In this article Gow explores the rhetorical dimensions of 138 of the most popular music videos shown during the 1980s. He argues that the rhetoric of music videos is a rhetoric of musical performance as opposed to rhetorics of storytelling or argumentation. Gow breaks the videos in his sample into six recurring formulas: antiperformance, pseudoreflexive, performance documentary, special effects, song and dance, and enhanced performance.

Harvey, Lisa St. Clair. 1990. "Temporary insanity: Fun, games, and transformational ritual in American music video." *Journal of Popular Culture* 24: 39–64.

Harvey writes an interesting article that examines music videos as cultural artifacts through a use of Durkheim's treatment of both ecstasy rituals and critical theory, most notably from Lacan and Barthes. The author argues that music videos provide viewers with a sort of dreamscape or dreamscript wherein through spectacle and excess viewers can work through internalized conflicts. Music videos, as a collective dream-text, have become yet another means of reinforcing the social order. They have gone beyond their own format to become included in viewers' material worlds (MTV clothes, MTV parties). The author argues that music videos provide us, as analysts, a candid picture of contemporary culture and its directions for the future.

Jones, Steve. 1988. "Cohesive but not coherent: Music videos, narrative and culture." *Popular Music and Society* 12: 15–30.

In this essay, Jones defines music videos as a type of "cultural bulimia" that devours images and regurgitates them in a random manner. More importantly, he focuses on the ways in which music videos restructure our visual perceptions of time and space. He distinguishes between two types of narrative structures, analog—information presented as a whole, in a continuous fashion—and digital—information presented in discrete steps with no necessary relationship to what it communicates. He finds that most music videos, aside from pure concert videos, have elements of digital narrative that necessarily change our perceptions of time and space.

Kaplan, E. Ann. 1987. *Rocking Around the Clock: Music Television, Postmodernism and Consumer Culture*. New York: Methuen.

This book is a set of six loosely related but mostly independent essays that examine music videos. The author uses a multiperspective approach including cultural criticism, psychoanalytic theory, feminism, and poststructuralism. She argues that music videos use themes, forms, and motifs from the history of rock and roll in a nonlinear fashion to create a postmodernist sensibility. Her main focus is the aesthetics of popular culture. Perhaps the most interesting part of the book is the essay in which she analyzes five types or categories of videos on MTV: romantic, socially conscious, nihilist, classical, and postmodernist.

Seidman, Steven A. 1992. "An investigation of sex-role stereotyping in music videos." *Journal of Broadcasting and Electronic Media* 36 (2): 209–216.

In this article Seidman investigates stereotyping of occupational roles and the behaviors of music video characters. Basing his analysis on a random sample of 182 music videos, he shows that males and females both continue to be shown in gender-typed occupations. In addition, males continue to be shown as aggressive and violent, while females continue to be shown as affectionate and dependent. He concludes by linking his findings to the literature that demonstrates that young females have more negative self-images and lower self-esteem than young males.

Sherman, Barry L., and Joseph R. Dominick. 1986. "Violence and sex in music videos: TV and rock 'n' roll." *Journal of Communication* 36: 79–93.

This article's focus is on the extent of violence and sexual content of rock music videos. The authors sampled for seven consecutive weeks MTV "Night Tracks," and "Friday Night Videos." The sampling procedure produced 366 videos, 200 of which were not analyzed because they were concert as opposed to concept videos. Results indicate that episodes of violence occurred in over half of the sampled videos, with males the aggressors three-fourths of the time and females victims of violence over three-fourths of the time. The authors find that sex in music videos is more implied than overt. Flirtation accounted for more than half of the coded sexual contact, with kissing, hugging, embracing, and intimate touching also represented.

Vincent, Richard C., Dennis K. Davis, and Lilly Ann Boruszkowski. 1987. "Sexism on MTV: The portrayal of women in rock videos." *Journalism Quarterly* 64: 750–755, 940–941.

This article is a study of 110 rock music videos recorded from MTV, from both day-and nighttime programming. Using a standard sexism scale, coders rated the videos as follows: (1) condescending—woman portrayed as less than human; (2) keep her place—displays traditional roles for women; (3) contradictory—traditional and independent at the same time; and (4) fully equal—women portrayed in nonstereotypical ways. Sixty out of 110 videos were coded as condescending, nineteen as keep her place, fourteen as contradictory, and seventeen as fully equal. The authors conclude by noting that perhaps portrayals of women in rock music videos are not significantly different from portrayals of women in other media forms.

Vincent, Richard C. 1989. "Clio's consciousness raised? Portrayal of women in rock videos, re-examined." *Journalism Quarterly* 66: 155–160.

This is a follow-up study to the one conducted by the author and his associates two years earlier (abstracted above). Using the same methods and analytic framework as before, Vincent finds that in the two years since his last study, some changes in the way women are portrayed in rock music videos has occurred. There was a 22 percent decline in the condescending category and a 173 percent increase in the fully equal category. He notes that the degree of sexism found in videos seems to vary by sex of the musician. That is, when female performers are present, the level of sexism decreases.

Collected Works

Frith, Simon (ed.). 1988. *Facing the Music*. New York: Pantheon.

Frith edited a collection of original essays that link the particular experiences of songs, artists or radio with the more general concern with how and why popular music works.

Frith, Simon. 1988. *Music for Pleasure: Essays in the Sociology of Pop*. New York: Routledge.

This book is a collection of articles and essays by Frith previously published in a variety of journals and magazines from the late 1970s through the mid 1980s. Probably of most interest sociologically are the reprints of "The Industrialization of Music" and "Why Do Songs Have Words?"

Frith, Simon, and Andrew Goodwin (eds.). 1990. *On Record: Rock, Pop and the Written Word*. New York: Pantheon.

This book is a collection of material previously published in a variety of places. The unifying theme is that the study of popular music should be taken seriously. The authors have brought together both theoretical and substantive analyses of the popular music industry.

Garofalo, Reebee (ed.). 1992. *Rockin' the Boat: Mass Music and Mass Movements*. Boston: South End Press.

The articles in this volume address the connections between mass music and mass movements. This volume is one of an increasing number of works which examine the political uses of rock and other forms of popular music from a global perspective. The list of contributors is impressive: George Lewis, Reebee Garofalo, Simon Frith, Cynthia Lont, and Peter Wicke, to name but a few. The articles focus on the political uses of popular music from the U.S. to China to Argentina to the former Eastern Bloc.

Koskoff, Ellen (ed.). 1989. *Women and Music in Cross-Cultural Perspective*. Urbana: University of Illinois Press.

This book features original articles that should be of interest to anthropologists, sociologists, and ethnomusicologists. The focus is on women's cultural identities and musical activities, either in private performance situations or in public settings.

Leppert, Richard, and Susan McClary (eds.). 1987. *Music and Society: The Politics of Composition, Performance and Reception*. Cambridge: Cambridge University Press.

This volume is comprised of original articles by sociologists, cultural theorists, and musicologists. The common theme of the articles is how music and society interact with and mediate one another.

Middleton, Richard and David Horn (eds.). 1981. Popular Music I: Folk or Popular? Distinctions, Influences, Continuities; 1982. Popular Music II: Theory and Method; 1983. Popular Music III: Producers and Markets; 1984. Popular Music IV: Performers and Audiences; 1985. Popular Music V: Continuity and Change. All volumes Cambridge: Cambridge University Press.

These volumes represent a useful series of original articles that focused on a particular topic or set of related topics each year. The international journal *Popular Music* grew out of this series. Middleton and Horn's edited volumes are international in scope and deal with a variety of types of popular music. Each volume has a mixture of ethnomusicological and sociological treatments of popular music.

Scheurer, Timothy (ed.). 1989. *American Popular Music: Readings from the Popular Press, Volume I: The Nineteenth Century and Tin Pan Alley Years*. Bowling Green, OH: Bowling Green State University Press.

This book is a collection of material previously published in *Popular Music and Society*, *Journal of Popular Culture*, or *Journal of American Culture*. The articles focus on the beginnings of American commercial music, from the turn of the century up to the dawn of rock and roll.

Scheurer, Timothy (ed.). 1989. *American Popular Music: Readings from the Popular Press, Volume II: The Age of Rock*. Bowling Green, OH: Bowling Green State University Press.

As above, Scheurer compiles a collection of previously published material. The articles trace the roots and evolution of rock music from the 1950s through the 1980s.

Contributors

D.E. Benson is associate professor of sociology at Kent State University. Benson's current research interests center on the exploration of structural influences on identity, processes involved in identity change, and the relationship between attributional processes and identity.

Venise Berry is an assistant professor at the University of Iowa School of Journalism and Mass Communication. She is the author of a variety of articles on African-American images in the media, particularly music, television, and film. Berry is currently working on two books: an edited volume, *Mediated Messages: Issues in African-American Culture,* and the authored *Race and Politics in the Early Film Industry: The Life of Joel Fluellen 1909–1990.*

Thaddeus Coreno is currently teaching and finishing his doctoral dissertation in sociology at Kent State University. His interests include social theory, religion, inequality, culture, and, of course, avant-garde/experimental music.

Daniel Dotter is associate professor of criminal justice at Grambling State University. His research interests lie in the intersection of popular music and deviance.

Emily D. Edwards's professional media experience includes television news reporting and producing for NBC and ABC affiliates in Alabama and Tennessee, public relations, and radio features produced for the Tennessee Tape Network. She completed a Ph.D. in mass communications at the University of

Tennessee at Knoxville in 1984. She served as director for the broadcasting sequence in the Department of Communications at the University of Alabama at Birmingham. Currently she is director of graduate studies for the M.F.A. sequence in film and video production at the University of North Carolina at Greensboro. Her other research on popular music has been published in *Popular Music and Society, Southern Speech Communications Journal,* and the *National Academy of Recording Arts and Sciences Journal.* Her documentary on Dead Head music subculture, "Dead Heads: An American Subculture," is distributed by Films for the Humanities and Sciences.

Jonathon S. Epstein is a Ph.D. candidate at Kent State University where he has taught courses in social inequalities, computer research methods, and the sociology of adolescence. As an instructor at Youngstown State University, he has taught courses on juvenile delinquency, social deviance, criminology, and the sociology of rock music. He has published in journals as diverse as *Deviant Behavior, Popular Music and Society,* and *The Journal of Alcohol Studies.* He is currently writing his second book, *Fatal Forms: Towards a Postmodern Formal Sociology.* In addition to his academic work, Epstein also serves as an associate editor for the nationally recognized rock music monthly *U.S. Rocker.*

Donna Gaines holds a Ph.D. in sociology from the State University of New York at Stony Brook. She is the author of *Teenage Wasteland: Suburbia's Dead End Kids* and a frequent contributor to the *Village Voice.*

Stephen B. Groce is associate professor of sociology at Western Kentucky University. He teaches courses on sociological theory and the sociology of popular music. He has published extensively on small-time popular musicians, their performances, and their audiences.

Lawrence Grossberg teaches communications and cultural studies at the University of Illinois at Urbana. His latest projects are *We Gotta Get Out of This Place* and an edited volume in cultural studies. He is also the international co-editor of the journal *Cultural Studies.*

Joseph A. Kotarba is an associate professor of sociology at the University of Houston. He teaches courses on social theory, ethnographic research methods, the sociology of health, and the sociology of rock 'n' roll. He is currently writing on the relationship between various social institutions (e.g., the family, religion, medicine, and sports) and rock music. Dr. Kotarba has conducted field studies on all-ages rock music clubs, the musical experiences of homeless adolescents, the delivery of emergency medical services at festival rock concerts, the shared rock music experiences of parents and their children, and rock music and youth culture in Poland since the fall of communism.

Jerry M. Lewis received his Ph.D. from the University of Illinois (Urbana) in 1970. He joined the faculty at Kent State University in 1966. In recent years his work on collective behaviors has focused on soccer crowds. Previously he wrote extensively on the May 4, 1970, shooting at Kent State University.

Jean Malone is an assistant professor of sociology at the University of North Carolina at Greensboro. She received her Ph.D. from the State University of New York at Stony Brook in 1990. Her areas of interest include research methodology, deviance, and gender.

Amy B. Mohan received a B.F.A. degree from the North Carolina School of the Arts in 1986. She is a guitarist and a songwriter. From 1989 to 1991 she managed and performed with an alternative band. She is presently completing a B.A. in sociology at the University of North Carolina at Greensboro.

Scott A. Reid is currently finishing his Ph.D. in the department of sociology at Kent State University and is an instructor at Youngstown State University. He has conducted research on exotic dancers and is currently involved in a project researching the identity salience and psychological centrality of professional body builders. His areas of specialty are sociological theory, social psychology, and the sociology of deviance. Additionally, he is an instructor of sociology at Trumbull Correctional Institution, a maximum/close-security prison.

Robert Sardiello is currently an instructor at Nassau Community College on Long Island while completing his Ph.D. at the State University of New York at Stony Brook. His current interests revolve around myths, rituals and cultural studies. His past work has appeared in journals such as *Deviant Behavior*. His current work is in the field of interpretive symbolic interactionism and nonterritorial subcultures.

Deena Weinstein is professor of sociology at De Paul University in Chicago. Her present work is located on the interface between the study of popular culture, particulary the study of rock music, and postmodernist critical theory. She is author of *Heavy Metal: A Cultural Sociology* and coauthor of *Postmodern(ized) Simmel*.

Index

C

D

E

F

G

H

I

J

K

L

Q

R

S

T

U

V

W

Y

Z